DIFFERENTIATED LITERACY INSTRUCTION
IN GRADES 4 AND 5

Also from Sharon Walpole and Michael C. McKenna

Cracking the Common Core:
Choosing and Using Texts in Grades 6–12
William E. Lewis, Sharon Walpole, and Michael C. McKenna

How to Plan Differentiated Reading Instruction,
Second Edition: Resources for Grades K–3
Sharon Walpole and Michael C. McKenna

The Literacy Coach's Handbook, Second Edition:
A Guide to Research-Based Practice
Sharon Walpole and Michael C. McKenna

The Literacy Coaching Challenge:
Models and Methods for Grades K–8
Michael C. McKenna and Sharon Walpole

Organizing the Early Literacy Classroom:
How to Plan for Success and Reach Your Goals
Sharon Walpole and Michael C. McKenna

Promoting Early Reading:
Research, Resources, and Best Practices
Edited by Michael C. McKenna, Sharon Walpole,
and Kristin Conradi

Differentiated Literacy Instruction in Grades 4 and 5

Strategies and Resources

SECOND EDITION

Sharon Walpole
Michael C. McKenna
Zoi A. Philippakos
John Z. Strong

THE GUILFORD PRESS
New York   London

Copyright © 2020 The Guilford Press
A Division of Guilford Publications, Inc.
370 Seventh Avenue, Suite 1200, New York, NY 10001
www.guilford.com

Printed in the United States of America

This book is printed on acid-free paper.

Last digit is print number: 9   8   7   6   5   4   3   2   1

Library of Congress Cataloging-in-Publication Data

Names: Walpole, Sharon, author.
Title: Differentiated literacy instruction in grades 4 and 5 : strategies
    and resources / Sharon Walpole, Michael C. McKenna, Zoi A. Philippakos,
    John Z. Strong.
Other titles: Differentiated literacy instruction in grades 4 & 5
Description: Second edition. | New York : The Guilford Press, [2020] |
    Includes bibliographical references and index. |
Identifiers: LCCN 2019028523 | ISBN 9781462540815 (paperback) |
    ISBN 9781462540853 (hardcover)
Subjects: LCSH: Reading (Elementary) | Individualized instruction.
Classification: LCC LB1573 .W33 2020 | DDC 372.4—dc23
LC record available at *https://lccn.loc.gov/2019028523*

To all of the teachers
who have allowed us into their classrooms to learn

About the Authors

Sharon Walpole, PhD, is Director of the Professional Development Center for Educators at the University of Delaware, where she is also Professor in the School of Education. She has extensive school-based experience designing and implementing tiered instructional programs. Dr. Walpole has also been involved in federally funded and other schoolwide reform projects. She is a recipient of the Early Career Award for Significant Contributions to Literacy Research and Education from the Literacy Research Association (LRA) and the Excellence in Teaching Award from the University of Delaware. In 2018, she was named the Jerry Johns Outstanding Teacher Educator in Reading by the International Literacy Association (ILA). Her current work involves the design and effects of the open educational resource *Bookworms K–5 Reading and Writing*. She has coauthored or coedited several books, including *How to Plan Differentiated Reading Instruction, Second Edition: Resources for Grades K–3; The Literacy Coach's Handbook, Second Edition;* and *Organizing the Early Literacy Classroom*.

Michael C. McKenna, PhD, was Thomas G. Jewell Professor of Reading at the University of Virginia until his death in 2016. He authored, coauthored, or edited more than 20 books, including *Assessment for Reading Instruction, Third Edition; How to Plan Differentiated Reading Instruction, Second Edition: Resources for Grades K–3; The Literacy Coach's Handbook, Second Edition;* and *Organizing the Early Literacy Classroom;* as well as over 100 articles, chapters, and technical reports on a range of literacy topics. Dr. McKenna also served as Series Editor, with Sharon Walpole, of *The Essential Library of PreK–2 Literacy.* His research was sponsored by the National Reading Research Center and the Center for the Improvement of Early Reading Achievement. He was a corecipient of the Edward B. Fry Book Award from the LRA and the Award for Outstanding Academic Books from the American Library Association, and was inducted into the Reading Hall of Fame in 2016.

Zoi A. Philippakos, PhD, is Assistant Professor in the College of Education at the University of Tennessee, Knoxville. Her research interests include reading and writing instruction for students in the elementary grades, strategy instruction and self-regulation, and professional development for classroom teachers. She has worked as an elementary school teacher and literacy coach, and she provides professional development to teachers on effective reading and writing strategies. Since 2010, Dr. Philippakos has codeveloped and organized the Writing Research Study Group at the LRA, and she is Chair of the Writing Task Force at the ILA. She is coauthor of several books, including *Developing Strategic Young Writers through Genre Instruction: Resources for Grades K–2* and *Developing Strategic Writers through Genre Instruction: Resources for Grades 3–5.*

John Z. Strong, PhD, is Assistant Professor in the Graduate School of Education at the University at Buffalo, State University of New York. Previously, he taught undergraduate and graduate courses in literacy education at the University of Delaware. A former high school English language arts teacher, his research interests include integrated reading and writing interventions for adolescents. His dissertation research investigated the effects of an informational text structure intervention on fourth- and fifth-grade students' reading comprehension and informative writing. Dr. Strong is a recipient of the Steven A. Stahl Research Grant from the ILA and the Richard L. Venezky Award for Creative Research in Literacy from the University of Delaware. He has coauthored articles published in *The Elementary School Journal, Journal of Adolescent and Adult Literacy, The Reading Teacher,* and *Reading Research Quarterly.*

Preface

The first edition of this book, published in 2011, was our apology to those upper elementary teachers who had been excluded from the series of federal reforms that targeted grades K–3. What a difference the years since have made! Even among veteran teachers, there are likely many who have forgotten that they used to be "left behind." It would be difficult to imagine schools' not viewing their upper elementary teachers as front-line supporters of reading and writing development, *and* of the knowledge building that underlies all real literacy.

We have certainly spent time in upper elementary classrooms to inform our work in this new edition. You will see that we cannot even address the topic of this book—differentiation—without a thorough attention to engaging and challenging *grade-level* instruction. We hope readers will understand that what teachers need to do to differentiate for students must be yoked to their grade-level goals. We think of grade-level goals as a fulcrum, and of efforts to differentiate for students who are struggling and for students who are ahead as weights that teachers and schools add to maintain balance.

We continue to be committed to equity for teachers and students. For that reason, we recommend practices that are inexpensive and reasonable to implement. We know this is the case because we have costed them out and tried them out in real classrooms. For us, the move away from expensive commercial materials for grade-level instruction makes sense on many levels. It is cheaper to use actual trade books. Trade books are more engaging for students. And trade books offer unlimited potential for change and adaptation.

We have long used Occam's razor to make decisions on how to plan instruction. This commitment reflects our respect for teachers. We want their jobs to be satisfying and reasonable. We want them to focus more of their attention on responding to their students during instruction than on scouring the research literature for evidence. We take that on as our role here. We *do* have time to scour the research literature. We have done our best to sort through it and choose those nuggets with the potential to add real value to the experiences of students, without overwhelming the teachers who work so hard to serve them.

As a "teaser" for this new edition, look for a brief history lesson in Chapter 1, along with a linking of differentiation efforts with response-to-intervention (RTI) efforts. Chapter 2 updates the nuts and bolts of scheduling and grouping with a new tool that teachers can use to evaluate materials. Chapter 3 is a fresh look at the research for upper elementary; you will notice that much of it is quite recent. Chapter 4 is our assessment chapter, and we hope that readers will have the same response to it that our ongoing teacher partners have: Less assessment is more, as long as that assessment constitutes a system.

After the first four chapters, we specialize by content. Chapter 5's emphasis on word recognition defines word-level skills for older readers to include syllable patterns and meaning patterns. The chapter sets up the preplanned multisyllabic decoding lessons that we include as an appendix at the end of the book (Appendix F). Chapter 6 continues our advocacy for fluency as a necessary part of the upper elementary literacy diet. A corresponding appendix of sample fluency lessons is presented in Appendix G. Chapter 7 provides simple guidance for making vocabulary instruction an essential (and essentially connected) aspect of all student text reading. All of the content chapters lead to Chapter 8—comprehension—because that is the heart of the matter. Sample lessons for vocabulary and comprehension are provided in Appendix I. Teachers can use these lessons directly or as models for planning their own lessons. Chapter 9 is entirely new for this edition, and it is a start at wedding reading and writing.

We know that teachers work hard, and we also know that teacher leaders work hard. In Chapter 10, we take the long view. To really change instruction, we have to really change curricula. And to really change curricula, we have to think ahead and pace ourselves. Chapter 10 is a synthesis and planning guide for those leaders who want to go further and spread new ideas across their upper elementary team.

Our author team is one man down. Mike McKenna's death in December 2016 still stings for us. The ideas represented here, though, are ideas he was working on with us when he died. We are glad to bring them to you and hope they make teaching easier. That's always been our goal.

Contents

CHAPTER 1

Differentiation and Tiered Instruction

The new edition of this book is evidence of our continued efforts to make differentiation work. It also represents our commitment to bringing writing into the mix. We know that meaningful, sustainable differentiation in reading *and writing* instruction is intimately tied to the real-life demands of classrooms and schools. Those demands include the nature of new standards; the content and structure of the grade-level curriculum; the needs of students for increased time devoted to math, science, and social studies each year; and the reality that we must continually engage all students in their learning.

You will see that as we bring writing into the mix, we must confront the fact that we will juggle two types of differentiation: content differentiation for reading, and process differentiation for writing. Over time, we may be able to embrace both content and process differentiation for reading and for writing, but not yet. You will also see that we cannot discuss differentiation without a very thorough dive into the grade-level curriculum.

The history of our work is important to understanding it now. We originally designed an approach to differentiation for early grades with brief, targeted instruction at four levels: (1) phonemic awareness and word recognition, (2) word recognition and fluency, (3) fluency and comprehension, or (4) vocabulary and comprehension. We planned for an individual teacher serving a mixed-ability group, typical of an early primary classroom. This design phase was the result of collaboration among a large group of administrators, teachers, and literacy coaches who were willing to pilot-test our lessons and then integrate them into a model of comprehensive literacy instruction. That original work was published as *Differentiated Reading Instruction: Strategies for the Primary Grades* (Walpole & McKenna, 2007), and then as *How to Plan Differentiated Reading Instruction: Resources for Grades K–3* (Walpole & McKenna, 2009).

One basic problem in that early work was that upper elementary teachers (and their students!) were left out. We rectified that problem in the first edition of this book, and we propose even more deeply contextualized support in this new edition. To get started, we review the basics of our K–3 model. We position it within the general models of tiered instruction and response to intervention to emphasize that our work is designed to integrate these mandates. Finally, we propose differentiation for all students—including students in the upper elementary grades.

THE K–3 DIFFERENTIATION MODEL

Our K–3 differentiation model was originally designed for the fast-paced, high-stakes reform setting that was Reading First. Reading First was a federal program that provided resources for curriculum, assessment, and professional development to kindergarten through third-grade teachers in struggling schools. Unfortunately, it did not address the needs of teachers and children in upper elementary grades, even though they were in the very same school buildings. The funding was first available in 2002. Schools had to commit to implementing new core reading programs aligned with findings from reading research. Figure 1.1 presents the five core components of reading development highlighted in all Reading First work. These components are still important now.

Phonemic Awareness	The ability to notice and manipulate the sound structure of words.	An individual with strong phonemic awareness can take orally presented words and segment them into speech sounds or take speech sounds presented orally and blend them into words.
Decoding	The ability to use letter-sound knowledge to pronounce unknown words.	An individual with strong decoding skills can read new words presented in lists or in context.
Fluency	The ability to read text accurately, with adequate rate and with appropriate prosody.	An individual with strong reading fluency can read text orally, attending to phrasing and punctuation, and at a rate that sounds like regular speech.
Vocabulary	The knowledge of the meanings of individual words and of the connections between words.	An individual's vocabulary knowledge increases across the entire life span, but children with strong vocabularies derive new word meanings from reading and from listening.
Comprehension	The ability to construct meaning consistent with an author's intention.	An individual's comprehension is a complex interaction among the demands of the text, the individual's prior knowledge, and the individual's reading purpose. Individuals with strong comprehension can engage in strategic behaviors when they need to.

FIGURE 1.1. Core components of reading development.

Reading First required substantial changes in the way schools were organized. They had to commit to extended time for reading instruction in uninterrupted blocks. They also had to commit to new assessment systems, providing valid and reliable data about reading achievement for all children at least three times each year. Unfortunately, this data analysis indicated that although some students' beginning skills were consistent with the expectations of their grade-level program, other students' skills were not: Grade-level instruction would either be too easy or, in many cases, too difficult for them. For students with more serious needs, schools provided intensive interventions in addition to the reading instruction they received in the classroom.

The model of differentiated instruction that we designed (Walpole & McKenna, 2007, 2009) was influenced by this setting. We were deep in it. We worked extensively with literacy coaches and principals to understand the challenges in and the potential for increasing early grades' reading achievement in the foundational skills of phonemic awareness, decoding, and fluency. At the same time, however, we knew that foundational skills instruction without attention to vocabulary and comprehension would not yield long-term literacy success. In the end, our model made several structural assumptions, and they are pictured in Figure 1.2.

We assumed that most teachers would group children within a classroom (as opposed to across classrooms). We assumed that grade-level teams would work together (and with the support of their school leaders) to decide exactly how to use their core program for grade-level instruction. Since we were wary that the texts in those programs were not especially rich, we assumed that we could add a read-aloud from children's literature to that grade-level time, providing an opportunity to build vocabulary knowledge and model comprehension strategies for all. After grade-level instruction and the read-aloud, we assumed that most teachers could divide their students by literacy achievement into three groups. They could meet briefly with each of the three groups every day while the others either worked together in literacy centers or engaged in meaningful individual reading practice. In Figure 1.2, the teacher's work is highlighted in the shaded blocks. As the teacher worked with each group, the other groups would be engaged in reading practice. Another way to think about this type of rotation is that the teacher functioned as a "center," with all groups rotating to the teacher for one of the three blocks of time devoted to the combination of differentiated instruction and reading practice. For pragmatic reasons, we

Children's Literature Read-Aloud Grade-Level Core Instruction		
Middle Group	Reading Practice	Reading Practice
Reading Practice	Lowest Group	Reading Practice
Reading Practice	Reading Practice	Highest Group

FIGURE 1.2. Assumptions about time.

designed our differentiation lessons in 15-minute segments, enabling a teacher to address the needs of three different groups in a 45-minute time period.

The within-class grouping model also allowed us to create a flexible differentiation model. The classroom teacher could easily group and regroup students, because they were all in the room. We wanted to help teachers to use data to design these differentiation groups and to monitor progress. For this reason, and because schools typically operate on 6-, 9-, or 12-week marking periods, we designed our model in 3-week or 6-week units. Every 3–6 weeks, then, a classroom teacher could change the focus of an intact group or move some children from one group to another. Groupings and instructional focus were only temporary for students; as their skills changed, they could move to more complex work during the differentiation time.

OUR STAIRWAY TO PROFICIENCY

Although attention to time for grade-level instruction, a children's literature read-aloud, and a grouping and rotation plan are essential components of our differentiation model, the real meat of the model is the specificity of the instructional focus for each group. Applying a developmental standard—the idea that students progress as readers in a predictable manner—we assumed that early reading proficiencies could not be "skipped" in favor of grade-level ones. That is, a student with no knowledge of letter sounds cannot simply begin to decode single-syllable words; a student with weak oral reading fluency cannot simply engage in independent comprehension of grade-level texts. As a result, we assumed that we had to use simple assessments to document those literacy skills that children had mastered, and that our differentiated instruction had to target the next most complex set of skills for each group. Because our model was coupled with grade-level instruction and a read-aloud, it could be entirely skills-based; there was no need for it to provide a balanced literacy diet. Rather, it provided a very concentrated dose of skills instruction. Figure 1.3 provides a simple set of choices for instructional focus that we have come to call the *stairway to proficiency*.

We use the stairway to remind teachers that their students are taking one step at a time, and that movement up a step is a strong sign that differentiation is working. In fact, our goal is that teachers' skills instruction is so effective that more and more students

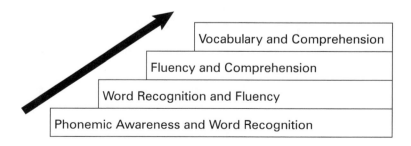

FIGURE 1.3. Stairway to proficiency.

reach the top step—differentiated attention to vocabulary and comprehension—at every benchmarking opportunity. If students are continuing to achieve at least benchmark scores in assessments of oral reading fluency, then we know that the grade-level instruction and read-aloud are sufficient in the area of basic skills. These students, then, can continue to build their vocabulary and apply comprehension strategies to an even wider variety of texts. Their differentiation time extends the curriculum. Our differentiation model, then, is not merely an intervention model. It is also a system for extending literacy learning for students with the strongest skills.

Our K–3 differentiation model became much more than just the broad conceptual focus of the stairway. Each step was elaborated with sets of lessons for what could be "logjams" for some readers. After trials in classrooms for several years, we made some adjustments (Walpole & McKenna, 2017). Figure 1.4 presents the logjams that we anticipated and for which we created sets of plans. These plans continue to be, for many schools, low-cost interventions.

We planned for three types of students in the phonological awareness and word recognition group. The first group, the basic alphabet knowledge group, comprises emergent readers who need to learn their letter names and sounds and to build their basic phonemic segmentation skills for initial sounds. It also includes print concepts if they are needed. The children in the letter sounds group know nearly all letter sounds in isolation, but need to learn to blend those sounds together to decode words. Children in the letter patterns group can decode words using letter sounds, but do so very slowly and need to take advantage of short-vowel patterns. In all three cases, the phonological awareness and word recognition lessons target only letters, words, and pictures in isolation. The groups needing to build very basic skills in phonological awareness and word recognition do only that.

Once students can recognize short-vowel words fairly reliably, they are ready to work in the word recognition and fluency group. For this group, we have matched specific

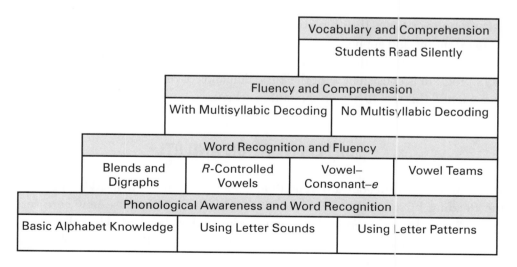

FIGURE 1.4. Skills progression in differentiation by assessed needs. From Walpole and McKenna (2017). Copyright © 2017 by The Guilford Press. Reprinted by permission.

types of phonics instruction with specific phonetic elements. The blends and digraphs and the *r*-controlled vowels lessons use synthetic sounding and blending phonics. The vowel–consonant–*e* lessons use compare-and-contrast phonics to introduce the idea that in most single-syllable words, short-vowel sounds are typically represented by single letters, and long-vowel sounds are marked by the use of two vowels. Finally, the vowel teams lessons use decoding-by-analogy phonics strategies to help students see that they can use patterns in known words to recognize unknown ones. In all cases, lessons for this group move from a targeted dose of phonics instruction, with a new set of words each day, to an application sequence of whisper, partner, and choral reading in a decodable passage written to build students' skills for decoding in context. In addition, all lessons include instruction in a small set of high-frequency words that are unknown by at least one member of the group.

Students who can read single-syllable words with vowel teams have acquired their basic decoding skills and no longer need the support of any decodable text. In fact, decodable text would likely hold them back. For those students, we have designed fluency and comprehension lessons with a very simple structure. Students read a variety of texts (including natural-language chapter books), in a structured sequence of choral and then partner or whisper rereading. Then they engage in a short comprehension discussion targeting important inferences. They continue with this concentrated dose of repeated reading and comprehension, with increasingly more complex texts, until their reading rates indicate that they can read grade-level text at rates associated with adequate comprehension.

Students with strong reading rates do not need the support of instruction in word recognition in isolation, decodable text, or repeated oral reading during their differentiation time. Rather, they need vocabulary instruction and opportunities to extend their use of text structures and comprehension strategies to understand more and more texts. They read narratives, informational texts of all kinds, and even web-based texts. The measure of the differentiation model in a given classroom is the increase in the number of children in this group over time: If differentiation on the lower stairsteps is effective, students move to extending and applying rather than shoring up their skills. Although this was not our original intent, if this differentiation model is fully implemented at a grade level, the school's program is consistent with the basic demands of response to intervention (RTI). We have found this fact to be very helpful in schools.

DIFFERENTIATION AND RTI

When we were designing our differentiation model, we were influenced by the demands of the Reading First legislation. We knew that teachers *had to* use new core reading programs in similar ways across classrooms; we knew that they *had to* have long and protected blocks of time for grade-level work; and we knew that they *had to* collect data to evaluate student achievement. Our differentiation model was designed to leverage these facts so that regular classroom teachers would find a small-group, data-driven model reasonable to implement every day for all students. Little did we know, but we were actually creating a viable model of tiered instruction. In fact, coaches, administrators, and teachers who work in schools with full implementation of our model will likely find absolutely no differences between it and RTI models.

One reason that we did not know that we were actually designing an RTI model is that RTI came onto the national educational policy scene at about the same time that we were designing our model, and it was influenced by some of the very same research that influenced us. RTI is an approach to integrating regular and special education in such a way that formal special education designations are really a last resort. Rather than identifying a child for special education because of a discrepancy between his or her ability and achievement, an RTI approach systematically rules out the possibility that increasingly intensive instruction can increase a student's achievement and eventually eliminate reading (or math or behavior) problems. The goals of RTI, then, are twofold: to reduce the number of students classified as special education who simply need targeted instruction, and to replace the discrepancy model for special education services.

There are two general RTI models: the *problem-solving* model and the *standard treatment protocol* model (McCardle, Chhabra, & Kapinus, 2008). In the problem-solving model, teachers meet with an intervention team to design specific, measurable "solutions" to individual student academic or behavioral problems. Teachers then implement their solutions and track their rate of success. The standard treatment protocol model opts for a set of procedures that can be used across classrooms, with all teachers actually engaging in the same set of interventions in response to data on student achievement. Our differentiation model is consistent with the standard treatment protocol model for RTI. It supports a system of tiered instruction and is far easier to implement on a schoolwide basis than the problem-solving model, especially in schools where many students need additional academic support.

Tiered instruction in reading requires a plan that increases in specificity and intensity when data reveal achievement concerns. It is a hallmark of the standard treatment protocol model for RTI, because students receive gradually more intensive instruction if data indicate that they are not "responding" to the intensity of the instruction that they are getting. Brown-Chidsey, Bronaugh, and McGraw (2009) provide a very readable description of the rationale for tiered instruction in the standard treatment protocol. They begin by equating intervention in RTI with instruction. All students need effective, grade-level core instruction (Tier 1) in the model. For students whose needs are not met, more intensive instruction (Tier 2) is the next step. That instruction is provided in a smaller-group setting. Once the Tier 2 instruction has been implemented for a reasonable amount of time, but it is found not to be effective, an even more intensive intervention (Tier 3) is called for. This instruction is provided in an even smaller group and for more time each day. Those students who do not respond to a high-quality tiered system (as evidenced in a system of progress monitoring) are likely to need special education, where some of their skill deficits will be accommodated rather than remediated. As schools work through their own RTI implementations, we will be able to reflect on the extent to which these systems realize their goals (Kovaleski & Black, 2010).

A pyramid is usually used to represent a tiered instruction system (see Figure 1.5). In this RTI structure, the breadth of each level of the pyramid represents the number

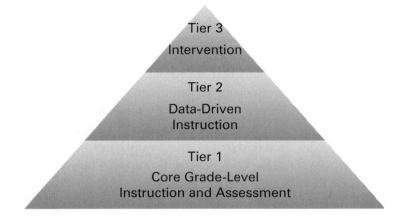

FIGURE 1.5. Tiered instruction pyramid: Differentiation for some.

of students who will need the instruction. The widest level is Tier 1, because all students are included. Only some students (those with below-grade-level performance) are included in the narrower layer of Tier 2. Even fewer require the third layer in the pyramid: intensive intervention.

This standard treatment protocol, with tiered instruction, was always embedded in our differentiation model for K–3, and we have included it in our extension to grades 4 and 5. Tier 1 instruction—consisting of grade-level core instruction plus an interactive read-aloud, planned consistently across classrooms and using high-quality materials and research-based procedures—is a basic feature. Our differentiation lessons, provided by the classroom teacher during the reading block, make up Tier 2. And we acknowledge that some students will need even more; that is, intensive interventions must be available outside of regular classroom instruction. We have not designed Tier 3 instruction, because we believe that it should be chosen from the research available on regular and special education interventions.

RETHINKING GRADE-LEVEL INSTRUCTION

When we first began our differentiation work, schools were still routinely purchasing commercial core programs. With the release of the Common Core State Standards (CCSS; National Governors Association Center for Best Practices [NGACBP] & Council of Chief State School Officers [CCSSO], 2010), those programs were immediately out of date; the standards changed dramatically what was expected in each grade level. The most salient changes were three: (1) specific expectations for text difficulty; (2) specific expectations for writing informed by text-based evidence; and (3) a focus on knowledge building of all kinds. Because the text excerpts in their current commercial programs were not difficult enough, districts and states began writing model lessons and posting them for shared use. We did too. The program that we worked on was originally called *Bookworms*. A second-generation version, with a full writing curriculum, is called *Bookworms K–5 Reading and Writing* (Open Up Resources, 2018). It is among the current family of open educational resources (OER). OER curricula are free to schools, and they are gaining in coherence, in popularity, and in sophistication. Beginning in 2020–2021, lesson plans for *Bookworms K–5 Reading and Writing* will be available digitally for free at *https://openupresources.org*. Schools will need to purchase the trade books that are used in the curriculum, but this expense is much less than what is required to purchase a new curriculum from traditional publishers.

We took on this work because we realized an important fact: What teachers do to differentiate their instruction can *never* make up for missed opportunities in their grade-level instruction. For that reason, in this book we show you how we have planned grade-level instruction in *Bookworms K–5 Reading and Writing* for shared reading, for interactive read-alouds, and for genre-based writing strategy instruction. Then we show you how we have planned differentiated lessons that add value to this strong grade-level instruction. We believe that showing you our behind-the-scenes planning strategies allows you either to use our plans with greater understanding or to generate your own. We give you a "teaser" in the section below.

DIFFERENTIATION FOR UPPER ELEMENTARY STUDENTS

Although our approach is used by many schools to meet the requirements of their states' RTI systems, our model differs in two important ways from the standard treatment protocol with the tiered instruction pyramid. First, we propose a system in which differentiation is provided for all (see Figure 1.6). We continue to believe that all students deserve Tier 1 (grade-level) and Tier 2 (differentiated) instruction every day. It is only intensive intervention that is reserved for a small number of students. For that instruction to be truly intensive, we believe that it cannot be provided by the classroom teacher while the other students wait. There simply isn't time.

We believe that intensive intervention should be provided by an additional teacher or interventionist, using very specialized curriculum materials. We have seen schools accomplish this in two ways. Figure 1.2 proposes grade-level instruction and then a rotation of practice and instruction for three groups. Now that we have designed a full grade-level curriculum, we can get much more specific. Figure 1.7 provides an overview of the choice that most schools we work with make. They provide 90 minutes of grade-level reading and writing instruction for all students, and then schedule differentiation

Tier 3	Intervention		
Tier 2	Below-grade-level instruction	At-grade-level instruction	Above-grade-level instruction
Tier 1	Grade-level instruction		

FIGURE 1.6. Differentiation for all.

45 minutes	Shared reading of grade-level texts			
45 minutes	Grade-level English language arts			
45 minutes	Differentiation for most			Intensive intervention for some
	Group 1	Text-based writing	Self-selected reading	Tier 3 curriculum materials
	Self-selected reading	Group 2	Text-based writing	
	Text-based writing	Self-selected reading	Group 3	

FIGURE 1.7. Allocating time for Tier 1, Tier 2, and Tier 3 instruction.

time and intensive interventions at the same time, with intervention providers pushing into classrooms or pulling students out so that they can serve students from multiple classrooms. The alternative choice accommodates intensive interventions that require 90 minutes. Those interventions take the differentiation time plus one of the other grade-level segments. We see this second choice as high-stakes, in that it replaces half of their grade-level instruction. This choice is sometimes called *replacement core instruction.*

In the fourth and fifth grades, which students receive differentiation for most, and which receive the intensive intervention for some? This is a school-based decision, of course. But we have a proposal based on what we know about development and on our reading of the new standards. Students who cannot decode nearly all single-syllable words have foundational skills consistent with late first grade; if they are in third, fourth, or fifth grade, they should have access to extremely intensive interventions. That will leave us three groups to plan for in our upper elementary classroom: students who need to apply what they know about single-syllable words and patterns to longer words; students with strong word recognition but problematic reading rates; and students with strong fluency who can continue to extend their vocabulary and comprehension. It is reasonable for a classroom teacher to serve the needs of all three of these groups of children.

LOOKING AHEAD

That's easy for us to say. A tiered instruction model for fourth and fifth grades must be grounded in good science and good sense. It will demand collaboration, and it will rely on assessments and progress monitoring. It will place heavy demands on teachers at first, but these demands will decrease over time as teachers become comfortable with the focus and management required for targeted skills work. In the chapters that follow, we walk you through the design of such a system and give you the tools you need to get started. We start, though, by providing you a window into the structural elements that we think should guide the design of an upper elementary program: time, groupings, and curriculum selection.

CHAPTER 2

Designing an Upper Elementary Literacy Program

We hope that many of you are reading this book along with the rest of your school-based team. We spend much of our time with teams, helping districts and schools make the transition from collections of individual classrooms to interdependent, collaborative units with a sense of collective responsibility for students' school experiences. The most exciting aspect of tiered instruction in RTI initiatives is that it compels schools to consider this type of systems thinking. In this chapter, we introduce concepts that we have learned in the course of our problem-solving work with school-based teams. We have the luxury of working across schools, districts, and states, so we share ideas that we have seen in our travels. We consider some of the nuts and bolts of planning: thinking though instructional time, grouping strategies, the introduction of the CCSS, and strategies for reviewing curriculum materials. You will see that we think of a literacy program as a thoughtful use of all available resources, including time and people, rather than a set of materials that are purchased. This series of program design tasks is best undertaken in the spring or summer to prepare for school opening in the fall, because each of them will require thought and teamwork.

INSTRUCTIONAL TIME AND INSTRUCTIONAL TEAMS

As you build an upper elementary literacy program, think about the instructional time that you have and how you want to use it. As we have told you in Chapter 1, we started our work in schools that had a 90-minute, protected block of time for reading instruction. Depending on the district and school, this was a more or less shocking requirement. Schools with less institutionalized respect for the concept of extended instructional time for their classroom teachers still give priority in planning to the schedules of their specialists (e.g., physical education teachers, speech–language pathologists, art and music teachers), making the slivers of time between specials very hard to use. Such schools are also likely to interrupt instruction with announcements and other noninstructional activities. And now we know that we need to give writing an equal seat at the table. Make no mistake about it: If you are to implement a truly differentiated curriculum in the fourth and fifth grades, you need to make time for reading and writing instruction. As you will see in the remaining chapters of this book, this does not mean that you must give up science and social studies; in fact, if you take our recommendations to heart, you will actually increase time devoted to science and social studies content by integrating more of it into your English language arts (ELA) time and by having students process it deeply through listening, discussing, reading, and writing.

The National Center for Education Statistics tracks time spent in core academic subjects. A report using the Center's data found that in third grade significantly more time was allocated to ELA and math instruction than other subjects (Hoyer & Sparks, 2017). Figure 2.1 summarizes those findings.

RTI mandates put further pressure on this already pressured distribution of time. Some states impose mandatory extra instructional time for students who need Tier 2 and Tier 3 instruction. What we have seen most frequently is the provision of "RTI time" for Tier 2 as an addition to ELA time. We have used that time, calling it *differentiation*. Instead of sacrificing content area instruction, we urge you to consider that time be scheduled daily for Tier 2 and Tier 3 instruction. If they happen at the same time, with students either participating in Tier 2 differentiation *or* in Tier 3 interventions, the total time required is lessened.

All scheduling decisions are costly. Figure 2.2 provides a potential schedule for a classroom. The instructional day depicted here is 6.5 hours long. We are taking 90 of these minutes each day for Tier 1 reading and ELA instruction, and 45 minutes for differentiation or intensive interventions. We reserve 90 minutes for math instruction, assuming that a differentiation period can be incorporated within those minutes. With a 45-minute daily special and 45 minutes for lunch and recess (together), there are still 75

	Minutes per Week	Minutes per Day
English Language Arts	594	119
Math	348	70
Social Studies	168	34
Science	174	35
Physical Education	102	20
Art and Music	108	22
Recess	108	22

FIGURE 2.1. Average time spent in different subjects in elementary schools.

Time	Focus
8:00	Differentiation and Intensive Intervention
8:45	Shared Reading
9:30	ELA
10:15	Special
11:00	Lunch and Recess
11:45	Math
12:30	Math
1:15	Science
2:00	Social Studies
2:30	Dismissal

FIGURE 2.2. Sample instructional schedule.

minutes to allocate to science and/or social studies each day. We realize that we have not included any passing or transition time, but such time would only be necessary between ELA and the specials period, between the specials period and lunch/recess, between lunch/recess and the start of math, and at school dismissal. Time for science and social studies could alternate, so that each subject could have fewer but longer sessions per week; either the subjects could be taught on alternate days, or days could be strung together for units that alternate.

What makes the schedule more complicated in the upper elementary years is the fact that many schools want their teachers to departmentalize and work in teams. In the schedule in Figure 2.2, there are really six 45-minute classroom blocks with 30 minutes left over: three literacy blocks, two math blocks, and one longer block for science and social studies. For teaming to work, the blocks have to be of equal length. Figure 2.3 depicts such a schedule. The problem is that one content area (in this case, social studies) cannot be assigned to one teacher or the other—both the literacy teacher and the science, technology, engineering, and math (STEM) teacher have to teach it. And it is only 30 minutes long.

One last schedule to consider is shown in Figure 2.4. It assumes a three-person team. One team member teaches 90 minutes of reading and ELA to each class each day. Another teaches 90 minutes of math. The final member has 90 minutes each day to teach either science, social studies, or both. All three have a 30-minute block of differentiation, so all participate to some extent in the literacy plan. Some schools may have strong enough achievement that they can shorten this block: Teachers can meet with two groups for 15 minutes each, instead of the three groups we serve in the 45-minute block.

Remember our argument in Chapter 1 that our approach to differentiation guides us to provide it for everyone. In all three of the schedules shown in Figures 2.2 through 2.4, students are getting either differentiation or intensive intervention. The time allotted in the instructional schedule must influence curricular choices for those interventions. If

Time	Literacy Teacher	STEM Teacher
8:00	Differentiation and Intensive Intervention	Math
8:45	Shared Reading	Math
9:30	ELA	Science
10:15	Special	Special
11:00	Lunch and Recess	Lunch and Recess
11:45	Differentiation and Intensive Intervention	Math
12:30	Shared Reading	Math
1:15	ELA	Science
2:00	Social Studies	
2:30	Dismissal	Dismissal

FIGURE 2.3. Instructional schedule with a two-teacher team.

you have 45 minutes in the schedule, the intervention has to be reasonable to accomplish in 45 minutes. If you have only 30 minutes, the same is true. It is unfair to ask a teacher to "shorten" a 45-minute intervention to 30 minutes.

Experienced teachers reading this book are likely to be shaking their heads and thinking about the other adults whose schedules must be accommodated: special educators and teachers of English to speakers of other languages. To make the best use of limited support staff, most schools adopt a staggered schedule. The key is typically to make

Time	Literacy Teacher	Math Teacher	Science and Social Studies Teacher
8:00	Shared Reading	Math	Science
8:45	ELA		Social Studies
9:30	Shared Reading	Math	Science
10:15	ELA		Social Studies
11:00	Special	Special	Special
11:45	Lunch and Recess	Lunch and Recess	Lunch and Recess
12:30	Shared Reading	Math	Science
1:15	ELA		Social Studies
2:00	Differentiation and Intensive Intervention	Differentiation and Intensive Intervention	Differentiation and Intensive Intervention
2:30	Dismissal	Dismissal	Dismissal

FIGURE 2.4. Instructional schedule with a three-teacher team.

differentiation occur at a different time at each grade level. This will allow the specialists to serve students at the same grade level in an organized way across the school day.

If you have compared these schedules with those in the first edition of this book, you will see that we have taken more time for literacy overall. That is because we know now that we have to have real time for writing instruction. Good sense, good science, and new standards require it. You will also see that we take the need for students to read and write informational text very seriously. Into our extended literacy time, we infuse much more attention to high-quality informational texts.

GROUPING STRATEGIES

As you build an upper elementary literacy program, think about grouping and be purposeful about your decisions. Although we have presented our favorite approach to grouping embedded in the rotation in Figure 1.2 (see Chapter 1), it is not the only one. Our favorite approach is to begin with a set of classrooms heterogeneous by achievement. Many schools accomplish this as a part of regular business by forming classrooms based on prior student achievement data. They review this data and ensure that each classroom has roughly the same number of students who are likely to need intensive intervention and the same number of students with very strong literacy achievement. Then, for different times in the instructional day and for different purposes, instruction is provided to groups heterogeneous by achievement and to groups homogeneous by achievement. We believe that planning for both types of groupings is healthy during an instructional day.

We recommend that schools provide grade-level reading and writing instruction—including high-quality read-alouds; structured shared reading of meaningful trade books; and grammar and writing instruction for narratives, informative texts, and persuasive texts—to groups heterogeneous by achievement. This instruction can be scaffolded by the teacher, making it a time of accessible knowledge building for all students. Even for the students with the strongest literacy achievement, the chance to enhance vocabulary and world knowledge is always a rationale for the read-aloud—and that is why we are so insistent that it be a read-aloud of challenging language and content. For those students whose literacy achievement is very close to grade-level expectations, the shared reading segment may be just right to build their fluency and to provide the level of challenge and support they need to coordinate their comprehension processes. For those students whose skills are well below grade level, scaffolding by the teacher through a skillful, interactive read-aloud and a well-supported shared reading of an interesting book provides access to grade-level vocabulary and concept knowledge, as well as modeling of the application of comprehension strategies. During genre-based writing instruction, a focused instructional opener and a specific product goal can get most students writing productively, while the teacher supports those who struggle with composition or transcription. In short, all students are served during grade-level instruction, but they are not served the same meal.

After this period of heterogeneous grade-level instruction, we move to a segment in which students are grouped homogeneously by achievement. Those who remain in the classroom for differentiation are grouped *within* the classroom; those who need Tier 3 instruction are grouped *between* classrooms. This means that they join other students with similar achievement profiles, so that they can work together with one intervention teacher and one intervention.

We often return to the metaphor of a diet as we think about student achievement and grouping strategies. We do this because we want to provide students with the diet most likely to keep them healthy. We understand that some teachers will disagree with this stance. As research has revealed, some teachers fear that grouping students by achievement for differentiation is stigmatizing (Moody, Vaughn, & Schumm, 1997). However, instruction that does *not* group students by achievement is particularly problematic for the lowest-achieving students; they tend to make almost no progress (Schumm, Moody, & Vaughn, 2000). Grouping students by achievement for at least some part of the day, even across grade levels, has long been associated with higher rates of growth (Slavin, 1987). When grouping is accompanied by differences in instructional strategies and materials, as we are proposing in this volume, achievement effects are highest (Lou et al., 1996).

An alternative to the basic within-class grouping format that we have described previously is the use of between-class grouping during differentiation. Many schools use this strategy. Basically, they use a whole-class, heterogeneous group for grade-level instruction, and then they move children into homogeneous groups across classrooms for differentiation. If four teachers teach at the same grade level, one would have the highest-achieving students (and the largest group); another would have high-average students; a third would have low-average students; and a fourth would have students needing intensive interventions. This plan may be attractive to many teachers, because they are only personally responsible for their grade-level instruction and for instruction for one group. They may view planning for multiple groups as too daunting. However, there are two basic costs to this approach: (1) Teachers do not provide instruction for a number of their own students, and (2) the group sizes will be much larger.

An upper elementary literacy program cannot be silent on the issue of grouping. We urge you to weigh your options, base your choice on what you predict will be best for students, and then use your professional development resources to make that option work for teachers as well.

PLANNING FOR STANDARDS

As you are working on an upper elementary literacy program design, your thinking must be influenced by the ELA standards in your state. At the very least, standards drive the design of state assessments, and state assessments have consequences for children, for teachers, and for schools. Standards also help us to ensure that our literacy programs are vertically articulated, that what we teach in one year is actually a logical precursor to the goals for the next year.

As noted in Chapter 1, the release of the CCSS (NGACBP & CCSSO, 2010) required major redesign of reading and writing programs in the upper elementary grades. There are 10 reading standards and 10 writing standards that run across the K–5 grade levels.

These are reproduced in Figure 2.5 and Figure 2.6, respectively. Some states have stayed with these standards, while others have created state-level versions that are largely consistent with them.

What really drew us to reconsider grade-level reading and writing instruction, and to commit to the design of *Bookworms K–5 Reading and Writing* (Open Up Resources, 2018), were the specific and rigorous texts and text characteristics required in the new standards at each grade level. You will see that we have used the CCSS throughout this book to guide our text and content selection. In the area of basic reading skills, the standards address word recognition and fluency content for K–5 as foundational skills. The concept that these skills are actually foundational for higher-order standards is consistent with our thinking about appropriate differentiation and intervention targets for the upper elementary grades. As you are building your program, read the standards that apply to your state and district carefully—looking not for how they reinforce what you are already

Key Ideas and Details	
1	Read closely to determine what the text says explicitly and to make logical inferences from it; cite specific textual evidence when writing or speaking to support conclusions drawn from the text.
2	Determine central ideas or themes of a text and analyze their development; summarize the key supporting details and ideas.
3	Analyze how and why individuals, events, and ideas develop and interact over the course of a text.
Craft and Structure	
4	Interpret words and phrases as they are used in a text, including determining technical, connotative, and figurative meanings, and analyze how specific word choices shape meaning or tone.
5	Analyze the structure of texts, including how specific sentences, paragraphs, and larger portions of the text (e.g., a section, chapter, scene, or stanza) relate to each other and the whole.
6	Assess how point of view or purpose shapes the content and style of a text.
Integration of Knowledge and Ideas	
7	Integrate and evaluate content presented in diverse media and formats, including visually and quantitatively, as well as in words.
8	Delineate and evaluate the argument and specific claims in a text, including the validity of the reasoning as well as the relevance and sufficiency of the evidence.
9	Analyze how two or more texts address similar themes or topics in order to build knowledge or to compare the approaches the authors take.
Range of Reading and Level of Text Complexity	
10	Read and comprehend complex literary and informational texts independently and proficiently.

FIGURE 2.5. Common Core State Standards (CCSS) anchor standards for reading. From NGACBP and CCSSO (2010). In the public domain.

Text Type and Purposes	
1	Write arguments to support claims in an analysis of substantive topics or texts, using valid reasoning and relevant and sufficient evidence.
2	Write informative/explanatory texts to examine and convey complex ideas and information clearly and accurately through the effective selection, organization, and analysis of content.
3	Write narratives to develop real or imagined experiences or events, using effective technique, well-chosen details, and well-structured event sequences.
Production and Distribution of Writing	
4	Produce clear and coherent writing in which the development, organization, and style are appropriate to task, purpose, and audience.
5	Develop and strengthen writing as needed by planning, revising, editing, rewriting, or trying a new approach.
6	Use technology, including the Internet, to produce and publish writing and to interact and collaborate with others.
Research to Build and Present Knowledge	
7	Conduct short as well as more sustained research projects based on focused questions, demonstrating understanding of the subject under investigation.
8	Gather relevant information from multiple print and digital sources, assess the credibility and accuracy of each source, and integrate the information while avoiding plagiarism.
9	Draw evidence from literary or informational texts to support analysis, reflection, and research.
Range of Reading and Level of Text Complexity	
10	Write routinely over extended time frames (time for research, reflection, and revision) and shorter time frames (a single sitting or a day or two) for a range of tasks, purposes, and audiences.

FIGURE 2.6. CCSS anchor standards for writing. From NGACBP and CCSSO (2010). In the public domain.

doing, but for how they can influence you to set even higher goals for yourself and for your students.

EVALUATING INSTRUCTIONAL MATERIALS

Many people would argue that the place to start in designing a literacy program is with the instructional materials themselves. We surely disagree. Without a notion of the amount of time you have, how you will group, and what your goals are, it makes no sense to select materials. Reading and writing programs do not come in boxes. In fact, with the OER revolution (of which *Bookworms K–5 Reading and Writing* is part), some are decidedly outside the box! Reading and writing programs are complex and organic. However, once you know what you want to do and what resources you have to spend, it makes sense to examine the extent to which new materials can make your job easier. Usually they can. Both commercial and OER reading and writing programs tend to sequence skills and strategies within meaningful texts and themes. They also tend to include both narratives and informational texts. Choosing among the programs requires that teachers have some concrete tools to guide their thinking. We know that many districts consult the free reviews available on EdReports (*www.edreports.org*). These reviews can be helpful, and the reports themselves provide a window into the specifics of instructional design for a program. We see the work of the EdReports team as a helpful first step in program selection. The reviews help teachers gauge the extent to which the texts are well selected, the instructional routines are coherent, and the supports for instruction and assessment are sufficient. The reviews are really about standards alignment and usability.

What EdReports does not do is evaluate the extent to which the instruction is consistent with reading and writing research. We think that this consideration is at least as important as the overall design elements. In fact, we believe that EdReports will produce some misleading guidance; it is possible for a program to score well on the EdReports rubric (largely because it is standards-based) but not be attentive to the collective work of reading and writing researchers. Luckily, there is a tool that does just that. It is called the *Rubric for Evaluating Reading/Language Arts Instructional Materials for Kindergarten to Grade 5* (Foorman, Smith, & Kosanovich, 2017). This tool is free and downloadable. Its recommendations are keyed to the Institute for Education Sciences Practice Guides (which are also available for download from the Institute's website, *https://ies.ed.gov*). As this document is public access, Figure 2.7 provides this rubric's items for upper elementary grades.

The process for reviewing a literacy program involves a team in a careful content analysis. Basically, given the teachers' editions and the program scope and sequence, teachers work together to evaluate the extent to which the items in the rubric are addressed. They provide rubric ratings with evidence. That procedure develops a deep understanding of the program's design, and it also highlights areas where teachers will have to work together to strengthen the program. The trick is to go through the process with your own colleagues, even after a district's adoption team has made a decision. If you are not working through these items with your core program and your teammates, you will not reap the benefits of the deepened understanding that comes from the analysis.

It may seem odd for a book about differentiating instruction to give such thorough attention to realizing the potential of grade-level instruction. Although we believe that this instruction is essential, we also want to emphasize that grade-level programs will *never* be enough. They cannot ensure a healthy literacy diet for all students. They neither sufficiently review for students who are experiencing difficulties nor sufficiently challenge students who are not. We need both a strong Tier 1 program in reading and writing, and an approach to differentiation that enhances its effectiveness. In the next chapter, we review the research that must underlie both.

Foundational Reading Skills
1.1.	Materials support development of advanced word analysis skills (for example, suffixes, prefixes, Greek and Latin roots, and syllabication patterns).
1.2.	Materials include guidance to provide small-group, differentiated instruction to students struggling with reading development.

Reading Comprehension for Literary and Informational Texts and Text Complexity
2.1.	The text and text complexity are appropriate for the reading level of students.
2.2.	Materials provide students extensive opportunities to encounter and comprehend grade-level text.
2.3.	Materials incorporate texts that require a careful and purposeful reading and rereading.
2.4.	Additional materials markedly increase the opportunity for regular independent reading of texts that appeal to students' interests to develop both knowledge and love of reading.
2.5.	Specific texts are included in materials for teaching various text structures (for example, sequence, comparison/contrast, and cause/effect) to support comprehension and careful reading of narrative and informational text.
2.6.	Materials contain questions and tasks that require students to use text-based evidence (including making inferences).
2.7.	Material cultivates student engagement in reading text carefully.
2.8.	Texts provide opportunity for students to build knowledge through reading and extended discussion.
2.9.	Materials include questions and tasks that require students to analyze information and evidence focused on the meaning of texts.
2.10.	Materials support instruction that teaches students to identify and describe or explain ideas for narrative text (for example, main idea and theme) and informational text (for example, connections between ideas and concepts) in a progressively more complex manner.
2.11.	Materials support instruction that teaches students to use the features of text to gain meaning from narrative text (for example, how chapters and scenes are used in types of literature) and informational text (for example, use of illustrations and graphs, and structural elements) with increasing complexity.
2.12.	Materials support instruction that teaches students to understand and analyze various points of view for narrative text (for example, author, narrator, and characters) and informational text (for example, what the author wants to explain and multiple accounts of the same event) with increasing complexity.
2.13.	Materials support instruction that teaches students to compare and contrast or analyze information within and across narrative text (for example, compare and contrast two versions of the same story and compare and contrast stories in the same genre) and informational text (for example, identify similarities and differences between two texts on the same topic and integrate information from several texts on the same topic to write about the subject) with increasing complexity.

(continued)

FIGURE 2.7. Upper elementary indicators for an evidence-based literacy curriculum. From Foorman, Smith, and Kosanovich (2017). In the public domain.

Writing Development and Skills
3.1. Materials include extensive practice with short, focused research projects that allow students to have multiple experiences with the research process throughout the year and facilitate development of the ability to conduct research independently.
3.2. Materials include activities that require students to analyze and synthesize text sources and present the analysis using well-defended claims and clear information.
3.3. Materials provide instruction in different text structures (for example, sequence, comparison, contrast, and cause/effect) and place a focus on argument and informative writing based on texts with these structures.
3.4. Materials include activities that provide opportunities to write routinely over extended time frames (time for research, reflection, and revision) and shorter time frames (a single sitting or a day or two) for a range of discipline-specific tasks, purposes, and audiences.
Speaking and Listening Development and Skills
4.1. Materials include opportunities to continue to build oral language and listening skills as students determine main ideas and supporting details, paraphrase, and summarize texts read.
4.2. Materials use multimedia and technology to support and engage students in understanding and verbally expressing details and themes in a text.
Language Development and Skills
5.1. Materials teach academic vocabulary prevalent in complex texts in the context of listening and reading activities.
5.2. Materials include activities for students to acquire and use grade-appropriate general academic and domain-specific words and phrases, including those that signal precise actions, emotions, or states of being (for example, *quizzed, whined,* and *stammered*) and that are basic to a particular topic (for example, *wildlife, conservation,* and *endangered* when discussing animal preservation).
5.3. Materials include instruction for students to determine or clarify the meaning of unknown and multiple meaning words and phrases based on grade-appropriate reading and content, choosing flexibly from a range of strategies.
5.4. Materials include instruction for students to understand figurative language, word relationships, and nuances in word meanings.

FIGURE 2.7. *(continued)*

CHAPTER 3

Research on Upper Elementary Readers and Writers

Since the first edition of this book was published, we have focused more of our own attention and research on reading and writing instruction for upper elementary students. Other schoolwide researchers have likewise shifted their focus to include the needs of readers and writers in the fourth and fifth grades. These researchers are an interesting bunch. In this chapter, we review recent findings from research in upper elementary grades to describe characteristics of fourth- and fifth-grade readers and writers. In the chapters that follow, we show how you can design instruction to maximize students' reading and writing growth during these early adolescent years.

STAGES OF READING DEVELOPMENT

It would be fair to say that we view literacy development as cognitively oriented stage theorists. Jeanne Chall's (1996) seminal book *Stages of Reading Development* proposed that readers acquire skills in six definitive reading stages. Stage theorists contend that qualitatively different behaviors are associated with specific stages. In the case of reading stages, Chall argued that what differs is how the reader attends to printed text. We present Chall's stages in Figure 3.1. Children are often introduced to aspects of reading before beginning formal education, focus on letter sounds and decoding words in early primary grades, confirm what they know about words to develop fluency, and then begin to read to learn new things beginning in fourth grade.

Chall's proposed reading stages are important. Although individual children might reach Stage 3 at different times, this is the stage at which students in the upper elementary grades should normally be reading. The difference between Stage 2 and Stage 3 has

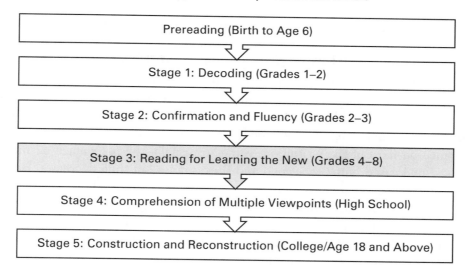

FIGURE 3.1. Chall's stages of reading development.

simplistically been called the transition from "learning to read" to "reading to learn." And fourth grade has traditionally been students' first real experience with the content area textbooks that they wrestle with through the rest of their schooling. Fitzgerald and Shanahan (2000) added critical reading and writing knowledge to each of Chall's stages, arguing that metaknowledge about comprehension, prior knowledge about content, knowledge about text structure, and procedural knowledge about reading and writing meaningful text are essential for readers and writers at Chall's Stage 3.

Fourth grade is also the first time that students are given the National Assessment of Educational Progress (NAEP) reading test, and the results have been consistently disheartening. Only 36% of fourth graders performed at or above the proficient level in 2017, and another 31% performed at the basic level. *Thirty-two percent of fourth-grade students performed below the basic level.* Unfortunately, there is no difference in the percentage of students below the basic level between the most recent results and those of a decade ago. Although the NAEP reading assessment is not given in the primary grades, conventional wisdom (likely stemming from a combination of Chall's reading stages, the somewhat problematic dichotomy between learning to read and reading to learn, and the NAEP scores) has led many to suspect that a large number of students begin to experience a dip in reading achievement in fourth grade despite adequate development through third grade. This trend is known as the *fourth-grade slump* and is particularly steep for students living in poverty. Compared with 18% of students not eligible for the National School Lunch Program, 46% of eligible students performed below the basic level on the NAEP.

THE FOURTH-GRADE SLUMP

An oft-cited study of the phenomenon of decreasing reading and writing achievement beginning in fourth grade (Chall, Jacobs, & Baldwin, 1990) tracked three cohorts of students experiencing poverty with measures of word recognition, spelling, word meaning, word analysis, oral reading, and reading comprehension. They also analyzed writing samples in several ways, including holistic ratings; analytic trait scores for content, form, organization, and handwriting; and measures of word production, syntax, vocabulary, and spelling. The data revealed that students' reading performance at second and third grades was adequate, but that knowledge of word meanings declined at fourth grade, and then that word recognition, spelling, and comprehension followed suit at seventh grade. Likewise, students' performance on most of the writing measures, especially the percentage of unfamiliar words used, increased between second and third grades but then decreased beginning in fourth grade. The fourth-grade slump, then, may begin with a slump in acquiring and using vocabulary knowledge, which may have wide-reaching negative effects.

There are several possible explanations for this trend. It may be fair to say that there are nontrivial differences in the reading and writing tasks children face in the primary grades versus the upper elementary grades. One difference may be the shift to informational texts. Narratives with strong story grammars have traditionally dominated the reading selections in first grade (Duke, 2000), and narrative writing is among the most common writing activities teachers have reported using in the primary grades (Cutler & Graham, 2008). Jeong, Gaffney, and Choi (2010) examined text use in second-, third-, and fourth-grade classrooms. As in Duke's study, they found very infrequent use of informational text, even in the fourth-grade classrooms.

In the years since the CCSS called for an increase in the use of informational text in the elementary grades, teachers have reported more frequent inclusion of informational text in their reading instruction (Ness, 2011) and writing instruction (Gilbert & Graham, 2010). In a survey of third- and fourth-grade teachers, Brindle, Graham, Harris, and Hebert (2016) found that narrative, informative, and persuasive writing tasks were all assigned monthly. Li, Beecher, and Cho (2018) found that fourth-grade teachers assigned informational text reading weekly, but more frequent informational text reading was not associated with better reading performance.

Although students may be reading more informational texts, upper elementary teachers may not be providing students with the support they need to read them well. Informational text poses different cognitive demands, often presenting one or more unfamiliar text structures. For example, students may read a text that combines compare/contrast, description, and listing in its overall structure, and students accustomed to a diet of fiction with a strong story map may be unaccustomed to these organizational patterns. Teaching students how to identify and use text structure can improve both reading comprehension (Hebert, Bohaty, Nelson, & Brown, 2016) and writing quality (Graham, McKeown, Kiuhara, & Harris, 2012).

Another reason for the fourth-grade slump may be the increasing demands of reading and writing vocabulary outside of normal speaking and listening vocabulary. In short, reading selections begin to contain a higher percentage of lower-frequency words. The words become more abstract and complicated, and some students may not be able to understand them in reading or use them in writing. This trend is evident in poor reading vocabulary performance at fourth grade, weak comprehension beginning at sixth grade, and a low percentage of unfamiliar words in writing from second through seventh grades. It should come as no surprise that the largest contributor to upper elementary students' informational text comprehension is vocabulary knowledge (Liebfreund & Conradi, 2016). It may be that opportunities for wide reading make it possible for more advantaged students to develop larger vocabularies that they can leverage as the demands of reading and writing increase.

A third reason why students' reading performance declines in upper elementary grades may be the influence of world knowledge on comprehension of informational texts (e.g., Best, Floyd, & McNamara, 2008). McNamara, Ozuru, and Floyd (2011) found that children without sufficient world knowledge have difficulty learning from challenging content area texts, due to their inability to integrate a weak knowledge base with knowledge from the text to make inferences. They are not alone in arguing that knowledge, not reading skills, is the key to successful comprehension of informational texts. Hirsch (2006) suggested that a focus on teaching comprehension strategies, rather than improving world knowledge and knowledge-related vocabulary, is to blame for children's poor reading achievement. Daniel Willingham, a psychologist at the University of Virginia, explained that "comprehension is intimately intertwined with knowledge" (2017, para. 11). In other words, comprehension strategies should be taught in the context of developing content knowledge (Rotherham & Willingham, 2010).

Motivation and attitude may also play a part. A survey of upper elementary students found a decline in their motivation to read fiction and nonfiction from third through sixth grade, with the steepest drop in their self-concept and value for reading after fifth grade (Parsons et al., 2018). Students who develop a low self-concept for reading will surely read less, missing chances for incidental vocabulary acquisition, and these missed opportunities will eventually manifest themselves in poor reading comprehension. The same can be said for writing, as fourth-grade students' self-efficacy and attitudes toward writing predict their writing performance (Graham, Kiuhara, Harris, & Fishman, 2017).

Fortunately, there are ways that teachers can work together to prevent these trends. Chall and colleagues (1990) addressed this issue head on, arguing that upper elementary teachers should provide opportunities for their students to read widely from a variety of challenging narrative and informational books, with appropriate instruction to increase their word recognition, fluency, vocabulary, and reading comprehension. Sanacore and Palumbo (2009) suggest specific actions to help counteract the fourth-grade slump: (1) Increase access to expository discourse throughout the primary grades; (2) engage children in more informational text reading by reading aloud to them and then providing them access to high-quality classroom library materials for independent reading; (3) teach meaning vocabulary directly; and (4) foster engagement and participation. A combination of direct vocabulary instruction, a focus on knowledge building, and development of a positive school culture should help to prevent the slump (Goodwin, 2011).

THE POTENTIAL FOR RETHINKING HIGH-QUALITY TIER 1 INSTRUCTION

The fact that researchers have produced evidence of a fourth-grade slump and that NAEP scores are at unacceptable levels does not mean that the situation is hopeless. It does mean that upper elementary teachers must be resourceful in their use of texts.

Teachers have reported lack of instructional time, lack of quality resources, limitations in school-adopted basal programs, and disengaged readers as obstacles to including more informational text in their classrooms (Ness, 2011). One third-grade teacher identified her weekly 30-minute science and 50-minute social studies blocks as the best time to use informational texts. Another third-grade teacher expressed frustration with a lack of informational texts written at an appropriate level for students with reading difficulties. Most teachers stated that the vocabulary, knowledge demands, and structure of informational texts are challenges for their students. A fourth-grade teacher described the extensive amount of time required to teach vocabulary and preview before reading about a new topic as a barrier. Clearly, many teachers want to provide more opportunities for their students to read informational texts, but the barriers they report are real impediments.

Creative approaches to using content area texts and core reading programs are one possible solution. Swanson, Edmonds, Hairrell, Vaughn, and Simmons (2011) describe a small set of comprehension strategies, including previewing, question generating, identifying the main idea, and summary writing, that teachers can use over and over again with different texts, keeping the focus squarely on the content. In fact, Willingham (2006–2007) advocates for quickly teaching three categories of strategies aimed at building knowledge: strategies designed to encourage students to (1) monitor their comprehension, (2) relate sentences to one another, and (3) relate sentences to things they already know. His strategy categories, influenced by the work of the National Reading Panel (2000), are summarized in Figure 3.2. You will see that we encourage many of these strategies as ways to facilitate the growth of even the highest-achieving readers in Tier 1 instruction.

We have been intrigued by a number of suggestions that stand in stark contrast to the status quo. Some researchers have questioned the large number of skills and strategies targeted in commercial programs, and have recommended using fewer strategies and focusing on content (see Dewitz, Jones, & Leahy, 2009). Others have tested the potential benefits of privileging knowledge building over strategy instruction. McKeown, Beck, and Blake (2009) compared a strategies approach, a content approach, and typical core instruction for fifth graders. The strategies approach included direct instruction of summarizing, predicting, drawing inferences, generating questions, and comprehension monitoring, while the content approach included guided discussion of the content of the text through open, meaning-based questions. All three approaches yielded adequate comprehension, but the content approach was slightly more effective. The authors have suggested that teachers target comprehension strategies quickly and then use them flexibly as students discuss text content. We have been convinced by their argument.

Elleman, Olinghouse, Gilbert, Compton, and Spencer (2017) conducted a similar study with students who struggled in grades 2–6. Students in the knowledge instruction group were taught how to use four strategies, which are the familiar components of reciprocal teaching (questioning, summarizing, clarifying, and predicting; Palincsar & Brown, 1984) to check whether the text made sense. The vocabulary group focused on target words in the texts, again using four strategies: determining the part of speech, word analysis strategies, context clues, and a look-up strategy. Finally, the content group

Strategy	Description
Strategies designed to encourage students to monitor their comprehension:	
Comprehension monitoring	Readers are taught to become aware of when they do not understand—for example, by formulating what exactly is causing them difficulty.
Listening actively	Students learn to think critically as they listen, and to appreciate that listening involves understanding a message from the speaker.
Strategies designed to encourage students to relate sentences to one another:	
Graphic organizer	Students learn how to make graphic representations of texts.
Question answering	After students read a text, the teacher poses questions that emphasize the information students should have obtained from the text.
Question generation	Students are taught to generate their own questions, to be posed during reading, that integrate large units of meaning.
Summarization	Students are taught techniques of summarizing—for example, deleting redundant information and choosing a topic sentence for the main idea.
Mental imagery	Students are instructed to create a mental visual image based on the text.
Cooperative learning	Students enact comprehension strategies—for example, prediction and summarization—in small groups, rather than with the teacher.
Story structure	Students are taught the typical structure of a story and learn how to create a story map.
Multiple-strategy instruction	Multiple strategies are taught—often summarization, prediction, question generation, and clarification of confusing words or passages.
Strategies designed to encourage students to relate sentences to things they already know:	
Prior knowledge	Students are encouraged to apply what they know from their own lives to the text, or to consider the theme of the text before reading it.
Vocabulary–comprehension relationship	Students are encouraged to use background knowledge (as well as textual clues) to make educated guesses about the meaning of unfamiliar words.

FIGURE 3.2. Categories of comprehension strategies. Adapted from Willingham (2006–2007). Reprinted with permission from the Winter 2006–2007 issue of *American Educator*, the quarterly journal of the American Federation of Teachers, AFL-CIO.

read the text and completed activities such as drawing pictures, using graphic organizers, matching vocabulary and definitions, and answering questions after reading. The results were not easy to interpret. Both strategy instruction groups performed better on vocabulary acquisition, but there were no differences between any of the groups on content knowledge acquisition, general vocabulary, or general comprehension. The content instruction treatment was more effective for older students. The authors concluded that a balanced approach to strategies and content instruction may be most effective for upper elementary students with reading difficulties.

College and career reading standards call for an increase in the difficulty of texts children are expected to read, a focus on answering text-dependent questions in writing, and an emphasis on building knowledge. The text difficulty shift has evoked contro-versy among some literacy researchers, especially for the youngest readers (e.g., Fisher & Frey, 2014a; Hiebert & Mesmer, 2013). For older readers who have learned to decode, however, Shanahan (2017) has argued in favor of increasing exposure to difficult texts, especially with instructional support from their teacher. We have chosen to embrace the potential of difficult text and to rethink the type and amount of instructional support teachers provide.

The approach to Tier 1 literacy instruction that we describe in this book, *Bookworms K–5 Reading and Writing* (Open Up Resources, 2018), makes challenging text accessible for all students by employing contextualized strategy instruction and a focus on building vocabulary and world knowledge through direct instruction and through high-volume reading. There are routines for building fluency (choral and partner rereading), com-prehension (direct explanation of word meanings, text structure instruction, brief com-prehension strategy modeling, meaning-focused discussion, and text-based writing), and vocabulary and knowledge (high-volume reading and listening through interactive read-alouds). An initial study of the effects of this Tier 1 program on oral reading fluency and comprehension for students in grades 3–5 in one school district revealed that students in *Bookworms* schools grew more in comprehension at all three grades than students in a comparison guided-reading district. *Bookworms* students in grades 3 and 5 also outper-formed their peers on fluency (Walpole, McKenna, Amendum, Pasquarella, & Strong, 2017). We take these findings to suggest that upper elementary teachers can improve their students' reading achievement through a combination of exposure to challenging text and supportive instruction. We use the general planning template for *Bookworms K–5 Reading and Writing* as a template for explanations in this book; we add our new writing template as well. Both Tier 1 planning templates are included in Appendix A.

THE ADDED VALUE OF TARGETED DIFFERENTIATED INSTRUCTION

Strong Tier 1 instruction alone cannot prevent the fourth-grade slump. Although foun-dational skills matter, comprehension instruction also matters. Both must be consider-ations in the design of differentiation. Results should not be surprising. A focus on word recognition benefits children with weak word recognition skills; a focus on comprehen-sion benefits children with strong word recognition skills. Wanzek and colleagues (2017) designed an intervention that yielded significant effects on comprehension, but not on word recognition or vocabulary. This study reminds us that comprehension instruction can improve comprehension, but that this improvement doesn't necessarily extend to word recognition; this conclusion is consistent with a review of upper elementary inter-ventions (Wanzek, Wexler, Vaughn, & Ciullo, 2010). Phonics instruction may be needed for students with word recognition difficulties, but a vocabulary and comprehension intervention may do the trick for children experiencing the fourth-grade slump. This is why we argue that upper elementary teachers must continue to use achievement data to make decisions about the focus of their small-group instruction. We describe our approach to assessment in Chapter 4.

A Focus on Fluency

Is fluency still important at the upper elementary grades? Rasinski, Rikli, and Johnston (2009) tested the relationship between fluency and comprehension at grades 3, 5, and 7, to examine the extent to which fluency exerted an influence on comprehension beyond the primary grades. Results indicated that fluency (measured to include both rate and prosody) was still related to silent reading comprehension beyond the ages at which Chall's (1996) stage model might predict. Students gained in fluency from grades 3 to 5, but then seemed to regress at grade 7. We continue to include fluency in our upper elementary model. If fluency is still developing in fourth and fifth grades, fluency interventions will still be important.

Repeated reading protocols, a mainstay of fluency interventions, have shown positive effects for fourth- and fifth-grade students. However, the findings are not always straightforward. Paired repeated readings led to fluency improvements in fourth-grade students in urban schools, but they still failed to meet end-of-grade benchmark goals (Musti-Rao, Hawkins, & Barkley, 2009). Paired repeated reading increased vocabulary, word reading, and comprehension, but not fluency. Vadasy and Sanders (2008) speculated that the students actually needed a word recognition treatment rather than a fluency treatment—a distinction that we address in the following chapters, and one that we believe is a hallmark of the need for intensive intervention. Yet other studies have demonstrated that multisyllabic word-reading interventions are effective for upper elementary students with reading difficulties (e.g., Toste, Capin, Vaughn, Roberts, & Kearns, 2017). In Chapter 6, we advocate an approach to fluency intervention that combines repeated reading with multisyllabic decoding instruction for students who need it.

You will also see that we continue to recommend the use of challenging text in these interventions. Other researchers are investigating the effects of text difficulty on intervention results. O'Connor, Swanson, and Geraghty (2010) found the same improvements in reading rate when students read text at their independent reading level or at a more difficult level. Another intervention documented greater gains in oral reading fluency and comprehension when students who struggled read texts two grade levels above their instructional reading level (Brown, Mohr, Wilcox, & Barrett, 2018). Taking these findings together and combining them with the evidence that vocabulary growth matters, we find no reason to restrict students' fluency practice to texts at their independent reading level, or their fluency instruction to texts at their instructional level. We focus instead on the scaffolds teachers can provide and the knowledge-building opportunities texts can afford.

A Focus on Vocabulary

The importance of vocabulary for upper elementary students cannot be overestimated. Vocabulary is essential for reading and writing. Strong vocabulary fuels comprehension, and strong comprehension builds vocabulary (Stanovich, 1986). Students with greater vocabulary knowledge also write better (Silverman et al., 2015). Vocabulary building is an important target for differentiation.

There are at least four routes to vocabulary building: wide reading, direct instruction in word meanings, modeling word solving, and using words in discussion (Fisher & Frey, 2014b). Direct instruction in vocabulary in the upper elementary grades has to include both use of context and morphology (Baumann, Edwards, Boland, Olejnik, & Kame'enui, 2003; Bowers & Kirby, 2010; Silverman et al., 2017). It can also include metacognitive training that helps readers to become more conscious of their own word learning and more strategic when they come across a word they do not know (Lubliner & Smetana, 2005).

Fourth and fifth graders' comprehension is related to their understanding of morphology; this is true both for native English speakers and for Spanish-speaking English learners (Carlo et al., 2004, 2008; Kieffer & Lesaux, 2007). These researchers recommend that we attend to four principles when designing instruction that builds students' understanding of morphology: (1) Teach students morphology in the context of their vocabulary and word learning; (2) teach students to examine morphology as a cognitive strategy; (3) build morphological knowledge both explicitly and in context; and (4) use Spanish cognates when appropriate. We have incorporated the first three principles into our vocabulary instruction; we focus on these issues in Chapter 7.

A Focus on Comprehension

Providing access to challenging informational texts is important for building comprehension. Researchers have demonstrated positive effects of using science texts for fifth-grade students with poor reading comprehension (Ritchey, Palombo, Silverman, & Speece, 2017). Some interventions have even integrated science and literacy instruction, finding positive effects on fourth-grade students' science understanding, vocabulary, and writing outcomes (Cervetti, Barber, Dorph, Pearson, & Goldschmidt, 2012). Concept-Oriented Reading Instruction (CORI) targets reading comprehension, fluency, content knowledge, motivation, and text-based writing within the domain of science. A test of CORI in fourth grade (Wigfield et al., 2008) documented its effectiveness in building comprehension, strategy use, and engagement. In fifth grade, CORI was effective in building comprehension, content knowledge, and word recognition skills, for both high- and low-achieving readers (Guthrie et al., 2009). All students read texts that dealt with ecological communities, but readers with low achievement read texts that were easier than the ones read by their peers with higher achievement. Because all of the texts were related in content, all students developed their content area expertise. Choosing informational texts with rich content, connected to the curriculum, may be especially important to upper elementary literacy development.

Allowing students to talk about text also matters. Clark (2009) analyzed postreading discussions of short stories among small groups of fifth-grade students with high achievement. She documented a host of strategic behaviors, but also found that they were not used with equal frequency. The most frequently used strategies were questioning and evaluating, but other strategies included interpreting, comparing/contrasting, noting author's craft, engaging in retrospection, contextualizing, using prior knowledge, summarizing, searching for meaning, stating a confusion, and inserting self into text.

How can teachers ensure that students use these strategies during text-based discussions? Hall (2012) found that readers below grade level in sixth-grade social studies classes were relatively silent during small-group discussions until they heard their peers struggling with ideas in the text and using strategies to facilitate comprehension. A recent study examined teachers' use of a set of discourse moves referred to as Support for Students' Learning from Text (SSLT; Dwyer, Kelcey, Berebitsky, & Carlisle, 2016). The SSLT discourse moves were related to higher engagement in discussions, as well as to higher reading comprehension and vocabulary achievement. Dwyer et al.'s coding scheme, which we have captured in Figure 3.3, provides concrete suggestions for

Type of discourse move	Description
Revoices	The teacher restates a student's statement in a way that makes it comprehensible to others, so that they can more easily respond to the contribution.
Clarifies students' ideas	The teacher asks questions or requests further explanation about a student's response/statement, to make sure it is understood.
Facilitates sharing of ideas	The teacher actively encourages children to share ideas or information.
Synthesizes/summarizes	The teacher synthesizes or integrates different student responses or ideas on a topic, to create a public and shared information base for the group.
Expresses interest in students' ideas	The teacher shows or expresses interest in students' contributions to a discussion—including (but not limited to) expressing an interest in students' ideas, actively engaging with students as they speak, and looking at children when they speak.
Facilitates reasoning	The teacher pushes students to explain, justify, or analyze their responses, often with questions following a student's comment.
Encourages students to provide evidence from text	The teacher asks students to find evidence in the text to support a comment or idea or to answer a question.
Prompts students to make text-to-self connections	The teacher actively encourages students to make personal connections with the text by asking them to think about how their experiences or knowledge relates to the topic.
Draws out students' knowledge and experience	The teacher elicits students' background knowledge and personal experiences that are likely to help them make personal connections to the topic or content of a text. This might set the stage for reading a text or deepen understanding of some topic under discussion.
Provides background information	The teacher provides information that will help students understand a text or topic under discussion.

FIGURE 3.3. Discourse moves to facilitate text-based discussions. Adapted from Dwyer, Kelcey, Berebitsky, and Carlisle (2016). Copyright © 2016. Adapted with permission of the University of Chicago Press; permission conveyed through Copyright Clearance Center, Inc.

engaging students in rich text-based discussions in the upper elementary grades. We include text-based discussions in our comprehension instruction in Chapter 8.

A Focus on Writing

Given that writing instruction improves the quality not only of adolescents' writing (Graham & Perin, 2007), but also of their reading comprehension (Graham & Hebert, 2010), a focus on writing serves two important masters. Much of the research on reading and writing interventions has focused on strategies that support self-monitoring and self-evaluation (Wehmeyer, Shogren, Toste, & Mahal, 2017). Metacognitive knowledge about writing, including the writing process and genres or structures, is positively related to upper elementary students' reading and writing performance (Englert, Raphael, & Anderson, 1992). One of the best-known approaches to writing strategy instruction, Self-Regulated Strategy Development (SRSD; Graham, Harris, & Mason, 2005), uses a specific procedure to teach students how to plan and draft in different genres. Teachers develop background knowledge about a genre-based writing strategy, discuss why it is important, model how to apply the strategy, support the use of the strategy with a collaborative writing experience, and then provide opportunities for students to use the strategy independently. SRSD has led to longer and better-quality stories and opinion essays than a writers' workshop approach for elementary students (Graham et al., 2005; Harris, Graham, & Mason, 2006). Interestingly, the effects even transfer to personal narratives and informative writing, which are not taught in the intervention. The writing strategies that can be used with SRSD instruction vary, but some strategies are commonly used. Common strategies for opinion, informative, and narrative writing, based on those presented by Ciullo and Mason (2017), are displayed in Figure 3.4. In Chapter 9, we describe the use of specific genre-based writing strategies in our approach to writing instruction.

THE NEED FOR CONTINUED INTENSIVE INTERVENTIONS

Who begins to experience reading difficulties in fourth grade? These students are a heterogeneous group (Lipka, Lesaux, & Siegel, 2006). A recent longitudinal study investigated the achievement profiles of late-emerging poor readers by looking back at their

Opinion: TREE	Informative: TIDE	Narrative: C-SPACE
Topic	Topic	Characters
Reasons	Ideas	Setting
Evidence	Details	Problem
Ending	Ending	Actions
		Conclusion
		Emotions

FIGURE 3.4. Genre-based writing strategies. Adapted from Ciullo and Mason (2017). Copyright © 2017 by SAGE. Adapted by permission of SAGE Publications, Inc.

word reading and reading comprehension achievement from kindergarten through grade 10 (Catts, Compton, Tomblin, & Bridges, 2012). While 29% of students were identified as having a reading disability in grade 2, that percentage increased to 44% in grade 4. Only another 2% of students were identified as having a reading disability in grade 8, and that was also true in grade 10. For students identified with reading difficulties in two grades, 52% were persistent poor readers, 6% had early reading problems only, and 42% were late-emerging poor readers. These late-emerging poor readers could be further classified into three types: Over half (52%) had problems in reading comprehension alone, over one-third (36%) had problems in word reading alone, and the remaining students (12%) had problems in both. Each of these three groups was truly experiencing a fourth-grade slump, one that would require intensive intervention. But the slumps were different.

The intensive interventions we choose at upper elementary grades must acknowledge these differences. Students with word-reading difficulties may need explicit, systematic decoding and morphology instruction; students with reading comprehension difficulties may need explicit instruction in comprehension strategies and vocabulary; and students with mixed reading difficulties may need multicomponent interventions (Spear-Swerling, 2016). But even students within these three types of reading difficulties may possess different strengths and weaknesses. Buly and Valencia (2002) investigated the achievement profiles of a group of fourth-grade students who had failed their state-mandated reading assessment. Results revealed six different types of students; these profiles are represented in Figure 3.5. Although we stop short of recommending specific Tier 3 interventions, we argue that these must actually be chosen for their match to late-emerging poor readers' specific needs. As Figure 3.5 demonstrates, these readers exhibit a variety of patterns.

INCLUDING ENGLISH LANGUAGE LEARNERS

With the growing population of English learners in American classrooms, understanding their literacy development is increasingly important. The achievement gap between English learners and native English speakers is wide; only 9% of English learners performed

Profile	%	Word Identification	Meaning	Fluency
Automatic Word Callers	18	Strong	Somewhat weak	Strong
Struggling Word Callers	15	Somewhat weak	Somewhat weak	Strong
Word Stumblers	17	Somewhat weak	Somewhat strong	Somewhat weak
Slow Comprehenders	24	Somewhat strong	Strong	Somewhat weak
Slow Word Callers	17	Somewhat strong	Somewhat weak	Somewhat weak
Disabled Readers	9	Weak	Weak	Weak

FIGURE 3.5. Profiles of fourth-grade students with reading difficulties. Based on Buly and Valencia (2002).

at or above the proficient level on the NAEP in 2017, when 40% of native English speakers met that goal. Lesaux, Crosson, Kieffer, and Pierce (2010) examined the influences of oral language and word-reading skills on the reading comprehension of Spanish-speaking English learners from grades 4 and 5. They found that oral language (vocabulary and listening comprehension) was a stronger predictor of reading comprehension than word-reading skills were. Not unlike native English speakers identified as late-emerging poor readers, English learners may develop proficient decoding ability and then begin to have comprehension difficulties in fourth grade due to low vocabulary knowledge. This is one reason why we are so adamant that upper elementary instruction must contain interactive read-alouds, with consistent attention to the development of vocabulary and listening comprehension, *and* the experience of reading connected text. Perhaps unsurprisingly, a recent meta-analysis found that instruction focused on both vocabulary and comprehension was most effective for upper elementary English learners (Hall et al., 2017).

As we look at recent research conducted with upper elementary students, we are convinced that high-quality vocabulary, comprehension, and writing instruction are necessary for all students. We also know that some students will need targeted help in fluency and in word recognition. To facilitate that work, our next chapter proposes an assessment model that has been useful in identifying these needs.

....

CHAPTER 4

Choosing and Using Reading Assessments

Our understanding of how to use reading assessments quickly to guide differentiation is the focus of this chapter. We address writing assessments in Chapter 9 as we describe Tier 1 writing instruction. We suspect that many classroom teachers view the idea of reading assessment as a complex and slightly mysterious process—one that involves giving an assortment of tests and applying daunting inferential strategies to arrive at diagnostic conclusions. Although there is some truth to this perception with regard to a small number of challenging cases, we wish to allay any fears you may be harboring about the assessment required to make small-group instruction successful in an upper elementary classroom. This perception may also stem from the fact that many teachers are forced to give assessments that are not actually used to make decisions. Others must give assessments that actually produce conflicting information. The fact is, only a few informal assessments are needed to group students for differentiated instruction and to gauge their growth.

TYPES AND PURPOSES OF ASSESSMENTS

Assessment serves a critical role in differentiated reading instruction. It guides the process first by grouping students with similar needs, then by helping to plan instruction, and finally by gauging the extent of student learning. A distinction is sometimes made between assessment *for* instruction and assessment *of* instruction. When we assess for instruction, we use the information we gather to target our teaching toward student needs. Assessment of instruction is conducted to determine whether our efforts have been successful. In our approach to differentiated instruction, both kinds of assessment are important. The fact that assessment has multiple purposes has led to more than one type of assessment, and we begin with an overview of the four basic types.

Screening measures provide an indication of achievement in a particular area. Screenings are common for word recognition, fluency, and comprehension. They are sometimes administered individually and sometimes to an entire classroom at once. These measures are limited in what they can tell us. Identifying a problem area is a good first step, but it does not suggest specific actions we might take to address the problem. To accomplish that aim, we administer *diagnostic measures*. These are follow-up tests that break down the area into teachable skills and strategies. For example, if a screening measure of word recognition indicated that a student was performing below expectations in general, a follow-up inventory of specific decoding skills would provide the information needed to identify and address the specific deficit. Screening and diagnostic measures work in tandem to provide the information teachers require in order to meet their students' needs. Our approach to differentiation in small groups for upper elementary students makes only limited use of diagnostic assessments. They would take on a more central role in selecting Tier 3 intensive interventions for students who are performing well below grade level.

Progress-monitoring measures are administered periodically to provide a teacher with feedback as to whether instruction is having the desired effect. The information they provide can be useful in adjusting approaches to instruction in order to improve learning. They answer the perennial educational question "Are they learning what I am teaching?" These measures are frequently the same as those used for screening. This is one example of how the same measure can serve different purposes. Sometimes, though, they are assessments related much more directly to the content of the instruction.

Finally, *outcome measures* help educators judge the effectiveness of instruction on a broader scale. They typically combine the results for many students to measure the achievement of classrooms, schools, districts, and the nation. They include (but are not limited to) the high-stakes tests that so often concern teachers and administrators. We believe that outcome measures serve an important purpose by providing stakeholders with the information they require. Because outcome assessments come near the end of the school year, it is too late to use them to plan instruction, but the results can shed light on how effective the overall instructional program has been and possibly suggest modifications for the next year. Our concern is that teachers make the best use of outcome measures—and that use is very limited. At best, they provide tentative screening information for the upcoming year, although it is frequently too dated to be of much use. Outcome measures do not provide information that is specific enough to guide instructional planning. Moreover, their use for progress monitoring would be cumbersome and inappropriate. What is troubling is that teachers in grades 4 and higher rely mainly on outcome measures (Torgesen & Miller, 2009). It is important to avoid this pitfall by becoming aware of the variety of available assessments and learning how to use them in concert.

ORGANIZING FOR ASSESSMENT

The thought of assembling a battery of useful assessments and then coordinating their use may seem daunting: There are so many types of assessments and so many possibilities for using them. As you will see, however, accomplishing this aim is not difficult. We begin with a few simple guidelines about reading assessment for small-group instruction.

• *Aim for the fewest assessments to answer the questions that are important.* We don't assess for the sake of assessing. An assessment system that is "lean and mean" is far preferable to one that generates a great many data points that no one will use. Because administering assessments takes time, a minimalist system helps to ensure that the time left for instruction will be maximized.

• *Assessments must be coordinated to account for the important aspects of reading.* Identifying a single area of need and directing all available resources toward meeting that need may not be enough to ensure that students become proficient. Too often, students are experiencing multiple problem areas, and it is crucial for teachers to arrive at conclusions concerning particular students' status in word recognition, fluency, and comprehension.

• *All students must be screened.* The fact that students in the upper elementary grades are performing at benchmark levels at the beginning of the year does not mean that no further assessments are needed: "Students must acquire many additional reading skills after third grade in order to be proficient readers in high school" (Torgesen & Miller, 2009, p. 10). This fact requires that we assess even students who are not presently struggling, in order to ensure that they continue to make progress.

• *Formative assessments are the key to successfully using data to guide instruction.* Formative assessments are informal measures that help teachers plan and adjust their instruction. There are three types of formative assessments: (1) those embedded in ongoing classroom instruction, (2) periodic benchmark assessments, and (3) screening and diagnostic assessments (Torgesen & Miller, 2009). All three have a place in our model of differentiated instruction. In curriculum-based measurement, we make a distinction between general outcome assessments, which are good for temporarily classifying students and for gauging their progress from time to time, and skills-based and mastery measures, which are useful for determining whether specific instructional objectives have been attained (Hosp, Hosp, & Howell, 2016). This distinction is very similar to the difference between screening and diagnostic assessments. The former are used to classify and monitor; the latter are short-term in nature and help us plan instruction from cycle to cycle.

We turn now to assessments useful in gathering information about the major dimensions of reading. In order to plan appropriate instruction, we need information in three areas. As you will see, however, the assessment burden is light.

Assessing Fluency

Oral reading fluency is the ability to read aloud grade-level text at an appropriate rate and with a high level of accuracy and natural intonation. This definition contains the three dimensions of fluency that are important to assess: rate, accuracy, and prosody. Most screening in the area of fluency targets the first two of these, and it is common to use a combined metric consisting of words correct per minute (WCPM). Since this metric only counts words read correctly, there is no need to measure the percentage of accuracy separately. Consensus benchmarks for each grade have been established and are presented in Chapter 6. A brief sample of oral reading, typically 1 minute, can provide a quick indicator of whether a particular student is performing below benchmark. Rasinski's (2003) spring benchmark for grade 4 was 118 WCPM and for grade 5 was 128 WCPM. Hasbrouck and Tindal's (2017) norms table reported a spring benchmark of 133 for fourth grade and 146 for fifth grade for students at the 50th percentile. The differences might be attributable to the increased attention paid to the importance of fluency over time. In both sets of norms, there is only a modest increase from grade 4 to grade 5, but the texts students encounter in grade 5 are more challenging.

We consider fluency to be a pivotal proficiency in students' reading development. This is because students who are dysfluent devote too much attention to word recognition and too little to comprehension. Fluency is therefore a prerequisite of comprehension, although it by no means guarantees that comprehension will be adequate. We assess fluency to identify it (or rule it out) as a cause for concern and as a target of instruction. For those students who fall below the fluency benchmark, it is tempting to assume that they are best served by evidence-based instructional approaches for building fluency. However, this is only the case when a full range of word recognition skills has been acquired. Deficits in skill acquisition are one cause of dysfluency, and it is important to determine whether these deficits exist. If they don't, fluency work is indeed appropriate. If they are present, addressing fluency alone is not likely to result in improved proficiency.

Assessing Word Recognition

When students reach the upper elementary grades, they should have received instruction on a full array of decoding skills. They will also have encountered many unfamiliar words in text, and they have attempted to apply their skills in decoding those words. By fourth grade, students should possess the skills needed to decode many multisyllabic words. Their ability to do so is grounded in more basic skills. Namely, they should be able to decode nearly every single-syllable word they encounter, and they should be able to recognize many thousands of words on sight without having to decode them consciously. A full diagnostic workup on children who are still struggling with these foundational skills would be time-consuming, to say the least. It would also require considerable expertise. We are not suggesting that fourth- and fifth-grade teachers conduct such detailed assessments. Far from it. When problems in word recognition appear to be causing dysfluency, we recommend only a brief decoding inventory. We have included such an inventory, the Informal Decoding Inventory, in Appendix E.

Figure 4.1 lists the components of our original version of the Informal Decoding Inventory, as it appeared in the first edition of this book. We structured this assessment so that it began with the more basic application of decoding skills in monosyllabic

Part I: Single-Syllable Decoding
• Short Vowels • Consonant Blends and Digraphs • *R*-Controlled Vowel Patterns • Vowel–Consonant–*e* • Vowel Teams
Part II: Multisyllabic Decoding
• Compound Words • Closed Syllables • Open Syllables • VC-*e* Syllables • *R*-Controlled Syllables • Vowel Team Syllables • C-*le* Syllables

FIGURE 4.1. Components of the original Informal Decoding Inventory.

words, followed by their application in multisyllabic words. In the first edition, we recommended that the most efficient way to administer this inventory for fourth- and fifth-grade students was to start with Part II. This practice saved time and avoided unnecessary testing. Only students who struggled with multisyllabic decoding were given Part I.

At this writing, we have simplified our protocol even further. In essence, we have created a screening that replaces the full administration of Part II of the Informal Decoding Inventory. The screening now appears in Appendix E as the Multisyllabic Words subtest, the final subtest in Part I; it is also presented in Figure 4.2 as the Multisyllabic Decoding Screening (which is what we call it when using it separately). The assessment strategy is simple: If a student in grades 4 or 5 is not meeting the beginning-of-year oral reading fluency benchmark, give the 10 items from the multisyllabic subtest. If that student pronounces 8 or more items correctly, you can assume that providing a fluency intervention, without word-level instruction, is appropriate. If a student does not pronounce at least 8 items correctly, administer the vowel teams subtest. That subtest contains both real words and pseudowords, with specific scoring criteria for each. A student who passes the Vowel Teams subtest in Part I, but not the Multisyllabic Decoding subtest, will benefit from a small dose of multisyllabic decoding instruction in addition to fluency work.

flannel	submit	cupid	spiky	confide	cascade	varnish	surplus	chowder	approach
							Total		

FIGURE 4.2. The Multisyllabic Decoding Subtest (which appears in the current version of the Informal Decoding Inventory as Multisyllabic Words, the final subtest in Part I; see Appendix E).

For upper elementary students who have not mastered vowel teams, a focus on more basic skills is required. Administering the full version of Part I of the inventory can help verify this need and identify specific instructional targets. However, we do not believe that Tier 2, classroom-based instruction in these basic skills is realistic in fourth and fifth grades. Our reading of current standards requires mastery of all single-syllable decoding skills in the early spring of grade 1. Students in upper elementary grades who need this instruction deserve Tier 3 intervention, not simply small-group instruction in the classroom. This advice should come as good news: It simplifies matters for the fourth- and fifth-grade teacher, and makes an assessment-driven approach practical and easy to manage. Commercial intervention programs in the area of decoding typically include their own assessments. Once informal assessments have indicated the need for such a program, these built-in assessments should be used to guide instruction (Torgesen & Miller, 2009).

Assessing Vocabulary

Although no one disputes the importance of vocabulary knowledge in reading, the problem of assessing that knowledge has proved difficult to solve. The National Reading Panel (2000) identified vocabulary assessment as an especially troublesome area. We have not seen much progress in informal assessments since then. There are dependable normed and standardized screening tests available, to be sure, but they are time-consuming and provide little information that is helpful in planning differentiated reading instruction. Diagnostic tests of vocabulary, in contrast, are nonexistent. This is because a diagnostic test delineates an area into the specific skills a student may lack. In the case of vocabulary, these skills are the equivalent of individual word meanings. That is, every new word is a "skill." Because there is no agreed-upon vocabulary curriculum for each grade, we cannot simply assess a student to determine which words need to be taught. Even if there were such a curriculum, it would contain too many words to make diagnostic assessment feasible.

We do think that strategies for assessing knowledge of taught words are important. Given new standards' linking of reading and writing, we believe that the most important evidence that a student has learned a word is the ability to use that word in a rich sentence-level context. We describe vocabulary instruction in Chapter 7, but we preview it here by sharing the rubric we've developed to assess it. Figure 4.3 attends to both the meaning of the word and the quality of the sentence-level context that a student generated for it.

Assessing Comprehension

Comprehension is unquestionably the most important dimension of reading—the bottom line—and yet assessing comprehension is difficult. However, screening measures, such as the comprehension subtest of a group achievement test, can be useful in determining how a student is performing relative to grade-level expectations. Although we have pursued the design of free curricula for teaching reading and writing, we have not found free

	4: Exceeds Standard	3: Meets Standard	2: Progressing	1: Developing
Meaning	Sentence demonstrates clear understanding and is written in a creative way.	Sentence demonstrates clear understanding.	Sentence demonstrates partial understanding.	Sentence does not demonstrate understanding.
Structure	The resulting sentence is compound or complex.	At least 3 questions are answered.	At least 2 questions are answered.	Either 1 question or 0 questions are answered.
Word usage		Word is used correctly.		Word is not used correctly.

FIGURE 4.3. Rubric for rating vocabulary use in context.

screening assessments of comprehension that are valid and reliable. Some schools will have purchased commercial comprehension assessments, but others will not.

Because states typically require outcome assessments yearly beginning at grade 3, spring assessments at the end of that year and the next may be useful as screenings for the fall. Many outcome assessments produce achievement levels in four bands, similar to the NAEP's. For students with spring scores of 3 or 4 (typically equating to meeting or exceeding standards), it is safe to assume adequate comprehension the next fall. For those with scores of 1 or 2, it makes sense to think diagnostically about their comprehension. In order to do that, we use a fluency screening, and, if necessary, the Multisyllabic Decoding subtest.

As is the case for vocabulary, there are no diagnostic tests of comprehension, but the reason is different. Attempts to delineate comprehension into specific skills and strategies have proved fruitless, because assessments of these skills are highly correlated (McKenna & Stahl, 2009). A student who scores high on one skill is likely to score high on others, for example. The best way to diagnose a comprehension problem is to examine the various factors that might contribute to that problem. These include difficulties with word recognition; limited vocabulary and background knowledge; lack of familiarity with various text and sentence structures; and the failure to apply comprehension strategies for specific purposes. We are not suggesting that assessments in each of these areas are needed to implement differentiated reading instruction, but comprehension assessment is nevertheless a part of our approach to differentiated instruction.

Let's begin by considering the two reasons to assess comprehension. One is to determine a student's overall level of proficiency; the other is to gauge the student's understanding of a particular text. These are very different goals, and both are important. Consequently, in our approach, two kinds of comprehension assessments are needed. The first is a screening measure designed to provide an overall level, usually translated into a performance level or Lexile—a metric used to rank students' ability on a scale ranging from beginning reading (a scale score of 200) well into advanced ranges (see *https://lexile.com*). A Lexile is a prediction of 75% comprehension when students are reading on their own. Figure 4.4 demonstrates how a teacher might judge the suitability of a particular book for use with a particular student or with a small group of students. In this case, the

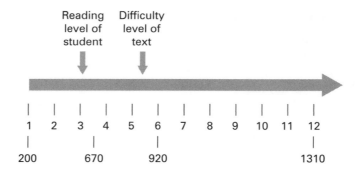

FIGURE 4.4. Using grade levels or Lexiles to judge the match between students and texts.

text is likely to be very challenging without support from a teacher—unless the student is reading about a topic about which he or she has very strong background knowledge.

We believe that comprehension metrics create the illusion of precision. In reality, they are merely estimates that must be weighed, together with teacher judgment. We are also convinced that a precise match between a student and a text is not important; getting reasonably close is good enough. And in some ways, a precise match may not always be desirable. Inspecting this example might prompt one to think that this hypothetical text is too difficult. Keep in mind, however, that in small-group instruction the teacher is in a position to provide considerable support that makes challenging texts appropriate.

The second comprehension assessment useful in small-group differentiated instruction is the day-to-day informal information a teacher derives while interacting with students. This information might come from asking questions or thinking about the questions students ask. If these examples seem imprecise, so be it. Comprehension of a particular text is difficult to reduce to a number or set of numbers even under the best of conditions, and certainly not in the give-and-take of small-group instruction. What is important is for teachers to judge whether comprehension is adequate. If it isn't, adjusting the level of support or switching to an easier text may be required.

As we have designed Tier 1 instruction in *Bookworms K–5 Reading and Writing*, we have designed assessments of comprehension of the grade-level curriculum. Much as we evaluate vocabulary with the vocabulary rubric we have shared in Figure 4.3, we use rubrics to evaluate comprehension. We assign text-based writing prompts to reading every day, and we evaluate one every two weeks. Figure 4.5 shares our rubric for scoring those responses in fourth grade; the fifth-grade rubric has the same format but uses the fifth-grade standards.

Given the imprecision inherent in comprehension measurement, we do not expect a teacher to chart gains in comprehension over the course of a year, and certainly not over a matter of weeks. The tools available for this purpose are simply not very good. Other than informally monitoring students' comprehension of each text they read, nothing more is needed. We focus instead on using assessments to address the underlying factors that impair comprehension and providing a rich diet of texts, high in vocabulary, text structures, and other nutrients.

	4: Exceeds Standard	3: Demonstrates Standard	2: Progressing	1: Developing
First, consider accuracy.		Answer is plausible.		Answer is not plausible.
↓	**4: Exceeds Standard**	**3: Demonstrates Standard**	**2: Progressing**	**1: Developing**
Next, consider evidence.	Response refers explicitly to what the text says and includes accurate quotes.	Response refers explicitly to what the text says and includes details and examples from the text.	Response refers explicitly to key details in the text.	Response refers generally to the text or is unrelated to the text.

FIGURE 4.5. Grade 4 rubric for scoring written responses as evidence of comprehension.

Assessing the Affective Dimensions of Reading

Affect is a dimension of reading development that is frequently overlooked. It involves how well students like to read, what they like to read, and what they think of themselves as readers. Given the well-documented downward trajectory of reading attitudes and habits, we believe that these factors have a place among the assessments classroom teachers use to improve their understanding of how their students function as readers. We confess that simply documenting that a student harbors a negative attitude or has come to view him- or herself as a poor reader is not of very much help in planning instruction. Other than selecting books that are engaging and accessible, we typically do not make the affective side of reading a primary target. We argue, however, that affect should instead be an indirect target. Supplying an abundance of interesting texts, facilitating students as they engage those texts, and working to build the skills and strategies needed to comprehend them can improve attitudes.

The chief usefulness of assessing affect lies in gauging changes over the course of a school year, not in planning instruction for a group. We suggest that three assessments are sufficient: an interest inventory, an attitude survey, and a self-perception survey. These are group assessments, given at the beginning and end of the year.

An interest inventory is simply a list of topics that might be of interest to students. It could follow a checklist format, allowing students to easily identify those topics about which they might be interested in reading. Some teachers prefer to use graduated responses so that students can indicate their degree of interest. For example, students might be asked to give each topic a "grade." Interest inventories are of two kinds: general and content-specific. A general inventory lists a range of topics and types of fiction. A content inventory lists aspects of a subject area that students might like. A science inventory, for example, might include subtopics of likely appeal (e.g., poisonous snakes, strange phenomena, black holes). Content inventories have utility beyond small-group instruction. The results can be useful in recommending books to students in connection with content area instruction. An example of a general interest inventory is presented in Figure 4.6. Note that it contains a few blanks. The reason is that an interest inventory is essentially

Name _____

Which topics do you like the most? Pretend you're a teacher and give each one of these a grade. Give it an A if you really like it, a B if you like it pretty well, a C if it's just OK, a D if you don't like it, and an F if you can't stand it! If I've missed some topics you really like, please write them on the lines at the bottom of the page.

_____ sports		_____ monsters
_____ animals		_____ horses
_____ magic		_____ detectives
_____ jokes		_____ love
_____ exploring the unknown		_____ famous scientists
_____ sharks		_____ ghosts
_____ camping		_____ other countries
_____ UFOs		_____ dogs
_____ spiders		_____ comic books
_____ the jungle		_____ the ocean
_____ drawing, painting		_____ music
_____ riddles		_____ science fiction
_____ friendship		_____ cats
_____ snakes		_____ families
_____ the wilderness		_____ the desert
_____ fishing		_____ computers
_____ manga		_____ video games

What other topics do you really like? Write them here:

_____

_____

_____

_____

_____

_____

FIGURE 4.6. Example of a general interest inventory.

a ballot, and every ballot should have a place for write-in candidates. Although you are welcome to duplicate the inventory in Figure 4.6, it is a good idea to create your own, so that you can modify it as needed. For example, you may find that some topics are rarely checked or that topics you overlooked are frequent write-ins. You can edit your inventory accordingly. Finally, you must be able to deliver the goods. It is pointless to include topics for which you have no texts to recommend or to use for small-group work.

A reading attitude survey asks students to respond to statements or questions that are matters of personal judgment and opinion. Questions such as "How do you feel about reading on a rainy Saturday?" are quickly rated on a Likert or pictorial scale. Summing the results provides an overall indicator of whether a student's attitude is positive, negative, or indifferent. A free attitude survey long popular in the upper elementary grades is the Elementary Reading Attitude Survey (ERAS), a pictorial instrument based on the cartoon character Garfield (McKenna & Kear, 1990; McKenna, Kear, & Ellsworth, 1995). It is group-administered and easy to score and interpret. It contains two subscales: one measuring attitude toward academic reading, and another assessing attitude toward recreational reading. The ERAS has excellent psychometric properties and has been used as the basis of numerous research studies. Kear, Coffman, McKenna, and Ambrosio (2000) also developed the Writing Attitude Survey (WAS) to measure students' attitude toward writing. Both may be downloaded free at *www.professorgarfield.org.*

An assessment of self-perception is designed to provide teachers with an idea of how students view themselves as readers. A free instrument specifically designed for grades 4–6 is the Reader Self-Perception Survey (RSPS; Henk & Melnick, 1995). The RSPS assesses four dimensions: (1) progress (how a student views his or her progress in becoming a more proficient reader), (2) observational comparison (how the student compares his or her proficiency with that of peers), (3) social feedback (input the student has received from peers and family about his or her reading), and (4) physiological states (internal feelings that the student experiences during reading, such as comfort or frustration). Like the ERAS and WAS, the RSPS is nationally normed, group-administered, and easy to interpret.

A COORDINATED PLAN FOR ASSESSMENT

Now that we have explored the characteristics of various assessment instruments likely to be useful in upper elementary grades, it is time to take stock of what we need and bring the components together in an assessment tool kit. Its contents are listed in Figure 4.7. The left-hand column lists the types of assessments you will need; the right-hand column indicates specific assessments that would be suitable (with room to write in specific instruments that might be available).

Using Assessments Systematically

These tools are enough to accomplish the principal goals of our differentiation model: (1) place students into appropriate small groups, (2) plan instruction targeted to the needs that group members share, and (3) gauge the impact of that instruction on student progress.

Assessments You Need	Assessments You Have or Can Get
Comprehension screening measure from previous year	
Comprehension performance measure	Figure 4.5
Vocabulary performance measure	Figure 4.3
Oral reading fluency screening	
Multisyllabic decoding screening	Multisyllabic Decoding Screening (Figure 4.2; also appears in Appendix E as the Multisyllabic Words subtest in Part I of the Informal Decoding Inventory)
Inventory of decoding skills	Informal Decoding Inventory (Appendix E)
Attitudes toward reading and writing	ERAS and WAS
Self-perception as a reader	RSPS

FIGURE 4.7. Assessment tool kit.

Forming small groups requires systematic use of a few basic assessments from our tool kit. Placement of students into groups is not a precise process. It involves estimation and compromise, but its benefits are considerable. It is useful to think of students with reading difficulties beyond grade 3 as falling into either of two broad categories (Torgesen & Miller, 2009). One includes students who are reasonably fluent but who lack the vocabulary, background knowledge, and comprehension strategies to understand grade-level text. The other includes students who are not fluent and who may lack the more fundamental decoding skills needed to become fluent. Fluency screening can help teachers in grades 4 and 5 quickly decide which category is the better fit for a given student. Students who fall in the second category (usually far fewer in number than the first) require additional informal assessment at the word level. Figure 4.8 represents our grouping process.

The point of giving formative assessments is to follow them with the kind of effective, targeted instruction that the assessments indicate (Torgesen & Miller, 2009). Once groups are populated, such instruction is determined by the focus of the group. As Figure 4.8 illustrates, there are only three types of groups, each with a dual focus: (1) vocabulary and comprehension, (2) fluency and comprehension, and (3) fluency and comprehension with multisyllabic decoding. There is an intended overlap of four areas in these three groups. All three groups have some attention to comprehension. Our top group, vocabulary and comprehension, includes both the students who are known to have strong comprehension and those who may have some comprehension weaknesses but have strong fluency. We can serve both types of students well in the same group. In the next four chapters, we discuss instruction in each of these four areas.

Using Assessments to Regroup

Formative assessments are most useful when they are given periodically, after regular intervals. In our approach to differentiated instruction for earlier grades, we recommend

3-week cycles. This length of time not only fits conveniently into marking periods, but it also guarantees that teachers will regularly take stock of student progress and adjust their instruction accordingly. For students in the upper elementary grades, though, a longer group membership is perfectly fine. That longer period allows teachers to use longer books.

After forming the groups, a teacher will embark on instruction for all groups. Each day will bring informal assessment information. Making a few notes about how individual students are responding to instruction will be useful. At the end of the marking period, the teacher is in a position to judge which group will best serve each student's needs going forward. These cycles continue throughout the year, and a combination of formal and informal assessments can determine group membership in a truly flexible way. Remember that students who are experiencing the combined effects of fluency building in Tier 1 and differentiation may improve and be better served by moving up to the vocabulary and comprehension group. Figure 4.9 illustrates this continuing process, beginning with initial screening and proceeding from cycle to cycle through the year, ending in outcome measures (including high-stakes assessments). We note that this year-long model, which is based on the one proposed by Torgesen and Miller (2009), occasionally includes a midyear screening assessment.

Maintaining Records of Assessment

We have deliberately created a Tier 2 instructional system in which assessment plays an important but limited role. Despite its limited nature, however, the information acquired

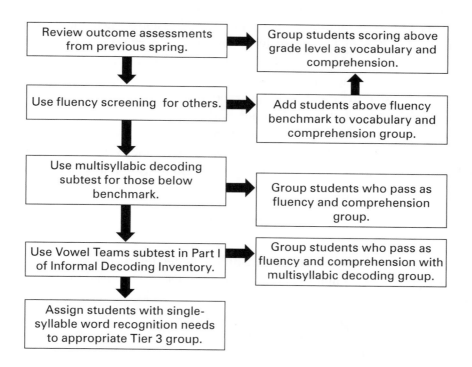

FIGURE 4.8. Using assessments to form groups.

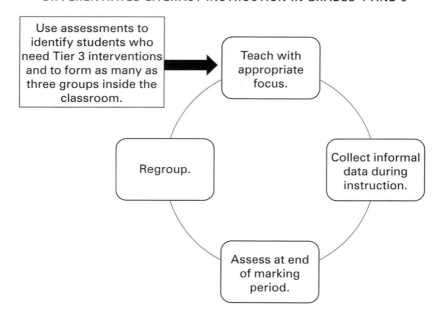

FIGURE 4.9. A year-long plan for using assessments. Based on Torgesen and Miller (2009).

for individual students is surprisingly extensive when we consider it across the course of the school year. This information allows us to track students and to gauge their progress at a glance. One might argue that as long as the general blueprint laid out in Figure 4.9 is followed, there is no pressing need to keep records over time. We disagree and can suggest three persuasive reasons for doing so. First, the decision a teacher must make at the end of each cycle, although based largely on the student's performance during that cycle, can also be affected by the longer history of small-group work. Second, this history will be useful as evidence of the need for Tier 3 intervention for the few students who do not progress. The decision to provide such instruction will probably be reached not by the classroom teacher alone, but in conjunction with a specialist or team, who will benefit from examining the student's history. Finally, maintaining records over time can play a role as part of a larger RTI plan. For example, if Tier 3 intervention proves effective, students can move to a fluency and comprehension group with multisyllabic decoding.

A FINAL WORD

Choosing and using assessments as part of a differentiated instruction plan is not difficult. Those required are few in number and easy to administer. They lead to straightforward group placement, and they provide the information needed to regroup appropriately. They also facilitate a simple long-term record-keeping system that allows a teacher to track the progress of students over time and make decisions about the kinds of instruction that will best meet their needs.

······························

CHAPTER 5

Building Word Recognition

In this chapter, we present a tiered instructional model for developing fourth- and fifth-grade students' word recognition. In order to introduce the model, we first present some foundational knowledge about the structure of words. For Tier 1 instruction, we argue that direct instruction in the sound, spelling, and meaning of a small set of words before students read can both improve their comprehension and build their understanding of the way words work. We also argue that for some students, more strategic and concentrated work on recognizing long words can be a reasonable segment of their differentiated instruction; we provide readers with a set of lessons to use, along with a systematic plan for engaging these students in analyzing words. Finally, we argue that upper elementary students who are still struggling with basic word recognition skills for single-syllable words must have access to Tier 3 intensive interventions.

FOUNDATIONAL KNOWLEDGE
ABOUT WORD RECOGNITION DEVELOPMENT

When we begin our work with upper elementary teachers, we hear a familiar refrain: "Wait! We never learned this!" We imagine that most fourth- and fifth-grade teachers will be relieved to know that they do not have to teach basic word recognition skills; in fact, they really will need to do little at the level of the individual sound. When we meet new words as skilled readers, we actually do not sound them out one sound at a time. Rather, we automatically look for ways to avoid that laborious process—using other words with similar structures as models, or looking for spelling patterns. For example, if the word *morpheme* is new to you, you will process its syllables (*mor* and *pheme*) to generate a pronunciation, using chunks around the vowels fairly automatically to divide and conquer the word, even as you wonder what it means. (A *morpheme* is a unit of meaning, by the way, just as a *phoneme* is a unit of sound.) If we then use the word *morphemic,* you will automatically recognize that this word has a suffix (-*ic*), and that the second syllable (*phem*) actually experienced an *e*-drop with the addition of that suffix and will still be pronounced with a long-*e* sound. See? You really do know it. This type of decoding, which we call *structural analysis,* is the focus of word recognition instruction for upper elementary readers. In order to understand how to teach children to attack long words, we first need to become conscious of how we ourselves, as skilled readers, have learned to recognize most words with relative ease—even long words and even the first time they are encountered in print. Figure 5.1 defines some important words about words that will help us in this quest.

Thinking about how words are built can be helpful in breaking them apart in order to read and understand them. The word *speech,* for example, is a free morpheme, or base word, because it is a meaningful unit that can stand alone. Because *speech* is a noun, we can create the word variants *speeches* (adding an inflected ending to indicate plurality) or *speech's* (adding an inflected ending to indicate possession). We can also derive a very different word—*speechless*—by adding a derivational suffix. This new word is an adjective. If we add another derivational suffix, we can retain the new meaning but change the word back to a noun: *speechlessness.* The root word *teach* offers additional possibilities. It is a verb, so it can be inflected as *teaching* or *teaches.* It can also be changed into a noun (*teacher*) by adding a derivational suffix. The meaning of the root word can be extended to *coteach* or *preteach* or *reteach* through the addition of common prefixes, or the part of speech can be changed to an adjective (*teachable*) through the addition of a common suffix. Clearly, the generative nature of prefixes and suffixes makes them key building blocks in students' vocabularies. And again, you *do* know these things as a mature user of words, even if you do not know the technical vocabulary. Figures 5.2 and 5.3 provide lists of common prefixes and suffixes, respectively, adapted from O'Connor (2014).

Advanced decoding is not about sounds; it is about chunks. The easiest chunks to recognize are those that represent meaning—root words and their affixes (prefixes and suffixes)—especially when those root words are unbound. Unbound morphemes, though, are not the only way that long words are built. Words are also built through adding suffixes to bound morphemes and through creating combinations of syllables that represent sound and not meaning. Bound morphemes are units of meaning, but they do not stand alone as words. The most common are the Greek and Latin roots, some of which are presented in Figures 5.4 and 5.5, respectively. Again, these are likely to be very familiar word parts to mature readers and writers—but not necessarily to the novice wordsmiths in our classrooms.

Upper elementary readers may not recognize these roots as units of meaning until they learn basic etymology. Instead, they will have to decode them. Decoding is the process by which we translate written words into their pronounced form. With long words, we don't do that sound by sound. We nearly automatically find syllables. Syllables are units of pronunciation that are easily isolated because they contain a vowel sound.

Syllable	A syllable is a unit of pronunciation that is easy to isolate because it contains one and only one vowel sound. The word *word* is a syllable; the word *pronounce* has two syllables (*pro-nounce).*
Morpheme	A morpheme is the smallest unit of meaning in a word. A word contains one or more morphemes. A morpheme can be free (meaning it can stand alone as a word) or bound (meaning it can only be used in combination with other morphemes). Prefixes and suffixes are bound morphemes, but so are Greek and Latin word roots that do not stand alone. For example, *listen* is a free morpheme. It stands alone as a word, and it can be combined with other morphemes to become *listening, listens,* or *listener. Audi* is a bound morpheme meaning *hear.* It cannot stand alone as a word, but it can be used in combination with other morphemes to make *audible* or *auditory.*
Root Word	A root or base word is a free morpheme to which prefixes and suffixes may be added. A root word with prefixes and/or suffixes is a derivative of that root. *Test* is a root word. Derivatives include *pretest, retest,* and *tester.*
Prefix	A prefix is a bound morpheme added to the beginning of a root word to change its meaning. Prefixes sometimes also change the word's part of speech. The prefix *en-* changes both meaning and part of speech when it is added to the root word *slave.* The prefix *pre-* changes the meaning but not part of speech when it is add to the root *view.*
Inflectional Suffix	An inflectional suffix is a bound morpheme added to the end of a root word to indicate plurality, possession, tense, person, or comparison. Inflectional suffixes do not change a word's part of speech. The inflectional suffixes are *-s, -es, -'s, -s', -ed, -ing, -er,* and *-est.*
Derivational Suffix	A derivational suffix is a bound morpheme added to the end of a root word to change its meaning. Derivational suffixes change a word's part of speech. The derivational suffix *-ly* changes *soft* from an adjective to an adverb.
Compound Word	A compound word is made up of two or more free morphemes (e.g., *cupcake*). In most compounds, the meaning of each word is retained and the meaning of the combination is clear. However, some compounds have obscure histories that do not help young decoders (e.g., *turnpike*). Although linguists often include compounds separated by a space (e.g., *high school*), we are not concerned with these because they present no decoding difficulties.
Contraction	A contraction is formed by replacing one or more letters with an apostrophe. It is possible sometimes to confuse contractions with possessives (e.g., *Tom's* could mean *belonging to Tom,* or it could be the contracted form of *Tom is*). Context resolves such ambiguities, which are surprisingly frequent. The contraction *she'd* could mean *she had* or *she would,* depending on the sentence context.

FIGURE 5.1. Words about words.

Remember that more than one vowel letter (and sometimes a vowel plus *y, w,* or *r*) can work together to make one vowel sound. *Hot* has one vowel letter, one vowel sound, and one syllable; *hotel* has two vowel letters, two vowel sounds, and two syllables. *Fountain* has two vowel sounds and two syllables, even though it has four vowel letters.

Syllables (whether they carry meaning or not) can be tricky to decode because vowel letters can represent more than one sound. We have to rely on syllable patterns to know which sound to use. Eldredge (2005) reports some interesting facts about words that may help convince you that the spelling system actually uses a relatively limited number of patterns; we define the six most common patterns in Figure 5.6. An analysis of the 3,000 most common single-syllable words in the language revealed that 45% have single vowels with short-vowel sounds, 38% have vowel teams or *r*-controlled vowel sounds, and 16% have vowel–consonant–*e*. A very small percentage (<2%) are single vowels pronounced with their long sound, as in *he, she,* and *we*. From these building blocks, represented in familiar one-syllable words, a virtually endless number of multisyllabic words can be built. When meaningful morphemes cannot be recognized, knowing the patterns used in most syllables is the key to multisyllabic decoding.

Prefix	Meaning	Examples
un-, in-, dis-	not	*unaware, incomplete, dislike*
re-	again	*redo, resurface*
en-, em-	to make	*enlarge, embolden*
non-	not	*nonsense, nonbinding*
in-	in	*inland, inlaid*
mis-	wrong	*misspell, misidentify*
sub-	under	*submarine, subzero*
pre-	before	*preschool, precaution*
im-, il-, ir-	not	*imperfect, illegal, irrelevant*
inter-	between	*interstate, interpersonal*
fore-	before	*foreshadow, forejudge*
de-	negate, away from	*degrease, declaw*
trans-	across	*transatlantic, transpolar*
super-, out-, over-	excess	*supermarket, outperform, overflow*
semi-	half	*semicircle, semiliterate*
anti-	against	*anticlimax, antihero*
mid-	in the middle	*midnight, midpoint*
bi-	two	*bicolor, bicycle*

FIGURE 5.2. Common prefixes. Adapted from O'Connor (2014). Copyright © 2014 by The Guilford Press. Adapted by permission.

Suffix	Meaning	Examples
-er, -or	one who, something that	*teacher, actor*
-ly	in the manner of (adverb)	*friendly, gladly*
-ful	full of	*wonderful, spiteful*
-ness	with	*kindness, happiness*
-less	without	*matchless, childless*
-tion, -sion	creates noun form	*construction, repression*
-ment	creates noun form	*government, enjoyment*
-able, -ible	able to (adjective)	*dependable, visible*
-al	creates noun from verb	*refusal, denial*
-y	inclined to be (adjective)	*funny, juicy*
-ity	creates noun form	*equality, electricity*
-ive	creates adjective form	*decisive, expressive*
-en	creates adjective form	*oaken, golden*
-ent	creates noun or adjective	*different, president*
-ant	creates noun or adjective	*pleasant, attendant*
-ous	full of	*adventurous, nervous*
-ian, -ist	one who studies	*historian, violinist*

FIGURE 5.3. Common suffixes. Adapted from O'Connor (2014). Copyright © 2014 by The Guilford Press. Adapted by permission.

	Meaning	Examples
ast(er)	star	*asteroid, astronomy*
auto	self	*autobiography, auto*
bio	life	*biography, biology*
chrono	time	*chronology, synchronize*
geo	earth	*geography, geology*
graph	write	*autograph, calligraphy*
path	feel	*empathy, pathetic*
phil	love	*bibliophile, philosopher*
phon	sound	*phonics, phonograph*
photo	light	*photograph, photosynthesis*
tele	far off	*telephone, telegraph*

FIGURE 5.4. Common Greek word roots.

	Meaning	Examples
audi	hear	*audio, audible*
bene	good	*benefit, benefactor*
dict	say	*dictate, dictionary*
gen	give birth	*generate, genetic*
jur/jus	law	*jury, justice*
luc	light	*lucid, translucent*
omni	all	*omnipotent, omnivore*
port	carry	*transport, portable*
scrib/script	write	*enscribe, transcript*
sens	feel	*sensitive, resent*
terr	earth	*territory, terrestrial*
vid/vis	see	*video, visible*

FIGURE 5.5. Common Latin word roots.

Syllable Type	Description	Examples
Closed	A single vowel is followed by one or more consonants and is pronounced with a short sound.	*trash* *tractor*
Open	A single vowel is at the end of a syllable and is pronounced with its long sound.	*she* *remote*
Vowel–Consonant–*e*	A final silent *e* marks the long-vowel sound in a syllable.	*time* *enrage*
	OR The final silent *e* is dropped when a vowel suffix is added, but the vowel is still long.	*blaming*
r-Controlled	A vowel and *r* are linked to make a vowel sound that is neither long nor short.	*shark* *purpose*
Vowel Team	Two vowels (and sometimes *w* or *y*) work together to represent one sound. It can be long, short, or neither.	*team* *contain* *boyish*
Consonant–*le*	A single consonant sound is followed by -*le* (representing the sound /ul/) in an unaccented syllable at the end of a word.	*candle* *enable*

FIGURE 5.6. Six syllable patterns.

Although this system of using morphemes and syllable types to recognize words will not account for the accurate pronunciation of every word in the English language, it works for many words. Typically, the problematic syllables are those unaccented ones in the middle of words. Think about the word *repeat*. It has two syllables: an open one (*re-*) and a vowel team (*peat*). It is easy to decode (although the vowel team *ea* can represent more than one sound). If we add an inflectional suffix *-ed*, to create *repeated*, we have also simply added a closed syllable. That closed syllable is also a morpheme signaling the past tense. But what about the noun form? *Repetition* is harder to solve as a decoding puzzle. *Re-pet-i-tion* or *rep-et-it-ion?* The second set of segments is more consistent with the sound. The vowel sounds in the first two syllables are unaccented, and the short-*i* sound before the suffix is accented. We don't believe that in-depth linguistic analyses are helpful. However, talking about this word and its morphemic relatives can make those spelling and pronunciation variables memorable for students, building their interest in words and how they work. The promise that "We will look at this word and see how it works" goes a long way.

The basic building blocks of morphemes and syllables provide a foundation on which to build upper elementary word recognition. Instruction, then, will teach students to recognize the units and to use them to attack new words. It will also teach them to be flexible. These skills are necessary so that students can both engage in fluent reading and encounter enough new words to constantly build their meaning vocabularies—a topic to which we turn in Chapter 7. For readers interested in learning more about the structure of words, Figure 5.7 lists some resources we find especially helpful. What we consider the best resources in this area have been generated by a team of scholars initially studying spelling development together at the University of Virginia. We have all been influenced by their initial pioneering work and by their ongoing efforts to inform decoding, spelling, and vocabulary instruction. If you dive into these resources, you will see that the spellings of words in English trace some of their idiosyncrasies to sound and pattern, others to history, and still others to our tendency to adopt words from other languages.

TIER 1 INSTRUCTION IN WORD RECOGNITION

We do not endorse the purchase of vocabulary and spelling workbooks to practice words in isolation. The key to efficient Tier 1 instruction for upper elementary readers is the link between a focus on individual words and the rest of the students' literacy diet: fluency,

---

Ayto, J. (2011). *Dictionary of word origins: The histories of more than 3,000 English-language words.* New York: Arcade.

Bear, D. R., Invernizzi, M., Templeton, S., & Johnston, F. (2016). *Words their way: Word study for phonics, vocabulary, and spelling instruction* (6th ed.). Boston: Pearson.

Ganske, K. (2008). *Mindful of words: Spelling and vocabulary explorations 4–8.* New York: Guilford Press.

Johnston, F., Invernizzi, M., Bear, D. R., & Templeton, S. (2018). *Words their way: Word sorts for syllables and affixes spellers* (3rd ed.). Boston: Pearson.

FIGURE 5.7. Resources about words.

vocabulary, comprehension, and writing. Texts at this level provide multiple opportunities to teach the pronunciation, spelling, and meaning of words directly. They also provide multiple opportunities for students to *generalize*—that is, to recognize longer words in context that have not been taught in isolation. The interesting, whole texts used in Tier 1 will provide ample opportunity for building word recognition. What we need to do is select specific words to teach and develop the teaching language that makes their meaning and spelling structure transparent.

Content

What we need to develop advanced word recognition is simple: words. Word recognition instruction at this stage must build flexibility and competence for meeting words in connected reading and for using them in speaking and writing. In the early primary grades, we choose the words for their orthographic features—but not in upper elementary. The *Rubric for Evaluating Reading/Language Arts Materials for Kindergarten to Grade 5* (Foorman et al., 2017) identifies "development of advanced word analysis skills (for example, suffixes, prefixes, Greek and Latin roots, and syllabication patterns)" (p. 14) as the foundational skills requirement for evidence-based instructional materials for the upper elementary grades. Such words and word parts are encountered in every grade-level text that students read.

All students, then, need a working knowledge of the six syllable types. They need to know that single vowels can be pronounced as short or long, or with the schwa sound; they also need to know that vowel teams and *r*-controlled vowels have specific pronunciations. They actually know these things from their single-syllable store of many thousands of words that they can recognize by sight. They need to know what a prefix, a suffix, and a root are. Again, they have a strong personal store of sight words that are inflected. To put this knowledge to work to decode unknown words, they need to learn some strategies that can help them to break words into chunks that are easily analogized to these underlying decoding keys. Figure 5.8 presents a series of steps that teachers can use to think aloud as they chunk multisyllabic words. These strategies are related to the specific building blocks (morphemes and syllable types) for each word.

There is one spelling generalization that is also essential for success during the upper elementary grades. According to developmental spelling theories advanced by our University of Virginia colleagues, students at this age are most likely working at the stage of syllables and affixes. This means that their attention is likely to be drawn to understanding the junctures of syllables, especially to whether consonants should be doubled or not. In fact, adults are still working on these junctures as they spell. For example, spellers will be wondering whether the word *commit* + *ment* will have two *t*'s or one. It has only one *t*, because the suffix -*ment* begins with a consonant. *Committed* has two, because the final syllable of the base word *commit* is closed, and we are adding a vowel suffix. Teaching students to use the doubling principle in context with actual words will build deep conceptual understanding. Application of the doubling principle, which guides spelling changes as suffixes are added to base words, forces students to understand and use concepts of syllable type. Figure 5.9, based on Ganske (2008), illustrates the doubling

Compounds	Closed–Closed	Open–Closed	Consonant-*le*
breakfast *myself* *snowstorm* *throughout* *folktale* *downpour*	*napkin* *happen* *magnet* *dentist* *plastic* *absent*	*music* *robot* *female* *fever* *human* *basic*	*table* *battle* *handle* *bugle* *cable* *sample*
Divide between words you know.	Divide between consonants.	Divide between the vowel and the consonant.	Divide before the C-*le* syllable.

Prefix Only	Suffix Only	Both Prefix and Suffix	
misjudge *pretest* *unicycle* *tripod* *nonsense* *extend*	*roughly* *weakness* *plentiful* *lengthy* *cautious* *craziest*	*unhappiness* *mistreatment* *subtraction* *pretreatment* *returning*	
Divide between the prefix and the rest of the word.	Divide between the suffix and the rest of the word.	Divide between both the prefix and the suffix and the rest of the word.	

FIGURE 5.8. Strategies for chunking words.

Base Word Patterns	Adding a vowel suffix	Examples
CVVC, CVCC *mail, jump*	Add the suffix with no change to the base.	*mailed, mailing* *jumped, jumping*
CVC-*e* *tape*	Drop the final *e* and add the suffix.	*taped, taping*
CVC *pin*	Double the final consonant and add the suffix.	*pinned, pinning*
V-y *play*	Add the suffix with no change to the base.	*played, playing*
C-y *dry*	Add -*ing* with no change; change the *y* to *i* before adding -*ed*.	*drying, dried*
Two-syllable words with accented last syllable *permit, divide, destroy*	Use the pattern in the final syllable to determine your action.	*permitted, permitting* *divided, dividing* *destroyed, destroying*
Two-syllable words with unaccented last syllable *edit, happen, offer*	Add the suffix with no change to the base.	*edited, editing* *happened, happening* *offered, offering*

FIGURE 5.9. The doubling principle. Based on Ganske (2008).

principle. Again, we don't intend for students to memorize the second column. Rather, we intend for them to use it again and again when they wonder about words.

Instructional Strategies

But how do we teach students to be wordsmiths? There are a few robust instructional strategies that teachers can use quickly and consistently in Tier 1. The first is thinking aloud, and it applies to both word recognition and spelling. In order to teach students to read words, we must teach them how words are spelled. You should think of this type of spelling lesson as conceptual. By this we mean that we are teaching principles of the spelling system, using specific words as examples, rather than a list of spelling words. For example, a teacher writing a vocabulary word on the board can model how to think through that word as he or she is spelling it:

> "I am thinking about how to spell *momentary.* I know that it comes from the word *moment.* I hear two syllables in *moment.* The first one sounds like an open syllable. This means that I can spell it with just the single vowel *o.* The second syllable sounds like a regular closed syllable. I'll try the spelling *-ment.* Now I have to spell the suffix, and it begins with a vowel. I can see that my base word ends with two conso-nants, so I can just add the suffix."

> "I am thinking about how to spell the word *combination.* I know that it comes from the root *combine,* so I will start there. I'm going to spell the schwa sound in the second syllable with an *i* to keep it consistent with the root. Now I'll think about the suffix. It starts with a vowel, so I'll drop the silent *e* from the root, and then add the suffix. I know that the suffix can have two different spellings: *-sion* and *-tion.* I have to decide which one looks right."

This same think-aloud strategy can be used in decoding:

> "Our first word today is *submit.* Say the word. It's a verb. One meaning of *submit* is to hand over. For example, 'You submit your writing pieces to me.' Let's look at how this word works. I see two single vowels, so I know that it has two syllables. I also see two consonants between the vowels, and they are not working together as a blend or a digraph, so I'll divide between them. Now I have two closed syllables. Easy to read, easy to spell. Since it's a verb, let's see what it looks like in other forms. For *submit-ting* or *submitted,* I'll have to double the final consonant because the final syllable is closed, and I want to keep that short-vowel sound. If I want to create a noun form, I can add a suffix. A paper you submit is your *submission.* Look at how that spelling changes. You can add a prefix to either the noun or the verb form. You can resubmit, and you will have a resubmission. So our first word today is *submit,* and it means to hand over."

For those of you who are skeptical about your own ability to do this type of think-aloud, Figure 5.10 provides examples from a sequence of fifth-grade word study lessons

Re-turn (open, *r*-controlled) can be used as a noun or a verb, but the meanings are very similar. *Return* means to go back or come back, or the act of going or coming back. That makes sense, because the prefix *re-* means again. If we use it as a noun, we could say, "The queen's return to the castle was quite fabulous." If we use it as a verb, we could say, "The prince returned to the very spot where we had first seen the princess." It's easy to add our verb suffixes: *returned, returning.*

Re-store (open, *r*-controlled) has the same prefix, so we know that it is going to have something to do with again. It means to bring something back to its original or perfect condition. We can restore an old house by painting it and repairing it. We can also restore our good feelings about someone who has made us angry if that person apologizes. *Restore* can be used as a noun, but we have to add a suffix: *restoration.* "The restoration of the house was quite expensive."

Com-fort (closed, *r*-controlled) can be a noun or verb and means to give relief or make more pleasant. You can comfort someone who is sad by hugging the person. The verb suffixes are added without spelling change. The adjective form is *comforted.*

De-fend (open, closed) is a verb that means to protect from harm. You should defend a friend if people are telling lies about this person. Verb suffixes are added without spelling change: *defended, defending. Defense* is the noun form. *Defensive* is the adjective form.

Re-spect (open, closed) is a noun and verb. We see the *re-* at the start of this word, but it's actually not a prefix. The word means being thought of highly. You respect people who are truthful and kind. We can add verb suffixes without spelling change: *respected, respecting. Respectable* is the adjective form.

Im-press (closed, closed) is a verb that means to make a strong positive impact on someone. You impress me when your interpretations of stories include figurative meanings. We can add verb suffixes without spelling change: *impressed, impressing.* The noun form is *impression.*

FIGURE 5.10. Word study examples for upper elementary students.

for the *Bookworms K–5 Reading and Writing* text *Walk Two Moons* (Creech, 1994). You will see that we start with syllable types to aid decoding, then address meaning, and finally include affixes. If you would like to see more examples, they are included each week in the curriculum for grades 4 and 5.

After consistent modeling during instruction, a teacher can move to guided practice, asking individual students to think aloud while they spell words. The best time to do this, of course, is when students are actually writing. A teacher can use an existing spelling error as a teachable moment, directing a student to look back at the word, pronounce it, and think it through. Using consistent language (e.g., "Try thinking about the syllable type," "Try thinking about the spelling pattern," "Try thinking about the root") ensures that students will get multiple opportunities to apply a small set of ideas.

Instructional Planning

Planning Tier 1 word study instruction for upper elementary students involves a decision about which words to explain. We think that the importance of the word to the selection is paramount. Put simply, any text hangs on a text structure skeleton. Some specific words are absolutely essential to getting the shape of that skeleton right. So it's not the orthographic characteristics of the words that matter; it's their position in the meaning making. Choose words that you think may be unfamiliar but really cannot be omitted in a retelling of the day's selection, whatever their spelling patterns. Then teach them quickly before reading.

We think that a simple, repetitive planning frame is preferable. Beginning now, and in the chapters that follow, we show you the planning frame that we have developed over time (see Figure 5.11). Initially, we used it to help teachers reduce time spent on isolated skills in favor of connected reading of the excerpts in their commercial programs. Then we applied it to the design of *Bookworms K–5 Reading and Writing* with full texts rather than excerpts. We call the time that students actually read new grade-level texts *shared reading*. We have found the frame to be entirely reasonable to use in planning, and we have seen teachers use the plans with students. The result has been increased time for successful work with challenging, interesting texts.

We have not reserved much time or attention to word recognition instruction during Tier 1 shared reading. That is because, developmentally, students who are working at or near grade level will not need much instruction. That does not mean that this small dose of instruction is necessarily easy for all teachers to plan. We recommend that teachers work together with colleagues to plan. The challenge lies in deciding where to divide words to make their spellings transparent and memorable to students. The dictionary syllable divisions will not always be the best way to present a word. For example, the word *universe* has three syllables. In the dictionary, they are divided as *u-ni-verse*. If you choose to divide it *u-niv-erse*, you will still arrive at the pronunciation, but the open, closed, and *r*-controlled syllables may make the spelling easier to remember.

Here are some strategies that may help as you are learning to think about words in ways that are helpful. Consider first isolating prefixes and suffixes. With what remains, discuss the division of syllables and the syllable types. Establish a consistent shared language about the structure of words, perhaps supported by a classroom chart that defines these word parts. Instead of trying to teach the syllable types and phonics terms up front, just use them until students see them as natural ways to discuss the components of words. We have provided a sample chart in Figure 5.12. If this is a daily part of instruction, students will come to internalize analysis as a part of learning a new word.

Time	Activity	Description
5 minutes	Review	
5 minutes	Word study	Introduce two new words, with attention to syllable types, meaning, and derivatives.
20–25 minutes	Fluency and comprehension instruction	
5–10 minutes	Discussion	

FIGURE 5.11. Template for planning shared reading with word study.

	When you are reading a new word, divide into syllables and conquer!	
When you look for syllables, some word parts should stay together.		When you look for syllables, some word parts should be divided.
Blends Digraphs Vowel teams C-*le*		Compound words Prefixes, suffixes, and base words Double consonants
Conquer your word by finding the syllables, saying the syllables, and blending the syllables.		

FIGURE 5.12. Classroom words about words.

Most students in the upper elementary grade levels will continue to build their word recognition with this fairly simple combination of attention to words in isolation and in the context of the week's interesting reading. For others, though, a more targeted daily segment of instructional time for small-group instruction will be necessary. This is our Tier 2 word recognition instruction.

TIER 2 INSTRUCTION IN WORD RECOGNITION

Tier 2 instruction in word recognition is appropriate for upper elementary students who do not meet oral reading fluency benchmarks and who struggle with multisyllabic decoding. As we have discussed in Chapter 4, teachers identify these students by first testing the entire class in oral reading fluency, and then testing those who are below the grade-level benchmark with the Multisyllabic Decoding subtest in Figure 4.2 and, if students do not demonstrate proficiency, the Vowel Teams subtest in Part I of the Informal Decoding Inventory in Appendix E. We are trying not to waste precious small-group time on skills that are either too simple or too complex.

Upper elementary students who are prime candidates for Tier 2 instruction in word recognition will have mastered single-syllable decoding through long-vowel teams, but perform poorly on multisyllabic tasks. For them, the explicit, opportunistic analysis of the selection of words targeted for instruction during Tier 1 may not provide enough examples of the same types of words to build underlying understanding of how words work. Researchers have demonstrated that direct instruction in syllabification and word recognition builds word attack skills and fluency, even for students identified with reading or learning disabilities (e.g., Diliberto, Beattie, Flowers, & Algozzine, 2009). We have designed a very brief multisyllabic decoding intervention consistent with this finding.

Content

As in Tier 1, the content in Tier 2 word recognition instruction is words. But the selection process is different. For these students, more practice with words with similar structures is necessary. The content, then, for Tier 2 instruction in word recognition is this: multisyllabic words with similar structures, combining the six syllable types with common prefixes and suffixes, and a set of explicit strategies about how to divide and decode words (Roberts, Torgesen, Boardman, & Scammacca, 2008). It is very difficult to think of words with common features without using any references. Word lists can help generate this content. Figure 5.13 presents a list of words that we have reorganized by their features. In this case, the words come from a fifth-grade list of words frequently taught in core reading programs (Taylor, 1989). They are presented in that text in alphabetical order, but we have reorganized the words beginning with *r* to group them by their possibilities for highlighting word parts.

Any grade-level word lists are good sources of content for word recognition lessons that highlight word parts. Fifth-grade science words beginning with *c* include *calcium, calorie, cell, cerebellum, cerebrum, characteristics, chemical, circulatory, circumference, cloud, cocoon, compass, compound, concave, conduction, connective, consume, consumer, controlled, convection, cornea, corrosive, crater, crystal,* and *cycle*. This short list includes all of the syllable types. Once you embrace the idea that direct teaching of the structure of words will build students' decoding skills, you will see opportunities for identifying word parts everywhere. Researchers also have demonstrated that direct instruction in decoding skills improves students' spelling skills, even for readers with disabilities (Wanzek et al., 2006).

A word to the wise: Do not avoid words that you cannot explain. As you work with longer words, you will see that many times the vowels in unaccented syllables are pronounced with a schwa sound, similar to a short *u*, rather than the short sound that their syllable type would suggest. It is better to address these syllables and to teach students to be flexible. Often, if they actually have the word in their listening vocabulary, pronunciation with the short vowel intact will cue the actual pronunciation of the word with its schwa syllable. For example, if students use their knowledge of syllable types to pronounce *cocoon* as *co-coon,* context will usually help them correct the long *o* in the first syllable and arrive at the true pronunciation. There are also syllables that are simply spelled irregularly. You can call these syllables "oddballs." For example, if you separate the word *pronunciation* into syllables, you will find *pro-nun-ci-a-tion.* The third syllable looks open, but the vowel represents the long-*e* sound rather than that long *i*. Despite the reality of these oddballs, the number of syllables that conform to the types is much greater than the number that do not.

The second content aspect of Tier 2 decoding lessons is strategies for division. Again, a flexible set of division options is probably more useful than a very complex protocol. Figure 5.14 is based on a protocol called DISSECT (Deshler, Ellis, & Lenz, 1979). Students work down through the protocol until they are confident that they have recognized the word. If you choose to create your own multisyllabic decoding intervention rather than using ours, DISSECT will be helpful to you.

Closed Syllables	Open Syllables	Vowel Team Syllables
ra*ll*y	ral*y*	raid
ram	r*a*ven	rail
ran*som*	recent*ly*	raw
ra*scal*	re*cess*	ray
ra*ven*	re*flect*	re*a*sonable
rea*son*able	re*freshment*	reed
re*cently*	re*gard*	refugee
re*cess*	re*gion*	re*gion*
re*ckon*	re*gret*	re*hearse*
re*flect*	re*hearse*	re*pay*
re*freshment*	re*ly*	re*staurant*
re*fuge*	re*mark*	re*view*
re*giment*	re*pay*	
re*gret*	re*putation*	
re*putation*	re*solution*	
re*solution*	re*view*	
re*staurant*	re*volution*	
re*volution*		
rhythm		
ri*diculous*		
rink		
ri*pple*		
ro*tten*		
ru*dder*		
ru*gged*		
rung		
rust		

VC-*e* Syllables	C-*le* Syllables	*r*-Controlled Syllables
ref*uge*	reason*able*	re*gard*
rhyme	rip*ple*	re*mark*
ridic*ulous*	remark*able*	ro*ller*
rove		ru*dder*

Prefixes	Suffixes	
*re*flect	reason*able*	
*re*flection	recent*ly*	
*re*freshment	reflec*tion*	
	refresh*ment*	
	regi*ment*	
	remark*able*	
	reputa*tion*	
	resolu*tion*	
	revolu*tion*	
	revolu*tionary*	
	ridic*ulous*	
	rol*ler*	
	rot*ten*	
	rug*ged*	

FIGURE 5.13. Fifth-grade words sorted by word parts.

	DISSECT
D	**D**iscover the context.
I	**I**solate the prefix.
S	**S**eparate the suffix.
S	**S**ay the stem.
E	**E**xamine the stem: If it begins with a consonant, underline three letters. If it begins with a vowel, underline two letters. If that doesn't work, redo without the first letter.
C	**C**heck with someone.
T	**T**ry the dictionary.

FIGURE 5.14. DISSECT division rules. Based on Deshler, Ellis, and Lenz (1979).

Instructional Strategies

To make instruction effective for students who are struggling, we have to be sure that it provides explicit instruction, more practice items, and a carefully sequenced set of lessons. Tier 2 instructional strategies build on the think-aloud strategy used in Tier 1 instruction, but include additional guided practice and every-pupil response. We have found optimal engagement when each child has his or her own word list. The model lessons included in Appendix F contain 10 or 12 words for each day's lesson, chosen for their common features. We recommend four simple instructional strategies: (1) marking up the words, (2) identifying syllable types, (3) reading the words with partners, and (4) reading the words chorally. In order to make room for both multisyllabic decoding practice *and* contextualized work on fluency, we challenge teachers to make these procedures entirely routine, so they take fewer than 4 minutes.

Generally, finding the correct division is the most challenging part of reading longer words. The first strategy that we have found useful is to have students quickly mark up the words independently. Students first circle any prefixes or suffixes they see. Then they work through the sequence of letters that remain, identifying syllables. Each syllable has to have one vowel sound. Teach the students to place a dot under each single vowel and to underline a vowel team. Then they can divide the syllables with a line, ensuring that each syllable has only one vowel sound. Because they are actually marking their words, it is easy to monitor their work by watching what they do. This is a form of every-pupil response and provides useful feedback about whether individual students are coming to understand syllable structures or not.

Once students have marked vowels and divided the words, identifying syllable types reinforces the fact that these are repetitive structures rather than simply individual words. To maintain a brisk pace and high engagement, use every-pupil response. Simple, repetitive teacher talk is helpful here:

> "You have divided your words. Point to your first syllable. When I say 'Go,' tell me the syllable type. Go. Next syllable. Go."

Students can answer in unison, and when there are errors, you can explain them. That way you will not waste time explaining syllables that all of the students have gotten correct. Here is a sample of the language you can use for error correction. One of the students has just said that the first syllable in *vintner* is open.

> "That first syllable is closed. I saw two single vowels separated by three consonants. I kept the *nt* blend together and divided between the single consonant and the blend, like this: *vint-ner*. Then the syllable had a single vowel followed by two consonants, so it is closed."

After students have marked words and identified syllables, they can read their words to a partner. We have found it useful for them to read each syllable separately and then to read them together. They can alternate reading words. For a list of open–closed words, then, they would read like this: *re-cent—recent, si-lent—silent, fo-cus—focus.*

Finally, a simple management system that creates yet another chance for the students to read the words is to have them read chorally with the teacher. For 10 words, this will take fewer than 20 seconds. They can use the same format as for partner reading (reading each syllable and then blending them to form the word), but this time the teacher's voice ensures that they read them together and that they have read each syllable and word correctly.

Instructional Planning

Generally, explicit instruction in any content area demands a scope and sequence of instruction and instructional tasks that progress in difficulty over time. In the word lists that we have constructed, we have taken the stance that meaning-based divisions are easiest. To teach meaning-based divisions, we first move from compound words to words with high-frequency prefixes and suffixes. Next, we move to combinations of syllable types, again working with the simplest ones first before moving to more complex examples. Figure 5.15 provides a scope and sequence for our lists, and the lessons are provided in full in Appendix F.

We have planned for 18 weeks of lessons. Readers of the first edition of this book may have used the longer diagnostic assessment we originally designed to assign students to multiple entry points. In practice, we found this level of differentiation difficult to manage. Instead, we have found it best to teach these lessons from the beginning (compound words) and go straight through. Starting with simple words will create initial confidence—both for you and for the students. We have provided the teacher talk to explain the features at the top of the lessons. You will see that some teacher talk goes

Week	Content	Patterns
1	Compound Words	
2	Prefixes and Suffixes	*un-, re-, -ful, -ly*
3		*over-, mis-, -ed, -ness,*
4		*pre-, dis-, -able, -er, -ar, -or*
5		*fore-, trans-, -ing, -en*
6		*under-, after-, -some, -ment*
7	Closed Syllables	CVC Syllable Pattern
8	Open and Closed Syllables	CVC and CV Syllable Patterns
9	Closed, Open, and VC-*e* Syllables	CVC, CV, and VC-*e* Syllable Patterns
10	*r*-Controlled Syllables	(*ar, or, or, ir, ur*)
11	Vowel Team Syllables	(e.g., *ai, ea, ou, oy*)
12	Consonant–*le* Syllable	
13	*-ed* and *-ing*	
14	Changing *y* to *i* or No Change	
15	Combinations of Syllable Types in Multisyllabic Words	
16	Accent and the Schwa Sound	
17	Accent in Two- and Three-Syllable Words	
18	Accent in Two- and Three-Syllable Words	

FIGURE 5.15. Scope and sequence for one series of multisyllabic decoding lessons.

across the entire week, and that some is specific to a day's lesson. You will save instructional time if you use this talk as written and follow the procedures (mark up, identify syllable types, pronounce with partners, pronounce chorally) in the same way every day. Remember that the goal for these lessons is that they are a very quick first segment of a fluency lesson. If you have more than 15 minutes total for small-group time, we have provided spelling practice. If you have only 15 minutes, omit the spellings to make time for fluency work.

At the end of 18 weeks, we have a comprehensive outcome assessment. Part II of the Informal Decoding Inventory (see Appendix E) has real words and nonsense words to test application of multisyllabic decoding strategies. This assessment is meant to be untimed. We have simplified our scoring interpretation since we first designed this assessment. These words are not taught in the intervention; they are true transfer words. We consider a score of 8 or more on real words to indicate proficiency. Nonsense words are more difficult, so use a criterion of 6 or more for proficiency.

If these lessons are not sufficient for your students, the key to planning additional ones is to organize words by their common characteristics, as we have done in Figure 5.13. You can use any available sets of words—spelling lists, word lists from commercial materials, or content area words from an upcoming unit. Simply decide on syllable combinations to target (e.g., closed–closed; closed–*r*-controlled), and sort your words into these combinations. If you can identify particular syllable patterns that are troubling your students, as indicated by their performance on the Informal Decoding Inventory, you can be diagnostic about your list design.

The most rigorous evidence that this instruction is working will come from measures of oral reading fluency. Students who have truly built their word recognition skills and strategies should read natural text more quickly and accurately. In the course of that reading practice, they will also be building their word recognition skills.

CHOOSING TIER 3 PROGRAMS FOR WORD RECOGNITION

We want to emphasize that a truly tiered program for upper elementary readers must have more than well-designed Tier 1 instruction and a plan for systematic Tier 2 instruction. Some students' needs in word recognition will not be met in this combination. Two groups of students will require Tier 3 programs: (1) those fourth and fifth graders who have not mastered single-syllable decoding through vowel teams; and (2) those fourth and fifth graders who have mastered single-syllable decoding but do not respond to consistent, high-quality Tier 2 instruction in multisyllabic decoding. Those students require more intensive and systematic instruction, and we argue that that instruction will likely require a commercial (or published) program provided outside of regular classroom instruction (Kamil et al., 2008). In many cases, a Tier 3 program will be comprehensive (incorporating more than just word recognition). In the area of word recognition specifically, the program is likely to be significantly more controlled and rules-driven than our Tier 2 lessons. Researchers continue to demonstrate that various interventions that target word recognition, or word study, for older students with reading difficulties or for older students with special education classifications can yield gains (Scammacca et al., 2007).

We stop short of recommending commercial programs, because we lack sufficient empirical evidence to recommend one over the other. In addition, as researchers turn attention to the needs of young adolescent students within an RTI framework, improvements in the efficacy of interventions are likely to be achieved. When we look for evidence about the effectiveness of interventions, we turn to two Internet sources that are updated frequently: (1) the Institute of Education Sciences' What Works Clearinghouse (*https://ies.ed.gov/ncee/wwc*) and (2) the National Center on Intensive Intervention (*https://intensiveintervention.org*). When you search either of these websites for evidence on the efficacy of intensive interventions for word recognition for upper elementary students, consider searching both in the early primary (K–3) section and in the adolescent (4–12) section.

CHAPTER 6
....

Building Fluency

This chapter focuses on fluency development and instruction. We define fluency, explain its development for students in fourth and fifth grades, and provide models for instruction for Tier 1 and Tier 2 instructional time. We believe that all fourth and fifth graders should participate in shared reading activities and engage in reading tasks (including wide and repeated reading) that support their fluency development. Students who need additional support can easily be served a double dose in differentiated, small-group instruction (Tier 2) that is both motivating and targeted to students' fluency needs.

Fluency is the ability to read with appropriate rate, accuracy, prosody, and endurance or stamina (see Figure 6.1). The term *appropriate* refers both to the age and development of the learner and to the complexity of the text; not all texts are built to be read the same way. Upper elementary students must practice reading demanding texts that stretch their

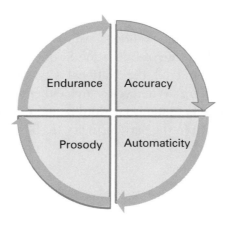

FIGURE 6.1. Components of fluency.

word recognition and meaning-making skills. Here's why: A first grader will read texts built from relatively short, simple sentences, containing relatively familiar content; an upper elementary student will read longer texts with a constantly shifting combination of simple, compound, and complex sentences, and these sentences will present challenging vocabulary and content. These grade-level texts provide important knowledge-building opportunities. We have come to realize that students should listen to and observe fluent reading, participate in supported fluency activities, and practice fluent reading in different structures. In this chapter, we provide illustrations that teachers can use to plan for this variety of reading and rereading for fluency building.

Before that, though, we would like to set the fluency record straight as we see it. Fluency work sometimes gets a bad rap as "speed reading" (see Deeney & Shim, 2016), with students engaged in a race to read a sentence, a page, a chapter, or a book. But fluency work is far from a race. It is more similar to a dance, incorporating appropriate rate, accuracy, prosody, and endurance or stamina. Think of fluency as a multifaceted attainment with very specific indicators. *Rate* in fluency refers to "how fast" a reader processes a text. *Accuracy* refers to "how well" a reader reads without making deviations from the words the author provided. *Prosody* refers to "how naturally" a reader reads and considers the extent to which the reader provides meaningful chunking of phrases and attention to punctuation. *Endurance,* or *stamina,* refers to "how long" the reader is able to read at a comfortable rate without feeling fatigue and resorting to avoidance strategies. Thinking of fluency as how fast, how well, how naturally, and how long an individual can read may help to explain its important relationship to comprehension.

Fluency is a means to an end—and that end is comprehension. Especially in the early elementary years, fluent reading is closely related to students' basic ability to decode words. In upper elementary grades, students may master foundational decoding but struggle with multisyllabic decoding. In either case, fluency practice in connected text should still engage nearly all of our time. Skills instruction alone cannot support students' reading for meaning (Meisinger, Bradley, Schwanenflugel, & Kuhn, 2010). As we work to support comprehension, we naturally keep an eye on fluency.

In grades 4 and 5, fluency can flourish nearly effortlessly if we use efficient routines. In the next sections, we propose a simple instructional diet for fluency instruction in grade-level text and in differentiated small-group instruction. We provide management suggestions that are widely applied in classroom settings, and that we have observed working well in our collaboration with schools. We also identify some routines that really must be avoided. Finally, we present resources to consider for students needing a Tier 3 curriculum.

FOUNDATIONAL KNOWLEDGE ABOUT FLUENCY DEVELOPMENT

Fluency is a necessary, but insufficient, first step toward unlocking an author's meaning when one is reading connected text. It makes sense, then, that fluency is a strong predictor of reading comprehension (e.g., Kim, Wagner, & Foster, 2011). Researchers hypothesize that a student who is able to process text with appropriate rate, accuracy, prosody, and endurance will allot cognitive energy to meaning making. The student's attention will be freed to shift from the word level to a more global understanding of the text and its features. A dysfluent reader, by contrast, will tediously work to decode words, with little attention left to attend to text meaning. Perhaps because reading is about extracting and *constructing* meaning (RAND Reading Study Group, 2002), fluency is the bridge between decoding and reading comprehension (Pikulski & Chard, 2005). Fluency allows readers to make semantic connections between words and across syntactic barriers. This process of meaning making requires cognitive effort, and that effort cannot be expended both on figuring out the words and figuring out the text at the same time (Kuhn, 2005; LaBerge & Samuels, 1974; Wolf & Katzir-Cohen, 2001).

While the strong relationship between fluency and comprehension has been documented extensively, that relationship is far from simple. Fluency and comprehension are reciprocal. It's a classic chicken-and-egg problem: Fluency functions both as a *product of* and as a *contributor to* comprehension (Strecker, Roser & Martinez, 1998). It is easier to see this when thinking about prosody. Especially with the complex text that upper elementary students read, it is very difficult to read aloud with prosody if they are not understanding the content and cannot make meaning. When students do read aloud with prosody, though, their comprehension can improve (Kuhn & Stahl, 2003). The routines we suggest to develop fluency, then, also promote comprehension.

Almost all students reading at fourth- and fifth-grade levels will have developed appropriate accuracy and rate. However, prosody, the meaningful chunking of phrases, is likely to need further development for this group of students. Text-level fluency is what fuels comprehension, and to develop such fluency, students need support to read with the type of expression that will enable meaning making (Petscher & Kim, 2011). Students reading below grade level, though, may still need to work on their accuracy and rate in word recognition; this group of students will need to be supported with additional instruction at the word level (see Chapter 5). Remember that we distinguish between students who need only a small dose of multisyllabic support, which classroom teachers can provide quickly, and those who struggle with single-syllable words and patterns. Again, we believe those students deserve an intensive decoding intervention.

Fluency is measured with assessments of rate, accuracy, and/or prosody. Reading *accuracy* targets a reader's ability to pronounce a word correctly within a given context. For example, a student reading the word *record* might say *reorder*—an obvious error—but might also read with the emphasis or stress on the wrong syllable. *Record* can be a verb ("I need to record the show so that I can watch it later") or a noun ("I keep a record of my choice reading"). Either reading a word incorrectly or reading it without the correct pronunciation for the context constitutes an error in accuracy, as it is a deviation from the text. When accuracy is reported separately from rate, it is typically expressed as a percentage. A student reading a specific text at less than 90% accuracy is very unlikely to comprehend that text, as too much energy is devoted to figuring out the words in the text and too many of those words are wrong.

It is also possible to measure rate and accuracy, or *automaticity*, at the same time. Measures of automaticity gauge a reader's ability to recognize or decode a sufficient number of words within a given time. These measures are captured through timed oral readings of unpracticed text, usually reported in words correct per minute (WCPM), as noted in Chapter 4. For example, if a student reads 90 words within 1 minute and makes 13 mistakes, you subtract the number of total mistakes and report 77 WCPM. The WCPM goals increase with the reader's grade level and time of year and are reported specifically on assessments of oral reading fluency. It is important to use the norms associated with the test used for assessment, because they were derived from the actual passages read for that particular test.

WCPM goals across time of year in grades 4 and 5 are presented in Figure 6.2 (Hasbrouck &Tindal, 2017). The data were derived from over 500,000 individual students taking one of three different fluency measures. If you examine the fall scores, you will see that the least automatic students had nearly identical scores in fall of grades 4 and 5, but that the least automatic fifth graders made better progress over time. You will also see that most fifth graders were more automatic than fourth graders at every time point, but that fourth graders tended to make more progress over time. These data do not suggest that a specific number of WCPM is optimal, but they do help us see that both variance and growth are evident during the upper elementary years.

Prosody, in which oral reading sounds like natural speech, is a term borrowed from the study of poetry. It refers to readers' expression and ability to read phrases in chunks that represent their meaning. Labored, word-by-word reading or inaccurate phrasing can pose obstacles to comprehension, and it certainly doesn't sound good. Prosodic reading sounds like natural speech; readers attend to meaning and conventional punctuation markers in the text, and their voices are unforced. The National Assessment of Educational Progress (NAEP) has developed guidelines for measuring prosody (Pinnell et al., 1995; see Figure 6.3). It is interesting to note that guidelines were developed with our target age group: fourth-grade students. A nationally representative subsample of 1,779 fourth graders was recorded while reading aloud a fourth-grade passage. Approximately 40% of the students were placed in the nonfluent range, because they lacked the expression that could assist meaning making.

Prosody can also be captured with the Multidimensional Fluency Scale (Rasinski et al., 2009; Zuttell & Rasinski, 1991), which was drawn from the NAEP measure of prosodic reading and includes three dimensions: phrasing, smoothness, and pace. Figure 6.4 provides the components for each dimension. There are similar scales with slightly

Percentile	Grade 4			Grade 5		
	Fall	Winter	Spring	Fall	Winter	Spring
90	153	168	184	179	183	195
75	125	143	160	153	160	169
50	94	120	133	121	133	146
25	75	95	105	87	109	119
10	60	71	83	64	84	102

FIGURE 6.2. WCPM goals by grade. Norms from Hasbrouck and Tindal (2017).

Fluent	Level 4	Reads primarily in larger, meaningful phrase groups. Although some regressions, repetitions, and deviations from text may be present, these do not appear to detract from the overall structure of the story. Preservation of the author's syntax is consistent. Some or most of the story is read with expressive interpretation.
	Level 3	Reads primarily in three- or four-word phrase groups. Some small groupings may be present. However, the majority of phrasing seems appropriate and preserves the syntax of the author. Little or no expressive interpretation is present.
Nonfluent	Level 2	Reads primarily in two-word phrases with some three- or four-word groupings. Some word-by-word reading may be present. Word groupings may seem awkward and unrelated to larger context of sentence or passage.
	Level 1	Reads primarily word-by-word. Occasional two-word or three-word phrases may occur—but these are infrequent and/or they do not preserve meaningful syntax.

FIGURE 6.3. NAEP Oral Reading Fluency Scale. From U.S. Department of Education, Institute of Education Sciences, National Center for Education Statistics, NAEP 2002 Oral Reading Study (*https://nces.ed.gov/nationsreportcard/studies/ors/scale.asp*). In the public domain.

different characteristics. For example, Klauda and Guthrie (2008) used a 4-point scale for five dimensions (passage expressiveness, phrasing, pace, smoothness, and expressiveness). Benjamin and colleagues (2013) developed a criterion-referenced assessment to address both automaticity and prosody.

Reading endurance, or stamina, may be especially important during the upper elementary years. Texts that students read at this time are longer and require more time on task and more thinking. They are likely to be peppered with new, longer words, new uses of old words, and entirely new concepts. In addition, these texts include longer sentences with more embedded clauses. Reading them fluently, then, requires the willingness and the ability to persevere, even though it will be difficult at times. Timed assessments that measure oral reading fluency in WCPM don't tell much about endurance; however, endurance might be assessed by measuring a student's rate and accuracy when the student is reading extended texts of varying length (Deeney, 2010).

To plan for fluency challenges and development, instruction must be influenced by the goals set by the department of education in your state. Although each state has developed standards to guide instruction, they are all influenced by similar sources. The CCSS for Reading: Foundational Skills (NGACBP & CCSSO, 2010) suggest that fluency development should begin with emergent-reader texts in kindergarten. Goals for grades 1–5 indicate that students should be able to read grade-level texts with appropriate fluency to support comprehension. In addition, early attention to sound-level fluency in kindergarten and first grade leads to word-level fluency and then to fluency at the text level in subsequent grades. We represent that progression for fluency development in Figure 6.5.

It makes sense to review the CCSS beginning at grade 3, to gain a better understanding of what is expected in the upper elementary grades. To understand the expectations

Use the following scales to rate reader fluency on the three dimensions of phrasing, smoothness, and pace.	
A. Phrasing	
1.	Monotonic with little sense of phrase boundaries, frequent word-by-word reading.
2.	Frequent two- and three-word phrases giving the impression of choppy reading; improper stress and intonation that fails to mark ends of sentences and clauses.
3.	Mixture of run-ons, mid-sentence pauses for breath, and possibly some choppiness; reasonable stress/intonation.
4.	Generally, well-phrased, mostly in clause and sentence units, with adequate attention to expression.
B. Smoothness	
1.	Frequent extended pauses, hesitations, false starts, sound-outs, repetitions, and/or multiple attempts.
2.	Several "rough spots" in text where extended pauses, hesitations, etc. are more frequent and disruptive.
3.	Occasional breaks in smoothness caused by difficulties with specific words and/or structures.
4.	Generally smooth reading with some breaks, but word and structure difficulties are resolved quickly, usually through self-correction.
C. Pace (during sections of minimal disruption)	
1.	Slow and laborious.
2.	Moderately slow.
3.	Uneven mixture of fast and slow reading.
4.	Consistently conversational.

FIGURE 6.4. Multidimensional Fluency Scale. From Zutell and Rasinski (1991). Copyright © 1991. Reprinted by permission of Taylor & Francis Ltd, *http://www.tandfonline.com.*

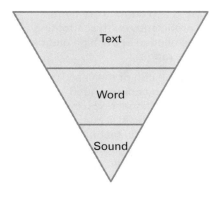

FIGURE 6.5. The development of fluency over time.

for fluency in each grade, we must look both at the fluency standards found in the foundational skills and at the standard for range of reading and level of text complexity (see Figure 6.6). This figure is worth close examination. While the fluency standards stay exactly the same across grades 3, 4, and 5, the text complexity standard does not. Notice the increases in text difficulty, genre specificity, and student proficiency goals across time.

By the end of grade 3, students achieving grade-level standards should be able to read text accurately and expressively at an appropriate rate. They can allocate their attention to identifying the type of text and the appropriate purpose for processing that specific text. Context can be used to confirm the accurate decoding of words, to select among multiple meanings of words, and to understand sentences, but *not* to guess words. This constellation of fluency, vocabulary, and comprehension skills allows readers to do the cognitive work that will assist in the meaning-making process. Specifically, these readers will detect when meaning breaks down and will self-correct by using fix-up strategies such as rereading.

Consistent with the standards in grades 4 and 5, students should read literature and informational texts both with teacher support and independently. Gradually, the goals

Grades 3–5 Fluency Standards	
General Goal	Evidence
The students read with sufficient rate, accuracy, and prosody.	Read grade-level text with purpose and understanding. Read grade-level prose and poetry orally with accuracy, appropriate rate, and expression on successive readings.
The students read with sufficient fluency to support comprehension.	Use context to confirm or self-correct word recognition and understanding, rereading as necessary.

Text Complexity Standards for Reading Literature and Informational Text		
Grade 3	Grade 4	Grade 5
By the end of the year, read and comprehend literature, including stories, dramas, and poetry, at the high end of the grades 2–3 text complexity band independently and proficiently.	By the end of the year, read and comprehend literature, including stories, dramas, and poetry, in the grades 4–5 text complexity band proficiently, with scaffolding as needed at the high end of the range.	By the end of the year, read and comprehend literature, including stories, dramas, and poetry, at the high end of the grades 4–5 text complexity band independently and proficiently.
By the end of the year, read and comprehend informational texts, including history/social sciences, science, and technical texts, at the high end of the grades 2–3 text complexity band independently and proficiently.	By the end of the year, read and comprehend informational texts, including history/social sciences, science, and technical texts, in the grades 4–5 text complexity band proficiently, with scaffolding as needed at the high end of the range.	By the end of the year, read and comprehend informational texts, including history/social sciences, science, and technical texts, at the high end of the grades 4–5 text complexity band independently and proficiently.

FIGURE 6.6. Fluency and text complexity standards from the CCSS. From NGACBP and CCSSO (2010). In the public domain.

are for students to become aware of and comfortable with a variety of text structures, and for their reading to be done not for practice but rather for gaining new understandings. What you must keep in mind is that as students advance to the upper elementary grades, text demands increase, *and* students are required to read more independently. The emphasis on informational texts will mean that both content and structure are unfamiliar. The standards require students to be able to read *both* informational and narrative texts with accuracy, prosody, and comprehension; what they don't tell us is how to plan instruction that will yield that level of reading competence. Students' fluency must become broader and more flexible. For students who do not continue to build fluency during this time, comprehension will surely not improve. The stagnation appearing fairly suddenly in grade 4 had been called the *fourth-grade slump* (Chall et al., 1990; see our discussion in Chapter 2) even before text complexity goals were increased. If we don't put fluency on the menu, more and more students will be captured in the slump.

Selecting books for fluency development and instruction need not be a challenging or time-consuming task. As you build your own skills and resources for book selection, connect yourself with those whose business is books: your school library media specialist and the librarians at your local public library, for example. They will have insights about what students are choosing to read, and you can leverage that interest.

You also have to consider the level of difficulty that texts pose for readers, as this is clearly a target of the standards. The Lexile Framework for Reading website (*https://lexile.com*) provides access to a quantitative system for leveling books. For example, a text on the site will be described with a number followed by the letter *L*. The number that is generated for a book is an indicator of the text's difficulty. Text difficulty is calculated on the basis of sentence length and word frequency. For example, the book *The Watsons Go to Birmingham—1963*, by Christopher Paul Curtis (1995), has a Lexile of 1000L. In the CCSS text complexity grade bands, the Lexile range in grades 4 and 5 is 740L–1010L (NGACBP & CCSSO, 2010), so this text would be a narrative at the high end of the upper elementary text difficulty band. Remember, though, that the system cannot evaluate text content. A book may be within the appropriate range of difficulty, but its content may not be appropriate for your students. Therefore, we urge you to read books prior to making your choices, rather than simply choosing with quantitative measures. You should keep in mind both the quantitative and the qualitative components for book selection.

The Lexile website can also generate book lists based on a Lexile range you provide. This method can assist you in selecting books for your classroom library and for your small-group instruction, or even for a summer reading list. Remember that students who are building fluency and improving their rate, accuracy, and prosody should be provided with many opportunities to read and reread different texts and stretch their endurance/stamina. This fluency practice has the potential to improve their comprehension, because they will be processing text as it was intended to be read. Always keep in mind that reading with appropriate intonation and phrasing supports the extraction and construction of meaning. It is not a waste of instructional or practice time. In the next sections, we discuss how you can support reading fluency during Tier 1 and Tier 2 instruction, and we will explain different organizational structures you may use to engage students in meaningful reading and rereading.

TIER 1 INSTRUCTION IN FLUENCY

All students in your classroom need Tier 1 fluency work. During Tier 1 instruction, you are likely to work in all areas of reading: word study, fluency, vocabulary, comprehension, and text-based writing. Fluency instruction will focus on the four components of fluency: rate, accuracy, prosody, and endurance/stamina. Emphasis on rate alone will not be enough to support fluent reading for comprehension (Rasinski, 2006). Reading that facilitates comprehension should engage all components of fluency at the same time. In this section, we describe the content, instructional strategies, and instructional planning required to support fluency.

Content

It may be odd to think about the content of fluency instruction. The content actually consists of the increasingly complex texts that students read accurately, automatically, and with appropriate phrasing and endurance/stamina. Because the texts that students must read in the upper elementary grades include both narratives and a wide variety of informational texts, your Tier 1 instruction must include modeling of fluent reading in these text types, as well as ample opportunities for student practice—with your support, in pairs and groups, and independently.

The *Rubric for Evaluating Reading/Language Arts Instructional Materials for Kindergarten to Grade 5* (Foorman et al., 2017) does not have a separate section for fluency in grades 3–5. Instead, the reading comprehension recommendations address the need to use complex texts that give meaningful opportunities for students to read and reread. These rubric sections target daily practice in reading fluency with the inclusion of reading strategies that encourage the students to reread when comprehension demands it. Furthermore, they suggest that students be exposed to both narrative and expository (or informational) texts and be prompted to reread after error corrections—a procedure that supports text-level fluency. In addition to opportunities for student rereading, the guidelines target teacher modeling of fluent reading. We interpret this recommendation to mean that upper elementary students still need modeling of appropriate prosody, rate, and accuracy during read-alouds and during shared reading of grade-level texts. Then they can apply their skills in wide and independent reading. We use the term *wide reading* to signal a breadth of reading choices in school, in classroom libraries, and in the school's media center. Our real goal, though, is independent, self-selected reading, where students go beyond the school's texts to read for their own learning purposes.

The *Bookworms K–5 Reading and Writing* program provides a real-life example of this simple model for text selection. Instead of an anthology of excerpts, the curriculum uses intact books. For instance, Figure 6.7 provides the selections for shared reading and for interactive read-alouds during the first 15 weeks of fourth grade, along with Lexiles and page numbers. Besides the fact that these selections meet criteria for genre variety and text difficulty, we have evidence that upper elementary students who listen to and read these texts increased their fluency and comprehension (Walpole et al., 2017).

	Books	Description	Lexile	Pages
Shared reading books	*Charlie and the Chocolate Factory,* Roald Dahl	A humorous fantasy takes a poor central character on the adventure of a lifetime when he wins a contest to visit the inside of a mysterious chocolate factory. His character, and those of other winners, are tested by the factory's owner, Willy Wonka.	810L	176
	Steal Away Home, Lois Ruby	This fiction tale has two plot lines—one set in the present and one in 1856. The protagonist in the present-day tale finds a skeleton and a diary behind the wall in her new house. Investigations reveal the life of a conductor in the Underground Railroad.	890L	208
	Blood on the River: James Town 1607, Elisa Carbone	This piece of historical fiction is richly sourced with primary source documents. It tells the story of a young boy who traveled to James Town and became the page of Captain John Smith. It paints a picture of the difficulties in the early settlement.	820L	256
Interactive read-aloud books	*Worst of Friends: Thomas Jefferson, John Adams, and the True Story of an American Feud,* Suzanne Tripp Jurmain	This picture book chronicles Jefferson and Adams as both political rivals and friends. The illustrations help to provide context and humor.	920L	32
	Freedom on the Menu: The Greensboro Sit-Ins, Carole Boston Weatherford	This piece of historical fiction is told by a child in the first person. It provides context for sit-ins in Greensboro, North Carolina, in 1960.	AD660L	32
	Earthquakes, Seymour Simon	This is a nonfiction book about the causes and consequences of earthquakes. It is richly illustrated with diagrams and photographs.	1,010L	32
	Go Straight to the Source, Kristin Fontichiaro	This is a nonfiction book about the types and uses of primary sources to understand history and to write research and reports.	890L	32
	My Life in Dog Years, Gary Paulsen	This book provides a series of chapter-length memoirs about the life of Gary Paulsen through his experiences with beloved dogs.	1,150L	137
	Hatchet, Gary Paulsen	This survival story traces the experiences of a boy who survives a plane crash in a remote Canadian forest and must learn to take care of himself.	1,020L	192

FIGURE 6.7. First 15 weeks: Books for shared reading and interactive read-aloud.

Instructional Strategies

Even though you may think that reading to students in grades 4 and 5 is not necessary because they are older, we retain our commitment to read-alouds, which will allow students to hear fluent reading. We know that silent reading is important for students as they progress in schooling; however, depending on their reading achievement, silent reading rates can differ and such differences can affect reading comprehension (Trainin, Hiebert, & Wilson, 2015). Modeling of fluent reading during whole-group instruction keeps everyone on the same page. When this fluency modeling is augmented with the discussions and strategy modeling we recommend in Chapter 8, it supports comprehension and provides students a model to emulate in their independent practice.

Teachers can model reading aloud at an appropriate rate, with words pronounced accurately, and phrases and sentences presented with prosody. Syntactic (or grammatical) cues signal modification of pace and pitch, always with the goal of making sense of the processed text. All readers make occasional errors, and these provide a natural opportunity to model word recognition strategies and rereading procedures when necessary, instead of "guessing" words based on context or "skipping" words and phrases. This modeling of good reading will help everyone know what real reading sounds like (Allington, 1983). It will also be helpful for your fluent-so-far-readers who still need to improve their prosody or grow in their reading stamina.

The texts that we now ask upper elementary students to read make additional, proactive attention to fluency building important. For example, consider reading aloud the following selection from *A History of Western Art* by Antony Mason (2007):

> The Mycenaeans are named after the ancient city of Mycenae, but there were a number of other similar cities on the Greek mainland, such as Athens, Tiryns, Pylos, and Thebes. Their warlike nature is reflected in the massive stone fortifications that they built to protect their palaces. Their art is similar to that of the Minoans, but is rather stiffer and more formal, and tends to focus on more aggressive themes, such as warriors and hunting. (p. 15)

This excerpt contains only three complex sentences. It requires readers to pay attention to commas and conjunctions, to understand how the series of cities are related and to recognize the tensions between Minoan and Mycenaean art. The sentences also include multisyllabic words such as *fortifications* and *nature* that may not be in students' lexicons. This is the type of text that students must be able to read independently as they progress through the middle grades. By reading such complex texts aloud, you can model syllable division strategies for any words that stump you, rereading for expression at the sentence level, and appropriate intonation and phrasing. In fact, if you read aloud from a text like this and stumble on words or phrasing, you will be able to talk to your students about this, showing them that all readers actually make word recognition and fluency errors and reread to fix them. Also, reading aloud will allow you to think aloud and model the use of comprehension strategies—a reading goal we examine in Chapter 8.

We consider read-alouds necessary, but not sufficient, for building fluency. Fluency develops through reading practice. Repeated oral reading that includes the teacher or peers can improve the reading fluency of all readers (Strickland, Boon, & Spencer, 2013). Repeated oral reading can build students' reading fluency. In our previous work, we have presented instructional strategies for repeated oral reading strategies on a continuum from most to least teacher support (Walpole & McKenna, 2017). This concept can still be applied with upper elementary students. Figure 6.8 presents three modes of student oral reading, presented from most to least supportive, that can provide foundational structures for building fluency. Choral reading is guided by the teacher, whose voice models fluent reading while the class participates in unison. Immediate partner rereading builds both fluency and comprehension. This rereading must have an authentic and meaningful purpose; otherwise, students will not thoughtfully engage in it. At times, individual whisper rereading can further enhance student fluency and comprehension. The goal is not for students just to process the text; the goal is to read "much" and purposefully (Allington, 1977).

We have hinted at the start of this chapter that we would share practices to be avoided. One of those practices is round-robin reading. Our visits to schools indicate that it is not always clear to teachers how to support classwide fluent reading, so they persist in round-robin reading. We often see round-robin reading (sometimes called *popcorn reading* or *popsicle reading*)—a system of oral reading with students abruptly being asked to take turns reading aloud individually. Although teachers may use this turn taking as a way of managing the group and covering the content, it is simply not a good practice. Round-robin reading may give the illusion that it supports students' fluency, but there is no evidence to suggest that it does (Ash, Kuhn, & Walpole, 2009). Studies examining the effects of round-robin reading found that it did not have any effects on students' fluency, vocabulary, or comprehension. It has also been found to be less effective than shared reading as a means of increasing accuracy (Eldredge, Reutzel, & Hollingsworth, 1996).

It is one thing to say that round-robin reading is not an ideal practice. It is another to say that it may be harmful. We actually find that round-robin reading can harm students'

	Strategy	Teacher's Role	Students' Role
More to Less Support ↓	Choral reading	The teacher leads an oral reading, in unison, supporting both word recognition and phrasing.	The students follow the teacher's lead, matching their voices to the teacher's voice as closely as possible.
	Partner reading	The teacher pairs students to read together and monitors and supports the work of the pairs, providing assistance if needed.	Students take turns reading aloud, with the silent partner following in the text and providing prompts if words are miscalled.
	Whisper reading	The teacher sets a purpose to reread to build fluency and comprehension.	Each student reads the text aloud in a quiet voice, such that only the student can hear the reading. All students in the class are reading at the same time, but at individual rates.

FIGURE 6.8. Strategies for oral reading.

reading fluency and their will to read. The practice may increase anxiety among students with weak oral reading fluency and direct their attention to reading ahead in order to practice silently, so that they will not be embarrassed when their turn comes (Kuhn, 2014). It can also lead to frustration for students with strong oral reading fluency who must listen to weaker readers. Therefore, whatever its name, round-robin reading is not a method you should keep in your tool box. Luckily, it can be replaced easily with choral reading, partner reading, and whisper reading procedures. In all cases, these alternative procedures increase the amount of text that all students read. For example, in a class of 20 participating in round-robin reading, all things being equal, each child would receive 5% of the time allotted for oral reading. Compare that with partner reading, during which each child would practice for 50% of the same allotted time. The teachers with whom we work find these data convincing, and they have successfully integrated these procedures while maintaining well-managed classrooms.

We suggest two different structures you may use to coordinate your instructional strategies for fluency building during Tier 1 instruction. Either one will facilitate supported repeated reading of challenging text. The first is a structured shared reading of the day's pages or chapter, systematically incorporating choral and paired reading. You will see that this shared reading structure fits easily into our Tier 1 planning template for *Bookworms K–5: Reading and Writing*, but that is surely not the only way for you to organize your time. The second one is a paired reading protocol called Peer-Assisted Learning Strategies (PALS). The criteria for selecting a structure can be based on the texts you will use and the management decisions you make. In fact, we know many teachers who use both procedures—one in shared reading, and the other in social studies and science. We describe the two formats next.

In the past, commercial reading programs have provided many suggestions for instruction and activities every day. We have come to see these choices as very difficult to justify with empirical evidence and as needlessly reducing reading volume. Our goal is that students read as much high-quality, complex text with support as possible every day. We suggest that instead of wrestling with time to include a wide variety of activities, you follow a repetitive format with a structured model for your daily instruction. If you need to make adjustments, always keep in mind that your goal in these grade levels is for students to wrestle with and conquer complex texts. Figure 6.9 presents our evolving lesson template, adding the fluency components to the word recognition work we have introduced in Chapter 5.

The planning is very simple. Once a teacher has a grade-level text to read, that text has to be chunked into reasonable segments. We want each segment to be read chorally and then reread with meaningful goals. You will see that we set a purpose for choral reading, and it is not related to fluency. Upper elementary students are unlikely to be motivated by skill building; they are likely to be motivated by rich text ideas. Fluency building is a byproduct of that motivated reading. We always direct students to read for meaning. Because we are assuming text complexity, that initial purpose should help students attend to the gist and focus on the most important information. Once the purpose is set, the choral reading can start, with the teacher reading at a natural pace and volume and the students reading along softly enough that the teacher's modeling is easily heard.

Time	Activity	Description
5 minutes	Review	
5 minutes	Word study	Introduce two new words, with attention to syllable types, meaning, and derivatives.
20–25 minutes	Fluency and comprehension instruction	1. Set a meaningful purpose. 2. Engage class in choral reading. 3. Briefly discuss first purpose. 4. Set a new purpose. 5. Engage class in partner rereading. 6. Briefly discuss second purpose.
5–10 minutes	Discussion	

FIGURE 6.9. Template for planning shared reading with fluency instruction.

Once the day's segment has been read once chorally, a brief discussion of the initial purpose keeps the text itself, with all of its affordances, at the forefront. Then the teacher can set a new, deeper purpose for partner rereading. For example, with a narrative, you can ask students to reread to consider the actions and feelings of a particular character or to examine the role that direct dialogue plays in the selection. You can ask them to visualize the events or to think about how the text is similar to one that they have previously read. In an informational text, you can ask students to focus on finding the main idea or on a cycle or sequence of events. You can ask them to consider questions that the text information raises for them. You can ask them to consider the role that the headings play in signaling the content of the text. The possibilities are virtually endless, and the standards for reading literature and information can guide you—but the important thing is to set a new purpose, connected to the actual text, with each successive reading.

There are two general ways for partner rereading to be structured. We use a simple structure for assigning partners, which we describe later. Students can either alternate (one reading a page and then another reading a page) or read chorally. If the two read chorally, that increases the number of words read aloud by each, but if they alternate, they get a chance to really listen to one another's prosody. You can even let the students themselves choose. And since the teacher has no role during this time, it provides an opportunity to drop in and listen to students reading, or to call together a small group who might benefit from a second dose of choral reading with the teacher.

We have extensive experience in planning and facilitating choral reading and partner rereading with upper elementary students. The trick is the timing. The text segment for choral reading is determined in advance. The time for partner rereading will be determined by the time left, although teachers need to make sure that there is still time for a discussion and closure. Once the procedures are firmly in place, 10 minutes of daily rereading can be a great boost for student fluency and comprehension. If fewer minutes remain in the period, though, it is better to shorten the rereading slightly than to miss the chance to discuss text ideas. Teachers can interrupt the rereading politely by returning to the second purpose and then launching a real discussion. All students will have had the same amount of time to reread, although they will be at different places in the text.

Another format that may be used is PALS. To use PALS exactly as designed requires 32 minutes. This model was designed by Douglas and Lynn Fuchs and their colleagues (Fuchs, Fuchs, Mathes, & Simmons, 1997; Simmons, Fuchs, Fuchs, Hodge, & Mathes, 1994). PALS supports the fluency and comprehension of students at different grade levels and with different levels of skills (McMaster, Fuchs, & Fuchs, 2006). Partners practice fluency and comprehension during a structured reading of connected text. The students are paired according to ability, with higher-performing students working with lower-performing ones. The pairs are assigned by rank-ordering the students based on reading ability (either fluency or comprehension scores) and then splitting the groups in half. Figure 6.10 presents this system. The class depicted has 20 students. The first column represents the top 10 readers in the class, and the second column the second half of readers, numbered 11 through 20 according to skill level. Rows represent pairs. The top reader is paired with the reader with the 11th best performance. Therefore, within each pair there is always a higher-performing student, but the distance between their performances is controlled. This allows the stronger readers (i.e., Reader A in each pair) to model for the weaker readers (i.e., Reader B) as they alternate in reading aloud and discussing the text.

During their reading, students work on both fluency and comprehension. Figure 6.11 presents the activities that students engage in during PALS. Note that the times are specific in the researchers' design. PALS takes 32 minutes, as noted above, and researchers recommend that it be used every other day.

PALS requires the teacher to teach students the roles and procedures for partner reading, retelling, paragraph shrinking, and prediction relay, and to keep time. The students use cue cards to remind them of the steps in each segment of the lesson. In addition, once the procedures are in place, the teacher motivates students by providing points for on-task behavior, for cooperation, and for catching one another's mistakes on score cards. In PALS research projects, these points have been exchanged for rewards. If you

Reader A	Reader B
1	11
2	12
3	13
4	14
5	15
6	16
7	17
8	18
9	19
10	20

FIGURE 6.10. Planning pairs for PALS.

Time	Activity	Description
10 minutes	Partner reading	The higher-performing student (Partner A) reads first for 5 minutes to model for the lower-performing student (Partner B); then the lower-performing student rereads that same section of text for the remaining 5 minutes.
2 minutes	Retelling	Students take turns reviewing what they have read in partner reading. They can use sentence frames and look back in the book: • The first thing that happened was . . . • The next thing that happened was . . . • The last thing that happened was . . .
10 minutes	Paragraph shrinking	The students alternate reading one paragraph and retelling its content in 10 words or less: • Name the who or what. • Tell the most important thing about the who or what. • Say the main idea in 10 words or less.
10 minutes	Prediction relay	The students alternate making a prediction about upcoming content, reading half a page, deciding whether their prediction was correct, and then using the paragraph-shrinking procedure.

FIGURE 6.11. Template for PALS instruction.

choose to use rewards, we hope that you will provide books or magazine subscriptions for your students' homes. We describe each of the PALS procedures in more depth next.

During partner reading, Partner A (the stronger reader) reads aloud for 5 minutes while Partner B plays the role of coach. Then the students switch roles, with Partner B rereading the text that Partner A has modeled, while Partner A takes on the role of coach. Figure 6.12 shows the two mistakes the coach will look for (careless mistakes and hard words) and the language the coach should use to help; the figure can be used as a cue card. In all cases, if neither student can identify a word, they should ask for the teacher's support. If students have their hands raised for assistance too often, this indicates that the text is too challenging, and a switch to choral reading may be in order.

After 10 minutes of partner reading, the pairs engage in 2 minutes of retelling with look-backs. The purpose of the retelling is to support comprehension. Partner A begins by retelling the first event, and then Partner B retells the second. The partners alternate retelling another event or fact until time is called. The questions used to prompt the retelling are meant to keep the partners involved and to support them in sequential recall. Figure 6.13 provides the types of questions asked during retelling.

The next segment of PALS, paragraph shrinking, requires reading additional text, paragraph by paragraph, and identifying the main idea. In narratives with extensive dialogue, the text may be chunked into half pages. Again, students take turns as reader and coach. The coach can monitor the partner's performance and provide feedback. Figure 6.14 presents the three-part procedure. Once the reader has answered the questions and has generated a main idea, the coach counts words in that main idea. If the main idea exceeds 10 words, the coach guides the partner to shrink the main idea.

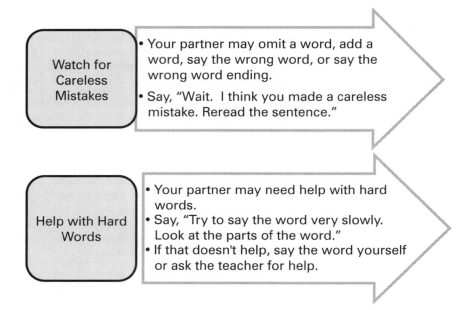

Watch for Careless Mistakes
- Your partner may omit a word, add a word, say the wrong word, or say the wrong word ending.
- Say, "Wait. I think you made a careless mistake. Reread the sentence."

Help with Hard Words
- Your partner may need help with hard words.
- Say, "Try to say the word very slowly. Look at the parts of the word."
- If that doesn't help, say the word yourself or ask the teacher for help.

FIGURE 6.12. Cue card for partner reading.

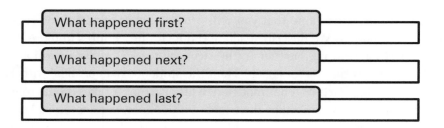

What happened first?

What happened next?

What happened last?

FIGURE 6.13. Cue card for retelling.

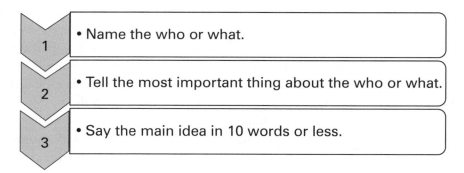

1
- Name the who or what.

2
- Tell the most important thing about the who or what.

3
- Say the main idea in 10 words or less.

FIGURE 6.14. Cue card for paragraph shrinking.

The next section of PALS combines prediction with paragraph shrinking, and the procedures are represented in Figure 6.15. The prediction students make is an immediate one: what they think will happen in the next half page. After the students complete the reading of this next section, they check whether their prediction was correct or not, and then summarize the information by using the paragraph-shrinking procedure again. In all instances, the students in each pair are both accountable for the task. To learn more about PALS, visit the researchers' website (*https://vkc.mc.vanderbilt.edu/frg/what-is-pals*).

Instructional Planning

A daily read-aloud and either structured shared reading or use of the PALS procedure within Tier 1 instruction have the potential to support students' reading fluency. Once you have established your classroom procedures, neither one of these systems requires much planning at all, at least not beyond selection of the instructional strategies. The only real planning required for Tier 1 fluency work will be selecting books to read aloud.

For your read-alouds, try to select books that will motivate and engage the students. The texts do not need to be narratives; you can also use informational texts and model fluent reading and meaning-making strategies. The texts can be connected by theme or with your instruction in science and social studies. It makes sense after devoting time to a topic in these content areas to read aloud a book with the same theme. Each grade-level team can choose a different set of engaging read-alouds. We encourage you to consider award-winning books. The Association for Library Service to Children (*www.ala.org/ alsc*) has classified lists of books by award. This is one resource you may want to consult before purchasing books or borrowing them from the library.

The Lexile website (*https://lexile.com*) can also assist you in selecting read-aloud texts in different genres, as well as books for use in shared reading or PALS, if you do not

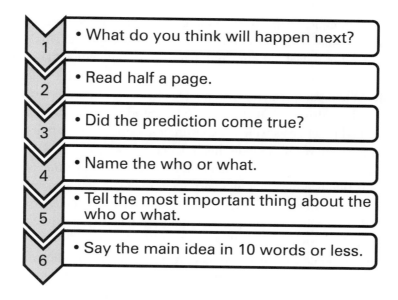

1. • What do you think will happen next?
2. • Read half a page.
3. • Did the prediction come true?
4. • Name the who or what.
5. • Tell the most important thing about the who or what.
6. • Say the main idea in 10 words or less.

FIGURE 6.15. Cue card for prediction relay.

already have books selected in your school's curriculum. From our experience, teachers are often reluctant to select challenging read-alouds, because they think that these texts will be too difficult for their students. Remember, however, that students are not reading these books on their own; their teachers are there to model and scaffold. Look back at Figure 6.7: We have chosen books for fourth-grade shared reading that are inside the 4–5 text difficulty band, and then we have chosen even more difficult ones for read-alouds.

Both read-alouds and shared reading are our fluency work in Tier 1, whole-group instruction. However, many students may need additional support with fluency. You can identify them easily with the procedures we have provided in Chapter 4. You will find two groups of students for this instruction. Both groups are below benchmark in your assessment of automaticity. One of those groups has also failed the Multisyllabic Decoding subtest provided in Figure 4.2. This latter group receives instruction in fluency and comprehension with multisyllabic decoding, and the other receives instruction in plain fluency and comprehension.

TIER 2 INSTRUCTION IN FLUENCY

Tier 2 instruction that supports fluency is nearly identical to Tier 1 instruction. If you look back at Figure 5.10, you will see that our multisyllabic decoding instruction is very similar to Tier 1 word study. It's just a larger dose, and we've planned it for you in advance. After that, both of our groups participate in another structured repeated reading.

Content

The key to addressing fluency problems is simple: It all comes down to engaged practice. You can work on all aspects of fluency at the same time. Your students may lack stamina; they may find long, complex texts overwhelming. They may be accurate in reading words in isolation, but they may struggle with texts with complex syntax. This lack of prosody can sound almost robotic, lacking phrasing, pauses, and intonation. They may struggle to match their reading rate to genre, reading a novel and a scientific informational text at the same rate. When good readers read poetry or stories or nonfiction, their prosodic attention differs; they also read at different rates. Students who need support in fluency need additional practice as well as exposure and opportunities to process different genres. It is relatively simple to provide this practice.

The content for students in Tier 2 fluency building is the very same content that was targeted in Tier 1: fluent processing of a very wide range of sentence structures within interesting texts. The difference between Tier 1 and Tier 2 fluency work is minimal; all students need extensive reading practice, and students who struggle with fluency need even more. We suggest that you choose an *additional, different* text to increase the number of words and sentences that students process successfully each day. In this way, they will do fluency work within their grade-level band *and* with a text that you have added for Tier 2 every day. The variety in text processing can better support students' understanding of genres, their engagement (as they will be reading texts that allow them to learn about an additional author or topic), and gradually their confidence (as they see themselves improve as readers and conquer fluency goals).

Instructional Strategies

Fluency instruction is very easy to manage. In small-group instruction, we use the core instructional strategies from Tier 1: choral reading followed by partner rereading. A teacher's oral reading is still the blueprint for students' intonation and expression. In Tier 2, though, the group will be smaller, and the teacher can attend more directly to the students. In addition, the teacher can schedule groups to maximize the pages read by staggering the work. Figure 6.16 shows what we mean.

In contrast to our differentiated fluency design for younger students, we now know that upper elementary students can accomplish their rereading tasks independently. In fact, this actually solves a management problem. If "teacher time" is either choral reading or discussion and then choral reading, time management is simple. All students are reading at the same rate (with the teacher), so they finish at the same time. Rereading, either with partners or as whisper reading, can be untimed. This allows for a more natural rereading, with pairs finishing when they finish, allowing the teacher to plan for more pages a day.

Days	Format	Activity	Teacher's role	Students' role
Day 1	With teacher	(Multisyllabic decoding practice, if warranted.) Choral reading.	Teacher reads the text with intonation and expression, modeling text processing.	Students follow the teacher's lead.
Day 1	Outside of the group	Partner or whisper rereading.	Teacher can serve another group or circulate to provide support.	Students reread the text with a partner, monitoring and supporting one another's reading, or independently.
Day 2	With teacher	(Multisyllabic decoding practice, if warranted.) Comprehension discussion of previous text segment; choral reading of new segment.	Teacher engages students in comprehension-rich discussion; teacher reads the text with intonation and expression, modeling text processing.	Students engage in targeted fluency practice for the purpose of supporting comprehension.
Day 2	Outside of the group	Partner or whisper rereading.	Teacher can serve another group or circulate to provide support.	Students reread the text with a partner, monitoring and supporting one another's reading, or independently.

FIGURE 6.16. Template for fluency practice.

Structuring the group this way also serves another master. Fourth- and fifth-grade students are capable of independent work and are likely to crave peer interactions. We can build their confidence and competence at the same time by assigning it with less direct monitoring. While rereading can be independent, the teacher's monitoring can be of comprehension—by planning and leading a meaningful discussion. This second meeting brings into focus the importance of the students' independent work and their purpose for rereading to comprehend the selection.

We have always favored the use of new texts or text segments every day in fluency-building programs, but we are softening that stance as students reach the upper elementary grades. You have to choose the length of your discussion. If you reserve 15 minutes to work with your group, you will be able to complete a choral reading of a substantial new segment of text and also lead a very brief discussion, or you can choose to read chorally for the full time one day, have the students reread later, and take the full 15 minutes for discussion the next day.

Because this plan is different from our plans for younger students, we would like to explain our thinking. Although we have always planned for both fluency and comprehension to be targets within a brief Tier 2 daily lesson in our K–3 instructional model, this may not be ideal in the upper elementary grades. You will find that many texts at those levels (especially interesting ones!) have such complex structures and content that their discussion simply requires more time. That is why we encourage you to use the full time allotted either for a brief discussion and a new text segment read chorally, or for choral reading and discussion on alternating days. The first choral reading of the text will still allow the students to work on the dimensions of fluency; in addition, if they can read more pages, they will view the content of the text as a whole and have a representation of the text's overall structure. When they reread the text immediately with their partners, you will have gradually released responsibility to them. Also, this concentrated attention to fluency building will guarantee that those students whose weak fluency has been the result of a lack of reading practice will get the practice they need.

Choosing this structure for our upper elementary Tier 2 fluency groups does come at a cost, and we would like to expose it so that you can choose a structure that makes sense in your classroom. In the *Bookworms K–5 Reading and Writing* program, in which our entire differentiation model is embedded, students in a fluency group will not have time for self-selected independent reading on the days when they are rereading with their partners. Their small-group lesson will be followed by their partner rereading and then by their written response to shared reading. On the alternate days, when they are discussing that text segment, they will have time for independent reading. We believe that wide, independent, self-selected reading is important. We want teachers to create classroom communities where students read by choice at home from texts selected from classroom libraries and the school's media center. Our goal in planning this extra dose of fluency is to increase students' fluency to such an extent that they no longer need the extra support.

What about those students who do not pass the Multisyllabic Decoding subtest provided in Figure 4.2? Your instruction for them is simple, because we have already scripted it in Appendix F. It is simply a very short dose of multisyllabic decoding instruction. Your goal should be to get it down to 4 minutes each day. There is a scripted teacher introduction; a word for you to use to model; a list of 10 words per day for students to actually mark divisions, pronounce in parts, and then blend; and 3 words for them to spell if time allows. To minimize your preparation and management, we suggest that you simply copy the lessons for the week, and distribute and collect the sheets each day. The students can spell the day's spelling words on the back of the sheet. Students need not even use the same copy each day. Figure 6.17 provides the routine; it is the same every day for 18 weeks.

Instructional Planning

For upper elementary students who need to build fluency, there are only three things to consider in planning: (1) whether the group needs a 4-minute multisyllabic decoding lesson or not; (2) what and how much they should read each day; and (3) what questions you can use to place comprehension at the forefront of the work. We suggest you select high-quality, authentic books for your work with these students. Remember that these texts must be engaging enough *to the students* that they will want to participate in repeated readings. They also must be difficult enough that fluency builds through repetition, but accessible enough that the students are not frustrated. The Lexile website can support you in making this choice, but book selection is never an exact science.

For fourth- and fifth-grade students in the fluency with multisyllabic decoding group, we suggest that you select books with Lexiles at the lower end of their grade-level range. Start with books that have Lexiles of 700L–850L, especially if you are also engaging them in more challenging texts in Tier 1. For students with strong multisyllabic decoding, you may select more difficult texts, but you need not match the texts precisely to your data. These students will be supported initially through choral reading and subsequently through their own repeated readings. The only real test of the fit between your readers and the texts you select is to try them. If you have made a poor choice, simply replace the text with a different one.

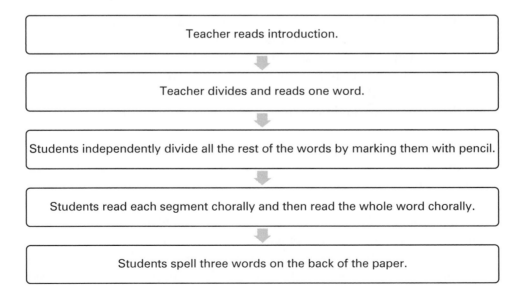

FIGURE 6.17. Multisyllabic decoding routine.

Once you have chosen a text, you have to match your goals for pages per day with that particular text. We have found a tried and true way to do that: Read it aloud and time yourself! That way you can get a sense of how to match the minutes you have with your group and the pages you can typically plan for. This is also important so that you can write a few excellent discussion questions.

We share model lessons in Appendices F and G. Remember that our multisyllabic decoding lessons are warm-up tasks for a Fluency and Comprehension group struggling in this area, but the rest of the lesson is exactly the same for both groups. In this chapter, we have described fluency development and instruction, and presented models you can use for Tier 1 and Tier 2 instruction. In the next two chapters, we complete our Tier 1 templates to include instructional strategies for vocabulary and comprehension to support upper elementary students. We acknowledge, however, that this combination of Tier 1 and Tier 2 instruction will not be enough for a small number of students whose word recognition and fluency achievement are much farther from grade level. Students with such needs will require access to Tier 3 interventions.

CHOOSING TIER 3 PROGRAMS FOR FLUENCY

Again, even if you provide strong and explicit Tier 1 and Tier 2 instruction, there will be students who will continue to struggle with fluency. For such students, you should first examine whether their fluency problems reflect difficulties with lower-level skills involving single-syllable word recognition. You can do that with the full Informal Decoding Inventory in Appendix E. We remind you that students will not show improvement if they are misplaced in a group that does not target their needs. However, if students are correctly placed in the Fluency and Comprehension group and make no progress in fluency and comprehension, they may need to receive intensive support outside your classroom from specialized personnel who can diagnose and address their needs.

Tier 3 interventions for fluency will have some similarities to our Tier 1 and Tier 2 strategies, but they are less likely to use whole natural texts and will address skills more specifically. For example, they are likely to have a series of shorter texts already selected and sequenced, perhaps repeating words and phrases across texts. They may include introduction and repeated reading of specific words and phrases before text reading. Some include computer-assisted modeling, as well as audio recording of students' practice.

As in Chapter 5, we do not provide a list of commercial programs for Tier 3 instruction. Recommendations for interventions for students in the upper elementary grades can be found on the Center on Instruction website (*www.centeroninstruction.org/index.cfm*), the Center on Response to Intervention website (*www.rti4success.org*) and the Institute of Education Sciences' What Works Clearinghouse (*https://ies.ed.gov/ncee/wwc*), which also provides evaluations of specific programs that address literacy (*https://ies.ed.gov/ncee/wwc/FWW/Results?filters=,Literacy*). These resources can help you identify programs and methods that can support additional needs in fluency and comprehension.

CHAPTER 7

Building Vocabulary

In this chapter, we present a tiered instructional model for developing fourth- and fifth-grade students' vocabulary. To introduce the model, we first present some foundational knowledge about vocabulary instruction and its importance. For Tier 1 instruction, we argue that direct instruction in the meanings of a small set of words before students read, exposure to multiple-meaning words in context while they read, and writing sentences using the words in a new context after reading can both improve their comprehension of a specific text and lead to incremental improvements in vocabulary knowledge. We provide a short list of strategies teachers can use to get started. We also argue that for students who have achieved grade-level standards in word recognition and fluency, building vocabulary is a reasonable (and important) goal for their Tier 2 instruction. Finally, we argue that a small number of upper elementary students, especially English learners, may also require intensive Tier 3 vocabulary instruction.

FOUNDATIONAL KNOWLEDGE ABOUT VOCABULARY DEVELOPMENT

Because there are so many types of vocabulary (e.g., listening, speaking, reading, and writing), it is important to be clear about the focus of this chapter. Our concern is with students' knowledge of word meanings, regardless of whether they encounter those words in oral or written language. We are interested in developing academic vocabulary—including both domain-specific words that students learn in their study of a particular discipline or content area, and general academic words that children may encounter in any text (Baumann & Graves, 2010).

The great problem with vocabulary instruction is that there are so many words to teach and so little guidance for choosing them. Some linguists argue that the English language contains more words than any other language, although the true number is unknown. Literacy researchers once estimated that children may encounter up to 88,500 distinct word families in school reading materials from grades 3 through 9 (Nagy & Anderson, 1984). Some experts contend that the number of words in the English language is almost limitless because of rules that allow us to coin new words. English language users follow set rules for coining new words, thus adding greatly to the number of potential words in the language. Consider this sentence:

> The mail carrier likes our street because it is dogless.

You probably have no difficulty determining why the mail carrier likes our street, even though the word *dogless* is not in the dictionary, and you are unlikely ever to have encountered it before.

Children learn new words at different rates and in different quantities, depending on aptitude and environment. Large differences in the meaning vocabulary of children have already developed before they reach kindergarten. Hart and Risley (1995) estimated that children of parents with professional careers averaged knowing about 1,100 words by age 3, compared with children whose parents lacked the same educational and economic advantages. These children possessed vocabularies that averaged about 500 words.

Long-term studies allow us to project an ever-widening gap in word knowledge as children pass through school. What are schools doing to narrow this gap and to ensure that all children have the vocabulary they need to succeed in school? According to Andy Biemiller (2012), very little: "In short, vocabulary levels diverge greatly during the primary years, and virtually nothing effective is done about this in schools" (p. 36). He maintains that the greatest gaps occur in the primary years, and that the rate of learning is about the same for the highest- and lowest-achieving children between grades two and five (Biemiller & Slonim, 2001). The size of a child's vocabulary is not just an abstract statistic. It bears directly on comprehension and consequently on school success. In 1997, Cunningham and Stanovich reported that oral vocabulary at the end of first grade was a significant predictor of comprehension 10 years later. Sparks, Patton, and Murdoch (2014) replicated these findings with a larger number of students, confirming the influence of grade 1 vocabulary knowledge on grade 10 reading skills. In another study, third- and fourth-grade students who made the largest gains in vocabulary also made the largest gains in comprehension (Shany & Biemiller, 2010). These stark findings indicate the true importance (and potential) of our efforts to build vocabulary.

Vocabulary knowledge is central to comprehending what we read, to a degree that might be surprising. Let's consider a famous example from a research study (Beck & McKeown, 1994). The following paragraph is from a fifth-grade social studies text. Read it and see if you have any comprehension difficulties.

> In 1367, Marain and the settlements ended a seven-year war with the Langurians and Pitoks. As a result of this war, Languria was driven out of East Bacol. Marain would now rule Laman and the other lands that once belonged to Languria. This brought peace to the Bacolean settlements. The settlers no longer had to worry about attacks

from Laman. The Bacoleans were happy to be part of Marain in 1367. Yet a dozen years later, these same people would be fighting the Marish for independence, or freedom from United Marain's rule.

As you may have suspected, there's a trick involved. Some of the key terms have been replaced by nonsense words. Even the four digits of the date were scrambled. Now take a look at the original text.

In 1763, Britain and the colonies ended a seven-year war with the French and Indians. As a result of this war, France was driven out of North America. Britain would now rule Canada and the other lands that once belonged to France. This brought peace to the American colonies. The settlers no longer had to worry about attacks from Canada. The Americans were happy to be part of Britain in 1763. Yet a dozen years later, these same people would be fighting the British for independence, or freedom from Great Britain's rule.

No doubt you found this version a little easier. However, the participants in the study were not teachers; they were fifth graders. Surprisingly, the students found both versions equally difficult! This little experiment illustrates how powerful an effect preteaching important words can have on the comprehension of children with limited prior knowledge.

How do we go about bridging this gap so that students leave the upper elementary grades for middle school with the vocabulary they need to succeed? In a meta-analysis of vocabulary intervention studies conducted mostly in grades 3–6, Hairrell, Rupley, and Simmons (2011) provided support for nine effective vocabulary practices recommended by the National Reading Panel (2000): mnemonics, explicit vocabulary instruction, incidental word learning, repeated practice or multiple exposures, computer-assisted instruction, contextual analysis, morphological analysis, semantic analysis, and multiple strategies. While we don't cover each of these in detail, we do describe those approaches that we have used extensively in our tiered vocabulary instruction. We tend to agree with Graves's (2006) suggestion that a comprehensive approach to vocabulary instruction should include rich and varied language experiences, direct instruction in word meanings, strategies for learning words through context, and opportunities to promote word consciousness.

One approach is direct instruction of word meanings. Although we strongly endorse this practice and offer suggestions for doing so in this chapter, there are simply too many important words to teach them all directly. Teaching relevant vocabulary may be more necessary for informational texts centered on a small number of content words (Armbruster & Anderson, 1988). For these and other texts, a complementary approach is to provide opportunities for incidental word learning through rich and varied language experiences. Researchers have documented that individuals learn about 15% of unknown words incidentally; however, the proportion of words learned is higher when they are reading to learn about a topic than when they are reading for pleasure, and high-ability readers are more likely than low-ability readers to learn words incidentally (Swanborn

& de Glopper, 1999, 2002). Stanovich (1986) and others have suggested that the relationship between vocabulary knowledge and reading is circular. On the one hand, knowing more words makes you a better reader; on the other hand, being a better reader enables you to read more and to develop a larger vocabulary through reading. Having a large vocabulary also influences writing. Elementary students with greater written vocabulary diversity compose narrative texts of higher quality (Olinghouse & Leaird, 2009; Olinghouse & Wilson, 2013).

We can think of this relationship in terms of a circle, depicted in Figure 7.1. Having a larger vocabulary makes you a better reader and writer; being a better reader makes it possible for you to read more; and then reading more gives you a larger vocabulary that makes its way into your reading comprehension and into your writing. This circular relationship tends to increase the difference in vocabulary size between good and poor readers over time. On the positive side, better readers tend to read more, acquire larger vocabularies, and become even better readers. On the negative side, poorer readers tend to read less, fail to develop large vocabularies, and find reading increasingly difficult as the vocabulary demands of the texts they must read increase (Stahl & Nagy, 2005). For this reason, we consistently encourage efforts to increase reading achievement *and* to promote high-volume reading for all students.

You might be tempted to conclude that wide reading alone is enough to acquire an adequate vocabulary. We obviously know thousands of words that were never formally taught to us in school. We picked up their meanings through incidental exposures. Krashen (2012) argues that many people have developed a large academic vocabulary without instruction, and that real reading is more effective and efficient than direct instruction. Researchers have hypothesized that most of children's vocabulary learning occurs in this incidental way (Nagy, Herman, & Anderson, 1985; Nagy, Anderson, & Herman, 1987). If this is the case, why bother teaching vocabulary at all? Why not provide children with opportunities to meet new words through reading and conversation? Wouldn't that be enough? Graves (2011) points out that there are different benefits of wide reading and direct instruction; while wide reading leads to knowledge of a larger

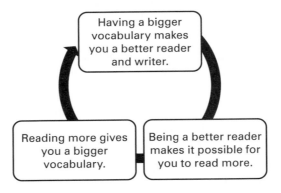

FIGURE 7.1. How reading fosters vocabulary growth and vice versa.

body of words over time, direct instruction is necessary if you want students to learn a specific set of words—namely, the important words in an upcoming reading selection. Marzano (2004) argues that there is no need to choose between the two approaches: "There is no obvious reason why direct vocabulary instruction and wide reading cannot work in tandem" (p. 112). We agree. And in the case of domain-specific academic vocabulary, direct vocabulary instruction may be a necessary part of the solution (Nagy & Townsend, 2012).

A third approach is to teach word-learning strategies. Because we can't possibly teach all the unfamiliar words students will encounter in text (and we can't guarantee that they will learn them incidentally), students have to be equipped with strategies to learn unfamiliar words on their own. Two strategies used individually or in combination—morphemic analysis (teaching meaningful word parts) and contextual analysis—have been shown to improve fifth-grade students' ability to infer the meanings of untaught words (Baumann et al., 2002, 2003). Students can be taught to first check whether there are context clues about the meaning of unfamiliar words when reading, next check whether they can use word-part clues to figure out the meaning, and finally check whether the meaning makes sense in context (Baumann, Ware, & Edwards, 2007). Figure 7.2 displays types of context clues and word-part clues students may be taught. To determine whether they have inferred the correct meaning of multiple-meaning words, students should also be taught how to consult a dictionary, either print or digital.

Clues You Can Use: Look for Both . . .	
Word-Part Clues	Context Clues
1. <u>Root:</u> The basic part of a word. It might be a whole word (e.g., uni<u>cell</u>ular) or a meaningful part of a word (e.g., <u>vis</u>ion, <u>vis</u>ible).	1. Definition: The author explains the meaning of the word right in the text.
2. *Prefix:* A word part added to the beginning of a word that changes its meaning (e.g., *uni*cellular means *one* cell).	2. Synonym: The author uses a word with a similar meaning in the text.
3. **Suffix:** A word part added to the end of a word that changes its meaning (e.g., venge**ful** means **full of** revenge).	3. Antonym: The author uses a word with an opposite meaning in the text.
4. Combine the meanings of the <u>root</u> and any *prefix* or **suffix** and see if you can infer the meaning of the word (e.g., *trans*<u>pir</u>**ation**).	4. Example: The author provides example words or ideas related to the word's meaning.
	5. General: The author provides other words or statements that give clues to the meaning.

FIGURE 7.2. Context and word-part clues. Based on Baumann, Font, Edwards, and Boland (2005) and Baumann, Ware, and Edwards (2007).

As we begin to consider instructional approaches, it is vital to note that our knowledge of words is not all or nothing. It is better to think of our understanding of any word as a matter of degree, ranging from no knowledge to a deep appreciation. Imagine an out-of-school context in which you must attempt to learn the meaning of a new word you hear someone else use. Think back to your first encounter with the word *Quidditch* in the Harry Potter series. You learned that it was a game, and this was helpful in learning the word. However, this first encounter was only a small step along the path to acquiring the full meaning of the word. In fact, you also had to learn the meanings of *Golden Snitch* and *Seeker* and *Quaffle*. Each encounter with a word helps us narrow a new word's meaning. As you read about a Quidditch match, your understanding deepened considerably. Beck, McKeown, and Kucan (2013) suggest a continuum of word knowledge. The ideal is a thorough appreciation of a word's meaning involving "decontextualized" understanding. That is, even without a specific context, the word alone calls to mind an abundance of useful associations. In between the extremes, our knowledge of a particular word may be relatively weak or strong. Figure 7.3 demonstrates this continuum.

As students reach grades 4 and 5, they are expected to continue acquiring a broad academic vocabulary, both general and domain-specific. They are expected to be able to use their word knowledge appropriately as they read and write. They are also expected to be able to determine the meanings of unfamiliar words by a number of means, such as using contextual clues, morphological analysis, and reference materials. These characteristics are embodied in the CSSS. Because there are almost no differences between the fourth- and fifth-grade standards, we have combined them in Figure 7.4.

We encourage you to continue building your knowledge of vocabulary instruction. The sources listed in Figure 7.5 are appropriate for individual professional reading or for group study with your colleagues.

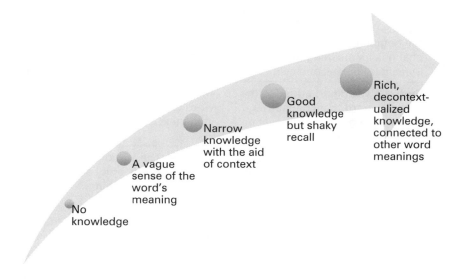

FIGURE 7.3. A continuum of word knowledge.

General Goal	Evidence
Grades 4 and 5	
The students determine word meanings.	Determine or clarify the meaning of unknown or multiple-meaning words through the use of one or more strategies, such as using semantic clues (e.g., definitions, examples, or restatements in text); using syntactic clues (e.g., the word's position or function in the sentence); analyzing the word's sounds, spelling, and meaningful parts; and consulting reference materials, both print and digital. Use a known root word as a clue to the meaning of an unknown word with the same root (e.g., *telegraph, photograph, autograph*).
The students understand word relationships.	Build real-life connections between words and their various uses and meanings. Define relationships between words (e.g., how *ask* is like and unlike *demand*; what items are likely to be *enormous*). Distinguish a word from other words with similar but not identical meanings (synonyms).
The students use words appropriately.	Use grade-appropriate general academic vocabulary and domain-specific words and phrases (in English language arts, history/social studies, and science) taught directly and acquired through reading and responding to texts.

FIGURE 7.4. Vocabulary standards from the CCSS. From NGACBP and CCSSO (2010). In the public domain.

Baumann, J. F., & Kame'enui, E. J. (Eds.). (2012). *Vocabulary instruction: Research to practice* (2nd ed.). New York: Guilford Press.
Beck, I. L., McKeown, M. G., & Kucan, L. (2008). *Creating robust vocabulary: Frequently asked questions and extended examples.* New York: Guilford Press.
Beck, I. L., McKeown, M. G., & Kucan, L. (2013). *Bringing words to life: Robust vocabulary instruction* (2nd ed.). New York: Guilford Press.
Blachowicz, C., & Fisher, P. J. (2015). *Teaching vocabulary in all classrooms* (5th ed.). Boston: Pearson.
Stahl, S. A., & Nagy, W. E. (2005). *Teaching word meanings.* Mahwah, NJ: Erlbaum.

FIGURE 7.5. Resources for vocabulary instruction.

TIER 1 INSTRUCTION IN VOCABULARY

Without a model to narrow the scope of vocabulary instruction, teachers would have little to guide them in choosing words and selecting instructional strategies. Thankfully, there are several models for planning systematic Tier 1 vocabulary instruction. There are at least four decisions that teachers have to make during Tier 1 time: what words to teach, when and how to teach them, what materials to use, and how to assess understanding of words (Johnston, Tulbert, Sebastian, Devries, & Gompert, 2000). Choosing words to teach is the essential first step.

Content

With all the potentially important words in a given text, how do teachers decide which words to teach? Not surprisingly, most guidelines do not include a list of words that all fourth and fifth graders should know. There are simply too many words (and too many opinions) to make that possible. Instead, researchers provide frameworks for choosing words to teach. You may already be familiar with the three tiers of words suggested by Beck and colleagues (2013). (We apologize in advance for the fact that this book includes attention to tiers of instruction and tiers of words.) Tier 1 *words* are basic words, such as *lucky,* that are commonly used and that most students are likely to know. Typically, these do not need to be taught. Most vocabulary instruction should focus on Tier 2 words, or general words that are important for understanding texts across content areas, such as *coincidence.* Tier 3 words are low-frequency, domain-specific words that are necessary for comprehension of texts in particular content areas. These words, such as *monarchy* or *atmosphere,* should be taught when students are reading informational texts about a particular topic. These three tiers of vocabulary provide a useful framework for prioritizing words for instruction.

Other researchers have provided additional guidance for which words (and how many) to select from texts. Graves and colleagues (2013) have described four types of words to teach: (1) essential words that are necessary for comprehending the text, (2) valuable words that have broad utility for reading and writing about text, (3) accessible words of high frequency that students with limited vocabulary knowledge are unlikely to know, and (4) imported words that don't appear in the text itself but may enhance understanding. From among these four types, they recommend teaching about 2–3 words per day, resulting in 8–15 words per week and 500–600 per school year.

We recommend choosing between two and four valuable, Tier 2 words when students are reading fictional texts. For informational texts, we recommend teaching the essential, Tier 3 words related to the topic. Accessible words might be chosen for English learners or students with developing vocabularies, regardless of text type. Imported words may help students make connections to key concepts in informational texts, or they may emphasize themes or character traits in narratives. Regardless of which approach you choose, Tier 1 *instruction* should begin with a careful examination of what words in a text will potentially be unfamiliar to your students. We also advise you to consider posting vocabulary words in the classroom to remind you (and your students) to review taught words often and notice when they occur in new contexts. Examples of each type of word, selected from *Ice to Steam: Changing States of Matter* by Penny Johnson (2008), are displayed in Figure 7.6.

Instructional Strategies

Effective vocabulary instruction depends on more than just providing the dictionary definitions before students begin reading. Two equally important decisions, we think, are how you will teach word meanings and when you will teach them. Vocabulary instruction is enhanced when teachers establish efficient and rich routines, provide multiple

	Tier 1	Tier 2	Tier 3
Essential			Melting Freezing Evaporating Condensing
Valuable		Describe Material Properties Temperature	
Accessible	Change Form Same Different		
Imported		Distributed	Precipitation

FIGURE 7.6. Types of vocabulary words. Based on Beck, McKeown, and Kucan (2013) and Graves et al. (2013).

exposures to words through ongoing review, give clear definitions and examples, and encourage all students to participate in word-leaning activities (Manyak et al., 2014). Below, we recommend a handful of routines that are likely to be useful in teaching the words that you choose from fiction and nonfiction texts.

Direct Instruction of Word Meanings

Only a limited number of words can be singled out for explicit instruction. For these words, Manyak and colleagues (2014) recommend a six-step approach based on the approach of Beck and colleagues (2013). First, present the word in the context in which it appears in the text. Then provide a student-friendly definition, followed by multiple examples of how to use the word in different forms of speech. After this, prompt students to use the word, show and briefly discuss a visual image representing the word, and conclude with an interactive word-learning activity. The procedure should be fast-paced and engaging, focused on providing multiple exposures in different contexts. Here's an example from an interactive read-aloud lesson for *Hatchet* by Gary Paulsen (1987):

> "In today's text, we heard the word *lurched*. What word? [Students say the word.] To *lurch* means to move suddenly without control. If I tripped on the sidewalk, I might lurch forward. In this chapter, we read that 'the plane lurched slightly to the right and Brian looked at the pilot.' To *lurch* means to move suddenly without control. You can use that word: 'When I tripped, I lurched and _____.' 'If I see someone who lurches, I _____.' What word?"

Here's another example from the word study component of a shared reading lesson for *Steal Away Home* by Matt Carter and Aaron Ivey (2017):

"*Suspected* is a verb that means thought, when you are talking about a mystery. 'I *suspected* you were not actually sick.' You can add verb suffixes with no change, because the root, *suspect,* ends in two consonants. The noun form is also *suspect,* and it means someone that you think committed a crime."

For the last two steps, presenting a visual image and providing interactive word-learning activities, we rely on a few effective approaches. Some words that are concrete, like the word *trench,* lend themselves well to finding photographs that enhance understanding. While showing a picture of the Rocky Mountain Trench, for example, you might explain, "If there were no water in the ocean, a trench in the ocean floor would look like a canyon or valley." More abstract words, such as the word *monarchy,* might require you to use a diagram or graphic organizer instead of a photograph to convey a more nuanced meaning. We describe two types of graphic organizers—*concept of definition* (COD; Schwartz & Raphael, 1985) and *semantic feature analysis* (SFA; Pittelman, Heimlich, Berglund, & French, 1991)—below. We also describe an interactive activity called *super sentences* that we use to deepen understanding of new words after reading.

The question of when direct instruction in word meanings should occur depends on the type of words and the text in which they appear. When students are reading informational texts, it is important to teach essential, Tier 3 words either just before reading or when the words are encountered during reading. Understanding the meanings of words such as *magma, lava,* and *eruption* will probably be necessary to comprehend an informational text about volcanoes. In the case of fictional texts, we recommend explicitly teaching valuable, Tier 2 words after reading. Teaching general words that may not be necessary to comprehend the text (but are important nonetheless) before reading may be distracting when students encounter them during reading. Instead, Tier 2 words that may have multiple meanings, such as *suspicion* or *tension,* can be discussed in the context in which they appear in the text. Imported words that are important for understanding literary concepts, such as *irony,* may also be explicitly taught and discussed after reading. What about accessible words you encounter in the text that students do not understand? Of course, we do not advocate ignoring the request of a student who asks the meaning of a word during reading. In these instances, we suggest a technique we call *quick scaffolding,* which involves quickly providing an explanation of the word's meaning without disrupting the flow of the text. To aid in direct vocabulary instruction, we also recommend using the strategies described below.

Concept of Definition

COD (Schwartz & Raphael, 1985) is a strategy based on the idea that a good definition has two components: It tells the category to which a concept belongs, and it provides features that enable us to distinguish the concept from other members of the same category. A *triangle,* for instance, is defined as a polygon with three sides and three angles. From this simple definition, we can see that *triangle* is a member of the category *polygon,* and we can distinguish it from other polygons by noting its features (i.e., three sides). COD utilizes these two components to directly teach important new words, especially in content subjects. This strategy relies on the creation of a semantic diagram and is sometimes called *word mapping.* The word map that is created in the course of this instruction makes explicit the connections between an unfamiliar word and known words. You can use a variety of materials to present a COD map. For example, it can be drawn on a traditional or interactive whiteboard, presented on a PowerPoint slide with a projector, or copied on paper for students to use. A simple word map has a space for the word in the center, a connecting line to the category to which it belongs, more lines to its characteristics or attributes, and some examples.

In the example provided in Figure 7.7, the key term is *cells.* Note that this concept belongs to the larger category of *units of life,* and that characteristics of cells appear below the key term. Examples of cells are connected at the side, and examples of units of life other than cells are linked to the concept of units of life but not to the key term. A COD map is introduced in this way:

> "Cells are the smallest unit of life. All living things are made of cells. An organ, like your heart, is also a unit of life, but it is not a cell. Cells have walls or membranes, a nucleus, and specific functions. Here are some examples: Your skin is made of skin cells; a plant is made of plant cells; some small living things, like bacteria, are a single cell."

This strategy is only useful when the target word is a member of a specific category. Fortunately, many content area terms are of this kind. The strategy is helpful both for

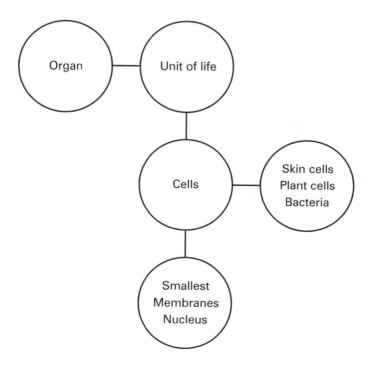

FIGURE 7.7. COD map of the word *cells.*

developing new concepts and for teaching children to generate definitions as they are learning new words. For example, a student can look at the completed diagram and say that a cell is "a unit of life that is small and has membranes and a nucleus." Note that this makeshift definition has the two characteristics of any good definition: It tells the category to which cells belong, and it provides features that enable us to tell cells from other units of life. That is why the approach is called *concept of definition*. It teaches the definition of particular words, but it also develops conceptual understanding of how to define a word.

Semantic Feature Analysis

SFA (Pittelman et al., 1991) is also based on the notion of a definition. It is a very simple instructional technique that is useful whenever new concepts belong to the same category and can be compared and contrasted on the basis of a set of features. You can begin SFA by creating a basic table with any word-processing program. In the upper left-hand cell, write the name of the category to which the concepts belong. List the members of the category in the left-hand column, and the features on which they are being compared across the top row. The individual cells in the table are filled in by writing a plus sign or a minus sign if the member of the category does or does not possess the feature listed at the top of the column. You can also write the letter *S* if a category member *sometimes* possesses a particular feature. Figure 7.8 presents a sample SFA chart based on the states of matter.

SFA can only be used with groups of terms that are members of the same category. Fortunately, these groups are often encountered in informational texts. If your responsibilities as a teacher include instruction in mathematics, science, or social studies, look for opportunities to use SFA in presenting and reviewing clusters of terms that are members of the same category. When you select informational texts to use in Tier 1 ELA instruction, look for texts that develop knowledge associated with your content area standards. Then use SFA as a means of quickly introducing category members and their distinguishing features. A useful approach is to leave a portion of the chart blank and to challenge the students to complete it as they read. A key to the success of this technique is to discuss the chart after it has been constructed, together looking for similarities and differences. In the example depicted in Figure 7.8, what conclusions can you help students reach about how solids, liquids, and gases are similar and different?

States of Matter	Made up of particles	Fixed shape	Fixed volume
Solid	+	+	+
Liquid	+	−	+
Gas	+	−	−

FIGURE 7.8. SFA chart of the states of matter.

Super Sentences

To really understand the meaning of a new word, students need to have opportunities to participate in interactive word-learning activities that allow them to try out the meanings of new words in different contexts. It's not enough to assume that if a student can match a word to its definition, the student has acquired the word's meaning. To really understand the meaning of a word, an assortment of contexts is needed, plus multiple exposures over time. Researchers estimate that 12–15 encounters with a word are needed for adequately learning its meaning (Stahl & Nagy, 2005). This is a long and winding road, indeed, and it is not traversed in a single day. Fourth- and fifth-grade teachers are, however, in a position to start their students down this road by increasing the number of times students meet new words in contextual settings.

We use a strategy called *super sentences* to help students construct a new sentence-level context when writing about their vocabulary words each day. Students create a semantic web or graphic organizer to plan a sentence. The target word is in the center, and the spokes are the journalistic questions that can be used to put the word into a meaningful context: *who, what, when, where, why,* and *how.* Students consider all of the possibilities and then use at least three to write a sentence using the target word that contains more than one clause. The target word can be used in any part of speech, and the sentence can be written in any syntactic structure. Figure 7.9 presents a semantic

FIGURE 7.9. Semantic web used to plan super sentences about influenza.

web used to plan a super sentence about the word *influenza*. The students are reading a book about the 1918 influenza pandemic.

Writing a super sentence demonstrates a student's ability to use new academic words in different contexts. It is surely a better way to ensure that children know the meanings of words than the ubiquitous practice of looking up definitions and writing them down. Super sentences require students to be selective, determining which are the most important details about the target word. A good super sentence nearly always has more than one clause. Here's an example: "The influenza pandemic that occurred from fall 1918 to early 1920 was unusually deadly, due to the severe symptoms that affected both the strong and the weak." Students can select different details from the same semantic web to write more than one super sentence, increasing variety in meaning and sentence structure. Here's another example, derived from the same web: "Because influenza is an airborne virus, people who displayed symptoms had to remain in quarantine."

Assessment

Giving vocabulary assessments to measure your students' knowledge of taught words is worthy of your instructional time. What we don't recommend, however, is devoting time to pretesting vocabulary words before teaching them. All students are likely to benefit from multiple exposures to important words in different contexts, even if they already have a working knowledge of their meanings. Remember that word knowledge exists on a continuum, culminating in rich, decontextualized knowledge. We consider the ability to use new academic words in new, sentence-level contexts to be a reasonable approach to vocabulary assessment in the upper elementary grades. Multiple-choice, fill-in-the-blank, or matching vocabulary tests are shallow measures of vocabulary *breadth;* in contrast, using a target word in a sentence that reflects semantically and grammatically correct understanding is a measure of vocabulary *depth* (Stahl & Bravo, 2010). Our advice for teaching and assessing vocabulary is simple. Teach two new words each day, and have students write a super sentence for each. On the last day of the week, instead of teaching new words, have students review their words and choose half to use in super sentences to demonstrate meaning. Figure 7.10 presents a rubric for scoring super sentences.

Instructional Planning

Incorporating these suggestions into Tier 1 instruction is a matter of choosing words from your interactive read-aloud and shared reading texts, selecting appropriate instructional strategies for each word, and providing opportunities for ongoing review and assessment of word meanings. You will be working within a whole-class schedule that includes components other than vocabulary, and we turn again to the planning templates we have introduced in Chapter 5. We have already suggested that part of Tier 1 word recognition instruction will require you to show how the words are built—identifying spelling patterns, syllable types, and any prefixes, roots, or suffixes. We have also recommended that you present derivatives.

	4: Exceeds Standard	3: Meets Standard	2: Progressing	1: Developing
Meaning	Sentence demonstrates clear understanding and is written in a creative way.	Sentence demonstrates clear understanding.	Sentence demonstrates partial understanding.	Sentence does not demonstrate understanding.
Structure	The resulting sentence is compound or complex.	At least 3 questions are answered.	At least 2 questions are answered.	Either 1 question or 0 questions are answered.
Word usage		Word is used correctly.		Word is not used correctly.

FIGURE 7.10. Super sentence rubric.

Our attention now is directed toward direct explanation of word meanings—for those same words. We are assuming that a fiction or nonfiction trade book will be the mainstay of instruction for the week. Each day, you will introduce a few words from the upcoming selection, providing student-friendly definitions and examples in multiple contexts. It is important to ensure that the definition you provide does not contain words that are unknown to your students. Begin by looking up the words and then, for words with multiple meanings, locate the definition the students will need when they encounter the word in the selection. Be prepared to revise the definitions to make them student-friendly. An example may help to underscore this point. A fifth-grade teacher who wished to teach the word *delinquent* used a definition she found in the dictionary: "showing or characterized by a tendency to commit crime, particularly minor crime." We suspect that few of her students found this definition very useful. A more useful definition might be "someone who disobeys the law and causes trouble."

Whether you are reading fiction or nonfiction will affect when and how you teach vocabulary. Remember that you will probably be choosing valuable, Tier 2 words for fiction and essential, Tier 3 words for nonfiction. In the case of a fiction selection, there may be no relationships among the word meanings. These words should be taught quickly during reading or after reading during your interactive read-aloud. There may also be opportunities later in the lesson to revisit the words briefly. In shared reading, teach them before reading as part of your word study. For nonfiction, the words will likely be linked conceptually in related clusters, inviting the teacher to help students think though the connections. They should be taught before reading and reviewed as you engage students in discussion about the important ideas in the text. Figure 7.11 displays the lesson template for interactive read-alouds of fiction and nonfiction texts. The lesson template for shared reading is displayed in Figure 7.12.

Note that we have provided a template to plan your interactive read-aloud in this chapter. We continue to argue for the place of read-alouds in the upper elementary curriculum, but to earn those precious instructional minutes, they must be planned. The purpose is to expose students to rich language, develop comprehension ability, expand

Time	Activity	Description
5 minutes	Review	
5 minutes	Teach Tier 3 vocabulary (nonfiction)	Introduce Tier 3 words, using COD or SFA charts.
20–25 minutes	Vocabulary and comprehension instruction	Pause to model comprehension strategies, ask inferential questions, and provide quick scaffolds of new words.
5 minutes	Teach Tier 2 vocabulary (fiction)	Provide direct explanation of meanings for two new words.
5–10 minutes	Discussion	

FIGURE 7.11. Template for planning fiction and nonfiction read-alouds with vocabulary instruction.

vocabulary, and build knowledge through an engaging read-aloud of challenging texts the students wouldn't be able to access independently. Your read-alouds can easily include both fiction and nonfiction texts. While both follow a before–during–after reading format, the key difference is in when to teach vocabulary. Again, Tier 3 words that are essential to comprehending nonfiction texts should be taught before reading, via strategies such as COD and SFA. Tier 2 words that are valuable but not essential to comprehending fiction should be explicitly taught after reading, so as not to distract students when you mention them during the read-aloud. The other important difference between fiction and nonfiction read-alouds is the focus on text structure. We discuss this further in Chapter 8, where our focus is on comprehension instruction.

During shared reading in *Bookworms K–5 Reading and Writing*, we have chosen to place vocabulary instruction before reading both fiction and nonfiction. We have done

Time	Activity	Description
5 minutes	Review	
5 minutes	Word study (fiction)	Introduce two new words, with attention to syllable types, meaning, and derivatives.
	Teach Tier 3 vocabulary (nonfiction)	Introduce Tier 3 words, using COD or SFA charts.
20–25 minutes	Fluency and comprehension instruction	1. Set a meaningful purpose. 2. Engage class in choral reading. 3. Briefly discuss first purpose. 4. Set a new purpose. 5. Engage class in partner rereading. 6. Briefly discuss second purpose.
5–10 minutes	Discussion	

FIGURE 7.12. Template for planning shared reading of fiction and nonfiction with vocabulary instruction.

this to make the procedures more consistent for both teachers and students. For shared reading of fiction, we include direct instruction of word meanings as part of word study. We can link spelling and meaning through direct explanation and morphological analysis. Attending to the relationships between root words, prefixes, and suffixes builds students' morphological awareness and ability to generalize to related words. Students will be exposed to the words again in multiple contexts: during reading and when they construct super sentences as part of their daily text-based writing. Figure 7.13 displays 1 week of vocabulary instruction during shared reading of *Charlie and the Chocolate Factory* by Roald Dahl (1964). You will notice that two Tier 2 words are taught during word study, and students use them in super sentences for each of the first 3 days of the week. On the fourth day, students review the six taught words and choose two to use in a single super sentence. We give a word study test (serving as both a spelling and a vocabulary assessment) on the fifth day, and ask students to select one word from the text they don't understand to use in a super sentence.

We have developed an eight-step process for planning shared reading and interactive read-alouds of fiction and nonfiction trade books. We have used this process extensively to plan lessons for upper elementary students in *Bookworms K–5 Reading and Writing*. Because of the focus on both vocabulary and comprehension, we introduce the first two steps here and the last six steps in Chapter 8.

1. *Size up the book.* The first step in planning Tier 1 instruction is to appraise the book carefully. Start by reading the book from beginning to end. Assess your own understanding of it, and think about your own comprehension. It is vital that you resolve any difficulties you may have encountered, so that you have a thorough understanding of the content. What portions of the book are difficult to understand and why? If you have difficulties, you can bet that your students will require support if they are to learn from the book. It may be that the book is simply too difficult for them, even with support. This is a judgment that you need to make early so as not to waste time. You are in the best position to judge whether there is an appropriate match between the book and your students. Once you judge the book to be an appropriate choice, read it again, this time attempting to empathize with your students. For fiction books, what words does the author use that are likely to be unfamiliar to your students, and which are worth teaching? For nonfiction

	Day 1	**Day 2**	**Day 3**	**Day 4**	**Day 5**
Teach meaning vocabulary	*Absurd* and *satisfy*	*Stammer* and *astonish*	*Nourishment* and *marvelous*	Review vocabulary words	Word study test
Assign written response	Use *absurd* and *satisfy* in super sentences.	Use *stammer* and *astonish* in super sentences.	Use *nourishment* and *marvelous* in super sentences.	Choose two words to use in one super sentence.	Choose one unfamiliar word to use in a super sentence.

FIGURE 7.13. Example of weekly vocabulary instruction for shared reading of fiction text.

books, what new technical vocabulary is introduced, and how is it linked to your curricular objectives in science or social studies? What text structure(s) has the author used to organize the book? These are critical questions, and we address them both here and in Chapter 8.

2. *Decide how to teach the key vocabulary.* While the words you choose from your fiction selection may be unconnected, most nonfiction trade books focus on a set of technical vocabulary words. Surprisingly, these words are easier to teach than an equal set of unrelated, general vocabulary terms, because you can take advantage of the relationships among the words. As you will recall, research has demonstrated that direct instruction of vocabulary improves comprehension, even for books in which the word meanings are clearly presented. There are good reasons why this is the case. First, learning new content from nonfiction text, even when it is read aloud, requires the use of sophisticated strategies. Fourth and fifth graders may have problems applying multiple strategies in concert independently, especially in a book written at a challenging level. Second, we have stressed that multiple exposures to new words are required for adequate understanding of their meanings, and a single read-aloud is hardly enough. Third, by teaching key words before reading, you can informally assess how much the students know and then modify your instruction to make meanings clear and to fill in gaps in prior knowledge. Fourth, you can employ visual images that will help the students understand how the terms are related. Fifth, you can tie the new terms to the science or social studies curriculum and to previous lessons in these subjects. You can use the graphics for this purpose—for example, by constructing an SFA chart that contains both familiar and new vocabulary. Finally, the materials you create, such as diagrams on chart paper, can be displayed for later review. Try to include ways for the students to contribute to creating diagrams or charts. Doing so will make the process interactive, and by drawing on their prior knowledge, you will be able to tell how detailed your explanation needs to be. Decide on materials (e.g., whiteboard, chart paper on easel), and plan to leave the graphics on display.

Remember that there is not a single formula to follow in teaching vocabulary. You must think carefully about the content of the selection and look for clear ties to previous instruction. A number of well-researched instructional strategies are available, and your only difficulty may lie in choosing among them. This is a good problem to have! They are incredibly versatile. You will find them useful not only in Tier 1 instruction but also in Tier 2 instruction, Tier 3 intensive interventions, and science and social studies instruction. In the next section, we describe how you might deliver more intensive vocabulary instruction in small groups.

TIER 2 INSTRUCTION IN VOCABULARY

Tier 2 instruction in vocabulary is appropriate for upper elementary students with acceptable fluency. It is difficult to screen in the area of vocabulary, and impossible to diagnose. Luckily, neither of these assessments is necessary. Remember that Tier 2 instruction occurs for brief intervals and is highly targeted at skills that impair comprehension. Although all students can build their vocabulary, we believe that this time is better spent shoring up fluency problems, addressing any underlying difficulties with multisyllabic decoding if students need it, and answering questions about specific vocabulary items that arise during reading or discussion. However, if fluency is not problematic, then small-group work in vocabulary and comprehension is the next step. Remember that students will continue to work on fluency during the shared reading component of Tier 1 instruction. It would be a shame to miss out on the opportunity to develop vocabulary and content knowledge in Tier 2. The success of your differentiated instruction will ultimately rest on the number of students you can move from multisyllabic decoding and fluency, to fluency and comprehension, and then to vocabulary and comprehension.

Content

Students who meet the fourth- or fifth-grade fluency benchmark still benefit from small-group instruction that extends their vocabulary. We recommend approaching such instruction in the context of reading increasingly complex texts rather than teaching word lists. In this way, vocabulary and comprehension can be developed together, and students can see how new words are used in context. In order to make useful selections of trade books, we refer you to our discussion in Chapter 6. The book selections will dictate which words you should teach. For fiction, these will be a small number of general vocabulary words, perhaps two per day. For nonfiction, the words will be technical terms associated with the content subject, and mindful selection of texts will allow you to link Tier 2 instruction to content area topics.

How and when you teach vocabulary will be the same as in interactive read-alouds. For fiction books, we advise against teaching vocabulary before reading. If students are unfamiliar with a few words, they can still usually manage to grasp the events of a narrative. In addition, highlighting the words in advance of reading is likely to cause them to look for these words when they begin to read, possibly impairing their comprehension. We advocate studying the words after the students read, returning to the text for examples of how each is used. For nonfiction books, the words we select are central to comprehension, so we teach them in advance. Because they are naturally clustered together, it is actually easier to teach them. We do not have to worry that their meanings are unconnected, because they are always closely related. The most effective instructional strategies take advantage of these connections.

Instructional Strategies

Instead of recommending a different approach for Tier 2 vocabulary instruction, we recommend using the same instructional strategies as in Tier 1, with greater intensity. Vocabulary work is intensified in Tier 2 by increasing the frequency of instructional sessions devoted to learning new words and reducing the group size. As in group work with fluency and comprehension, group work with vocabulary can be staggered to maximize the number of pages students will be able to read. Figure 7.14 displays a small-group planning template for vocabulary and comprehension practice.

You will notice its similarity to the planning template for fluency and comprehension practice. The time management is similar so that you can see all of your groups each day. "Teacher time" is spent in either teaching meaning vocabulary or discussion, and then teaching meaning vocabulary before assigning a new text segment. Since reading is done independently, with or without a reading guide (which we cover in Chapter 8), it can be untimed. This allows students to read at different rates. It also allows teachers to continue to build fourth- and fifth-grade students' confidence and competence for engaging in independent reading with less direct monitoring. As in fluency and comprehension practice, we continue to monitor comprehension by engaging students in a rich, text-based discussion about the meaning and structure of the previous day's text segment (which we cover in Chapter 8) before assigning a new one.

Again, you will have to choose the length of time for discussion. If you reserve 15 minutes to work with your group, you will have at least two options. The first option is to teach meaning vocabulary, have students read silently for 7 minutes, and lead a very brief discussion each day. Then students will be able to engage in self-selected independent reading when you are not working with them. We prefer the second option: If you take the full 15 minutes to teach meaning vocabulary and engage in discussion before assigning a new text segment for students to read the next day, you will be able to have a much richer discussion. This additional time for discussion may be necessary for upper elementary texts with complex structures and content. Students will also be able to return to their

Days	Format	Activity	Teacher's role	Students' role
Day 1	With teacher	Teach meaning vocabulary (nonfiction); assign text segment.	Teacher introduces two new words, using SFA or COD charts.	Students follow the teacher's lead.
Day 1	Outside of the group	Silent reading of assigned text segment.	Teacher can serve another group or circulate to provide support.	Students read the text independently.
Day 2	With teacher	Teach meaning vocabulary for previous segment (fiction) or new text segment (nonfiction); assign new text segment.	Teacher introduces two new words, using direct explanation, SFA charts, or COD charts.	Students follow the teacher's lead.
Day 2	Outside of the group	Self-selected, independent reading.	Teacher can serve another group or circulate to provide support.	Students read the text independently.

FIGURE 7.14. Template for vocabulary and comprehension practice with vocabulary instruction.

seats to read at different rates. As in fluency and comprehension practice, though, choosing this structure may limit the amount of time for wide reading. In the *Bookworms K–5 Reading and Writing* program, students in a vocabulary group, especially those who read at slower rates, may not have time for self-selected independent reading after reading the assigned text segment on their own. Their small-group vocabulary lesson will be followed by their silent reading and then their written response to shared reading. On the days when they are discussing that text segment, they will have time for independent reading.

Remember that you will be applying these strategies in small groups with readers who are fluent. Your task is to introduce them quickly to key words and their relationships to each other. Your goals are twofold: (1) to help them acquire the word meanings, and (2) to facilitate their comprehension of the selection. Routines for building comprehension in Tier 2 are discussed in Chapter 8. Unless you are required to collect data for RTI purposes, we do not recommend pretesting the students. First, it is a time-consuming process. Second, multiple exposures are required to learn the meaning of any word. This means that whether one student may have encountered the word several times already and another has no familiarity with it, both will benefit from instruction.

Instructional Planning

Vocabulary differs from word recognition, in that there is not a clear sequence of instruction. The word meanings you teach will be driven by the books you select. Instructional planning entails choosing the best method (1) for introducing the words and making time for instruction before the students read, and (2) for reviewing the words afterward. Planning will differ for fiction and nonfiction books for two reasons. First, we introduce the words before reading in the case of nonfiction books and afterward in the case of fiction. Second, there are more instructional approaches available to us for information books, and we will need to choose among them.

Let's examine planning for a fiction book first. Consider the example of a short trade book that the students can read in 5 days during Tier 2 time. At the beginning of each small-group session, you might identify two words from the previous day's text segment, providing a student-friendly definition of each and returning to the point at which it was used in the text. Each day, you might review the two words from the day before, as well as introduce two new words. On the fifth day, you might review all the words taught that week instead of introducing new words. Figure 7.15 illustrates how this process would work across the week.

This simple, repetitive structure has several advantages. It can be used with any fiction trade book—including one that will not be finished in 1 week. It ensures a useful routine that will allow students to develop expectations about the lesson. It also builds in cumulative review. Notice that the review each day includes words from several text segments. Their inclusion requires hardly any additional time, because with each successive lesson, the earlier words go faster and faster. Students receive distributed practice (brief, periodic review), which is likely to result in superior retention of word meanings. For vocabulary learning, distributed practice requires that you also remember the words you have taught and take advantage of every opportunity to review their meanings and use

Day 1	Day 2	Day 3	Day 4	Day 5
Assign Day 1 text segment.	Teach two words from Day 1 segment.	Review Day 1 words and teach two words from Day 2 segment.	Review Day 1 and Day 2 words and teach two words from Day 3 segment.	Review words from Day 1, Day 2, and Day 3 segments.

FIGURE 7.15. Teaching general vocabulary during Tier 2 time.

them in new contexts. It may be helpful to display vocabulary on a word wall, so that any time the word is encountered, you can remember to review the definition and provide a new, off-the-cuff sentence context.

Now let's consider how to plan the vocabulary portion of a nonfiction book lesson. As with fiction, you usually must plan over a number of days to cover an entire trade book. You may also need to vary how you introduce each day's new words, depending on how they are related. The big difference, though, is that the words are taught prior to reading. Because their meanings are closely connected, we suggest updating an anchor chart each day to keep track of how Tier 3 words are related. Ask questions to review the anchor chart and word meanings before students read the next segment. Figure 7.16 shows how a week's small-group lessons would be structured.

CHOOSING TIER 3 PROGRAMS FOR VOCABULARY

As we have done for word recognition and fluency, we stop short of recommending commercial Tier 3 programs for vocabulary, because we lack sufficient empirical evidence to recommend one over another. In addition, as researchers turn their attention to the needs of young adolescent students and include those learning English within an RTI framework, improvements in the efficacy of interventions are likely to be made. When we look for evidence about the effectiveness of interventions, we turn to four Internet sources: (1) the Institute of Education Sciences' What Works Clearinghouse (*https://ies.ed.gov/ncee/wwc*), (2) the Center on Instruction (*www.centeroninstruction.org*), (3) the Best Evidence Encyclopedia (*www.bestevidence.org*), and (4) the Center on Response to Intervention (*www.rti4success.org*). When you search for evidence on the efficacy of

Day 1	Day 2	Day 3	Day 4	Day 5
Teach Tier 3 words from Day 1 text segment, using anchor chart.	Review anchor chart and add words from Day 2 text segment.	Review anchor chart and add words from Day 3 text segment.	Review anchor chart and add words from Day 4 text segment.	Review anchor chart and add words from Day 5 text segment.

FIGURE 7.16. Teaching technical vocabulary during Tier 2 time.

intensive interventions for vocabulary for upper elementary students, consider searching at a range of grade levels in order to make your search as broad as possible.

English Learners

As a final note, it is important to consider the vocabulary needs of English learners. Fortunately, they are likely to be served by the same approaches we recommend for Tier 1 and Tier 2, with greater intensity. A meta-analysis of reading instruction for English learners in upper elementary and middle grades recommends intensive vocabulary instruction focused on both academic vocabulary and comprehension (Hall et al., 2017). Not unlike instruction for native English speakers, effective vocabulary instruction for English learners includes (1) multiple exposures; (2) opportunities to demonstrate knowledge of word meanings in new contexts; (3) using words in discussion and writing; (4) using examples, nonexamples, synonyms, and antonyms; and (5) using visual images and student-friendly connections to words. In addition, English learners benefit from two types of first-language supports during instruction: drawing on knowledge of *cognates* (words that are morphologically similar in two languages) and providing translations of English words and texts in students' first language. We hope you feel that the strategies in this chapter will help you build a language-rich environment to spur the vocabulary development of students with weak vocabulary knowledge, including English learners.

CHAPTER 8

....

Building Comprehension

In this chapter, we offer background and approaches to improving the comprehension proficiency of fourth and fifth graders. We acknowledge from the start that our work in word recognition, fluency, and vocabulary means nothing if it doesn't contribute to comprehension. We once again follow our tiered approach, beginning with grade-level core instruction and moving to more intensive instruction in small groups. We start with background information on the complex development of comprehension. We argue that although research can guide our efforts to develop student comprehension in both Tier 1 and Tier 2 settings, we will never fully accomplish our task; rather, comprehension development is a lifelong pursuit, building on a constantly expanding set of background knowledge, vocabulary knowledge, and strategic processes.

FOUNDATIONAL KNOWLEDGE
ABOUT COMPREHENSION DEVELOPMENT

What happens when we comprehend? For proficient adult readers, the process of comprehending has become second nature. Indeed, it is so accomplished, so apparently effortless, that it is difficult to appreciate how it happens, and it is harder still to empathize with the problems encountered by readers who struggle. Researchers have studied the comprehension process for decades, and many questions about it remain, but we know enough to assist students in their efforts to become better comprehenders.

In order to gain awareness of how comprehension occurs, a simple, introspective example may be helpful. As you read the following sentence, think about how you make it meaningful:

The wolf is a carnivorous mammal that inhabits much of Europe, North America, and Asia.

114

We suspect that you have little difficulty in understanding this sentence. There are no unfamiliar words, and the background knowledge you need is available to you in memory. As you read, the words trigger connections in long-term memory. We might compare these connections with electrical switches that are turned to the "on" position as you read. In fact, this is not a mere metaphor. It is exactly what happens in the brain during reading. When you reach the word *wolf,* your "wolf" switch is activated, and all of the connections stored in your memory either enter your conscious thoughts or are available in the wings as needed. This bundle of connections, called a *schema,* includes the pronunciation of *wolf;* visual images of wolves; definitional knowledge; and anecdotal memories such as television shows, books you may have read, visits to museums, and so on. In short, the concept of *wolf* is associated in your memory with an impressive array of connected information. As you read to the end of the sentence, you probably encounter information that is consistent with your prior understanding about wolves.

In an example like this one, where the information you read is well aligned with prior knowledge, the content is easily assimilated. The fact that it is easy, however, does not mean that it is simple! As you read, additional schemas are activated. You have well-developed schemas for *North America,* for *carnivorous,* and so on, and each of these concepts has its own complex network of associations in your memory. This means that many more switches are turned on as you read.

But it isn't enough for you to turn on all of the switches. Something more is needed. Because your mind is preprogrammed to process language, you are able to perform a remarkable feat: You are able to link the concepts according to the blueprint provided by the sentence. This blueprint is governed by a set of grammatical rules that we begin to learn as infants. These rules guide us in connecting the concepts represented by words in ways that make sense. We use the same set of rules when we construct sentences as we speak or write, and we can be confident that other English speakers will use those rules to interpret what we express accurately.

In our example of the wolf, the meaning you are able to construct by using the rules of grammar to link concepts is not only consistent with your prior knowledge; it is probably contained within it. That is, the sentence tells you nothing that you don't already know. You may find the experience reinforcing but not particularly enlightening. But let's continue:

> The wolf is a carnivorous mammal that inhabits much of Europe, North America, and Asia. **Wolves live in groups called packs. By working together, a wolf pack can bring down a large animal, such as an elk or a moose. When game is scarce, however, a wolf may be lucky to find a small field mouse.**

The information contained in this continuation is also easy to assimilate. It is consistent with what you already know about wolves. This time, however, you may encounter a fact that you did not know before—for example, that a wolf may prey upon an animal as small as a mouse. Although mildly surprising, this new information does not contradict your prior knowledge of wolves and can be rather easily added to your wolf schema. This process of assimilating new information into prior knowledge is central to learning, but there are occasional bumps in the road. One such bump involves confronting information that is clearly at odds with prior knowledge. Again, let's continue our example:

> The wolf is a carnivorous mammal that inhabits much of Europe, North America, and Asia. Wolves live in groups called packs. By working together, a wolf pack can bring down a large animal, such as an elk or a moose. When game is scarce, however, a wolf may be lucky to find a small field mouse. **Wolves are dogs. Although they are wild and difficult to domesticate, they are still dogs. They are just as intelligent as other dogs, and they are not very dangerous to humans, despite the popular myth to the contrary. The fact is, there have only been six fatal wolf attacks on humans in North America in the 21st century. Two were actual predatory attacks; two were attacks in failed attempts to domesticate wolves; two were fatalities from rabies after wolf bites.**

We suspect that this continuation of the passage presents information contradicting what you may have previously believed about wolves. Most people are unaware that a wolf is a dog, and most believe that wolves are dangerous. When confronted by information that contradicts prior knowledge, readers cannot simply assimilate it. If readers choose to accept the new information, their schema for *wolf* must be substantially altered. Piaget referred to this process as *accommodation*. It represents another kind of learning. Whether the new information is assimilated or accommodated, learning has occurred and knowledge is acquired.

Walter Kintsch (1994) has offered a good description of the comprehension process. As you make your way through the passage, from clause to clause and sentence to sentence, you are building an internal representation of the passage's meaning. As you continue reading, you also expand and refine this structure. If someone asks you a question after your reading, you will refer to this internal structure to answer it. We can compare that structure to a house: You build it from the ground up, on a foundation of prior knowledge, and it has an overall design or blueprint plus numerous details (such as the individual boards, bricks, and shutters). Just after you finish reading the passage, chances are that you can clearly recall many of the details, in the same way you may envision details of the house or building in which you now live. However, after a time your memory for details of the passage will fade, although you may still be able to remember its gist. Think back to a house you lived in long ago. It is likely that a similar process has occurred with respect to your memory. You still retain a general idea of what the house looked like, but many of the details elude you. The same is true of the "reading house" you construct as you read. Over time, its details become fuzzy, but a general impression may remain in your memory.

We have been discussing processes that are typical of proficient readers like yourself. Now let's consider these processes from the perspective of someone with reading difficulties. When you read the first sentence of the passage, a number of schemas are activated, and you can link them appropriately on the basis of sentence structure. However, what if a few of the key schemas were poorly developed or nonexistent? For example, what if you were unfamiliar with the word *carnivorous?* What if you had only a very vague idea about the location of Europe and Asia? Your comprehension would be seriously jeopardized. Students with limited vocabulary and little prior knowledge often find themselves in this situation. Because they lack the conceptual knowledge that authors assume their readers possess, they are unable to link concepts appropriately. To put this another way, they are unable to build a solid mental structure of the content because they lack many of the building blocks that the author requires. They end up living in a reading shack!

Many of the building blocks to which we are referring here are bits of knowledge. It is important to make a distinction between vocabulary and background knowledge. Knowledge of word meanings, or vocabulary, is essential to comprehension, but it is only one component of the knowledge necessary to comprehend. Such knowledge may also include experiences and individual impressions that cannot be captured by a single word, and that amplify and enrich one's definitional knowledge.

The effects of limited vocabulary and background knowledge depend on the size of the gap between what a student does know and what is necessary to know in order to comprehend. If the gap is too large, it may not be possible for a teacher to facilitate adequate comprehension. Imagine having to read a technical research report in the field of medicine. Limitations of your prior knowledge base may well be impossible to overcome. Even with the assistance of a tutor who is knowledgeable about the topic, the amount of background building required may be prohibitive. In the case of a student, reading materials containing a large number of unfamiliar words—and referring to ideas and experiences that are also unfamiliar—are likely to be frustrating, no matter what the teacher does. In such cases, it is better to locate alternative materials. However, in cases where that gap is not impossibly wide, a teacher may be able to bridge it by preteaching the vocabulary and by building the prior knowledge needed to comprehend. Figure 8.1 demonstrates the relationship between prior knowledge and comprehension. As gaps in a student's prior knowledge are reduced, comprehension improves. We have introduced strategies for reducing that gap through vocabulary instruction in Chapter 7.

Of course, familiarity with the topic and with the words an author has chosen is not all that a reader requires to comprehend. In order to build a mental representation of text content, the reader needs to be able to approach the reading task strategically. Just as a carpenter must be able to use strategically a variety of tools in building a house, a reader

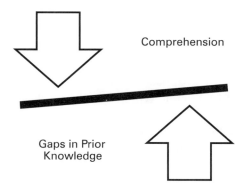

FIGURE 8.1. The relationship between prior knowledge and comprehension.

must employ a variety of strategies if a sound reading house is to be constructed. Even with assistance, the final product may be problematic. The reading house may need work. Like a master carpenter overseeing the work of a novice, a teacher can help a student improve the mental representation of text content even after reading has been completed. All of this is to say that teachers have three opportunities to improve text comprehension. The actions they take before, during, and after reading can do much to ensure adequate understanding of a particular text and to demonstrate the procedures skilled readers use to create strong mental representations. The understanding constructed and the procedures demonstrated also may assist in the next comprehension opportunity.

This discussion may seem very theoretical, but the implications for the classroom are enormous. In a short story, for example, if the protagonist enters a fast-food restaurant, the author will not bore you with details about how the character orders, what the restaurant looks like, how expensive it is, or how healthy the food is. The author will expect your schema for fast food to be activated instantly. However, imagine a reader who hasn't had this experience; this reader's comprehension of the text may be compromised. Anderson and Pearson (1984) used schema theory to explain the strong relationship between prior knowledge of ideas and concepts contained in a text to an individual's ability to comprehend that text. They took the restaurant example a bit further. Let's assume that the protagonist has been eating in an upscale restaurant. When does the character pay for the food? A reader who has had some experiences with restaurants of this kind knows that the check is paid after the meal, but readers who haven't been to this type of restaurant may not. The only restaurants they may know are fast-food establishments, where food is paid for before it is received. Their limited experience constrains their schema for the concept of a restaurant, and their comprehension is also constrained. Schemas, then, can be developed through experience in the world and through experience with text, as long as that text is understood fully.

Schema theory can also be applied to entire texts. For example, skilled readers have many schemas related to the organizational structures used in informational texts (Meyer, 1987). They have developed one schema for problem/solution, another for comparison, another for causation, yet another for description, and so on. When they begin reading a text employing one of these structures, they activate the appropriate schema. This schema involves knowledge about how main ideas in the text are typically structured. This knowledge helps the reader select and organize ideas in memory, which in turn aids comprehension. As an example, read the following comparison of humans and amoebas from *Animal Cells and Life Processes* by Barbara A. Somervill (2011):

> The simplest explanation for what makes humans different from amoebas is our cells. Human bodies contain 210 different types of cells. Amoebas have only one cell. Our bodies use different cells to form blood, bones, organs, muscles, and so on. The cells that make up a heart are different from cells in the brain or lungs. For amoebas, there is only one cell to carry out all the functions of blood, bones, organs, and muscles. (p. 28)

We suspect that your schema for comparison is well developed. Because we have just told you that what you are about to read is a comparison text, you are able to activate knowledge about how it will be structured. This knowledge includes the expectation that the text will present ideas about humans and amoebas that are similar or different in one or more aspects. In this case, the aspects being compared are the number and functions of cells that make up humans and amoebas. Think about how your attention would be different if we told you we were presenting a story about a human and an amoeba: You would expect characters, a setting, and a narrative structure. This example illustrates how important it is for readers to begin with a clear set of expectations about how texts are organized. This insight has led to effective instructional techniques for providing students with knowledge of text structures. It is an example of how theory can inform and improve practice.

To sum up, comprehension involves using prior knowledge to make sense of text. This knowledge includes word meanings, conceptual background, and an understanding of how sentences are structured and how texts are organized. This process involves extracting information from the text, interpreting it within a framework of prior knowledge, and constructing a mental representation of the text's meaning. These actions occur simultaneously, and the reader coordinates them purposefully. The RAND Reading Study Group (2002) has defined comprehension elegantly as "the process of simultaneously extracting and constructing meaning through interaction and involvement with written language" (p. xiii).

The RAND Group's definition creates both problems and opportunities as we attempt to sort through the issues related to comprehension instruction. On the one hand, the group's notion of comprehension as construction opens the door to multiple interpretations of what we read—the kind appropriate to the reading of literature such as stories, drama, and poetry. It also suggests, however, that no text has a single meaning, the one based only on an author's intention. Rather, meaning is always influenced by the particular construction process that a reader engages. This implication suggests that extensive latitude should be given to students, and that assessing their comprehension exclusively in terms of how closely they come to realizing the author's intended meaning is inappropriate. Most of the teachers, administrators, and policymakers whom we have met, however, prefer to think of comprehension as more a matter of extraction than construction.

An easy way to view the process of extracting and constructing meaning is to think of comprehension as occurring at successive levels. Although several approaches have been suggested, we believe that the most straightforward involves three levels, illustrated in Figure 8.2.

At the literal level, the reader extracts ideas that have been explicitly stated. In our wolf passage, the fact that wolves are dogs is expressed clearly. It is not a point requiring speculation and conjecture. Questions posed at the literal level are easy to ask and answer, but they privilege superficial comprehension rather than real understanding. This is a trap for the unwary teacher. To see just how misleading literal-level questions can be, consider again the following sentences from *Animal Cells and Life Processes* (Somervill, 2011):

Human bodies contain 210 different types of cells. Amoebas have only one cell. (p. 28)

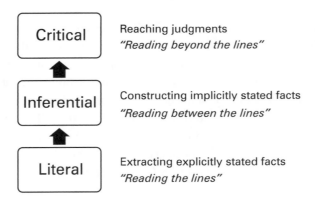

FIGURE 8.2. Levels of comprehension.

Most students are perfectly capable of answering questions like these without really thinking:

"How many different types of cells do human bodies contain?"
"How many cells do amoebas have?"

But these correct answers may not actually signal understanding of the basic premise that the variety of animal cells allows for high levels of complexity in the biology of animals. This is also not to say that literal-level questions are not useful. They can be springboards to inferences and critical judgments. It is only when they become ends in themselves that problems arise, for it is easy to be fooled into believing that the ability to answer questions like these means that comprehension has taken place.

At the inferential level of comprehension, the reader is still concerned with factual information. However, because this information is not explicitly stated, but merely implied, the reader must construct it by combining logically the facts of a given text with each other and/or with facts that are stored in prior knowledge. You may tentatively conclude, for example, that because North America, Europe, and Asia are mentioned as wolf habitats, no wolves are to be found in Africa. Africa is not mentioned in the passage, but you can construct this inference on the basis of passage content *and* prior knowledge.

In contrast, the critical level requires adequate comprehension at the levels below, so that defensible judgments can be reached. Appraising the quality of an informational article is one example of a critical judgment. It is not possible to undertake this task without first extracting factual aspects of the article and constructing a mental representation of it. In the wolf example, imagine that you have been charged with drafting a policy statement concerning "wolf awareness"—that is, making the general public aware that wolves are not very dangerous. Successfully meeting this charge will require (at a minimum) an adequate grasp of the facts expressed in the passage. Of course, critical judgments will vary considerably from reader to reader, based on taste, philosophy, cultural background, and related factors. For this reason, it is inappropriate to expect all students to arrive at the same critical judgment. What is important is that they can explain *how* they arrive at their judgments. No one disputes that reaching critical judgments is a constructive process. By its nature, it is divergent rather than convergent, which is why most assessments of reading comprehension tend to ignore the critical level and focus instead on the literal and inferential levels.

By the time children reach the upper elementary grades, many have begun to experience comprehension difficulties. We have discussed some of the key factors that may be to blame: limited prior knowledge and vocabulary, unfamiliar text structures, weak decoding and fluency, and ineffective use of comprehension strategies. There are other factors as well, however, including motivation, intelligence, and the ability to attend. The RAND Reading Study Group depicts these as *internal* factors (see Figure 8.3). That is, they are problems that reside within students, and, clearly, some are more susceptible than others to the efforts of teachers.

The RAND group also reminds us of the influence of context on comprehension. They define reading comprehension as a cognitive process (the bull's eye in Figure 8.4) that is influenced by the union of the characteristics of the text chosen; the reader's characteristics in relation to that text; and the activities that the reader will engage in before, during, and after reading. In school, all of these things happen in the classroom, which is a particular sociocultural context.

As an example, let's consider Peter, a fifth grader whose internal characteristics are reasonably good. That is, Peter's fluency is at benchmark, he has an average vocabulary for his age, and he is motivated to read. It is tempting to think that whenever Peter is asked to read a fifth-grade selection, his comprehension will be adequate. According to the RAND Group's model, however, this expectation may be wrong. A particular text may present unfamiliar concepts or have a confusing structure, despite its overall level of difficulty. The teacher may require an unusual task in response to the reading, such

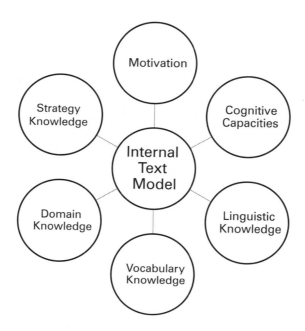

FIGURE 8.3. The RAND model of internal factors affecting comprehension.

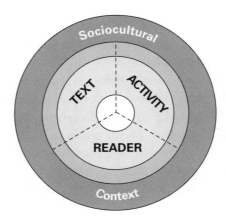

FIGURE 8.4. The RAND model of comprehension.

as solving a difficult problem or writing an essay. Or Peter may be required to work with students with whom he does not get along very well. Any of these factors can impair his comprehension. Given this litany of woes, it may sound as though comprehension is a fragile flower indeed, easily plagued by a host of problems. The good news is that most of these factors can be accounted for by skillful instruction. In teaching, the key is to become aware of which factors can be addressed through instructional planning. As a teacher, you are in a position to make decisions that can take advantage of these factors in ways that help students like Peter in their quest to comprehend.

One factor over which teachers can exercise some control involves the strategies their students use to extract and construct meaning as they read. By fostering the use of a few key strategies, and by returning to these strategies repeatedly in a variety of contexts, teachers in the upper elementary grades can provide their students with the tools they need to succeed. Although writers on this subject have produced slightly different lists of strategies, there is general agreement that students must be able to visualize events and settings, to arrive at logical inferences, to make and check reasonable predictions, to retell the important events of a narrative, to distill main ideas, to summarize content, and to synthesize across sources. Strategies such as these have replaced comprehension "skills" (e.g., noting a literal sequence of events or inferring causal relationships) in most curriculum materials. Skills may be important, but that is because they eventually achieve almost automatic status, while strategies must be consciously applied. Distinguishing skills from strategies is important, and Tim Shanahan (2018) offers the following distinction on his blog:

> Basically, the term comprehension skills tends to refer to the abilities required to answer particular kinds of comprehension questions. Skills would include things like identifying the main idea, recognizing supporting details, drawing conclusions, inferencing, comparing and contrasting, evaluating critically, knowing vocabulary meaning, and sequencing events. . . . The basic premise of strategies is that readers need to actively think about the ideas in text if they are going to understand. And, since determining how to think about a text involves choices, strategies are tied up in meta-cognition

(that is, thinking about thinking). Comprehension strategies are not about coming up with answers to particular kinds of questions, but they describe actions that may help a reader to figure out and remember the information from a text. . . . These kinds of actions—these strategies—are used intentionally by readers to increase the chances of understanding or remembering what one has read. Comprehension strategies need to be practiced too; however, they aren't learned by repetition and reinforcement, but by gradual release of responsibility (including modeling, explanation, guided practice).

As Shanahan's description suggests, strategies need to be applied intentionally, with a focus on understanding texts that require effort to comprehend. Good teachers scaffold strategies, too. They model them and then support students in their attempts to apply them. But the goal is for students to apply them on their own. Strategy use does not always come naturally, but it can be taught. Regardless of the strategies a teacher decides to target, strategy instruction is nearly always accomplished in the same way. Teachers employ a gradual-release-of-responsibility approach (Duke & Pearson, 2002; Pearson & Gallagher, 1983). That is, at the start, the teachers maintain most of the responsibility and control. They define and model the strategy for students, showing the strategy in action. Next, teachers move to a series of guided practice opportunities during which they share responsibility for employing the strategy. They provide students with relatively simple contexts to use the strategy, and they provide feedback quickly. They ratchet up the difficulty level of the context over time, still providing feedback (and noticing levels of student comfort and success). Finally, they release responsibility totally to the students, providing authentic opportunities to employ the strategy.

Research confirms that an instructional focus on comprehension strategy instruction is worth the effort! By the time students reach fourth and fifth grades, they have already received instruction in the key strategies. Teachers at these grades should make it their goal to revisit them many times in the new and challenging texts their students face. Essentially, then, the gradual release model is occurring over the elementary years. Teachers in grades 4 and 5 are providing very brief modeling and extensive guided and independent practice of a host of strategies. Doing so will not only assist students with reading difficulties, but will enable readers like Peter to continue to grow as comprehenders.

Like vocabulary, comprehension is an open-ended proficiency. As Peter and his classmates progress through grades 4 and 5, they are expected to continue improving their comprehension ability. One way of estimating this positive trajectory is in grade-level terms. Because comprehension is the end product of so many components, the framers of the CCSS do not attempt to delineate it. Instead, they use a grade-level index to gauge proficiency. We present these "bottom-line" standards in Figure 8.5. Note that the key difference between grades 4 and 5 is in the level of text complexity students are required to comprehend.

There are many valuable resources for building your knowledge of comprehension instruction. Whether you engage in individual professional reading or in book studies with your colleagues, we believe you will find the resources listed in Figure 8.6 helpful. In the sections that follow, we show you how we have used comprehension research to influence our planning.

General Goal	Evidence
Grade 4	
The students demonstrate proficiency at reading texts at appropriate levels of complexity.	Students focus on reading literature and informational texts independently and proficiently at the fourth- through fifth- grade level of text complexity, with scaffolding likely to be required for texts at the high end of this range.
Grade 5	
The students demonstrate proficiency at reading texts at appropriate levels of complexity.	Students focus on reading literature and informational texts independently and proficiently at the fourth- through fifth- grade level of text complexity.

FIGURE 8.5. Comprehension standards from the CCSS. From NGACBP and CCSSO (2010). In the public domain.

Duffy, G. G. (2014). *Explaining reading: A resource for explicit teaching of the Common Core Standards* (3rd ed.). New York: Guilford Press.
Israel, S. E. (Ed.). (2017). *Handbook of research on reading comprehension* (2nd ed.). New York: Guilford Press.
Klingner, J. K., Vaughn, S., & Boardman, A. (2015). *Teaching reading comprehension to students with learning difficulties* (2nd ed.). New York: Guilford Press.
McNamara, D. S. (Ed.). (2007). *Reading comprehension strategies: Theories, interventions, and technologies*. New York: Erlbaum.
Pressley, M., & Allington, R. L. (2015). *Reading instruction that works: The case for balanced teaching* (4th ed.). New York: Guilford Press.
Swan, E. A. (2002). *Concept-oriented reading instruction: Engaging classrooms, lifelong learners*. New York: Guilford Press.
Sweet, A. P., & Snow, C. E. (Eds.). (2003). *Rethinking reading comprehension*. New York: Guilford Press.
Willingham, D. T. (2006–2007). The usefulness of brief instruction in reading comprehension strategies. *American Educator, 30*(4), 39–50.

FIGURE 8.6. Resources for comprehension instruction.

TIER 1 INSTRUCTION IN COMPREHENSION

The approach to Tier 1 instruction described in this book, *Bookworms K–5 Reading and Writing*, is different from core programs in two important ways. First, it uses only intact, authentic books instead of an anthology of reading selections. Second, all of the texts are consistent with the CCSS grade-level bands for text difficulty (see Figure 8.7); there are no easy texts. The selections in grades 4 and 5 are approximately half narrative and half informational texts. The books used for read-alouds are well above grade level, allowing teachers to model comprehension strategies and increase students' background knowledge. The books represent a deliberate range of genres and text structures, in order to prepare students for the increasingly challenging world of text that awaits them in middle school. The same evidence-based instructional routines are used each day, ensuring that even students who struggle if asked to read grade-level material independently will eventually comprehend and contribute constructively to discussions and writing activities.

Content

As in our chapters on fluency and vocabulary, books are the first content consideration for designing comprehension instruction. The books used in *Bookworms K–5 Reading and Writing*, our continuing example of curriculum design, were selected for their quality, content, and likelihood of building world knowledge and motivation. But the texts themselves are not the essential ingredient in Tier 1 instruction. They are merely vehicles used to foster continuing comprehension growth. The real content of Tier 1 instruction in comprehension lies in the instructional routines that teachers provide as students engage in the reading of each text.

As in previous chapters, we encourage you once again to refer to the *Rubric for Evaluating Reading/Language Arts Instructional Materials for Kindergarten to Grade 5* (Foorman et al., 2017). The rubric for grades 3–5 values purposeful reading and rereading of complex grade-level texts, with an emphasis on developing knowledge and a love of reading. A curriculum consistent with these recommendations should include narrative and informational texts that allow for teaching students how to identify and use a variety of text structures (e.g., sequence, compare/contrast, cause/effect, and problem/solution) and text features (e.g., charts, diagrams, and other graphics). Students should be taught strategies for engaging in reading texts carefully, focusing on text meaning, main idea or theme, and points of view. Comprehension instruction should include tasks that aim to build knowledge through reading and discussion, including the use of inferential questions that require text-based evidence and comparing information within and across multiple texts. Below, we recommend instructional routines for incorporating these features within shared reading and interactive read-aloud lessons.

The other content consideration for design of comprehension instruction is actually which strategies to name, model, and release responsibility for to students. We believe that it is more important to have a list than to quibble over exactly what should be on the list. As we have planned lessons, we have become convinced that all comprehension strategies are structured forms of inference making. In *Bookworms K–5 Reading and Writing*, there are seven: making connections, asking questions to aid understanding, creating sensory images, inferring, determining importance, synthesizing, and self-monitoring. We don't see these strategies (or any other list) as magical. Instead, starting with a list of strategies and an outline of strategic talk allows those writing lessons to be consistent and maximizes opportunities for students to try the routines repeatedly. Duffy's (2014) *Explaining Reading*, now in its third edition, has been a go-to resource for us since its first publication in 2003. Once you have a set of great texts to engage students and a list of comprehension strategies to model and practice, you can choose and use *instructional* strategies to maximize opportunities for instruction and practice.

Instructional Strategies

Providing a Focus for Reading

It may sound simple, but providing a specific focus before students read improves comprehension. Setting a purpose for reading helps readers activate prior knowledge and relevant schema before reading, select important information during reading, and participate in discussion after reading (Blanton, Wood, & Moorman, 1990). We believe that the focus provided to students before reading should always involve meaning. Setting a purpose that is too narrow in scope, such as reading to practice a strategy, can actually misdirect readers from understanding important information; it will certainly not engage students who may be reluctant. Comprehension instruction should always include setting a purpose before reading and revisiting the purpose in postreading discussion. In Chapter 6, we have discussed routines for reading and rereading grade-level text. When students engage in multiple readings, we always provide a new focus before the second reading. For example, when students are reading the first chapter of *Blood on the River* by Elisa Carbone (2006), the focus of the first reading might be to pay attention to the main character and find things out about his life. After reading, teachers can quickly discuss this first purpose and set a new one for rereading in partners. The second focus might be to think about what clues the author provides about the setting and the characteristics of the time period. Just remember that the focus should always be related to understanding the meaning of the text.

Comprehension Strategy Modeling

We have signaled our view that teaching comprehension strategies is a good idea, consistent with evidence from research. Strategy instruction comprises a variety of instructional actions with shared characteristics. All strategy approaches identify and name a complex cognitive process; they all provide a series of concrete steps that an individual uses to accomplish this process; and they all explicitly identify when and why the strategy is helpful. Modeling a strategy improves comprehension by showing developing readers how you (a proficient reader) apply the strategy as you think aloud during reading (Pressley & Wharton-McDonald, 1997). Modeling, rather than prompting students to use the strategy, enables them to learn the procedures for applying each strategy from a good comprehender. We suggest stopping once during choral reading or even more often when reading aloud to model one of the strategies you have chosen as guiding your planning. In Figure 8.7, you will see that we have provided a list of strategies *and* specified the steps in each strategy. This is the key to modeling: You have to know what it is you want to model and how you want to model.

All comprehension instruction involves thinking aloud, but thinking aloud is not actually easy to do on the fly. Remember that think-alouds are about you; you are the reader who is solving a comprehension problem. We plan our think-alouds in advance. All of them are structured similarly. We actually tell students what the strategy is, explain how we are using the procedure to increase our comprehension, and then tell why we use that strategy. For example, a fourth-grade teacher might stop during reading *Can't You Make Them Behave, King George?* by Jean Fritz (1977) to model inferring, saying,

"I can make an inference here. The text says, 'Sometimes George sulked under so much instruction' [p. 9]. Since George had tutors trying to teach him how to have good manners and to know math and history and Latin, I can figure out that they expected the king to be a role model. So even though he was going to become king just because of his family, the job of king would still be hard and demanding. Now I understand that he was sulking due to these high expectations."

We see this type of very brief modeling as key to demonstrating cognitive strategies while not distracting students from text meaning. This approach is very different from those in which teachers have strategy units and students must memorize the components of the strategy rather than demonstrate understanding of the text.

Discussion

Effective questioning strategies are an essential comprehension instructional routine. Asking questions during a read-aloud, or leading a discussion after shared reading, engages students with content and continues to model how proficient readers ask questions to aid in understanding. Most questions should be at the inferential level. Answering inferential questions often requires using multiple pieces of information or combining text-based evidence with prior knowledge. The benefits of asking inferential questions

Strategy	Procedure
Making connections	Identify information in the text, think about information you already know, and explicitly link the pieces of information.
Asking questions to aid understanding	Identify a surprise or inconsistency in the text, use that information to ask a question, and answer the question if the necessary information has been provided (or say that it might be provided by reading further).
Creating sensory images	Identify words used as sensory details in the text, explain what you know about the meaning of those words, and combine the words with what you know to describe how you visualize a sensory image.
Inferring	Identify information in the text, think about information provided previously or from prior knowledge, and link them together to create an idea that is not explicitly stated in the text.
Determining importance	List important and unimportant information, label information as important or unimportant, and tell why and how you determined importance (based on text structure and/or prior knowledge).
Synthesizing	Identify details within the same text or across different texts, group details into categories and subcategories by topic or text structure, and then construct a statement that links categories.
Self-monitoring	Identify a surprise or misunderstanding in the text, tell why it is surprising or confusing, and say you will reread or read on to check whether your understanding is correct.

FIGURE 8.7. Procedures for modeling comprehension strategies.

are clear: Answering "why" questions about the information in the text improves reading comprehension (Menke & Pressley, 1994; Wood, Pressley, & Winne, 1990). Many teachers we know are fearful of these high-level inferential questions, because they can actually stump students. They prefer to ask lower-level questions that students can answer easily. We don't see this as an either–or scenario. Figure 8.8 shows a simple procedure for using discussion starters and leading a natural, inferential discussion based on students' responses. There are many opportunities to expand on this foundation during a discussion. Here are four:

1. When a student cannot answer an inferential or critical question, drop to the literal level and ask for an explicitly stated fact that is useful in answering the higher level question. For example, suppose a fifth-grade teacher asks why a fictional character made a particular decision. When a student is unable to answer, the teacher asks what happened to the character just before the decision.
2. Remember that higher-order questions do not result in rapid-fire responses. They require thought, and when students do not respond immediately, providing some "think time" can be an effective way to foster a reasonable answer.
3. Turn the tables from time to time by asking students to pose questions. Question generation is an evidence-based way of improving comprehension, and postreading discussions provide many chances to elicit such questions.
4. Consider asking some questions for one student to answer aloud and others for students to discuss between partners. Partner and small-group discussions provide modeling of how peers make sense of text, and this modeling can add value to our more distant adult modeling language.

Text Structure Instruction

Text structure knowledge provides readers with a plan for how to recognize and remember the important information in a text. Over time, this knowledge also provides fourth- and

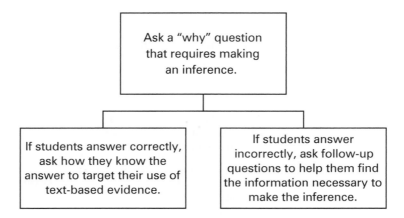

FIGURE 8.8. Steps for leading an inferential discussion after reading.

fifth-grade writers with choices for how to communicate ideas. Most approaches to teaching text structures use graphic organizers either to preview a text's structure before reading or to record important information after reading, but they can also be used to guide students in organizing their own text-based writing (Hebert et al., 2016; Roehling, Hebert, Nelson, & Bohaty, 2017). Text structure graphic organizers are physical representations of how ideas in a text are organized. Many classroom teachers we work with refer to them as *anchor charts*. When students are reading fiction, it is often unnecessary to preview the text's structure before reading. Narratives are usually structured according to a familiar sequence of events. However, organizing details by using a story map anchor chart that you update after reading each day can improve comprehension (Davis & McPherson, 1989; Reutzel, 1985). Figure 8.9 presents a story map for recording story elements after reading.

Nonfiction texts are usually more difficult for upper elementary readers to comprehend. Part of what makes them difficult is that authors use a variety of different text structures, often employing multiple structures in the same text (Williams, Hall, & Lauer, 2004). We have identified and defined in Figure 8.10 the six most common informational text structures. In *Animal Cells and Life Processes*, for example, the author uses

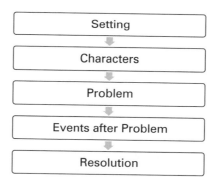

FIGURE 8.9. Story map anchor chart.

Structure	How It Works
Sequence	An author presents topics or ideas in chronological or time order.
Compare/contrast	An author describes how two or more topics or ideas are similar and/or different in one or more features.
Cause/effect	An author explains how one or more events cause, or lead to, one or more effects or results.
Problem/solution	An author presents a problem and one or more potential or actual solutions.
Description	An author describes a topic or idea and its attributes.
Listing	An author lists topics or groups them together in collections.

FIGURE 8.10. Basic informational text structures. Based on Meyer, Young, and Bartlett (1989).

listing to present different organelles, sequence of events to explain the digestive system, and compare/contrast to show how some of the cells that make up the human body are similar and different. When students are reading nonfiction, using a graphic organizer to preview a text's structure before they begin reading is likely to improve comprehension of important information (Boothby & Alvermann, 1984). We have provided graphic organizers for each of the most common structures in Appendix H. It is our hope that fourth- and fifth-grade teachers will introduce (or review) *all* of them early in the year and then refer to them flexibly all year long—during read-alouds, shared reading, and writing instruction. In fact, we hope that fourth- and fifth-grade classroom walls will be littered with evolving anchor charts representing the structures and content of texts that students are reading.

Instructional Planning

We again use our planning templates to demonstrate how to incorporate these suggestions into two components of Tier 1 instruction: interactive read-alouds and shared reading. To clarify our language, Figure 8.11 provides a comparison of the two types of reading as they are used in *Bookworms K–5 Reading and Writing*. If we start with how the types of reading are different, you will see that the planning for comprehension instruction is the same in many ways.

Figure 8.12 displays the planning templates for interactive read-alouds of fiction and nonfiction texts. The planning templates for shared reading are displayed in Figure 8.13. This template integrates what we have previewed about vocabulary instruction in Chapter 7.

When we plan for full text to be read aloud, the same fiction or nonfiction trade book is used for many days, and the instructional routines are the same each day. The only difference is on the first day. Because the selection is unfamiliar, the teacher must introduce it by building background knowledge and piquing the students' interest. On the following

	Shared Reading	Interactive Read-Alouds
Text selection	Within grade-level difficulty bands	Independent of grade-level difficulty bands
Vocabulary	Preselected only	Opportunities to insert additional explanations
Comprehension strategy modeling	Planned to minimize disruption	Both planned in advance and naturally occurring
Discussion	Only after each student reading	During and after teacher reading
Text-based writing	Assigned after reading to be completed later by students	Assigned after listening to be completed immediately, either as teacher modeling, in groups, or individually

FIGURE 8.11. Planning differences between shared reading and interactive read-alouds.

Time	Activity	Description
5 minutes	Review	Introduce book or review text structure anchor chart.
5 minutes	Teach Tier 3 vocabulary (nonfiction)	Introduce Tier 3 words, using concept of definition (COD) or semantic feature analysis (SFA) charts (see Chapter 7).
20–25 minutes	Vocabulary and comprehension instruction	Pause to model comprehension strategies, ask inferential questions, and provide quick scaffolds of new words.
5 minutes	Teach Tier 2 vocabulary (fiction)	Provide direct explanations of meanings for two new words.
5–10 minutes	Discussion	Lead the class in a brief, inferential discussion.

FIGURE 8.12. Template for planning fiction and nonfiction read-alouds with comprehension instruction.

days, introducing the selection is unnecessary, but brief reviews are important; this distinction is represented in Figure 8.12. This is the key difference between read-alouds of fiction and nonfiction. Before a fiction read-aloud, the teacher should briefly review events up to the point at which the previous day's read-aloud left off. Before a nonfiction read-aloud, the teacher should either introduce or review the text's structure, using an anchor chart to keep track of how ideas are organized. For both fiction and nonfiction, the teacher then reads aloud a new text segment each day, pausing to model comprehension strategies, pose inferential questions, and provide quick scaffolds of unfamiliar words. After the read-aloud, the teacher leads a brief inferential discussion. Every effort

Time	Activity	Description
5 minutes	Review (nonfiction)	Preview text structure anchor chart.
5 minutes	Word study (fiction)	Introduce two new words, with attention to syllable types, meanings, and derivatives.
	Teach Tier 3 vocabulary (nonfiction)	Introduce Tier 3 words, using COD or SFA charts.
20–25 minutes	Fluency and comprehension instruction	1. Set a meaningful purpose. 2. Engage class in choral reading. 3. Briefly discuss first purpose. 4. Set a new purpose. 5. Engage class in partner rereading. 6. Briefly discuss second purpose.
5 minutes	Review (fiction)	Update text structure anchor chart (story map).
5–10 minutes	Discussion	Lead the class in a brief, inferential discussion.

FIGURE 8.13. Template for planning shared reading of fiction and nonfiction with comprehension instruction.

should be made to use every-pupil response techniques (e.g., talking to a partner or polling the class), to ensure that all students participate in the discussion instead of relying on volunteers.

Interactive read-alouds can work in concert with shared reading to provide opportunities for comprehension instruction. Like interactive read-alouds, the structure of lessons differs slightly by genre. For nonfiction, we have chosen to place a preview of the text's structure, again using an anchor chart, before reading. Again, this is because following the author's structure is essential to understanding how ideas are organized, and it is very simple to do. For fiction, the text structure anchor chart (usually some form of a story map) can be updated *after* reading, to summarize the day's reading and bring the lesson to natural closure. For both types of text, we provide two comprehension-related purposes for reading. During the first reading, the teacher leads students in reading chorally, stops once for comprehension strategy modeling in context, and briefly addresses the first purpose for reading upon completion of the day's text segment. A new comprehension-related purpose for reading is set before students reread with partners. After the second reading, the teacher briefly addresses the second purpose and leads an inferential discussion.

Using challenging text every day can be a daunting goal, especially if students have typically struggled to meet grade-level expectations. From our work implementing shared reading lessons in real schools, we have learned about ways to differentiate the process of Tier 1 instruction. For those classrooms with push-in support, we suggest conducting lessons in a parallel teaching format. In parallel teaching, the general educator may lead whole-class instruction while the special educator delivers the same instruction in a teacher-led small group within the classroom (Friend, 2016). In a shared reading lesson, both teachers may read chorally with their students during the first reading. During the second reading, the general educator may facilitate partner reading with one group, while the special educator rereads chorally with students who need more support. Both teachers may lead separate inferential discussions at the same time, allowing for more opportunities for all students to participate and to receive appropriate scaffolding based on their responses during the discussion.

Planning shared reading and interactive read-alouds will require some time. Although the process may seem daunting at first, we are actually asking that you decide what opportunities a text provides for you to highlight the importance of text structures and comprehension strategies to support understanding. Your choices will come from a small set of high-utility structures and strategies that can be used repeatedly. In Chapter 7, we have begun the planning process with an eye to vocabulary development. We have first offered suggestions for sizing up the book and for deciding how to teach key vocabulary. These are Steps 1 and 2 of the planning process. We now turn to comprehension and continue with Step 3. Figure 8.14 lists all eight steps for easy reference.

3. *Decide how to build necessary background knowledge.* As they write, authors make certain assumptions about what the reader already knows. Consider a science book that begins, "The earth's crust is made up of three basic kinds of rocks: igneous, metamorphic, and sedimentary." In introducing these terms, the author is assuming that the

1. Size up the book.
2. Decide how to preteach the key vocabulary.
3. Decide how to build necessary background knowledge.
4. Decide whether to highlight one or more text structures.
5. Decide whether to highlight one or more comprehension strategies.
6. Decide what to say and do during reading to model and encourage thinking.
7. Decide what to say and do after reading to deepen understanding.
8. Develop a follow-up activity in which the children write to demonstrate or deepen understanding.

FIGURE 8.14. Steps in planning an interactive read-aloud of an information book.

reader already knows what the earth's crust is. Of course, no author can possibly predict who will actually read a book or listen to it being read aloud. Because prior knowledge of a topic differs greatly from reader to reader, it is possible that some students will not know what the earth's crust is. Consequently, their comprehension will be impaired because they will not be able to link the new ideas to their background knowledge. It is up to you as the teacher to anticipate possible gaps between what students actually know and what an author assumes they know. You must then try to fill those gaps both before and during reading.

This cannot be a sure-fire process, because background knowledge is individual. You can nevertheless try to anticipate gaps and take steps to make the book comprehensible. These steps include the following:

- Considering what content has previously been taught. (Have the students been introduced to the earth's crust?)
- Choosing where to add information. (Is it better situated before reading or as "asides" during the reading?)
- Choosing how to introduce background information. (Is it best accomplished by simply telling important facts, by adding to the chart or diagram discussed in Chapter 7, or by some other means?)
- Monitoring children's understanding as you read. (Do they appear to have the background needed to respond to questions, make comments, and pose questions?)

4. *Decide whether to highlight one or more text structures.* Begin analyzing the organization of the book by looking for key patterns. It is rare for informational books at fourth- and fifth-grade levels to be organized around a single pattern. Instead, you will find that they are combinations of two or more of the basic patterns. For the book you have chosen, consider whether a single structure is dominant or whether multiple structures are used in complex ways. Then decide whether highlighting the structure will afford a clear-cut lesson about text organization. There may be one portion of the book that provides a good example of an organizational pattern. Indicating the pattern

to students can serve as a brief and valuable lesson about text structure. Over the course of numerous books, your students will gain an appreciation of how each pattern works through exposure to a variety of examples.

5. *Decide whether to highlight one or more comprehension strategies.* Like text structures, strategies are more effective when they are taught as a tool box for readers and writers. Again, as in the case of text structures, it is our hope that teachers will review *all* of the comprehension strategies early in the year, and then refer to them flexibly all year—during read-alouds and shared reading. Planning for strategy modeling within a particular text is not difficult. Remember first that not all strategies are equally appropriate for a given text. Consider carefully when and where strategies can be applied. Look for clear-cut opportunities where understanding the text can be facilitated by a particular strategy. Do this by recalling the principal strategies we have highlighted and their most effective uses:

- Making connections (linking information in the text with information you know).
- Asking questions to aid understanding (using text information to ask and answer questions).
- Creating sensory images (visualizing mental images using sensory details).
- Inferring (combining stated facts or previously known facts to arrive at unstated facts).
- Determining importance (distinguishing more important from less important information).
- Synthesizing (linking information within the same book or across more than one book).
- Self-monitoring (rereading or reading on to clarify misunderstandings).

Having a text structure and a comprehension strategy goal does not ensure that reading will be productive. The real test is in the clarity and appropriateness of teacher modeling. In our experience, there is a steep learning curve for this aspect of instruction. Mature readers employ comprehension strategies fairly flexibly, and it is difficult to access the procedures involved and to share them with fourth and fifth graders. We suggest that you display a chart of strategies in your classroom and refer to it often, using clear, repetitive talk.

6. *Decide what to say and do during reading to model and encourage thinking.* Shared reading books will provide numerous opportunities for think-alouds at strategic points. A think-aloud is a model of how a proficient reader thinks through a difficult situation in order to comprehend. For example, let's assume that our wolf selection appears in a fourth-grade nonfiction trade book. On Day 1, when the teacher engages students in choral reading, think-alouds are especially appropriate because the students are unfamiliar with the selection. When the teacher reads, "and they are not very dangerous to humans," a dramatic pause may follow. "Wait a minute," the teacher might muse aloud, "I need to self-monitor here. I know that wolves are dangerous animals, so that sentence doesn't make sense. I will need to figure it out. When I am confused like this, I recognize

the confusion and read on to see if it is resolved." After reading aloud that there have been only been six reports of fatal wolf attacks in North America in the 21st century, the teacher concludes the think-aloud: "Well, I guess my original information was wrong. Wolves aren't as dangerous as I thought. Sometimes if we just keep reading, it will solve a problem we have in understanding. The trick is to notice the problem in the first place and keep it in mind until it is resolved." This last sentence is the point of the think-aloud. The fact that students have experienced think-alouds before does not dilute their instructive power. Just the reverse, in fact. After encountering them in a wide variety of texts over the course of several years, students will internalize the fix-up strategies of rereading and reading ahead that think-alouds are designed to teach.

Read-alouds also afford many opportunities for you as the teacher to make the experience interactive. The most obvious is to pause to ask questions, but there are many alternatives that can add variety to how the students interact with the content. Here are just a few of these:

- Asking for predictions.
- Prompting students to *pose* questions.
- Encouraging students to contribute to a summary up to a given point.
- Soliciting additions to a chart or diagram that was started before the read-aloud began.
- Prompting interpretations of the chart or diagram.
- Conducting think-alouds at points of possible confusion.

In planning where to pause during a read-aloud and what to do at each point, we recommend these steps:

- Choose points in the text where you can think of ways to invite interaction. These points will be examples of how one or more strategies can be applied.
- Frame what you will say, and consider inserting notes in your book to remind you.
- Be sure to include think-alouds at points where the author presents information that may be confusing to students or in conflict with their prior knowledge. (Remember our wolf example.) Use these opportunities to model fix-up strategies (what we call the "four R's"): Rereading, Reading ahead, Reflecting, and Referring to outside sources.
- Make sure that the pauses involve a variety of ways for students to interact. Do not, for example, rely on questions alone.
- Be sure to include every-pupil response techniques in order to maximize engagement. Asking each student to share with a partner, for example, ensures more engagement than calling on just one student.
- Include references to the graphic organizers you have used to introduce the text selection. Remember that you have kept these on display. Whenever appropriate, engage students in adding to or modifying the anchor charts.

One confusing thing about comprehension is that it can continue once the book is closed. Often, only knowing the full picture allows a reader to realize which initial ideas were important. In addition, comprehension of text is different from memory of text; a reader may understand a text during the read-aloud, but may not actually do the cognitive work that is necessary to store important ideas in memory.

7. *Decide what to say and do after reading to deepen understanding.* When you reach the last page, you may be tempted to share a "The End" moment, without fostering further interaction among the students. We believe that it is a mistake to close the book and move on to other lessons. Plan for enough time to take advantage of the fact that the content is still fresh in the students' minds. Begin by conducting a discussion that focuses on inferential thinking, drawing conclusions, and "take-away" lessons. Review the completed graphic organizer you have started before reading. Even a brief time for closure can help students think of themselves as readers and thinkers.

8. *Develop a follow-up activity in which the students write to demonstrate or deepen understanding.* A reading lesson of this nature takes planning, and its potential for building knowledge and skills should not be wasted. Follow-up activities allow teachers to reduce the number of independent activities that must be planned to facilitate differentiated reading instruction, build children's fluency and flexibility in writing, *and* allow them time to process text ideas deeply enough to facilitate their integration in students' memory. You will see in Chapter 9 that we think of these opportunities for text-based writing as extremely important.

To sum up, our big ideas about planning for comprehension instruction are designed to make complicated processes visible for students and reasonable to explain for teachers. We can leverage the potential of great texts in shared reading and in interactive teacher read-alouds to provide consistent, quick modeling for a small number of strategies. The differences in the ways we plan each component are actually contained in Chapter 6. Because we want to ensure that students are building fluency and stamina, we limit comprehension-oriented disruptions of connected reading in shared reading. We do not impose that same restriction on interactive read-alouds, though. We see this balance of support for comprehension as a reasonable way to plan, consistent with evidence, to support all students' comprehension.

TIER 2 INSTRUCTION IN COMPREHENSION

Because Tier 2 time is limited, we believe it is best spent in filling gaps in the basic skills (e.g., word recognition and fluency) students need to comprehend, not in developing comprehension directly. We also believe that all students must be served during Tier 2, including those without appreciable gaps in reading development. Consequently, the students we target for comprehension at Tier 2 are those with adequate fluency. Remember that comprehension, like vocabulary, is an open-ended proficiency: Our students should never cease to grow as comprehenders. Tier 2 time is an opportunity to stimulate such growth for fourth- and fifth-grade students whose fluency is adequate.

In many ways, our Tier 2 group of students in vocabulary and comprehension is more diverse than any other group at any grade level. You will have readers who are entirely fluent but very different in their general comprehension abilities. We have made this choice on purpose. Background and vocabulary knowledge are individual and resistant to meaningful diagnostic assessment. Luckily, though, as we have argued in Chapter 7, word knowledge grows through direct instruction and through incidental exposure, so we provide additional opportunities for both in this group. Construction of meaning, too, is entirely individual. For this group, we provide additional opportunities to do this construction with text read independently and silently, plus brief scaffolding before and after reading in discussion.

Our planning template from Chapter 7 for small-group instruction focused on vocabulary and comprehension is presented again in Figure 8.15. Again, you will notice its similarity to the planning template for interactive read-alouds and shared reading. This time, though, we keep procedures the same for comprehension instruction with fiction and nonfiction. On Day 1, we quickly introduce and build background knowledge for a new book; we review events or content on subsequent days. Before reading, we describe the structure of the day's text segment and suggest a comprehension-related focus for

Days	Format	Activity	Teacher's role	Students' role
Day 1	With teacher	Teach meaning vocabulary (nonfiction); preview text structure; assign text segment.	Teacher introduces two new words, using SFA or COD charts; teacher describes structure and sets a purpose for reading segment.	Students follow the teacher's lead.
Day 1	Outside of the group	Silent reading of assigned text segment.	Teacher can serve another group or circulate to provide support.	Students read the text independently, with or without a reading guide.
Day 2	With teacher	Engage in comprehension discussion for previous text segment; teach meaning vocabulary for previous segment (fiction) or new text segment (nonfiction); assign new text segment.	Teacher engages students in comprehension-rich discussion; teacher introduces two new words, using direct explanation, SFA charts, or COD charts.	Students follow the teacher's lead; students engage in text-based discussion for the purpose of supporting comprehension.
Day 2	Outside of the group	Self-selected, independent reading.	Teacher can serve another group or circulate to provide support.	Students read the text independently.

FIGURE 8.15. Template for vocabulary and comprehension practice with comprehension instruction. (Note that this is the same template as the one presented in Figure 7.14.)

reading. This reading differs from shared reading and interactive read-alouds: We allow students to read silently, giving them the opportunity to apply what they know about reading strategies when reading independently. Sometimes, we continue to scaffold their use of strategies with a reading guide. You will recall from Chapter 7 that there are two options for planning the reading and discussion. Some teachers send students back to their desks to read while the teacher is working with other students. After students have finished reading (or after a set amount of time), the teachers will reconvene students to update a text structure anchor chart and lead an inferential discussion. Other teachers will update the text structure anchor chart and lead an inferential discussion about the previous day's text segment when meeting with students the following day. These two plans can be applied with a wide variety of texts, although we encourage you to consider informational texts with links to your science and social studies curricula, or narratives that expand your students' experiences from shared reading with the same authors or themes. Because the students are adequately fluent and because you will support them during Tier 2 time, you can still select challenging texts. While we stop short of restricting text choice, remember that a text that builds knowledge for this group actually has to contain knowledge that they don't already have.

Instructional Strategies

For Tier 2, we chose to focus on two effective instructional strategies to guide independent reading. Each can also be used on a whole-class basis in science and social studies. Instruction in these subjects provides additional opportunities to read informational text and will help prepare your students for the reading they will be expected to undertake in the middle grades.

Reading Guides

A key difference between Tier 1 and Tier 2 instruction is that students can be provided with a reading guide to engage with a challenging text segment independently. A reading guide is like a map. It contains directions for strategies to use, questions to answer, charts and diagrams to complete, and other tasks that students can undertake while reading. A reading guide may also contain page numbers and subheadings to help students keep their place as they read. You can use Tier 2 time to introduce both the selection and the guide, and then work with other groups as the students begin to read the selection and complete the guide. At first blush, the use of reading guides may not appear to be an inspired approach, but their advantages are considerable. McKenna, Franks, Conradi, and Lovette (2011) list the following:

- They improve comprehension by focusing students' attention on important aspects of content.
- They make reading an active rather than a passive process.
- They cause students to translate the material into their own words, phrases, and sentences.

- They are means of integrating reading and writing.
- They produce useful tools for review.
- They provide blueprints for postreading discussions and give students valuable discussion aids.
- They model strategic, purposeful reading.
- They model effective note taking.

The fear that students will only read what is needed to complete a guide is easily allayed. We certainly agree that asking questions or presenting other tasks that simply require copying verbatim information from the text will encourage students to approach the reading at a superficial level. If a teacher truly believes that students will be tempted to focus only on what the guide requires, they are admitting what a powerful tool a guide can be. The solution is to pose questions and tasks that require higher-order thinking. When students must make inferences, categorize information, and reorganize ideas and thoughts, they need to process the content rather deeply. We argue that if a teacher is satisfied that the tasks contained in a guide require adequate comprehension, then it does not matter if the students "only" read to complete those tasks.

Writing a reading guide is a straightforward task, and you will get better at it over time. Keep your eye on the goal so you won't make too much of the task: A reading guide is there to help (not monitor) your students as they read independently. Begin by closely reading the material you expect your students to read. Decide what it is you wish them to take away from the reading. Once you do this, your choice of tasks will seem much clearer. Develop your guide in a linear fashion, moving from page to page and from section to section. Be sure to include visual landmarks (page numbers and subheadings, if available). Do not avoid literal-level tasks altogether. Explicitly stated information can be useful in arriving at inferences and making critical judgments. Opportunities to engage in these higher-level tasks should follow literal-level fact gathering. In this way, the guide models for students the hierarchical thinking process that is the basis of good comprehension: literal to inferential to critical.

Employing reading guides requires that you teach students how to complete them. You can model this process the first time your Tier 2 group uses one. Because guides are rarely used before grade 4, your students will probably need this instruction. When students begin to catch on to the way guides work, you can introduce more examples, but this time provide them with their own copies. Once you have modeled moving back and forth from reading to jotting down information required on a guide, you can provide guides that the students complete with partners. At this stage, you will need to monitor their work to ensure that they are using the guides as support. Finally, you will be able to give students a chance to complete guides independently.

Make sure that guides become a part of postreading discussions. When you return to your Tier 2 group, ask students to have their completed guides in front of them for reference. They can serve as powerful prompts. Above all, be critical of your own guides. Keep an eye out for trouble spots that can be improved the next time they are used. And remember that a guide is a teaching tool meant to direct attention and support comprehension. It is not a worksheet to keep students accountable.

Teaching about Text Structure

Before we go on, it is important that we distinguish between *genre* and *text structure*. Genres are associated with text structures, of course, but text structures exist on a more basic level, as building blocks for genres. That is, a single genre may employ several text structures. A short story or fiction trade book, for example, will have an overall genre but will also have an overarching story structure that includes presenting the setting and characters, revealing a problem faced by the protagonist, and unfolding how the problem is approached and solved. Information texts are members of a genre, but they can have a wide variety of text structures.

In our discussion of Tier 1 planning, we have listed the basic structures used by authors to organize their writing. We have suggested that Tier 1 time might afford opportunities for quickly reviewing one or more of them, especially if they are used in combination. Tier 2 time affords further opportunities for students to examine how the basic structures are often used in combination. This time, students can observe in their own copies how complex blends of text structures are signaled in writing. Let's consider some examples in which the basic structures have been combined:

- Gail Gibbons begins her 1992 book *Recycle!* (fifth-grade readability) by describing the problem posed by ever-increasing amounts of trash. She does this by tracking the movement of trash from the curbside to the landfill, employing a sequential pattern to present the problem. She then turns to recycling as a major solution to this problem. However, the solution is broken down into the types of materials to be recycled. She uses listing to present them: paper, glass, cans, plastic, and polystyrene. A four-page section is devoted to each type. For this book, then, the overall text structure is problem/solution, but the problem component relies on a sequential structure and the solution component on listing.
- The author of a trade book that describes sources of energy may use listing to present the sources, but follow these with a section that compares and contrasts them.
- A book on the problem of the disappearing rain forest may use listing to present possible solutions, at the same time comparing them. In this case, listing is combined with problem/solution and compare/contrast.

Remember that fourth and fifth graders have probably received instruction in basic text structures. The keys in the upper elementary grades are to review and refine their knowledge of these structures, to teach them to recognize complex combinations, and to help them use their developing knowledge of text structures to plan their writing.

Instructional Planning

Like vocabulary instruction, comprehension instruction has no clear sequence. The text structures examined are, of course, determined by the selection. The comprehension strategies included in reading guides are determined by what is appropriate for the selection. In planning, we link vocabulary and comprehension. In Chapter 7, we have discussed the need to choose words from the selection. A joint focus on vocabulary and comprehension begins by carefully examining the selection to choose (1) the strategies to highlight in a reading guide, (2) a method of discussing the text structure, and (3) important vocabulary (general words for fiction, technical words for information text).

Because these fourth or fifth graders will be reading the selection silently, it is helpful to use a teacher-prepared reading guide. When students are reading silently, they are also reading asynchronously. If you stop them at the same time, they won't be in the same place in the text. Merging vocabulary with comprehension instruction presents opportunities to blend instructional approaches. For example, a reading guide, which is primarily concerned with supporting comprehension and modeling strategies, may contain an SFA chart (see Chapter 7) to construct or complete. We hope to convey the idea that there is not a single best approach, nor is there a universal, cookie-cutter plan that will work for all groups and selections. This is good news, however, because it provides you with a chance to plan creatively by mixing and varying your approaches to instruction. Over time, your choices will keep your planning fresh and your abler students engaged. They will also give you the chance to gauge the more effective combinations of instructional approaches.

Now let's consider how to plan for Tier 2 vocabulary and comprehension instruction. Remember that we usually must plan over many days to cover an entire trade book written at the fourth- or fifth-grade level. Figure 8.16 shows how a week's small-group lessons could be structured. We have assumed a 5-day plan for purposes of illustration. A specific trade book will likely require more time to complete. You will also see in Appendix I that we have used reading guides and focused on teaching text structure in our model lessons based on fiction and nonfiction trade books.

The plans for both fiction and nonfiction provide for cumulative review of vocabulary and content. In comprehension, we encourage you to look for ways to bridge backward to previous content so that students can link the new with the familiar. Discussions

	Day 1	**Day 2**	**Day 3**	**Day 4**	**Day 5**
Text structure	Introduce Day 1 text segment and preview text structure.	Review content and structure from Day 1, and preview text structure from Day 2 segment.	Review content and structure from Day 1 and Day 2, and preview text structure from Day 3 segment.	Review content and structure from Day 1, Day 2, and Day 3, and preview text structure from Day 4 segment.	Review content and structure from Day 1, Day 2, Day 3, and Day 4, and preview text structure from Day 5 segment.
Reading guide	Highlight a strategy that will be helpful in Day 1 text segment.	Highlight a strategy that will be helpful in Day 2 text segment.	Highlight a strategy that will be helpful in Day 3 text segment.	Highlight a strategy that will be helpful in Day 4 text segment.	Highlight a strategy that will be helpful in Day 5 text segment.

FIGURE 8.16. Teaching comprehension during Tier 2 time.

that are cumulative (i.e., not limited to the text segment of a single day) are an excellent means of helping students forge these links (McKenna & Robinson, 2011).

Finally, we offer a few points about apportioning time. First, note that once these students begin to read, you are free to attend to other groups. You will need to schedule all of your small groups skillfully in order to take advantage of this flexibility. Again, you can choose to have students read silently for 7 minutes with the reading guide before reconvening for a very brief discussion, or you can give students more time to read and lead a longer discussion focused on the content and structure of the text segment the following day. You may find it more convenient to conduct the postreading portion of these small-group lessons on the next day, blending the discussion of one text segment with an introduction to the next. Doing so provides greater flexibility, but there may be a cost in terms of the freshness of the words and content in your students' minds.

CHOOSING TIER 3 PROGRAMS FOR COMPREHENSION

As in previous chapters, we stop short of recommending commercial programs for Tier 3 instruction, because we lack sufficient empirical evidence to recommend one over the other. In addition, as researchers turn their attention to the needs of young adolescent students within an RTI framework, new, effective interventions will be developed. When we look for evidence about the effectiveness of interventions, we turn to four Internet sources that we have mentioned in earlier chapters: (1) the Institute of Education Sciences' What Works Clearinghouse (*https://ies.ed.gov/ncee/wwc*), (2) the Center on Instruction (*www.centeroninstruction.org*), (3) the Best Evidence Encyclopedia (*www.bestevidence.org*), and (4) the Center on Response to Intervention (*www.rti4success.org*). When you search for evidence on the efficacy of intensive interventions for comprehension designed for upper elementary students, consider searching at a range of grade levels (including the middle grades) in order to make your search as broad as possible.

We encourage you to think carefully about the implications of an intensive intervention program in comprehension. Our approach, based on the cognitive model of reading assessment, is to identify the basic factors that may be impeding comprehension for particular students and to intervene at that level. Cases of pervasive comprehension difficulty when all of the factors influencing comprehension are within normal limits are mercifully rare. For this reason, most of the commercial interventions do not target comprehension exclusively, but focus also on underlying causes. The assessments that accompany these programs are therefore multidimensional, and the hope is that when proficiency is improved in an underlying area, improvements in comprehension proficiency will also be realized.

CHAPTER 9

Building Writing Competence

We focus in this chapter on effective writing instruction. Unfortunately, writing has been characterized as the "neglected R" (National Commission on Writing in America's Schools and Colleges, 2003), and for years it was not given adequate attention in federal policies (e.g., the No Child Left Behind Act of 2001). This lack of attention may have led schools to gradually reduce the time allotted to writing instruction (Cutler & Graham, 2008) and teachers' professional development for writing instruction (Troia & Graham, 2016). Consequently, students may underperform on national assessments (National Center for Education Statistics, 2012), and there is a genuine national concern about writing instruction. In fact, the first edition of this book had no writing chapter; we remedy that error now.

In this chapter, we address two different types of writing. Specifically, we first examine principles for supporting writing in response to reading, and then describe writing to demonstrate thinking and learning in longer authentic tasks. Next, we describe our processes for planning Tier 1 writing instruction. Finally, we provide suggestions for Tier 2 instruction and Tier 3 writing intervention.

FOUNDATIONAL KNOWLEDGE ABOUT WRITING DEVELOPMENT

Writing requires the coordination of several foundational skills, and as a form of communication it can serve multiple purposes (Graham, Bollinger, et al., 2012). To write, students must be able to develop ideas, organize them in a way that will clearly communicate with readers, and actually produce a clear message on paper or screen. During elementary grades, especially at the beginning stages of learning about reading and writing, teachers may place a greater emphasis on spelling and grammar and on the presentation of the written message than on its content and communicative purposes. But writing is far more than the application of foundational spelling skills and sentence-level grammar (even though these skills are important).

There are important developmental issues to consider. Figure 9.1 provides a preview. A beginning writer will have far more to coordinate than a student in the upper elementary grades will. For a first grader who is still learning how to apply the alphabetic principle, spelling and handwriting may significantly stress working memory and interfere with developing ideas and transitioning from ideas to a coherent message for a reader (Berninger & Winn, 2006). Students in upper elementary grades will not typically struggle as much with the application of foundational handwriting and spelling skills, but they still have some juggling to do. These students draw on large stores of words they can spell automatically, and handwriting is typically not an issue. However, they will need to apply spelling patterns and knowledge of derivations, syllable types, and affixes in order to correctly spell words that are not automatic. Furthermore, they will need to have a good understanding of different types of writing, so that their responses satisfy the needs of the task, purpose for writing, and audience (National Center for Education Statistics, 2012; NGACBP & CCSSO, 2010). They will also have to evaluate and synthesize information they have acquired through reading. Their reading comprehension will influence the quality and ease of their writing. Despite the scope of these challenges, teachers can support students through writing instruction.

The CCSS clearly set expectations for writing outcomes. Because there are few differences between grades 4 and 5, we have combined them in Figure 9.2. The standards'

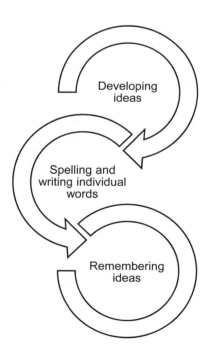

FIGURE 9.1. Challenges for beginning writers.

General Goal	Evidence
colspan="2" Grades 4 and 5
The students write for a variety of text types and purposes.	• Students write opinion texts that support a point of view with reasons and information, including introducing a topic or text, stating an opinion, creating an organizational structure, providing reasons supported by evidence, using linking words to connect opinion and reasons, and providing a conclusion. • Students write informative texts that convey ideas and information, including introducing a topic, grouping related information, including formatting, using linking words to connect ideas, using precise vocabulary, and providing a conclusion. • Students write narrative texts that develop real or imagined events, including establishing a situation, introducing characters, sequencing events, using narrative techniques (e.g., dialogue, description, and pacing), using transition words, using concrete language and sensory details, and providing a conclusion.
The students produce and distribute writing.	• Students produce genre-specific writing in which the development and organization are appropriate for the task, purpose, and audience. • Students develop writing using the writing process (e.g., planning, revising, and editing), with scaffolding from both peers and adults. • Students produce and publish writing using technology, including using the Internet and typing one to two pages in a single sitting, with scaffolding from adults.
The students conduct research to build and present knowledge.	• Students conduct short research projects using multiple sources on a topic to build knowledge. • Students gather information from a variety of sources by taking notes, summarizing or paraphrasing information, and providing a list of sources. • Students draw evidence from texts to support analysis, reflection, and research.
The students participate in a range of writing.	• Students write over extended time frames, including time for research, reflection, and revision, and shorter time frames (e.g., a single sitting), for a range of discipline-specific writing tasks, purposes, and audiences.

FIGURE 9.2. Writing standards from the CCSS. From NGACBP and CCSSO (2010). In the public domain.

implementation requires instruction that promotes reading and writing connections (NGACBP & CCSSO, 2010). The standards also set specific expectations for text types and purposes, production and distribution of writing, research to build and present knowledge, and a range of writing. According to the standards' guidelines, upper elementary students must demonstrate three types of writing: opinion writing, informative writing, and narrative writing. Students' development and organization of ideas need to be appropriate to a range of assignments, and students should respond to writing tasks by applying the writing process, including using technology to produce and publish (or share) writing. Most importantly, this writing need not be constrained by students' background knowledge and experiences; it must also be informed directly by single and multiple text readings. Students need both to provide short written responses to readings and to conduct research projects on a topic. They must learn to take notes from multiple sources and summarize or paraphrase to present information. Finally, they must learn to cite evidence and give credit to sources.

The standards set demands on instructional design and require schools to make and invest time for writing instruction. In many schools, teachers collaborate to give students opportunities to write across their instructional day. For instance, in science students may conduct preliminary research on topics with note taking, evaluation of sources, and development of ideas prior to writing (Philippakos & Williams, 2018). There is much to learn about writing instruction that we cannot fit into this chapter. Figure 9.3 provides a list of resources that you may use to broaden your knowledge about writing and writing instruction in the elementary grades.

TIER 1 INSTRUCTION IN WRITING

As we plan Tier 1 writing instruction, we start with the end in mind. We think about what students are reading, and then we think about authentic tasks that can be informed by that reading. Luckily, we can access research on writing and on specific approaches that support students' written production as well as their motivation to write. Figure 9.4 provides a preview of targets for effective writing instruction.

Evidence-based approaches support teachers and address the needs of all students (Harris et al., 2017; Graham, 2018; MacArthur, 2011). Graham, Bollinger, and colleagues (2012) have also provided a set of recommendations on writing instruction

---

Coker, D. L., & Ritchey, K. (2015). *Teaching beginning writers*. New York: Guilford Press.
Graham, S., & Harris, K. (2005). *Writing better: Effective strategies for teaching students with learning difficulties*. Baltimore: Brookes.
Graham, S., MacArthur, C., & Fitzgerald, J. (2015). *Best practices in writing instruction* (2nd ed.). New York: Guilford Press.
Graham, S., MacArthur, C., & Hebert, M. (2018). *Best practices in writing instruction* (3rd ed.). New York: Guilford Press.
Harris, K., Graham, S., Mason, L., & Friedlander, B. (2008). *Powerful writing strategies for all students*. Baltimore: Brookes.
MacArthur, C. A., Graham, S., & Fitzgerald, J. (Eds.). (2016). *Handbook of writing research* (2nd ed.). New York: Guilford Press.
Philippakos, Z. A., & MacArthur, C. A. (2019). *Developing strategic young writers through genre instruction: Resources for grades K–2*. New York: Guilford Press.
Philippakos, Z. A., MacArthur, C. A., & Coker, D. L. (2015). *Developing strategic writers through genre instruction: Resources for grades 3–5*. New York: Guilford Press.
Saddler, B. (2012). *Teacher's guide to effective sentence writing*. New York: Guilford Press.
Troia, G. (2009). *Instruction and assessment for struggling writers: Evidence-based practices*. New York: Guilford Press.

FIGURE 9.3. Resources for writing instruction.

Extensive practice with short, focused research projects and tasks.	Activities that require students to analyze and synthesize text sources.
Instruction in different text structures, and focus on argument and informative writing based on texts with these structures.	Opportunities to write routinely over extended time frames and shorter time frames, such as a single sitting.

FIGURE 9.4. Instructional targets for writing. Based on Foorman, Smith, and Kosanovich (2017).

that address time, instruction, foundational skills, and the development of a community of writers. These inform the content and instructional strategies of Tier 1 writing instruction.

Content

The content of Tier 1 writing instruction is the combination of appropriate writing tasks with systematic support for the writing process and with grammar instruction. To plan this writing instruction, we begin with the writing assignments themselves. Students must write for multiple purposes, using multiple genres. While the standards clearly target opinion, informative, and narrative writing, upper elementary students should learn to identify the purpose of a task and the audience for their work, as this knowledge should affect tone and word choice when the students are attempting to convey meaning (Graham, Bollinger, et al., 2012). Students need to be thoughtful in their analysis of a reading and writing assignment and to think carefully about audience and purpose, both when they read to retrieve information and when they write by integrating information (Philippakos, 2018). As students are learning to understand writing purposes and types, instruction should provide models and systematically guide students to develop their writing competence.

The writing assignments teachers construct should reflect these goals and support students' ability to apply what they are learning about audience and purpose. They must construct writing assignments or tasks that take advantage of opportunities in the texts students are reading. Reading and writing should be connected across the elementary grades, but these connections are particularly salient in the upper elementary standards. For grades 4 and 5, we take seriously the expectation that reading standards will be demonstrated in written responses. For instance, students may write to compare and contrast themes or character traits within or between texts. To do this, they need to find evidence from text to justify their claims. Students must also compose longer written products and research projects. Figure 9.5 provides examples.

Once teachers have worthwhile writing assignments planned in a variety of genres, they must build time for writing into their regular routines. Reviews of research on writing indicate that writing must take place daily and that students must have time for it. Graham, Bollinger, and colleagues (2012) recommend 1 hour daily, including 30 minutes of instruction and 30 minutes of practice. Given the crowded school day, students may

Brief, On-Demand, Text-Based Writing Prompts	Longer, Fully Processed Writing Tasks	Research Projects
In *Charlie and the Chocolate Factory,* we have just read about the history of the factory. Think about Willy Wonka's decision to close and then reopen the factory. Do you think he was in the right? Give reasons for your opinion.	For the next several days, you are going to write a narrative mystery piece based loosely on *Steal Away Home,* but your story will need to be different from Lois Ruby's story. You and your family will be the characters. Imagine that you have just moved into an old house. Your parents have decided to knock down a wall to make a room larger, and someone discovers something very strange hidden in the wall. You are going to write a mystery telling about how your family tries to solve the mystery of how this strange item came to be.	Today you are going to choose one natural disaster to begin researching. Before we start researching, you will need to pick which natural disaster interests you the most and makes you want to learn more about it.
In *Walk Two Moons,* we have just read about Sal and her grandparents' meeting with a strange boy. How did the boy's actions show that he was a complex character? Use examples from the chapter.	Today we will start another compare/contrast writing. We will use the information we learned in *Aunt Harriet's Underground Railroad in the Sky,* along with information we will learn about the Underground Railroad from an article that we will read today.	Today we are going to start a research unit on the Civil Rights Movement to help us learn even more about this period of our history. The question we will answer is this: What was it like to live during the Civil Rights Movement? We will spend several days gathering information from a variety of sources. We will take notes on the information we learn and organize our notes into similar categories. Our final project will be a newspaper article that could have appeared in a paper in the 1960s.

FIGURE 9.5. Sample writing assignments to address new standards in grades 4 and 5.

need to be able to write across the curriculum. In *Bookworms K–5 Reading and Writing*, students practice writing in daily text-based responses to their reading for at least 15 minutes every day, and they alternate between full 45-minute instruction and practice periods and 30-minute periods of grammar instruction and teacher modeling of writing. We have learned that we must keep this time protected, and that this can be challenging to do.

However, merely allotting time for writing is not enough. Students also need to understand the writing process and use it flexibly (Graham, Harris, & Chambers, 2016). Figure 9.6 provides a preview. Writing is a process with steps that researchers have addressed singly and in concert. Instruction must target planning, drafting, revising, editing, and publishing systematically. Although these steps may seem like too many to target, students develop independence when teachers gradually release responsibility for completing the steps along the way. Generally, we plan for initial teacher modeling, and then for collaborative practice with peers to allow students to develop the knowledge they need in order to finally work independently. We can teach strategies for different components of the writing process and support students in learning to select and use them flexibly. In this learning context, writing assignments need to also allow students to move flexibly back and forth across the steps of the writing process.

Instructional Strategies

All upper elementary teachers know students who are reluctant writers even when the teachers have planned meaningful assignments and provided adequate time for the students to complete their work. These students may need support in their foundational writing skills. They may need to move from handwriting to typing fluency, and they may need to continue to develop their spelling skills. Nearly all students need to continue to expand their sentence construction skills. For example, some students may benefit from using sentence frames to develop their ideas (e.g., "One reason _____"). Others will benefit from support with sentence-level grammar through expanding, combining,

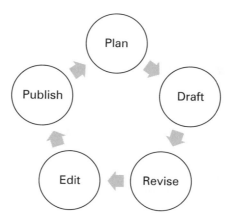

FIGURE 9.6. Writing process.

and imitating sentences (Graham, Bollinger, et al., 2012). Figure 9.7 provides sentence-level grammar prompts that we have written to build students' competence. In *Bookworms K–5 Reading and Writing*, these sentence-level grammar prompts are taken from each day's read-aloud to provide the students with meaningful context.

We see appropriate writing tasks, flexible process writing, and continued support for foundational skills in writing as best achieved in an engaged classroom community of learners. In fact, this book is itself evidence of the power of writing accomplished jointly. When a teacher takes time in class to write and to model writing, students see that the teacher views writing both as an opportunity for growth and as something that always requires time and effort. Students can be taught to give and receive feedback to and from peers at all stages of the writing process. Finally, at the publishing stage, students should relish opportunities to share their work in various forms and in ways that allow them to bring their work out of the classroom.

One of the most effective, evidence-based approaches in writing is *cognitive strategy instruction* (Graham, 2006; Graham, McKeown, et al., 2012; MacArthur, 2011). Strategy

	Grade 4	Grade 5
Sentence expanding	*Daddy and I shared big grins.* Let's add dialogue with correct punctuation at the end of a sentence. *Daddy and I shared big grins, shouting, "_____!"* Notice that I keep the exclamation point inside the quotation.	Each year people kill hundreds of millions of rats. This is a controversial statement. Some of you will think it's good, and others may think it's bad. Let's show that with an introductory word: *Fortunately* or *Unfortunately.* When we start a sentence with a word like that, we set it off with a comma.
Sentence imitating	*The larger the quake, the larger the wiggle.* *The larger the quake, the larger the _____.*	*By day, the bat is cousin to the mouse.* Let's think about verb tense here. The poet is communicating that this happens always. He is making a statement that is timeless. What if I want to say that it happened yesterday? *Was.* What if I want to say that it will happen in the future? *Will be.*
Sentence combining	*She got arrested at the lunch counter. She's in jail.* Let's use a new verb form here. *She got arrested at the lunch counter, so she _____ be in jail.* Would it be *may be, can be,* or *must be*? Think about the meaning you are trying to convey when you combine sentences.	*Matt took the time to listen.* *Matt took the time to learn their language.* *Matt took the time to make friends.* Think about the relationship of ideas. Are these similar things? Does one cause another? Are they in time order? Are they contrasting? Your choice of linking words has to be driven by meaning. You also want to be sure that you are not repeating information unnecessarily.

FIGURE 9.7. Sentence-level grammar instruction samples.

instruction attends to the cognitive processes and specific skills that students need to apply in order to complete a task. There is strong evidence that cognitive strategy instruction has large positive effects on writing quality. Research findings also point out that when cognitive strategy instruction is combined with self-regulation, and when students are supported in developing ways to overcome cognitive challenges through metacognitive processes and thinking, their writing production and writing quality improve even more (Graham, McKeown, et al., 2012).

The goal of cognitive strategy instruction is to support students in the completion of challenging writing tasks through using strategies for the steps of the writing process. Teachers share metacognitive strategies that help students develop language and procedures to overcome writing bottlenecks. In strategy instruction, the goal is not just the completion of a specific day's writing task; the ultimate goal is development of self-talk that writers can call upon whenever they write. Teachers explain and model thinking and use of tools to enable communication with an audience (Englert, Mariage, & Densmore, 2006; Englert, Raphael, Anderson, Anthony, & Stevens, 1991; Harris & Graham, 2009). The instructional framework of strategy instruction usually involves specific steps, provided in Figure 9.8.

Steve Graham, Karen Harris, Charles MacArthur, and many colleagues have systematically studied the effects of strategy instruction and self-regulation on students of all ages and of all instructional needs for more than three decades (e.g., Graham, McKeown, et al., 2012). Several researchers have been also studying processes for

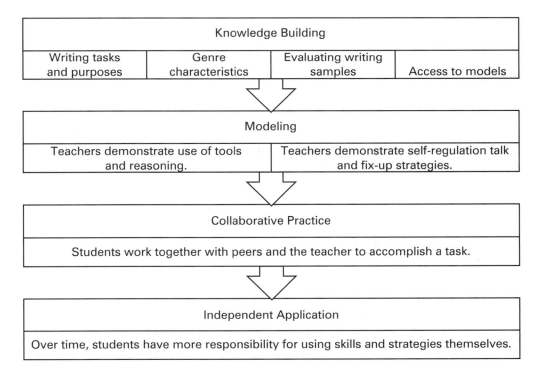

FIGURE 9.8. General steps in strategy instruction with self-regulation.

developing strategic writers, as well as other ways to support components of the writing process. For example, Philippakos and MacArthur (2016) examined the effects of using genre-specific evaluation criteria to give feedback on the revision and composition quality of fourth and fifth graders' opinion essays. In their work, they focused on evaluation. They provided instruction to all students on the genre and on its evaluation, using a rubric (with a 3-point scoring guide) that included these sections: Beginning, with a topic and opinion; Middle–Me, with reasons and evidence to support the writer's point of view; Middle–Others, with a presentation of the opposing position and its reasons, along with a rebuttal; and End, with a restatement of the position and a message for the reader to think about the topic. Students were then randomly assigned to different groups. The groups that practiced using the specific genre criteria to give feedback made more effective revisions and wrote papers of better quality. Similar practice embedded in strategy instruction was used with younger students, also indicating the effects of the use of genre criteria for evaluation and the value of evaluation in revision (Philippakos & MacArthur, 2019; Philippakos, MacArthur, & Munsell, 2018). Coker and Ritchey (2015) have described a similar genre-based strategy approach for younger writers, and have also recommended sentence-writing strategies. As we read the work of these writing researchers, we are struck by the fact that a well-sequenced set of lessons can make writing a much less daunting task for students.

Instructional Planning

We have surely not done writing research justice here. We have devoted four full chapters to reading and only one to writing! But we must learn to marry the two in our planning for tiered literacy instruction. We can use what we have learned in the planning of *Bookworms K–5 Reading and Writing* to give insight into how to plan Tier 1 writing instruction for upper elementary students.

First, the scope and sequence matter. We have planned daily, on-demand, text-based writing, based on the opportunities we see in each day's text. Each of those brief assignments can be structured with elements of opinion, informative, or narrative writing, but students have to analyze the assignment themselves. We have chosen to be proactive in our longer writing pieces. We want students to experience all three of our target genres each marking period, so that they can respond across all writing types. Figure 9.9 provides insight into how this particular writing curriculum is organized.

This is surely not the only way to sequence writing instruction. Once you decide how to sequence writing, you must decide how to engage in some form of cognitive strategy instruction. In *Bookworms K–5 Reading and Writing*, typical tools for this instruction include graphic organizers and checklists for each genre. When each type of writing is introduced, students first use their previous writing experience to brainstorm ideas about the genre, and the teacher adds ideas as needed to create a list of genre elements. Next, the teacher and students read various texts; using the genre elements list, they determine whether the texts they read reflect that type of writing or not. Teacher and students then engage in a collaborative discussion about the elements and about their presence in those texts. Students continue this practice and engage in collaboration with peers to determine whether a text represents the genre, and if not, why not.

Modeling of writing processes is the next thing to plan. We have reserved time for teachers to model quick composition of short text-based responses after read-alouds, and then to model processes of writing more extensively. In our early primary lessons, teachers model the use of graphic organizers specific to each genre to plan before writing; in grades 4 and 5, they teach students how to make their own organizers. Teachers model how to complete each section of the graphic organizer for each genre. Students also contribute as the lessons shift to a collaborative completion of each graphic organizer.

Once students have been introduced to the different genres, they revisit each one and spend a longer time working through the writing process. Students plan their work, write it, and use a rubric to evaluate it. Then they work with their peers and share comments with one another. Finally, editing is addressed through the use of an editing checklist.

Grade	Week	Instructional Focus
Grade 4	Week 1	Narrative writing
	Week 2	Opinion writing
	Week 3	Sentence-level grammar and modeling
	Week 3	Informative writing
	Week 5	Sentence-level grammar and modeling
	Week 5	Poetry
	Week 6	Narrative writing (mystery)
	Week 8	Sentence-level grammar and modeling
	Week 9	Sentence-level grammar and modeling
	Week 10	Sentence-level grammar and modeling
Grade 5	Week 1	Narrative writing
	Week 2	Opinion writing
	Week 3	Sentence-level grammar and modeling
	Week 3	Informative writing
	Week 6	Sentence-level grammar and modeling
	Week 6	Fictional narrative writing
	Week 8	Sentence-level grammar and modeling
	Week 8	Poetry
	Week 9	Sentence-level grammar and modeling
	Week 9	Compare/contrast informative writing
	Week 10	Sentence-level grammar and modeling

FIGURE 9.9. Instructional sequence for writing in grades 4 and 5.

To develop writing competence, students need cumulative practice and review of the types of writing. Therefore, after the initial introduction of the types of writing, the students revisit them and are given opportunities to provide shorter and longer essays that are based on real readings. As students become more and more competent and comfortable in their writing, they may be better able to collaborate and engage in discussions about the types of readings they do and the types of writing the authors use. Throughout this process, the teacher's role is to model the completion of the writing tasks and of the thinking processes, and to provide explicit explanations and opportunities for practice before students are asked to complete tasks alone.

TIER 2 INSTRUCTION IN WRITING

As we have previewed in Chapter 1, our approach to differentiation in writing is different from our approach in reading. More research is needed in writing differentiation and on instruction for Tier 2, but promising work is coming (e.g., Wilson, 2018). In reading, we have proposed content differentiation. Based on screening and diagnostic data, we have described instruction for three groups: (1) fluency and comprehension with multisyllabic decoding, (2) fluency and comprehension, and (3) vocabulary and comprehension. Since the actual instructional routines are different for each group, and since we expect that all three groups would be found in any classroom, this is a form of content differentiation. For writing, though, we recommend process differentiation.

A common practice to support differentiation in writing instruction is the use of accommodations; however, the decision-making process for providing accommodations can be challenging, and their application may not be systematic (Gilbert & Graham, 2010). In writing, teachers meet and confer with students in order to identify and address their specific needs. This conferencing process is definitely valuable, as students learn much through teachers' individualized and immediate support. Teachers can also learn about their students' understanding of writing tasks and the challenges they may face with the writing assignments. However, conferences can be time-consuming, and it is possible that by the time a teacher reaches a student, that student will not be motivated to backtrack and revise.

For Tier 2 work, we encourage teachers to work with students in small groups during writing work sessions. For students who may be challenged by components of a writing task, Tier 2 instruction can be provided inside or outside the general education classroom by means of flexible groupings (Philippakos & FitzPatrick, 2018). The main difference between groups is in the explicitness of the information provided. Teachers can be very specific as they support students' completion of a day's writing task. This type of differentiation allows all students to progress at a relatively similar rate to complete their writing assignments (Philippakos, MacArthur, & Coker, 2015; Philippakos & FitzPatrick, 2018). Also, all students see themselves as writers within the community of writers, and all writers are able to share their work and go through the process of evaluation with their peers. If the process of small-group work and differentiation connects with goal setting and allows students to reflect on their work and on the ways the strategies help them complete their goals (self-regulation), the benefits of small-group work will be long-lasting (Philippakos, Overly, Riches, Grace, & Johns, 2018).

There are different ways to group students. The most obvious way is observation. Students who seem uncertain about the day's task can be immediately supported. However, teachers, especially teachers honing their writing instruction skills, may accidentally miss students in need. Another way that may be more efficient is to use recently completed writing tasks diagnostically, identifying groups of students who struggle with specific genre elements or demands (Philippakos & FitzPatrick, 2018; Philippakos et al., 2015). This second process allows flexibility in group assignments as students gradually improve. After the completion of the next writing task, different students may need support, or the same students may need support in a different area.

CHOOSING TIER 3 PROGRAMS FOR WRITING

For students who struggle significantly with writing, a very explicit instructional approach will be effective. We do not recommend instruction at a slower pace, and we do not suggest lowering the standards. On the contrary, we recognize that writing needs are not the same for all students, and that not all programs are meant to serve all students. Thus some students may need a more rigorous approach to learn to plan their ideas and develop their sentences, or take notes when they read to write. The Self-Regulated Strategy Development (SRSD) model can help students who need Tier 3 support, and many studies have shown its positive effects for students with disabilities and behavioral disorders (e.g., Gillespie & Graham, 2014; Graham, Harris & McKeown, 2013; Rogers & Graham, 2008). SRSD has been used as a Tier 2 program as well (e.g., Lane et al., 2011).

You can visit the SRSD website (*https://srsdonline.org*) to learn more about the work of Harris, Graham, and their colleagues, or can consult two of their their coauthored books: *Powerful Writing Strategies for All Students* (Harris, Graham, Mason, & Friedlander, 2008) and *Writing Better: Effective Strategies for Students with Learning Difficulties* (Graham & Harris, 2005). We are pleased to say that the website and both books provide many resources that you can use to develop and support strong writers. We hope that you will be intrigued by the ideas we have introduced in this chapter and willing to read more about effective writing instruction.

CHAPTER 10

Putting It All Together

Our school-based work is always motivated by a desire to embed research findings within the realities of today's classrooms. In our independent work, Sharon Walpole and Mike McKenna did this with their coaching research, with their design of primary-level differentiation, and with the original *Bookworms* lessons. Sharon has continued that work in *Bookworms K–5 Reading and Writing*. John Strong has made his mark in the design of content area text sets for middle and high school classrooms and in an intervention program for increasing text structure knowledge. Zoi Philippakos has specialized in the design and teacher support required for excellent writing instruction that improves student writing outcomes. In this book, we have drawn upon these individual strengths to produce something that no one of us could have done independently.

Classrooms are like that, too. Each classroom has its own personality, influenced by the teacher and by the mix of students that year. The schools and communities in which classrooms are nested also represent more differences today than they ever did. There are meaningful differences in the needs of students and teachers. There are meaningful differences in the resources provided to them. For evidence-based instruction to become a reality in all classrooms, it has to be described clearly and with many possible examples, and its planning and implementation must be reasonable for those teachers who are tasked to use it. This is the reason why we are highlighting *Bookworms K–5 Reading and Writing* as a curricular example in this book. Its release as an open educational resource will ensure that *all* teachers can access the lesson plans for free; its use of trade books (much less expensive to adopt than the excerpt-driven anthologies that have typically driven the curriculum market) makes it a reasonable investment for schools.

A new curriculum has to be presented with support, through ongoing in-service work and coaching and through fair, meaningful teacher evaluations. Once an instructional model is understood and implemented, it actually has to yield the dividends that matter: classroom communities where teachers and students are actually engaged in purposeful and interesting learning every day, *and* where that engagement is associated with improved knowledge and skills for all, demonstrated on valid and reliable assessments.

We believe that the model for literacy instruction we have presented here is a realistic one for upper elementary teachers, and in this chapter our goal is to help you see what it would mean to adopt it in its full form. Full adoption will enable you to answer the two questions that are most important:

1. Under what conditions is this model reasonable for teachers?
2. Under what conditions is this model effective for students?

Because of the rhythm of schools, we present the answers within the framework of a school calendar. And because we tend to be systems thinkers, we present it with grade-level teams, rather than individual teachers, in mind.

SPRING: MAKE STRATEGIC CURRICULUM DECISIONS

There is a set of basic resources (see Figure 10.1) that is required to implement our model for coherent tiered instruction in upper elementary grades. Time must be allocated the entire year before implementation to select, purchase, and organize these resources. The first decision that will drive many others is the purchase or design of a core curriculum. The core curriculum must be consistent with research, which we have presented in this text through reference to Foorman et al.'s (2017) rubric. This rubric is meant for wide use and can be easily accessed online. You can use it in either or both of two ways: to provide an external blueprint for designing a core curriculum for your school (or district), or to evaluate the extent to which an externally designed curriculum is consistent with empirical evidence about reading and writing instruction.

There is certainly something to be said for designing a Tier 1 curriculum yourself. It allows free choice from the newest and best authentic texts, can be customized for the norms and traditions of a community, and can be modified as teachers and students use it. But do not minimize the time required to take on such a project. We know, because we've done it. Curriculum design for reading and writing requires full-time work for a team. If you don't have that time or team, you must use resources that are already developed.

There are resources available to help you to narrow the field so you can reasonably make informed choices. Let's start with some alphabet soup. First of all, the No Child Left Behind Act (NCLB) of 2001 has been fully replaced by the Every Student Succeeds Act (ESSA) of 2015. ESSA is a mechanism for states to receive federal funding. ESSA is less restrictive than NCLB but requires attention to high-quality instructional materials (HQIM). HQIM must be aligned to a state's standards. We have used the CCSS throughout this text, because new standards in states are more similar to it than different from it. You should use your own state's standards.

Resources	Reasoning
Core curriculum	A core curriculum consists of the scope, sequence, and general lesson plans that promote consistency among classrooms at the same grade level, and that direct text and vocabulary selection for Tier 1 instruction.
Shared reading and read-aloud texts	A complete classroom set of student copies of authentic, interesting, challenging narratives and informational texts will be essential for building vocabulary, text structure knowledge, comprehension strategy flexibility, understanding of complex sentence structures, and motivation to read. A rich set of single read-aloud copies of authentic, interesting, challenging narratives and informational texts will be essential for building vocabulary, text structure knowledge, comprehension strategy flexibility, understanding of complex sentence structures, and motivation to read.
Small-group sets of narratives and information texts for differentiated instruction	Small-group instruction for students with needs in fluency and comprehension and in vocabulary and comprehension will require multiple copies of texts. Teachers in the upper elementary grades can share these texts and the lesson plans they make for them if they are organized in a common library.
Organized classroom libraries of single titles	Wide, engaged reading of interesting and diverse texts can build vocabulary, background knowledge, knowledge of sentence and text structure, and positive attitudes toward reading and writing.
Multisyllabic decoding lessons	Students with needs in word recognition and fluency in the upper elementary grades will need to learn to attack complex words.
Access to intensive interventions	Students with needs in word recognition and fluency who do not respond to multisyllabic decoding instruction will need intensive instruction in single-syllable decoding and will not be able to accelerate their achievement sufficiently within short small-group rotations.

FIGURE 10.1. Resources required for differentiated instruction.

There are tools to help you make HQIM choices. To engage in the review locally, consider Foorman and colleagues' (2017) rubric. It will focus your attention to research. You can also use Educators Evaluating the Quality of Instructional Products (EQuIP). EQuIP is available for free online (*www.achieve.org*). It contains tools for evaluating lessons and unit and tasks. Achieve the Core also provides the Instructional Materials Evaluation Tool (IMET), which is also available for free online (*https://achievethecore.org*). If you would like to access completed reviews, visit EdReports (*www.edreports.org*). These reviews have their own rubrics, accessible at the site, and the reports themselves have extensive notes. States are also launching their own review processes. As an example, access the Louisiana reviews (*www.louisianabelieves.com*). Then check the state of Washington's OER reviews (*www.k12.wa.us/OER*). Check your own state's reviews, too, of course. It is likely that these open-access reviews will be available on the websites of many states' departments of education.

While the process of reviewing carefully at a district or school provides invaluable insight into the design of any curriculum, there is a tradeoff. Teachers certainly can do it if the district provides them ample time; in our experience, though, there is rarely time or money available. If adequate time and money are not available, it makes sense to review the work of other groups and teachers. We hope that adoption committees will resist the temptation to rely on the vendors themselves to do the convincing. Vendors have a vested, commercial interest in presenting their wares as panaceas to cure all ills.

Restriction of the curriculum to the most essential items in Figure 10.1 is strategic in many ways. We have worked in schools where teachers hoard old materials and pull them out when heads are turned. If those materials are truly better, then all students at a particular grade level should be using them; they should become the core curriculum. In reality, though, teachers tend to bring out these materials from force of habit or as a means to fill time. We prefer classrooms filled with books that are used for different purposes. For the teaching of reading, we emphasize connected reading rather than the skills-oriented tasks, which may be more appropriate for younger students. This emphasis saves teacher time and district money that would be wasted on trivial, low-level resources. It compels teachers to build classroom communities where students have the personal discipline, motivation, skills, and opportunity to build their literacy skills by reading and writing.

SUMMER: MAKE STRATEGIC ASSESSMENT AND GRADING DECISIONS

As we have argued in Chapter 4, very few assessments are actually needed to implement our model. What we have not mentioned there, however, is that we are often faced with schools or districts that are committed in theory to our differentiation model but simply cannot make the break from their previous assessment systems. We have seen the problems that this causes. First, too much assessment is incredibly wasteful in terms of both time and money. It can frustrate teachers as they see instructional time being devoted to exhaustive testing. Even worse, too much assessment causes confusion, especially when the assessments yield different results.

One nonstrategic assessment decision is the commitment to use weekly comprehension tests for the books or selections students are reading. Teachers initially tell us that they use them to assess the extent to which their students are learning the comprehension skills and strategies targeted for their grade level. The design of those tests, though, does not address this issue. Rather, when weekly tests assess students' understanding of a selection that has been read and discussed collaboratively across a week, we regard the test as a mere memory task and not a comprehension or strategy task. As a case in point, what if a student with intensive word recognition problems could earn a high score on that test after participating in shared reading and discussion across the week, but still could not actually read the core selection? Does this mean that reading comprehension does not require decoding and fluency skills? Our experience is that in many cases, these tests are used to generate inflated grades rather than to influence instruction for the next week. If this is the case, it may be better to craft a new system for generating grades and to save the time it takes to give and grade the core-embedded weekly assessments.

Another nonstrategic assessment decision is to use both external screening tests with strong psychometric properties *and* teacher-made district benchmark tests with no psychometric validation. Teacher-designed tests are important. They allow individual teachers to construct performance tasks that are directly related to their instruction, and the person who creates and interprets the test is the same one who provided the instruction and who will be providing instruction in the future. Such tests can influence instruction in important ways. We know that when we create tests ourselves, in our own university classes, they are sometimes flawed. That is, there are sometimes questions that almost no one answers correctly, and we assume this is because either we have taught poorly or students have tested poorly. We drop those questions from the mix for grades and for the next semester and reteach the material. The same applies to the teacher-generated tests, which often serve as district benchmarking. Because the items are not pilot-tested, they are subject to multiple sources of error. We believe that they should not be used to make high-stakes decisions across classrooms.

Another nonstrategic assessment decision we often face is that districts can be quick to add additional assessments but slow to remove old ones that no longer serve any useful purpose. One example is the use of informal reading inventories to group students on the basis of their reading levels after they read orally and answer a handful of comprehension questions. This approach, although time-honored, is fraught with measurement problems (Walpole & McKenna, 2006). Our system employs a more dependable approach. Students with adequate fluency receive instruction that builds vocabulary and comprehension. We assume that these students are of two types: (1) those with strong fluency and strong comprehension and vocabulary, and (2) those with strong fluency and weak comprehension and vocabulary. We assume that more gains will be realized for both types of readers by providing more challenging texts, because those texts provide more authentic opportunities for teachers to build both vocabulary and comprehension.

To truly adopt our model, then, many classrooms (and schools and districts) will have to reduce their assessment requirements considerably. Many will have to redo their report cards. They will have to think critically about the information yielded by each assessment and the decisions made because of it. This is a task, like curriculum selection, that is best performed before the school year starts, so that policies about curriculum selection and scheduling, administering, grading, and reporting to parents can be carefully thought out in advance.

EARLY FALL: MAKE STRATEGIC MANAGEMENT DECISIONS

If you were to adopt our differentiation model, you would need time in your schedule for Tier 1 instruction and time for differentiated instruction. During that differentiated time, you would have students spending some time with you and the other students in their group, and some time in independent work. In *Bookworms K–5 Reading and Writing*, Tier 1 shared reading and ELA instruction require 90 minutes of instructional time, and the differentiation described in this text requires an additional 45 minutes. During that time, students' independent work comprises the text-based written responses from their shared reading lessons and then a chance for self-selected reading from the classroom library.

To enact this model, the first 2 weeks of school are critical. It does not work to begin the year with only a whole-group model and then change quickly to a small-group differentiated model. Rather, you should begin with the end in mind. You have to teach your students to use the full differentiation period. First, think about setting up a classroom environment that communicates your goals to your students. Create an organization system for your classroom library that is both attractive and utilitarian. Set up areas on your whiteboards that are always used for the same purposes. Choose a chime or a bell to signal transitions between activities. Set up a computer logged on to an online dictionary, and teach children to use it. Post procedures for important daily activities on chart paper: choral reading, partner reading, choosing a book from the library, or writing an appropriate response. Post procedures for important cognitive activities on chart paper: graphic organizers, strategies for dividing words into syllables, syllable types, and common prefixes and suffixes. Post characteristics of genres that can help your students target their writing. Think about ways to reduce students' dependence on teachers to manage the classroom, and to encourage them instead to develop self-monitoring and management skills.

The most effective teachers take the time to explicitly instruct their students in the behaviors and procedures they expect (Brophy, 1983). For this reason, we suggest that even before your instruction is differentiated, you begin the year by establishing the procedures that will allow your students to maximize their time in meaningful literacy tasks. Doing so will allow you to maximize your time in teaching small groups. Before you engage in real differentiation, randomly assign the students in your class to groups of equal size. Then engage them in the procedures that will be essential to your instructional block. Figure 10.2 presents potential goals for the first days of school.

We actually believe that it is better to hold off on actual differentiated instruction until the procedures are comfortable both for you and for the students. It is better to spend more time on procedures than to begin differentiation with multiple distractions. If you are meeting with your class one-third at a time, you have a chance to conduct initial attitude and interest inventories, make personal book recommendations, gather book reviews that you can display in the classroom environment, and conduct fluency screenings. If students are writing in response to listening, you have the chance to collect initial natural writing samples that can provide useful insights into the students' skills and attitudes. If they use a composition book and date their daily responses, you will have an organized, concrete record that shows their progress across time. And if you use your first small-group meetings to gather the necessary assessment data, you can begin to differentiate before the first month of school has passed.

Teacher activity	Purpose
Read aloud from an engaging trade book.	• Set the expectation that listening and interacting are inherently interesting. • Prove to your students that they will learn interesting things from books.
Assign and model written responses.	• Establish a place and format for students to write their responses. • Teach the students that writing in response to listening will be a daily expectation.
Engage in cycles of choral, partner, and whisper reading.	• Establish comfortable, repetitive procedures that will not have to be reintroduced every day. • Build your students' reading stamina.
Meet with each of three groups while the other two groups either complete their written responses or read from the classroom library.	• Build the expectation that all students will be engaged in either reading or writing when you are working with a group. • Create signals and procedures for how students will switch from one activity to another. • Get to know your students as you talk with them in small groups.

FIGURE 10.2. Initial activities and their purpose.

LATER FALL: BUILD THE DIFFERENTIATION MODEL

You will know that you are ready to begin our differentiation model in the fourth or fifth grade when you can confidently sort your students into three potential groups: students who need work with fluency and multisyllabic decoding, students who need work with fluency and comprehension, and students who need to build vocabulary and comprehension. If you have students in all three categories, it is almost certain that the groups will be of unequal size. This cannot be helped. It is more important for each student to obtain the instruction that is needed than for the groups to be of uniform size. Alternatively, you may only have two of these three groups represented in your class. In this case, you can have larger groups or differentiate further by dividing the larger of your groups into two.

Although we have discussed word recognition, fluency, vocabulary, comprehension, and writing separately in previous chapters, we encourage you to look across the content for your differentiation time. Figure 10.3 shows each of the three groups across one instructional period. All students participate in your Tier 1 read-aloud or in process writing. All engage with you in Tier 1 word study, vocabulary development, fluency development, and comprehension work during shared reading. Then they begin their differentiation time, during which some students can receive intensive interventions outside of regular instruction, and the rest can have two segments of independent work and one segment of small-group instruction with you. One of those segments is always used to complete the written response to the day's shared reading. If students finish that work and their partner rereading or their silent reading, they will always be able to choose a book to read from the classroom library.

Tier 1 Shared Reading, Read-Aloud, and Writing Instruction for All			
MS/F	Written response	1. Multisyllabic decoding practice 2. Discussion of last section 3. Choral reading of new section	Partner reading of new section	
F/C	1. Discussion of last section 2. Choral reading of new section	Partner and whisper reading of new section	Written response	Tier 3 intensive interventions, inside or outside the classroom
V/C	Written response	Silent reading of new text section	1. Discussion of last section 2. Review previous vocabulary 3. Introduce new vocabulary 4. Provide comprehension focus	

FIGURE 10.3. A reasonable differentiation model. MS/F, multisyllabic decoding and fluency group; F/C, fluency and comprehension group; V/C, vocabulary and comprehension group.

The multisyllabic decoding and fluency group includes those students whose weakness in fluency is partially explained by an inability to divide and decode multisyllabic words. For that reason, they begin their small-group lesson with targeted multisyllabic decoding practice. For fluency, they read new text each day, with strong teacher support through choral reading. After their small-group lesson, they continue this fluency focus by rereading that day's selection with partners. The next day, in their small group, after multisyllabic decoding practice, they have a brief comprehension discussion before they begin the next segment in choral reading.

The fluency and comprehension group includes those students whose weakness in fluency seems to stem from a lack of reading experience or practice rather than from weak decoding skills. For that reason, they read and reread texts in addition to their shared reading selection. Like the multisyllabic decoding and fluency group, the fluency and comprehension group reads new text (a segment or chapter) each day, with strong teacher support through choral reading. After their small-group lesson, they continue this fluency focus by rereading that day's selection with partners. The next day, in their small group, they have a discussion before they begin the next segment in choral reading.

Students with no fluency problems do not need the support of choral, oral, or repeated readings. These students, moving up to the vocabulary and comprehension group, read additional texts. In this case, though, all of their small-group time is used to learn new vocabulary and to discuss the meaning of the texts. There is no need for teacher support for their reading, so they do it silently and independently, away from the teacher. They can use reading guides to prepare for their comprehension discussion. The teacher time is spent in supporting students' comprehension and vocabulary rather than modeling or supporting fluency.

Taken together, and listed like this, there seem to be few differences among the groups. In several senses, this is true: All three groups produce a daily written response to shared reading; all three groups discuss the additional book they are reading when they work with the teacher; and all three groups read on their own, away from the teacher. The differences, though, constitute the heart of differentiation.

The first difference is obvious. Only the multisyllabic decoding and fluency group engages in decoding practice during small-group time. All three groups have engaged in this practice as part of word study in shared reading, when the teacher has helped them identify syllable types in the vocabulary words, analyze the words, and list derivatives by adding prefixes and suffixes. These words, chosen for their meanings, will be unlikely to have much in common in terms of their structure. The additional small-group practice, though, includes practice with a list of words that are similar in structure.

The second difference is less obvious. The books that the three groups are reading may be different in their level of difficulty. We have used Lexiles to identify them, but you can also use the general idea of texts below, at, or above grade level. The multisyllabic decoding and fluency group may benefit from a slightly below-grade-level text, so that the decoding and fluency demands will not be overwhelming. The fluency and comprehension group can read a text at or near grade level. The vocabulary and comprehension group can read a text at grade level. In all three cases, the text can be narrative or informational.

The modes of reading are the same for the multisyllabic decoding and fluency group and the fluency and comprehension group. These students read chorally with the teacher, then reread with partners. The movement from choral to partner rereading is a gradual release of responsibility to the students. Within that gradual release, we embed repeated readings, a hallmark of all fluency-building programs. You should be able to see students becoming more confident and fluent across chapters, because many words are actually repeated within one book and then across books as the additional reading practice bears fruit.

When chapters in the book are too long to allow completion of choral reading within the time allotted, one of two solutions can be implemented. First, you can decide to simply break the chapter into sections, reading only as much as time allows. Second, you can decide to alternate days. On Day 1, you can do only the choral reading (with follow-up partner reading). Then on Day 2, students can discuss that section and have extra time for independent reading that day.

The vocabulary and comprehension group reads silently. These students have fluency work in the shared reading each day, and your assessments indicate that they are not struggling with fluency. Because they do not need additional fluency support, there is no reason for them to read out loud; they can read silently and independently. This also provides time for the teacher to thoroughly engage in comprehension and vocabulary support during small-group time.

The similarities among the groups are just as important as the differences. All three groups engage in discussion about the books that they are reading, sharing and deepening their comprehension. In all three cases, we favor inferential questions and prompts. There is no reason for the comprehension discussion in the multisyllabic decoding and fluency group to be less meaningful, although it may have to be shorter in order to accomplish the rest of the lesson in the time allowed. This will require that the teacher questions be even more thoughtful, so that they are not simply low-level questions.

Two final cautions: Do not make your groups of equal size, and do not force-fit your students into this grouping configuration. Use data to truly consider their needs. You may have three groups of multisyllabic decoding and fluency students. You may have two groups of vocabulary and comprehension students and one group of fluency and comprehension students. Over time, you should be aiming to reduce the number of students in the multisyllabic decoding and fluency group, and to increase the number in the vocabulary and comprehension group. But begin wherever the data lead you.

ALL YEAR: ENGAGE IN MEANINGFUL COLLABORATIONS

If your differentiation model is truly schoolwide, you and your colleagues can and should work together to do the planning necessary. The collaboration that will make differentiation easier (and the model truly schoolwide) is the lesson planning for the small-group texts. Of course, it is possible to plan for these lessons by staying one chapter ahead in all three groups. That is not ideal, though. It is better to have the whole book planned in advance. To do this, you would decide on a format for apportioning time, pick a group, and then write the lessons for an entire text. In your collaborative grade-level team, you would begin by planning for all three of your own groups, all reading different books. Then you would meet to discuss how those books are working. Once a group has finished a book, you could either plan a new one or use a set of plans that a colleague has already tried. Besides saving time, this system allows all teachers to talk about the books and the students, and to share insights they are gaining as they make differentiated instruction work for them. It also ensures that the students are all conversant in the same body of literature. Over time, a shared book room, with the plans already made, can be established. This will result in more text choices for everyone.

AN INVITATION

We invite you to be strategic about your curriculum, your assessments, and your management. We invite you to build your differentiation model so that it is comfortable for you and your students. We invite you to collaborate with your grade-level teammates to make lesson planning simpler. To assist you, we have created a set of sample materials to start with. In the appendices that follow this chapter, we provide what you need to get started.

In our experience, upper elementary teachers do not have an Informal Decoding Inventory and a set of multisyllabic decoding lessons, so we are providing them for you in Appendices E and F, respectively. There are directions for administering the Informal Decoding Inventory, beginning with multisyllabic words. Remember that you will only give the Multisyllabic subtest to those students who do not meet your fluency benchmark. Those who do well on the Informal Decoding Inventory will be assigned to the fluency and comprehension group; those who do poorly will be placed in the multisyllabic decoding and fluency group or in a Tier 3 intervention.

We have also included a set of text structure graphic organizers (Appendix H). All too often, the teaching of text structures is a rare component of instruction in the upper elementary grades (Beerwinkle, Wijekumar, Walpole, & Aguis, 2018). Graphic organizers like these can actually link all of the parts of your day. They can be used with read-alouds, shared reading, differentiated texts, and content area texts. They can be used to document comprehension and to plan writing. Again, use them however you like. When laminated and used as posters, graphic organizers can be used and reused to make notes about texts that you have read together. You can also create electronic versions that you can use and reuse interactively.

Finally, we present model lessons for each of our three groups in Appendices G and I. We have selected texts that differ in their reading level and that we think fourth- and fifth-grade students will enjoy. If you would like to use our lessons, obtain the books and give them a try. These lessons may help you to focus your attention on the management and procedural aspects of differentiation at first. They may also help you to see what we mean when we say that discussions should be targeted and inferential. Surely you may decide to jump in and plan your own lessons, but ours are provided as models if you want them.

We have enjoyed our visits to classrooms as we have been planning and writing this book. If differentiation is new to you, please know that we are committed to a model that is reasonable for teachers as well as effective for students. We are always humbled by our work with teachers who persevere regardless of the pressures they face. We hope that this book will make their work a tiny bit easier.

Reproducible Classroom Materials

Tier 1 Planning Templates

Shared Reading Planning Template

Activity	Description
Review: 5 minutes	
Word study (fiction): 5 minutes	Introduce two new words, with attention to syllable types, meanings, and derivatives.
Teach Tier 3 vocabulary (nonfiction): 5 minutes	Introduce Tier 3 words, using direct explanation, concept of definition (COD) charts, or semantic feature analysis (SFA) charts.
Fluency and comprehension instruction: 20–25 minutes	Set first purpose.
	Choral reading with comprehension strategy modeling.
	Revisit first purpose and set new purpose.
	Partner rereading.
Discussion: 5–10 minutes	
Assign text-based writing	

(continued)

Interactive Read-Aloud Planning Template for Nonfiction

Activity	Description
Review: 2 minutes	
Teach Tier 3 vocabulary (nonfiction): 5 minutes	Introduce Tier 3 words, using direct explanation, COD charts, or SFA charts.
Vocabulary and comprehension instruction: 10–12 minutes	Read aloud with frequent, planned stops to model comprehension strategies, define words in context, and ask inferential questions.
Sentence composing: 10 minutes	
Shared writing: 10 minutes	

(continued)

Interactive Read-Aloud Planning Template for Fiction

Activity	Description
Review: 2 minutes	
Vocabulary and comprehension instruction: 10–12 minutes	Read aloud with frequent, planned stops to model comprehension strategies, define words in context, and ask inferential questions.
Vocabulary instruction: 5 minutes	Teach two Tier 2 words.
Sentence composing: 10 minutes	
Shared writing: 10 minutes	

Sample Tier 1 Nonfiction Shared Reading Instruction

The lesson plans below bring concepts from this book together. This is a 7-day shared reading plan from *Bookworms K–5 Reading and Writing*. To see more open-access lessons of this type, please contact the publisher, Open Up Resources (*https://openupresources.org*). Each day's lesson requires 45 minutes.

The book required for this lesson, *Animal Cells and Life Processes* by Barbara Somervill, is a nonfiction text published in 2011 by Heinemann. The text is 48 pages, with rich illustrations and extensive opportunity for knowledge building. The Lexile for this text is 860L.

DAY 1

Word Study

Cells are the smallest units of life. An organ, like your heart, is also a unit of life, but it is not a cell. Cells have walls or membranes, a nucleus, and specific functions. Here are some examples: Your skin is made of skin cells; a plant is made of plant cells; some small living things, like bacteria, are each single cells.

Cells (closed) is a noun that means the smallest unit of life. All living things are made of cells. The adjective form is *cellular.*

Nu-cle-us (open, open, closed) is a noun that means center or most important part. Cells have a nucleus. The adjective form is *nuclear.*

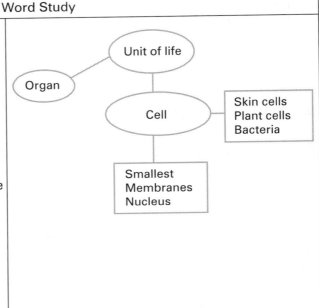

Discuss Text Structure

We are going to use a nonfiction text to learn about cells. Turn to the table of contents to see how the entire book is organized. Notice that all of the chapter titles are questions. Why do you think the author has chosen to organize her work this way? Let's turn to the glossary. How is it organized? How is the index different from the glossary?

We are going to read the first chapter today, but it will be helpful if you look at it before we read. What text features has the author chosen to include? When you read nonfiction, you have to make some choices about the order that you will use. I tend to think it is best to read the running text first for two pages, and then to go back and read any boxes and captions before turning to the next page.

(continued)

Provide a First Focus
[pp. 4–7] Pay attention to information that is truly new to you.

Choral Reading
[p. 4. You have just lost millions of cells.] We have enough information to make an inference here. We know that a single drop of blood is very small. The text says that the drop contains millions of cells. So we can figure out that a cell is a very tiny thing.

Provide a New Focus for Rereading in Partners
This time, stop after each heading. Reread the heading and see whether you can provide a simple answer to the question.

Comprehension Discussion
1. You know what a microscope is. What does it mean to say that a cell is *microscopic?* 2. Why would an adult have to have more cells than a small child? 3. Where did Robert Hooke first see cells? Why did he get to name them? 4. What does it mean to say that every living thing is made up of one or more cells? 5. Look at the boldfaced words on page 6. Each one is followed by information in parentheses. What does that mean? 6. Compare the information in parentheses to information in the glossary. 7. Why do you think the microscope was called *compound?*

Written Response
1. Use *cells* and *nucleus* in super sentences. 2. Take notes for this chapter. When we study something new, it is helpful to write a summary of information in your own words. Write each question in the chapter subheadings, and then write a short answer that will help you to remember the information. Reread, but then use your own words.

DAY 2

Review Written Responses
Pair-share written responses.

Word Study
Today we are going to read about cell parts, or *organelles.* I can see two parts in this word. *Organ-elles.* I know that an organ is a part of my body, like my heart. The suffix *-elle* means smaller. So I can figure out that an organelle is like an organ, but smaller. The names of the organelles may seem challenging, but we can get the pronunciations right if we use our syllable types. Dividing new words into syllables is the key to pronouncing them.

(continued)

nu-cle-us
Gol-gi body
cy-to-plasm
cell mem-brane
mi-to-chon-dri-a
vac-u-ole
ri-bo-some
en-do-plas-mic re-tic-u-lum

Or-gan (*r*-controlled, closed) is a noun meaning a group of cells that accomplishes a function. Your heart is an organ that pumps blood. Your skin is an organ that protects your body.

Or-gan-elle (*r*-controlled, closed, suffix) is a noun meaning a part of a cell that has a specific function.

Discuss Text Structure
There is a lot of information in this chapter, but it will help to look first at the structure. It looks like the author is just listing. Each of the organelles is a subheading, and there is a short paragraph underneath. So we will learn about one at a time.
Provide a First Focus
[pp. 8–13] For this first reading, try to get a general picture of the organelles.
Choral Reading
[p. 9, after looking at the illustrations] These illustrations really don't make sense to me yet. I have to self-monitor. I can see that there is a nucleus in both drawings, but the other organelles are only in one drawing or the other. I am going to have to read on to see if all cells have all of these organelles, or if some just have fewer.
Provide a New Focus for Rereading in Partners
This time, stop after each heading. Reread the heading and see whether you can come up with a simple description.
Comprehension Discussion
1. Why do you think cells have to work 24 hours a day? 2. Why is it helpful that the cell and the nucleus are surrounded by membranes? 3. Some people say that a cell is like a city. Let's look at each organelle and see if we can think of a part of a city that does a similar job.
Written Response
1. Use *organ* and *organelle* in super sentences. 2. Take notes for this chapter. Write each organelle's name, then a simple description. At the end, try to draw a cell and label its parts.

(continued)

DAY 3

Share Written Responses
Pair-share written responses.

Word Study

This section is about a body system called the *digestive* system. Other body systems are the *circulatory* system and the *nervous* system. Characteristics of the digestive system are that it uses organs (mouth, stomach, intestines) to break food into chemicals that cells need. Examples of those chemicals are carbohydrates, nucleic acids, proteins, and fats.

Di-gest-ive (open, closed, suffix) is an adjective that means having to do with breaking down food into chemicals. Our mouth, stomach, and intestines are all parts of the digestive system. *Digest* is the verb form. *Digestion* is the noun form.

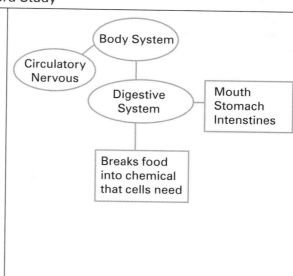

Discuss Text Structure
This next section is about food processes. It will help you to understand it if you know that the author is using some sequences of events. She is telling what happens in order. Try to look for number and order words (*first, second, then, finally*). Those help you to see the sequence and keep track of it.

Provide a First Focus
[pp. 14–23]
Be on the lookout for the sequence of events.

Choral Reading
[p. 15]
I see that the author is trying to help us know how much food different animals need to eat. She is telling us in *kg.*, or *kilograms.* We usually think about food in units of pounds or cups. I know that a kilogram is a metric unit of measurement in England and many other countries, and this book was originally published in England. So, as Americans, we have to do some math to understand this chart. One kilogram is 2.2 pounds, so we have to multiply.

Provide a New Focus for Rereading in Partners
This time, stop after each subheading and discuss the sequence of events. Remember that you can always reread if you aren't sure.

(continued)

Comprehension Discussion
1. Look at the table on page 15. Which animal needs to eat the most food each day?
2. Why do you think some animals can get all of their nutrients from one type of food and others need different foods?
3. What happens when you chew food?
4. How is a molecule different from a cell?
5. What is a nutrient?
6. What is the difference between a simple and a complex carbohydrate?
Written Response
1. Since this section is a sequence of events, it makes sense to use that sequence in your notes. Number and list the events that happen as you eat food and it becomes food for your cells.

DAY 4

Share Written Responses
Pair-share written responses.
Word Study
Today we are going to learn about unicellular organisms. An organism is a living thing. We can figure out what unicellular organisms are by breaking the word into its prefix, root, and suffix. The root is *cell.* We know what that is. The prefix is *uni-. Uni-* means one. A unicorn has one horn. A unicycle has one wheel. So a unicellular organism must have just one cell.
Or-gan-ism (*r*-controlled, closed, closed) is a noun that means a living thing. Human beings are organisms, but so are bacteria. We can see that the root word *organ* is used in many other terms.
Discuss Text Structure
This section is a simple listing. We are going to learn about three different unicellular organisms. Look at the headings and see what they are before we start to read.
Provide a First Focus
[pp. 24–27]
Think about how these unicellular organisms are similar to one another.
Choral Reading
[p. 24. Single-celled organisms are not that different from an elephant.]
I am going to have to ask myself a question here. How can that be? I know that an elephant is a large animal. I know now that animals are made of many cells. How can something made of many cells be not very different from something with only one cell? I am going to have to read on to find out.

(continued)

Provide a New Focus for Rereading in Partners
Now think about how the organisms are different. Stop after you read about each one and discuss it.

Comprehension Discussion
1. Why does the author compare a single-celled organism to an elephant? 2. Look up the word *protist* in the glossary. 3. How can you remember what an amoeba is? 4. How is a euglena different from an amoeba? Contrast these two organisms. 5. Why does a paramecium need to live in a pond?

Written Response
1. Use *organism* and *digestive* in super sentences. 2. For notes today, list the three organisms, and provide a brief description of each in your own words.

DAY 5

Share Written Response
Pair-share written responses.

Word Study
We are going to learn about some of the different cells that make up the human body. It will help if we use a chart to track them. *Pig-ment* (closed, closed) is a noun that means natural color. Many plants have green pigment. Paint is often made from pigments. *Re-pro-duce* (open, closed, VC-*e*) is a verb that means make another copy of. The prefix *re-* means again, and the root *produce* means make. Living things need to reproduce. We can also reproduce nonliving things, like pictures, by copying them. The noun form is *reproduction.*

	Carry things	Protect us	Have pigment	Reproduce
White blood				
Red blood				
Skin cells				
Nail cells				
Hair cells				
Neurons				
Bone cells				
Barrier cells				

(continued)

177

Discuss Text Structure
This next section uses the structure of compare and contrast. Remember that when you compare and contrast, you have to pay attention to how things are the same (compare) and how they are different (contrast).

Provide a First Focus
[pp. 28–33] Look for how a human is similar to and different from an amoeba.

Choral Reading
[p. 33. Most organs that deal with digestion have barrier cells.] I can synthesize here. We learned that cells have membranes on the outside, and that the nucleus also has a membrane. We learned that skin cells protect the body. We learned that organs have barrier cells. So I can put these things together to say that living things have many ways to control movement of chemicals and foods and waste.

Provide a New Focus for Rereading in Partners
This time, fill in the chart. Stop after each cell is described. Put a plus if the characteristic applies, a minus if it doesn't, and a question mark if you can't tell. Add a few more columns.

Comprehension Discussion
1. Why is it important that all living things have a way to reproduce? 2. Why do you think blood has three components? 3. Describe the process of skin cell renewal. 4. How are neurons different in shape from blood cells? 5. Why is the work of neurons important? 6. Why can't old bone cells just flake off like skin cells? 7. Why do you think the digestive organs need barrier cells?

Written Response
1. Use *pigment* and *reproduce* in super sentences. 2. Use your completed chart to write a sentence about each of the cell types: 　A _____ is a type of cell that _____ , but doesn't _____ .

DAY 6

Share Written Responses
Pair-share written responses.

Word Study
This section ends with a description of the two ways that cells divide: mitosis and meiosis. These words are easy to read by using syllable types. If you use this chart, it will also be easy for you to understand what they mean.

(continued)

Mei-o-sis (vowel team, open, closed) is the process of cell division that involves eggs and sperm. Some organisms reproduce with meiosis.

Mi-to-sis (open, open, closed) is the process of cell division that means division into two exact copies. Some organisms reproduce with mitosis.

	Type of cell division	Creates a full copy of DNA	Creates a half copy of DNA	Unites with another half copy of DNA
Meiosis				
Mitosis				

Discuss Text Structure

This next section is really about how cells inside organisms know when to produce more cells. There are two parts: How does the cell know when the organism needs more cells? And how are those cells formed? If you keep those two questions in mind, you will be able to remember more of the information in this section.

Provide a First Focus

[pp. 34–39]

Look for all of the amazing things that cells help organisms to do.

Choral Reading

[p. 34. Cells send messages day and night to keep an animal's body in good condition.]

That doesn't make sense to me. I need to ask myself how a cell can send a message without being able to use any words or language. There must be other ways to do it. I'll have to keep that question in my mind.

Provide a New Focus for Rereading in Partners

This time, fill in your mitosis/meiosis chart. Stop and talk about each decision.

Comprehension Discussion

1. How do you think cells can send messages?
2. Why does sweat help you cool off?
3. Why is it important that some cells can repair themselves?
4. How do your blood cells work together to make sure that you have enough blood?
5. Why do organisms need genes in order to grow and develop?
6. How does meiosis help you to inherit traits from both your father and your mother?

Written Response

1. Use your mitosis/meiosis chart to write a good definition for each.
2. Why do humans need to use both meiosis and mitosis?

(continued)

DAY 7

Share Written Response
Pair-share written responses.

Word Study
Have a vocabulary assessment.

Discuss Text Structure
The author is giving us this last bit of information today. We can use the question and answer structure to keep track of it.

Provide a First Focus
[pp. 40–43] Think about how important it is to get waste out of cells and out of your body.

Choral Reading
[p. 41. 8 240 ml glasses of water a day.] I remember that this author is British and is using metric measurements. I think I know enough to guess how much 240 ml is without using a calculator. I know that we are supposed to drink 8 glasses of water a day, and a glass of water is usually a cup, or 8 ounces. A cup is the amount of milk in a school milk carton. So we must need about 8 of those a day.

Provide a New Focus for Rereading in Partners
Stop this time after each subsection, and see if you can answer the question in your own words. Remember to reread if you need to.

Comprehension Discussion
1. Why is water so important to life? 2. Why do some animals need to drink more water than others? 3. Let's go back to page 8 and reread the descriptions of each organelle. Now we can think about how they are involved in managing the body's waste. 4. Let's read the glossary. It will help us to remember all of the new words we have learned in this book.

Written Response
1. For notes today, write the subheading questions and answers in your own words.

Sample Tier 1 Interactive Read-Aloud Instruction

The lesson plans below bring concepts from this book together. This is a 27-day inter-active read-aloud plan from *Bookworms K–5 Reading and Writing*. To see more open-access lessons of this type, please contact the publisher, Open Up Resources (*https://openupresources.org*). Each day's lesson requires 45 minutes.

The book required for this lesson, *Alabama Moon* by Watt Key, is a fictional coming-of-age text first published in 2006 by Farrar Straus Giroux and republished in 2010 by Square Fish (a Macmillan imprint). The text is 320 pages, with a Lexile of 720L. We include this sample plan because this particular text has been the hands-down favorite in *Bookworms K–5 Reading and Writing*.

DAY 1: CHAPTERS 1 AND 2

Read-Aloud

As we begin our book, think about the main character's responsibilities. I will give you a chance to write about them later.

[Chapter 1, after: But now Pap was dead and things were not the same.] What do you think about the main character? He was only 10 years old, and he was burying his father alone.

Why do you think Pap told this story about death?

[After: He'd said the government was after us ever since I could remember.]

I can make a connection here. We know that these two were living out in the wilderness alone. Now it says that Pap hated the government. I know that some few people who hate government live outside of it, so that they don't have to pay taxes or follow laws. I think that Pap must have been like that.

[Chapter 2, after: If they sold out to smaller landowners, we'd likely be found.]

Why was it a problem that the land had been sold?

[After: "You're too old to read out loud anymore."]

Why do you think Pap was treating the narrator differently?

[After: "What do you two have for me?"]

What does the author do so that we can learn the main characters' names?

Teach Tier 2 Words

One of the words from our book today was *stoop*. What word? *Stoop* means to bend your head down and to the side so that you can get under something. [Demonstrate!] You might have to stoop to get into a cave. In our book, it says that Pap had to stoop

(continued)

to enter their shelter. I suspect that Watt Key included this detail to help us picture how unusual the shelter was. *Stoop* means to bend over. You can use that word: "I had to stoop when I _____ because _____." "Older people seem to stoop more because _____." What word?

Another word from our book today was *reflection*. What word? *Reflection* means throwing back light or sound. You can see your reflection in the mirror. An echo is a kind of reflection of sound. In our book, it says that they couldn't carry anything shiny around outside to avoid a reflection being seen from a plane. I suspect Watt Key meant to tell us that Pap was really careful, because someone spotting a reflection from a plane would be very unlikely. *Reflection* means throwing back light or sound. You can use that word: "I look in a _____ to see my reflection." "I looked in a pond and saw a reflection of _____." What word?

Sentence Composing

Expand:

Tree roots had come down into the shelter.

Let's add two phrases: one starting with *where,* and another starting with *when.*

Imitate:

We walked back up the road and into the forest.

We walked back _____ and _____.

I've removed two prepositional phrases that tell where. Let's substitute others. Start one with *down,* and the second with *under.* Then we'll come up with others.

Text-Based Writing

Write about the main character's responsibilities. Remember, he was just 10 years old. Was this fair?

DAY 2: CHAPTER 3

Read-Aloud

There is an interesting word in this chapter that gives a really important clue about Pap's motivations. It's *homesteading*. Homesteading was a practice in the early days of the settlement of the United States. People could have land for free if they would build homes and farms. Homesteading is not a common way to get land today, but some people do it in places with very few people.

As I read, think about whether Pap loved Moon. You can write your opinion later.

[After: I'd always wanted to do it again.]

If it had been winter for 2 months, what had changed? Why was the time important?

[After: . . . we bound his leg with the leather shoelaces from my moccasins.]

(continued)

I can make an inference here. In the last chapter, it said that things started to go bad the summer before Pap's accident, because the new owner started building the house. Now it says that Pap broke his leg. That must have been the accident.

[After: He didn't make any noise because it was nighttime.]

What does the author mean by "white-knuckle"?

[After: "Somethin' like this leg won't heal."]

Why was Pap not going to get better? Why did he make Moon review his reasons for living in the woods?

Why did Pap want Moon to travel until he found another group of people living in the woods? Do you think this was a good plan?

Teach Tier 2 Words

One of the words from our book today was *butchered*. What word? *Butchered* means cut up for meat. All of the meat that we buy in the supermarket has been butchered so that only the healthy parts are there. In our book, Moon's chores included skinning and butchering animals that he caught in traps. He did that so he could sell the meat. This was just one of Moon's skills. *Butcher* means to cut up meat. You can use that word: "I had to butcher a _____." "I watched a hunter butcher a _____." What word?

One of the words from our book today was *routine*. What word? *Routine* means a set order for doing things. We have a routine in the classroom. It helps us to organize our day. You probably have a morning routine to make sure that you are ready for school on time. In our book, it says that Moon tried to keep his regular routine when Pap was sick, but then it got too hard. I suspect Watt Key meant to tell us that even though Moon had lots of survival skills, he wasn't ready to be alone. *Routine* means a set order for doing things. You can use that word: "I need a routine for _____." "My routine for _____ changed because _____." What word?

Sentence Composing

Imitate:

Even when Pap let us burn it all night, the heat was barely enough to keep our breath from streaming in front of our faces.

Even when Pap let us burn it all night, the heat was barely enough _____.

I have removed a series of prepositional phrases that all work together. Let's change the meaning by adding one or more different prepositional phrases.

Expand:

How will I get answers from the smoke?

I think we need to add more about what kind of answers and what kind of smoke. We can just add an adjective in front of *answers.* We can add a phrase after *smoke* beginning with that.

(continued)

Text-Based Writing

Do you think that Pap loved Moon? Write and tell why or why not.

DAY 3: CHAPTERS 4 AND 5

Read-Aloud

In these next chapters, we are going to get another view of the life that Pap and Moon had. There are times when children are left without a parent, and we have families who are willing to take children into their homes so that they won't be alone.

As I read, think about Mr. Abroscotto. You'll get a chance later to write from his perspective.

[Chapter 4, after: Love, Moon] Why do you think Moon wrote the letter? Why do you think the author chose to put the letter in this chapter?

The text says that Moon's parents were Mr. and Mrs. Oliver Blake. But Pap told Mr. Abroscotto that his name was George. I am going to keep this question in my mind as I read on: What was Pap's real name?

[After: . . . and stacked them beside the shelter.]

Why did Moon throw out the dead raccoons? Why didn't he save the skins?

[Chapter 5, after: ". . . didn't want you comin' after a doctor."]

How would you describe Mr. Abroscotto's reaction to Pap's death?

[After: ". . . and find these people on your own?"]

What did he think of Moon's plan to travel to Alaska?

[After: "I'm gonna turn you loose now, okay?"]

Why did Moon attack Mr. Abroscotto?

Why was Moon running for the trees at the end of the chapter?

Teach Tier 2 Words

One of the words from our book today was *storage*. What word? *Storage* means space available for keeping things. Our classroom has a storage area for books and supplies. In our book, Moon took Pap's personal storage, which was a locked metal box. *Storage* means space for keeping things. You can use that word: "I need more storage for my _____." "My mother puts _____ into storage." What word?

One phrase from our book today was *sense of reality*. What phrase? *Sense of reality* means the ability to make good plans that make sense. Sometimes I lose my sense of reality when I plan a science experiment. It takes much longer than I thought it would. You probably have wanted something too expensive because you didn't have a clear sense of reality. In our book, Mr. Abroscotto was worried about Moon's sense of reality because he didn't think it was likely that Moon could travel alone to Alaska and find homesteaders.

(continued)

Sense of reality means the ability to make good plans that make sense. You can use that phrase: "I increased my sense of reality by _____." What phrase?

Sentence Composing

Expand:

I would have nightmares if I slept.

Let's add a reason beginning with *because.* When we start a clause with *because,* it's a fragment on its own, but it can be added to a complete sentence at either the beginning or the end.

Combine:

There were two coons.

They were dead.

They had stiff hides.

They had matted hides.

Let's think about how the first two sentences are related. What does the pronoun *they* represent? So how could we combine those two sentences?

There were two dead coons.

Let's take the third sentence and turn it into a prepositional phrase.

There were two dead coons with stiff hides.

Now what information is added with the very last sentence?

Text-Based Writing

Put yourself in Mr. Abroscotto's shoes. What do you think he should have done? Give your reasons.

DAY 4: CHAPTER 6

Read-Aloud

In this chapter, we'll learn more about Moon's character. A good author helps us get to know a character by describing the character's thoughts and actions. As I read, think about how things changed for Moon in the space of just one day.

After we read today, I'll ask you to write a letter from Moon to Pap. Start thinking about what you might say.

[After: . . . so that no one would see the smoke.]

This action tells us a lot about the kind of person Moon was. Why did Moon burn the letter?

(continued)

[After: . . . until I was shaking and crying.]

Remember that we also learn about a character by reading about thoughts and feelings. How did Moon feel?

[After: . . . then ran on again beneath the tall pines.]

How did Moon feel now?

[After: . . . I almost closed my eyes while I chewed.]

How did Moon feel now?

[After "Interesting."]

What new information have we learned about Moon's life? Share it with your partner.

[After ". . . than that constable I met yesterday."]

Let's take a vote. Did Mr. Wellington do the right thing? Why?

[After: "We'll take him to the home and get him cleaned up."]

I have enough details to make a visual image. We know that Moon had been out in the woods for 8 years. We know that he had clothes made of animal skins. We know that he and Pap had no bathroom or laundry. The text says that Moon smelled and needed a haircut. I can picture a boy who was very dirty, who was dressed in animal skins, and who looked wild. Can you?

[After: "Gyaa!" he yelled as he jumped away.]

Why do you think Moon threw up?

Let's take another vote. Do you think Moon did the right thing? Why?

Teach Tier 2 Words

One of the words from our book today was *clutching*. What word? *Clutching* means grabbing tightly or quickly. If someone tried to take something from you, you might clutch it. In our book, Moon ran through the woods, scared, clutching tree roots to climb. He was clutching them so that he could keep moving quickly. *Clutching* means grabbing tightly or quickly. You can use that word: "When I woke up, I was clutching _____." "I saw a girl clutching _____." What word?

Another of the words from our book today was *dwelling*. What word? A *dwelling* is a place where people live. A house is a type of dwelling. A teepee is a type of dwelling. In our book, it says that the surveyors had found a primitive dwelling. They were calling Moon's shelter a primitive dwelling. That means that it was not very comfortable, but people could live there. A *dwelling* is a place where people live. You can use that word: "I learned about dwellings that _____." "I saw a _____ dwelling." What word?

Sentence Composing

Expand:

I hugged my knees together.

(continued)

Let's add a reason beginning with *because.* Remember that when we start a clause with *because,* it's a fragment on its own, but it can be added to a complete sentence at either the beginning or the end.

Combine:

My door opened.

Mr. Gene grabbed me by the shoulder.

He shook me gently.

These are three events that happened in a particular order. As we combine these, let's be sure to choose linking words that tell our reader what that order was.

We could use *first, then,* and *finally.*

Text-Based Writing

Think about Moon's situation now. Write a letter from Moon to Pap, providing details about what happened to him and how he felt about it.

DAY 5: CHAPTERS 7 AND 8

Read-Aloud

This next section is still action-packed. To understand it, you really have to think about the events from Moon's point of view. Remember that he was only 10 years old and had lived his whole life away from other people.

After we read today, I'll ask you to write a short paragraph summarizing the events to this point.

[Chapter 7, after: . . . travel that direction in less than half a day.]

What did it mean to say that the closest paved road was "three miles to a bird"?

[After: . . . and it reminded me to get on my way again.]

Why did it take Moon so much time to reach the road?

[After: . . . and then looked over at the wheelbarrow.]

I can make an inference here. It says that Moon recognized the police car from pictures. That means that he had never seen one before. That must have been because he had lived in the woods since he was 2, and was never on the road or in a car where he could see one. His father must have shown him pictures so that he could always hide from police.

[Before beginning to read, after inference above.]

What does it mean that the policeman was "like a flared turkey"?

[After: . . . I heard him splat in the mud behind me and felt my ankle gripped again.]

Why did Moon try to escape again?

(continued)

[After: "I hope I busted those sunglasses good, too." I said.]

Let's vote. Was the constable's reaction appropriate? Why?

[Chapter 8, after: . . . and I could tell he was nervous about something.]

Why do you think Moon described the policeman's clothes as tight?

[After: . . . a sink with running water and a flush toilet.]

Why was jail the best place that Moon had ever been?

[After: "Maybe two at once."]

Do you think Moon's thinking was realistic? Why?

Why did Moon say, "Never mind"?

Teach Tier 2 Words

One of the words from our book today was *juvenile center*. What word? A *juvenile center* is like a jail for people who are under 18. It is less strict than a regular jail, and it has a school in it, but the people are still locked inside. In our book, it says that Moon might be sent to a juvenile center. A *juvenile center* is like a jail for people who are under 18. You can use that word: "I will never go to a juvenile center because _____." "I imagine a juvenile center would be _____." What word?

One of the words from our book today was *assaulting*. What word? *Assaulting* means attacking. If you assault someone, you are trying to hurt him. Assaulting someone is a crime. In our book, Earle said that Moon might be charged with assaulting a police officer. That is a serious crime. *Assaulting* means attacking. You can use that word: "If I saw someone assaulting another person, I would _____." "Assaulting someone is bad because _____." What word?

Sentence Composing

Combine:

I made a last desperate leap to get away.

I wasn't able to break his hold.

Are these two sentences two related facts? If so, we should combine with a comma plus *and.* If they are contrasting, we should combine with a comma plus *but.*

Imitate:

I figured the whole outside world was just what Pap had warned me about.

Let's change this into a direct quotation. What could Pap have actually said? Let's figure out something that would make sense, and then we can punctuate it.

(continued)

Text-Based Writing

Write a paragraph that tells the main events of the story so far. Remember that when you write a summary, you need to decide what's important and what's not. You include only the most important facts.

DAY 6: CHAPTERS 9 AND 10

Read-Aloud

We're going to read two chapters today. The first one is about Sanders and Moon. You will see that Sanders had a prejudice. A *prejudice* is a feeling about a whole group of people. He was prejudiced against people he called "white trash." These were poor white families who had to rent their houses and couldn't find jobs.

The second chapter is about Moon's first transfer into the juvenile center. Do you remember what that phrase means?

After we read today, I'll ask you to speculate about what life would be like for Moon in juvenile detention.

[Chapter 9, after: "You didn't make it past 8th grade, did you, Sanders?"]

Why did Sanders treat Moon so poorly?

[After: "At least put some shoes and a jacket on the kid!" Obregon called after us.]

Why did Obregon stick up for Moon?

[After: "Pap gave me that rifle!"]

Why wouldn't Moon get his rifle back?

[After: "Seein' you in and out of jail all your life."]

I can make a connection here. It says that Sanders thought that he would see Moon in and out of jail all his life. I know that kids who have not gone to school and don't have parents to take care of them have a hard time finding jobs, so they might commit crimes.

[After: "The hell I don't. I've seen him!"]

Why was Sanders so negative about Pap?

[After: . . . with pee flowing down my leg.]

Let's vote. Do you think Sanders was right to squeeze Moon? Why?

[After: "That's white trash," Sanders said.]

What did it mean when Sanders asked whether his granddaddy had left him the land? What did that reveal about his own feelings about work?

[Chapter 10, after: I didn't reply.]

Who were the people asking Moon questions when he got out of the car?

[After: "What size shoes you wear?"]

(continued)

What do you think the special color meant?

[After: "You don't look too mean to me."]

Why do you think the TV said that Moon was mean as a snake?

What did Moon mean when he said he wouldn't talk about it?

Teach Tier 2 Words

One of the words from our book today was *militia*. What word? A *militia* is a kind of army of people who group together. People who are living together in the woods might form a militia. A militia is not made to protect a country, but to protect itself. In our book, Sanders called Moon "militia trash." He meant that as an insult, but Moon didn't know what the word meant. A *militia* is a kind of army. You can use that word: "A militia would need _____." "A militia would be _____." What word?

Another of the words from our book today was *gristle*. What word? *Gristle* means the tough, dry part of meat. We don't like to eat gristle. In our book, it says that Moon bit Sanders like he was made of gristle. I suspect Watt Key meant to tell us that Moon bit him as hard as he could. *Gristle* means the tough, dry part of meat. You can use that word: "Gristle tastes _____." "I don't like gristle because _____." What word?

Sentence Composing

Expand:

Soon we came to a closet, where we stopped.

Let's add a phrase beginning with *because.* We will be telling why we stopped. Remember that a phrase that begins with *because* can be added to the beginning or the end of a sentence, but it is not a complete sentence on its own.

Imitate:

They say you're mean as a snake.

Mean as a snake is a simile, because it is comparing a person to a snake. It's a common descriptive phrase. Why would snakes be especially mean? Why do you think the author chose this particular simile?

Let's imitate by changing the animal first, and then by changing both the adjective and the noun.

They say you're mean as a _____.

They say you're _____ as a _____.

Text-Based Writing

Moon had never had any friends. What do you think life would be like for him in juvenile detention? Explain your reasoning.

(continued)

DAY 7: CHAPTERS 11 AND 12

Read-Aloud

Today we get to see how different people treated Moon inside the juvenile center. Think about what their motivations might be. Motivations are the reasons why characters act the way that they do. Authors create characters with specific motivations so that we can anticipate their actions.

After we read today, I'll ask you to write a letter to Pap from Moon about life in prison. Be thinking about Moon's perspective.

[Chapter 11, after: Mr. Carter stood there holding a club.]

Why did Moon and Hal get into the fight?

[After: ". . . said she'll ring the upper bell in 10 minutes."]

Why did Mr. Carter only punish Hal?

[After: "Look down and shut your eyes."]

Why didn't Moon recognize the prayer?

[Chapter 12, after: . . . and brought Pap's box from the floor and set it on the desk.]

Why do you think Mr. Gene met with Moon?

[After: . . . before he could go touch the shelter and get back.]

How do you think Moon felt when the kids were asking him questions about his life?

Think back over today's chapter. Now it's your turn to ask a question. Think of a good one and raise your hand.

Teach Tier 2 Words

One of the phrases from our book today was *property of the state*. What phrase? *Property of the state* means something that belongs to the government instead of to a private person. Highways are property of the state. In our book, Mr. Gene told Moon he would be property of the state unless a relative came. He meant that the state would take care of him in some sort of prison until he was 18. He meant that kids can't live alone. *Property of the state* means something that belongs to the government instead of to a private person. You can use that phrase: "If someone said I was property of the state, I would feel _____." What phrase?

Another phrase from our book today was *foster home*. What phrase? A *foster home* is a real family that agrees to take care of another child who has no parents. Foster parents take children who are property of the state so that they don't have to live in juvenile facilities. In our book, Mr. Gene said that Moon might get to live in a foster home if he was lucky. A *foster home* is a real family that agrees to take care of another child who has no parents. You can use that word: "A foster home would be important if _____." "Foster homes can be special because _____." What phrase?

(continued)

Sentence Composing

Combine:

I took one more quick bite.

Then I got up.

Then I returned my plate.

This is a sequence of events. Let's choose linking words that make the sequence very clear to our reader.

Combine:

Some of the boys mumbled complaints.

They made their way back to their beds.

This is not a sequence of events. These two things were happening at the same time. We will have to choose different linking words here to be precise about that.

Text-Based Writing

Write a letter to Pap from Moon about life in prison. Make sure to include both events and facts, and also feelings.

DAY 8: CHAPTERS 13 AND 14

Read-Aloud

We have a sense now of a set of characters. Let's think of some details that would help us describe them. Moon we know. What about Mr. Carter? Mr. Gene? Hal? Kit?

Given what we know so far about the characters, setting, and events, what do you think the problem was?

As I read, think about Moon's escape plan. I'll ask you to write about it later.

[Chapter 13, after: . . . he was thinking about the deerskin hat.]

What did Kit's actions reveal about him?

[Chapter 14, after: . . . and smiled back at them.]

Why did the boys laugh at Moon when he came into the trailer?

[After: . . . she asked suspiciously.]

Why was Mrs. Crutcher suspicious?

[After: . . . learning some things in here.]

Why didn't Mrs. Crutcher believe that Moon would be leaving?

[After: "Here comes Mr. Carter."]

Let's vote. Do you think Moon would be punished for hitting Hal? Why?

(continued)

192

Now that Moon had beaten Hal twice, I have to keep a question in my mind. I know that Hal was a bully and everyone was afraid of him. I know that Moon was not afraid and wouldn't back down. So how would they be able to live together?

Teach Tier 2 Words

One of the words from our book today was *motioned*. What word? To *motion* means to move your hands to make a signal. You might motion to greet someone with a wave or to call someone over to you. In the book, Mrs. Broomstead motioned for Moon to come into the kitchen, and then to sit down. To *motion* means to move your hands to make a signal. You can use that word: "When I want you to _____, I motion." "In our classroom, the motion _____ means _____." What word?

One of the words from our book today was *jittery*. What word? *Jittery* means anxious and wiggly. You might be jittery if you are scared. In our book, Moon was jittery when the teacher asked him to talk about himself. I think he was jittery because everyone was looking at him and he was embarrassed. *Jittery* means anxious and wiggly. You can use that word: "I was jittery because _____." "If you eat too much _____, you might feel jittery." What word?

Sentence Composing

Expand:

Standing around Hal.

This is a sentence fragment. How can we expand it to make it a complete sentence?

Combine:

My eyes searched for a stick.

There was none nearby.

Let's think about whether these are two related ideas or two contrasting ideas. If they are related, we use *and.* If they are contrasting, we use *but.*

Text-Based Writing

Moon said he had discovered part of his escape plan. What do you think he meant?

DAY 9: CHAPTERS 15 AND 16

Read-Aloud

In these next chapters, we learn a lot about Moon's skills and character. Think about how independent he was.

After we read today, I'll ask you to write a summary of the book so far. You'll have to stick to the most important events.

[Chapter 15, after: . . . and look out the window.]

(continued)

193

Why do you think Moon wanted to look out the window?

[After: "They're scared of you."]

Why was it so easy for Kit and Moon to become friends?

[After: . . . and imagined that I was someplace else.]

Remember that we can learn more about a character through his actions. When Moon switched with Hal, what did it reveal about his character? Talk to your partner.

[After: . . . talking about making me president.]

Why do you think the boys wanted to make Moon president?

[Chapter 16, after: . . . he looked back at me.]

Let's predict. Do you think Kit would be able to do his part? Let's vote. Why?

[After: "I don't need it anymore."]

The author has mentioned Kit's medicine several times, but we don't know what he was taking it for. I think that this is going to be important later. One way to determine what facts are important is to notice when unusual things are repeated.

Do you think it was a good idea to bring everyone to the bus? Why?

Teach Tier 2 Words

One of the words from our book today was *hesitated*. What word? To *hesitate* means to pause briefly because you aren't sure. If someone asked you to pitch in a game, you might hesitate because you aren't sure you are good enough. You might hesitate to walk around in a dark house. In our book, Moon asked Kit about the medicine, and he hesitated for a second before saying he didn't need it. I think he was not 100% sure. To *hesitate* means to pause briefly because you aren't sure. You can use that word: "I hesitate when _____." "I wouldn't hesitate to _____." What word?

One of the words from our book today was *twitched*. What word? *Twitch* means to jerk or pull a little bit. Your face might twitch if you are about to cry. A sleeping dog might twitch if he is dreaming. In our book, it says that Hal's face started to twitch when Moon was explaining the escape plan. I think the author wants us to think that Hal was excited and a little bit scared. *Twitch* means to jerk or pull a little bit. You can use that word: "I felt _____, so I twitched." "I was scared, so my _____ twitched." What word?

Sentence Composing

Unscramble:

towards the bunk room/I started back/ following me/with Kit

Let's look first for a subject and verb. *Towards the bunk room* is a prepositional phrase telling where. *I started back* is actually a kernel sentence. It has a subject and verb.

I started back

(continued)

Towards the bunk room
Following me
With Kit

We can actually make more than one complete sentence here. When we have prepositional phrases to work with, we can put them in different orders.

Combine:

I was able to press against the deadbolt latch.

The cage door popped loose and swung open.

Let's think about how these ideas are related. Are they just two events in a sequence, or does one cause the other? If one causes the other, we can link with *because* or *since,* and we have different choices for ordering the ideas.

Text-Based Writing

Write a paragraph telling the main events of the story so far. Remember that when you write a summary, you need to decide what's important and what's not. You include only the most important facts.

DAY 10: CHAPTERS 17 AND 18

Read-Aloud

As I read today, I want you to look for all of the great examples of Moon's leadership skills.

Later today, I'm going to ask that you write another letter. This time it will be a letter from Moon to Pap telling about the escape.

[Chapter 17, after: . . . that tries to catch us and tell us what to do.]

Do you think this was a good plan? Why or why not?

[After: "We'll get in too much trouble."]

I think that it is important that the boys were crying and complaining already. They had not been away from Pinson very long at all. Life in the woods was very hard. I think that this is important because it showed that they wouldn't be able to live the hard life that Moon had lived.

[After: . . . had their blankets and pillows and were following behind me.]

Do you think the other kids would be safe in the bus? Why?

[Chapter 18, after: . . . and we set out for the fire tower again.]

What would have happened to Kit and Hal if Moon wasn't there? Why?

Your turn to ask a question! I want you to think of a good question to ask about what we've read today. Then ask the rest of us.

(continued)

Teach Tier 2 Words

One of the words from our book today was *trembled*. What word? *Tremble* means to shake slightly. An earthquake can cause the earth to tremble. Your hands could tremble if you were nervous or afraid. In our book, Moon's hands trembled when all of the kids were safe on the bus. He was so happy to be leaving. *Tremble* means to shake slightly. You can use that word: "If I saw _____, I would tremble." "I trembled because _____." What word?

Another of the words from our book today was *rig*. What word? *Rig* means to set something up quickly or to make something out of unusual materials. You might rig a fishing pole out of a stick and some string. You could rig a set of goals for a soccer game in your yard. If you have to rig something, it means that you don't have quite the right equipment. In our book, Moon said that he could rig traps. That meant he could make them out of things that he found in the woods. *Rig* means to set something up quickly or to make something out of unusual materials. You can use that word: "I wish that I knew how to rig _____." "In an emergency, we might have to rig _____." What word?

Sentence Composing

Expand:

I started up the tower ladder.

Let's add a phrase that tells when and a phrase that tells why. For when, we can start our phrase with the word *when,* or we can use a prepositional phrase. For why, we should probably start with *since* or *because.* Let's construct a few different phrases, and then we can see whether they should be added to the beginning, middle, or end of the sentence and whether they require commas.

Combine:

Hall and Kit fell behind.
I made my way off a small hill.
The hill was matted in pine needles.

Let's think about how these events are related before we choose our linking words. The first two sentences are events happening at the same time. How can we combine them to be specific about this? Can we use *as* or *while?*

The third sentence gives more details about the hill. How can we add it?

Text-Based Writing

Write a letter from Moon to Pap telling about the escape. Remember to include events and also Moon's feelings.

(continued)

DAY 11: CHAPTERS 19 AND 20

Read-Aloud

Moon was back in the woods where he felt safe and at home. Look for evidence that this was home to him.

After we read today, I'll ask you to write another brief summary of events.

[Chapter 19, after: Kit nodded, "I'm ready."]

Of the three boys, who seemed to be the toughest? Let's vote. Why did you vote the way you did?

[After: "That's when I get my hat?" Kit asked.]

Why did Moon say that they needed to make new clothes?

[After: ". . . He's still a mile or so back."]

Why was it scary that they could hear a dog coming?

[Chapter 20, after: "I figure he's hornet-mad I busted out of there."]

Do you think that Snapper was going to lead Sanders to the boys? Why?

[After: "All right," Hal said, sighing, "Let's go."]

I can make an inference here. We know that Sanders was cruel to Moon. We know that he was also cruel to the man that he visited who owed him money. This was his dog, but he was very friendly to strangers. Maybe that's because Sanders treated him badly because he was a mean man.

Time to predict! Do you think that Sanders was going to catch them? Raise your hand if you think so. Why?

Teach Tier 2 Words

One of the words from our book today was *thicket*. What word? A *thicket* is a dense group of bushes or trees. They grow together really thick—get it? So they're called a thicket. You would not be comfortable walking in a thicket. The going would be tough. In our book, the boys came to a thicket, and Moon made them put their blankets inside their jackets. He did that because the blankets kept getting caught in the sticker bushes. A *thicket* is a dense group of bushes or trees. You can use that word: "If I have to walk through a thicket, I _____." "I saw a _____ hiding in a thicket." What word?

Another of the words from our book today was *loping*. What word? *Loping* means walking or running with long strides. Animals like cheetahs can lope, because they can take long strides. Tiny birds can't lope because their legs are very short. In our book, it says that Moon imagined the dog loping toward them. I suspect Watt Key meant to tell us that Moon thought that the dog was going to be able to catch them. *Loping* means walking or running along with long strides. You can use that word: "A _____ can lope along." "If I saw a dog loping toward me, I would _____." What word?

(continued)

Sentence Composing

Combine:

I felt myself getting hungry.
I started making plans to get food for all of us.

How are these ideas related? Does one cause the other? If so, we should choose *because* or *since* or *so* to link them. What are the choices?

Expand:

Since Sanders is coming.

This is a fragment that is telling why. How can we expand it to create a complete sentence? When we start with a linking word, we need a comma and a complete sentence after that first phrase.

Text-Based Writing

Write a paragraph telling the main events of the story so far. Remember that when you write a summary, you need to decide what's important and what's not. You include only the most important facts.

DAY 12: CHAPTERS 21 AND 22

Read-Aloud

These next chapters combine a series of events with a lot of character information. Make sure that you are keeping track of both.

After we read today, I'll ask you to write about how Hal felt about the journey.

[Chapter 21, after: We both knew he didn't mean it, and smiled.]

How do you think Moon felt teaching Kit and Hal to survive in the woods?

[After: . . . his eyes burned with mischief.]

Why do you think Hal was picking on Kit? Tell your partner.

[After: Kit looked up at me.]

I think this is important. You determine importance as you go along by figuring out what information is new. We already know that Moon loved the woods and knew all about them, so new details about that are not as important. What is new here is that we are getting some of Hal's story and Kit's story. That will help us to understand their characters and interpret their actions.

[After: ". . . another year before I was better and they sent me to Pinson."]

What do you think Kit's medical problem was? Why?

[After: Go to sleep.]

(continued)

198

What do you think Hal meant when he said that Moon wouldn't be cussing at Sanders while he was around?

[Chapter 22, after: I can't climb a tree.]

What would happen if Hal wouldn't run?

Help me summarize the events we read about today.

Teach Tier 2 Words

One of the words from our book today was *ravine*. What word? A *ravine* is a deep place between two mountains. You can imagine it to have steep sides. Most of the action in these chapters takes place in a ravine. That's one of the reasons that the boys are moving slowly. They have to do a lot of climbing. A *ravine* is a deep place between two mountains. You can use that word: "A ravine might have _____." "I went to the ravine because _____." What word? [You may wish to search online for a picture of a ravine.]

Another of the words from our book today was *jowls*. What word? *Jowls* are the fat places at the bottom of a person's or an animal's cheeks. I had an uncle who was very large. His face had big jowls, right here. Animals have jowls too. Here's a quote from the book: "Snapper lay between them with his chin on the ground and his jowls flayed out." *Jowls* are the fat places at the bottom of a person's or an animal's cheeks. You can use that word: "My _____ has big jowls." "A _____ has big jowls." What word? [You may want to search online for a picture of a dog with jowls.]

Sentence Composing

Combine:

The sky was clear.
The forest flicked with life.

Let's think about how these two ideas are related. They are both providing description of the setting. We can probably just link with a comma plus *and*.

Expand:

We can stop and set some traps.

Let's add some details here. We can tell where by adding prepositional phrases. We can tell why by adding a phrase starting with *because* or *since*.

Text-Based Writing

How do you think Hal was feeling about the journey so far? Provide evidence.

(continued)

DAY 13: CHAPTERS 23 AND 24

Read-Aloud

The events in these chapters introduce a new twist for Hal's character. Once you've heard what happened, I bet you will say that the author did just the right thing with Hal. We can trace his decisions back to other details in the story.

You'll be writing another letter today, this time from Hal to Moon. Start thinking about how Hal felt about Moon.

[Chapter 23, after: "It's a puma track."]

Why was it a good thing that they saw a puma track?

[After: . . . and chewed on some of the leftover cattails.]

Why do you think Hal wouldn't eat the snake? Tell your partner.

[After: "I don't think Hal likes it out here," Kit said.]

How do you think Kit felt?

[After: "I don't want him to go," I said.]

Let's predict. How many of you think Hal was going to go? Why?

[Chapter 24, after: "Shut up, Moon!" Hal yelled.]

Hal told Moon to shut up. I think this is important. If Hal didn't trust Moon, he was going to be more and more unhappy, and he would leave. But he didn't really know how to survive, so that would be dangerous. Remember that we determine importance when we read novels by watching for things that characters do that are totally new.

[After: . . . and the forest was overcast and dripping.]

Why do you think Moon woke up early to make the shelter?

Let's vote. Thumbs up or thumbs down. What do you think of Hal's decision?

Teach Tier 2 Words

One of the words from our book today was *roiling*. What word? *Roiling* is a word that refers to water. It means turning so quickly that the sand or mud gets sucked up. In our book, Moon heard a swollen creek roiling. This meant that the rain had been very hard. The storm must have been worse than he thought. *Roiling* water is turning quickly. You can use that word: "When a storm is roiling, I _____." "If I saw water roiling suddenly, I would _____." What word?

Another of the words from our book today was *lick*. What word? You already know you can lick with your tongue, but *lick* also means to touch gently. In our book, Moon watched the fire lick the bark that he was using to send a message to Pap. *Lick* can mean touch gently. You can use that word: "My foot licked the _____." "If my elbow licked the edge of the table, it would feel _____." What word?

(continued)

Sentence Composing

Expand:

I want to hitch a ride.

Let's turn this into a quotation. Who would actually say this? How would we communicate that to our reader? Let's practice all the ways that we could punctuate that.

Combine:

The storm slowed to a dark drizzle.
It was early morning.

The second sentence just tells when the first sentence happened. Can you turn that information into a prepositional phrase? Where can we place it?

Text-Based Writing

How do you think Hal was feeling about Moon? Write a letter from Hal to Moon telling how he felt and why. You'll need to write from Hal's point of view.

DAY 14: CHAPTERS 25 AND 26

Read-Aloud

These two chapters are almost like their own story. Moon and Kit were facing a series of problems, one after another. We learn more about their characters, and we get a sense of some possibilities for unexpected turns.

After we read today, I'll ask you to make a prediction and write about what you think would happen when Kit and Moon found Sanders.

[Chapter 25, after: I was relieved to have our shelter finished.]

It says that Moon was relieved to have the shelter built. How do you think Kit felt?

[After: We laughed at Kit's joke.]

Do you think that Hal was safe? Why?

[After: . . . would shoot an arrow with enough force.]

I think this was important. To us, this is new information. Remember that when you are reading a novel and you read something unexpected, you can assume that the author put it in because it was important. This is the very first time that we have heard Moon doubting himself.

[After: . . . but I had never had it until then.]

Were you surprised that he got the doe on the first try? Why?

[After: . . . hung from a branch to use as trap bait.]

(continued)

Do you think Moon's knowledge of how to use the deer parts was impressive? Why or why not?

Do you think the boys were in danger or that Sanders was in danger? Let's vote. Now give me some reasons.

Teach Tier 2 Words

One of the words from our book today was *diverted*. What word? *Diverted* means sent in a different direction. You can divert traffic through a detour, or you can divert water by building a dam. In our book, the roots of the giant pine tree diverted water as it went downhill. That means that their shelter would not get washed out. *Diverted* means sent in a different direction. You can use that word: "There was an accident, so our car was diverted _____." "We diverted the water from our _____." What word?

Another of the words from our book today was *brittle*. What word? *Brittle* means hard and breakable at the same time. If sticks are brittle, you can step on them and they will snap. In our book, Moon was walking and felt brittle leaves under his feet. That means that they were frozen hard, but they broke easily when he stepped on them. I think the author used that detail to show us that things were going to get really cold soon. *Brittle* means hard and breakable at the same time. You can use that word: "The _____ felt brittle to me." "If my bread was brittle, I would _____." What word?

Sentence Composing

Combine:

I knew the voice was Sanders.
It set my heart to pounding in my chest.

How are these ideas related? Are they just two similar details, or does one cause the other? Let's see if we can preserve the relationship in our choice of linking words.

Combine:

Kit was collecting firewood.
I got back to the campsite.

These are two events. They are happening at the same time. Let's see if we can preserve the sequence in our choice of linking words.

Text-Based Writing

What do you think was going to happen when Kit and Moon found Sanders? Give your prediction and your reasons for making it.

(continued)

DAY 15: CHAPTERS 27 AND 28

Read-Aloud

In these two chapters, focus your attention on Moon as I read. Look for actions consistent with the character, and also for things that stand out as different or surprising.

As I read, start thinking about whether Kit and Moon would make it to Alaska. You can write your prediction later.

[Chapter 27, after: He kept walking.]

Why do you think that Kit was acting more uncomfortable about going after Sanders?

[After: "Snare him,"]

What does it mean that they planned to snare him?

[After: I turned and ran down the deer trail.]

Why did Sanders chase after Moon? Talk to your partner.

[After: "Come on," he begged.]

What is surprising to you about Moon's behavior?

[Chapter 28, after: "We can't leave for Alaska without plenty of supplies."]

Why do you think Kit was so anxious to get moving to Alaska?

[After: "I think we should have some just in case."]

Do you think that they would really be able to find medicine in the woods? Why or why not?

[After: "I don't think he is comin' back."]

This doesn't make sense to me. If it had been 2 weeks since they saw Sanders, why hadn't he come back? He was a policeman, and he knew where they were. Maybe he never made it out of the forest. Or maybe he was just still planning how to capture them. I'm going to have to read on. That's usually a good idea when things don't quite make sense.

Now I want you to think of a good question to ask about what we've read today. Then raise your hand and ask it.

Teach Tier 2 Words

One of the words from our book today was *assured*. What word? *Assured* means to make someone sure that what you are saying is true. It's like promising that you are not lying. In our book, Moon assured Kit that it would be okay to take Sanders's gun. Kit was afraid, and Moon made him feel more comfortable. *Assured* means to make someone sure that what you are saying is true. You can use that word: "I felt assured when _____." "I assured my friend because _____." What word?

One of the words from our book today was *bearings*. What word? Your *bearings* are your sense of direction. It means that you know where you are and where other things

(continued)

are. Once I stayed overnight in someone else's house, and when I woke up I needed to take a second to get my bearings. It can also mean that you know the longitude and latitude where you are. In our book, Moon stopped to get his bearings when he saw where Sanders was. He wanted to be sure that he could find him again easily. *Bearings* means your sense of direction. You can use that word: "I need to get my bearings when _____." "_____ can help you get your bearings." What word?

Sentence Composing

Expand:

I slept with the pistol beside me.

Why did this happen? Let's add details. Start with *since* or *so.* What kind of pistol?

Expand:

Lay in the treetop platform.

This is a fragment. There is no subject. Who or what lay there? We have to have a subject.

Text-Based Writing

Do you think that Kit and Moon would make it to Alaska? Why or why not?

DAY 16: CHAPTERS 29 AND 30

Read aloud

In the next two chapters, you will see that the author has provided all of the clues we need to know about what was going to happen, but he also distracts us enough that we will really be surprised.

As I read today, see if you learn anything surprising about Hal. You can write about it later.

[Chapter 29, after: . . . for a fire without whittling each piece of firewood to the core.]

How do you think Moon was feeling as Kit got sicker and sicker?

[After: ". . . and I never should have done it."]

This is a surprising thing. Everything that Moon says about his father is really positive— but now he is saying that he shouldn't have let him die. I am going to have to keep reading to see whether Moon was willing to go against his father's wishes.

[After: "I'm gonna find a road and some help."]

Why is it so surprising that Moon decided to take Kit back to the road?

[Chapter 30, after: . . . doubting all the things he told me were right.]

Why was Moon doubting the things that his father told him?

[After: They just wanted me locked up somewhere.]

(continued)

204

Do you think the description that the reporter gave is fair? Let's vote. Why?

Was Hal's father what you thought he would be like? Why?

Teach Tier 2 Words

One of the words from our book today was *evasion*. What word? *Evasion* means doing everything you can to get away. It's like hiding, but also moving around. Moon and Pap were skilled at evasion. In our book, Moon heard the reporter say that he was wanted for evasion of the law. That means that police were trying to arrest him because he was hiding out. *Evasion* means doing everything you can to get away. You can use that word: "I needed some evasion skills because _____." "I wish I were better at evasion so that _____." What word?

Another of the words from our book today was *fugitive*. What word? A *fugitive* is a person who is hiding or running away. In a way, Moon had been a fugitive all of his life. In our book, Moon also heard the reporter describing him as a fugitive. A *fugitive* is a person who is hiding or running away. You can use that word: "If I saw a fugitive, I would _____." "I might need to be a fugitive if _____." What word?

Sentence Composing

Expand:

Sanders coming on television and telling everyone how dangerous I was.

This is a fragment. We can fix it in two ways. We can use it as a phrase that tells why something else happened and add a complete sentence to the beginning or end, or we can change the verbs *coming* and *telling* into a different verb tense. Let's try both fixes.

Expand:

Kit developed a sniffle that would not go away.

Let's expand this sentence by adding a clause starting with *even though.* That means that we have to add a complete sentence that actually provides contrasting information. Why was it strange that Kit was sick now?

Text-Based Writing

Think about what you learned about Hal today. Is it surprising that he came back and rescued Moon? Explain your reasoning.

DAY 17: CHAPTERS 31 AND 32

Read-Aloud

We've seen what Moon did to be happy in the forest. In these chapters, we are going to learn more about Hal and where he felt at home.

(continued)

As I read today, you'll see that lots of events were happening fast. Later I'll ask you to make some predictions.

[Chapter 31, after: ". . . and red bugs, this feels pretty good."]

Do you think Moon was feeling at home? Why?

[After: "I can't make everything Kit needs."]

How had friendship changed Moon's feelings? Talk to your partner.

[Chapter 32, after: "You ain't the only one that knows about stuff."]

I can synthesize here. When Moon came to Pinson, he took away Hal's position. Then, when they were in the forest, Moon knew how to survive and Hal didn't. Now Hal was saying that Moon wasn't the only one to know things. I think this means that Hal wanted Moon to know that he did know some things that Moon didn't know, like how to go mudding in a truck.

[After: "Guess you don't."]

How did Mr. Mitchell get money?

Why do you think Moon shared his feelings with Hal?

Teach Tier 2 Words

One of the words from our book today was *machine gun*. What word? A *machine gun* is not used for hunting. It is a gun that can shoot a lot of bullets very quickly. It is used in a war. In our book, Mr. Mitchell let the boys shoot a machine gun—a gun that should only be used by people in the military. That makes me feel as if he might not be a very good parent. A *machine gun* is a gun that can shoot many bullets in a very short time. You can use that word: "Machine guns are dangerous because _____." "If I saw a machine gun, I would _____." What word?

One of the words from our book today was *throbbing*. What word? *Throbbing* means beating with a regular rhythm. Your heart throbs, because it has a regular beat. Sometimes a pain might throb every time your heart beats. Or an engine might make a throbbing sound. In our book, Moon felt the wiener dog throbbing against him. This means that he could feel the dog breathing and feel his heart beating. It must have made him feel safer after feeling so lonely. *Throbbing* means beating with a regular rhythm. You can use that word: "If I felt a throbbing pain, I would _____." "My heart was throbbing quickly because _____." What word?

Sentence Composing

Combine:

I sucked in my breath.
I took aim.
I turned every bottle in the line to glass splinters.

(continued)

These are three events that happened in a specific order. Let's combine with linking words that communicate the order to our readers.

Expand:

I don't want to be by myself.

Let's turn this into a direct quotation. Who do you think said it? How can we add words and punctuation to make that clear? Let's try several different ways.

Text-Based Writing

We have lots of unsettled things to think about. Do you think Moon would be able to get back together with Kit? Do you think he would be going to Alaska? Do you think Sanders would find them? What do you think was going to happen? Predict and give your reasons.

DAY 18: CHAPTERS 33 AND 34

Read-Aloud

What do you really think the theme of this story is? Is it about survival in the woods? Is it about friendship and the challenges it causes? Is it about whether Moon should have lived as his father taught him, or tried to make a life in the regular world? Think about it from Moon's perspective. Since he is the main character, the theme usually revolves around him.

Today there will be lots more action. Later I'll ask you to make another prediction.

[Chapter 33, after: "I hope I'm done whippin' up on people."]

Do you think Moon would want to talk to Mr. Abroscotto about his father? Why or why not?

[After: . . . and we both napped under the pine needles.]

How were Pap and Mr. Mitchell different?

[After: "All right."]

What did the letter reveal about Moon's feelings?

[Chapter 34, after: . . . and then I'd start recognizing things.]

Do you think it was safe for Moon to be going back to town? Let's vote. Why?

[After: Hal helped me put it in the bed and then we set out again.]

Why do you think he wanted the wheelbarrow?

[After: "Supposed to be in Alaska by now."]

How do you think Moon felt about his shelter being destroyed?

[After: "Somethin' like that."]

I can synthesize here. Mr. Mitchell was in the Vietnam War. That's why he had the

(continued)

machine gun. And now we know that Pap was also in Vietnam. If people fight in a war that they don't believe in, they might not fit into their regular life again. Maybe that's why Mr. Mitchell let Hal live so freely, and that's why Pap couldn't live in a town.

[After: "You're all messed up."]

How was Sanders different from Pap and Mr. Mitchell?

Now I want you to think of a good question to ask about what we've read today. Who's first?

Teach Tier 2 Words

One of the words from our book today was *inspecting*. What word? *Inspecting* means looking at something very carefully. You might inspect a melon before buying it. Adults have to get cars inspected to be sure that they are safe. In our book, Moon inspected an abandoned squirrel's nest. He said that squirrels make good pets. That reminds me that he would have never had a pet. *Inspect* means look at something very carefully. You can use that word: "Before I _____, I do some inspecting." "I can inspect your work to check for _____." What word?

Another word from our book today was *peered*. What word? *Peer* means to look very sneakily. You might peer around a tree if you were playing tag. A rabbit might peer out of its burrow to see if a predator is nearby. In our book, Mr. Abroscotto peered over the counter to see if it was safe to stand up, with Moon there with a gun. *Peer* means to look very sneakily. You can use that word: "I peered out the window and saw _____." "If I was being careful, I would peer at _____." What word?

Sentence Composing

Expand:

I'm trying to talk sense into your hard little head.

Let's turn this into a direct quotation. Who do you think said it? How can we add words and punctuation to make that clear? Let's try several different ways.

Combine:

He kept looking in the rearview mirror.
He did it for a while.
He relaxed.

These are three events that happened in a specific order. Let's combine with linking words that communicate the order to our readers.

Text-Based Writing

There are some important new twists today. Mr. Abroscotto knew that Moon was back. Sanders was still after him. And Moon had a gun. What do you think was going to happen? Use what you know about the characters as evidence for your prediction.

(continued)

DAY 19: CHAPTERS 35 AND 36

Read-Aloud

We are going to learn more about Pap today. It will help you if you know the word *draft*. For the Vietnam War, men were drafted to go into the army. This means that they didn't volunteer. Instead, they had a number, and if it was called they had to go. Today in Iraq and Afghanistan, the soldiers who are fighting chose to join the army. But that wasn't the case in Vietnam. Many did not want to go, and they were drafted.

After we read today, I'll ask you to write and tell me whether you would rather be in jail or live alone. This book makes it a hard choice.

[Chapter 35, after: "Especially the government."]

What was Moon's theory about why his father thought the government was after him?

[After: . . . I felt my soft mattress and the blanket and I was glad to be where I was.]

I can make an inference here. We know that Moon used to hate sleeping inside. Now he was saying that he liked being in the bed with a warm blanket. I think that he was getting more used to normal life and he wouldn't really want to live alone in the woods.

[After: . . . drug off into the forest with no roads goin' to it.]

How was the trailer idea a compromise between living in the woods and living in a normal town? Talk to your partner.

[After: ". . . maybe I'd rather go to Hellenweiler with you."]

What had really changed about Moon?

[Chapter 36, after: He turned and began to walk up the hill.]

Do you think that Mr. Mitchell was taking good care of Hal? Why or why not?

What do you think would happen when they tried to see Kit?

Teach Tier 2 Words

One of the words from our book today was *installing*. What word? *Installing* means putting something in place. You might have a light installed in your house. Some people get Internet service or cable TV installed. In our book, Hal found an old police car and took the light off the top and installed it on his truck. *Install* means to put in a part. You can use that word: "I learned to install _____." "I wish I could install _____." What word?

Another of the words from our book today was *civilization*. What word? *Civilization* means complicated, organized systems for life, including government and schools. We study ancient civilizations, like the Greeks and the Aztecs. We also live in a civilization. In our book, Mr. Mitchell told Moon that he might be able to find people who knew Pap and could tell him about Vietnam if he came back to civilization. By this, he meant if Moon decided not to live in the woods any more. *Civilization* means complicated, organized systems for life, including government and schools. You can use that word:

(continued)

"I like to study ancient civilizations because _____." "I learned that ancient civilizations _____." What word?

Sentence Composing

Combine:

The sound was so loud I covered my ears.
The sound echoed across the bottom of the clay pit.
The sound went skyward.

These are three events that happened in a specific order. Let's combine with linking words that communicate the order to our readers. Let's also make sure that we are not repeating words.

Expand:

Across the clay pit at the top of the pines.

This is a fragment. It's three prepositional phrases. We have to add a subject and a verb, at least, to make it into a complete sentence. There are lots of ways to do that.

Text-Based Writing

Would you rather be in jail or living alone? Why?

DAY 20: CHAPTERS 37 AND 38

Read-Aloud

Today, think about the relationships among the characters in these chapters. Decide if the characters were acting as we would expect them to, given what we know about them.

Sometimes we have to think carefully about what a character says if we want to infer the meaning. I'll give you an opportunity later to write about something Sanders said.

[Chapter 37, after: . . . and walk past the nurses' station to the hall on my left.]

Why did Moon have a hard time finding the fourth floor?

[After: "You can make just about anything else."]

Why was it so important for the boys to find a way to be together? Tell your partner.

[After: . . . just like we'd been there a week already.]

Do you think the plan was reasonable? Let's vote. Why?

[Chapter 38, after: "You lied about us!" I yelled.]

It is so surprising to me that Sanders could treat Moon so badly. He was a policeman, and he was supposed to keep children safe. But if I think back, I can see that Sanders was just a cruel person. So even though the information is surprising and causes me to self-

(continued)

monitor—that is, to stop and check my understanding—I think my reasoning is right, so I should just keep reading.

Help me summarize what's happened today.

Teach Tier 2 Words

One of the words from our book today was *jostled*. What word? *Jostle* means to push or bump roughly. Someone might jostle you in line by hitting you with an elbow. In our book, Sanders jostled Moon in front of the reporters while he was hanging upside down. He did that because he was so mean and because he had everyone convinced that Moon was dangerous. *Jostle* means to push or bump roughly. You can use that word: "If I jostle someone, _____." "I was carrying a glass of water, and someone jostled me, so _____." What word?

One of the words from our book today was *reasoned*. What word? *Reasoned* means thought about logically. When you reason something out, you think about it step by step. In our book, Moon reasoned that he needed to be in a familiar place if he was going to escape from Sanders, so he told Sanders that the gun was in his old shelter. *Reasoned* means thought about carefully and logically. You can use that word: "When we do math, we reason _____." "When my work is hard, I stop to reason because _____." What word?

Sentence Composing

Combine:

I realized I would have to get Sanders out into the forest.
I would have to get him lost.
I would have to trap him.

These are three events that happened in a specific order. Let's combine with linking words that communicate the order to our readers. Let's also make sure that we are not repeating words.

Combine:

Sanders chuckled.
Sanders spit into his cup.
Sanders did it again.

Let's combine these without linking words. Combine the first two first, and then add that last detail.

Again Sanders chuckled, spitting into his cup.

Text-Based Writing

What did Sanders mean when he said, "For that sickly kid's sake, you better hope you ain't lying"

(continued)

211

DAY 21: CHAPTERS 39 AND 40

Read-Aloud

Today we are going to see a character whom we've only met briefly. We don't know much about this character, and we are going to have to work hard to interpret this character's actions.

After we read today, I'll ask you to make more predictions. So put on your thinking caps!

[Chapter 39, after: He draped the canteen over me again and I began to walk.]

Why did Sanders need Moon to lead him to the shelter?

[After: ". . . before I write you up for obstructin' justice."]

Why did Sanders think he could get Mr. Wellington to leave, even though he had seen what Sanders was doing to Moon?

[After: Everybody I cared about was in trouble because of me.]

What did it mean when Moon thought the forest was full of animals that were turning their heads on him and speaking about him in whispers? Talk to your partner.

[After: I stared at Mr. Wellington blankly.]

Why was it surprising that Moon returned to Mr. Wellington's house?

[After: "That's a bad combination to be facing."]

I have to self-monitor here. It doesn't make sense to me that Mr. Wellington would think Moon was in a bad situation. Even though Sanders was a bad man, and his father was a judge, Moon hadn't really done anything bad. Mr. Wellington should have been able to help him, because he was a lawyer. I'll have to read on and see if Sanders could be defeated.

Now I want you to think of a good question to ask about what we've read today. Then ask your partner that question.

Teach Tier 2 Words

One of the words from our book today was *canteen*. What word? A *canteen* is a special water bottle used in camping or hiking. Soldiers carry canteens when they march long distances. In our book, Sanders hung a canteen around Moon's neck, but he didn't let Moon drink from it. A *canteen* is a special water bottle used in hiking or camping. You can use that word: "I would need a canteen if _____." "A canteen is like a water bottle because _____." What word?

Another word from our book today was *yanked*. What word? *Yank* means to pull hard and quickly. If you yank someone's arm, you could hurt him. In our book, Sanders put a dog collar around Moon's neck, and Moon had to lead him to the shelter. Sanders yanked the leash when he needed to rest. He did this because he was cruel. *Yank* means to pull hard and quickly. You can use that word: "It is not nice to yank _____." "If someone yanked my arm, I would _____." What word?

(continued)

Sentence Composing

Combine:

No one showed.
I drove out and found Sanders' car.

These are two events that happened at nearly the same time. How can we use when as a linking word here?

Combine:

I could have talked to you.
I could have been your friend.

Let's think about meaning first. If these are two similar ideas, we should combine with a comma plus *and*. If they are contrasting, we should use a comma plus *but*.

Text-Based Writing

Think about what Mr. Wellington had told Moon about himself. What do you think his motivations were for helping Moon? Do you think he was going to be successful? What do you think was going to happen?

DAY 22: CHAPTERS 41 AND 42

Read-Aloud

In these next chapters, we will see that Moon first became hopeful about Mr. Wellington and then lost hope. Think about why Moon was so confused.

Later today, I'll ask you to write a letter from Moon to Pap describing what happened. Pay attention to what Moon knew and didn't know.

[Chapter 41, after: ". . . and people are chasin' me all over."]

I think this is very important. It's new information about Moon. Mr. Wellington was talking about the law and why some people don't like it. It's about rules. Moon asked how people get to know the rules. I know that Moon followed the rules that his father had taught him, and he had no way to know that it is very serious to attack a policeman, even one as evil as Sanders. So Moon was actually following the rules that he was taught.

[After: "That's right."]

Why do you think Mr. Wellington was taping Moon's story?

[After: "Now," he said, "take me to where you met with Sanders."]

Why did Mr. Wellington take the log?

[After: "Okay, then, I'll see what I can do with this."]

Why do you think Mr. Wellington was taking these pictures?

(continued)

[After: "You dreamin' about dog cobbler?"]

Why were the other prisoners teasing Moon?

[After: "Yeah, get out of here, you idiot!" someone said.]

How did the other prisoners change their attitude toward Moon when Sanders was there?

How are you feeling about our characters?

Teach Tier 2 Words

One of the words from our book today was *tact*. What word? *Tact* means politeness in dealing with people. Tact is what keeps us from saying hurtful things, even if they are true. In our book, Moon said that Mr. Wellington looked very old. Mr. Wellington told Moon that he had to get some tact before coming in front of a judge. This means that he had to learn that there are some things that are impolite to say. *Tact* means politeness in dealing with people. You can use that word: "People with tact _____." "My family teaches me tact because _____." What word?

Another of the words from our book today was *advice*. What word? *Advice* means suggestions or recommendations for the future. You get advice from your parents and other adults. In our book, Mr. Wellington was talking to Moon about what happened, and Moon said that his Pap told him he could beat up anyone as long as he had enough adrenaline. Mr. Wellington said that he wished Moon would stop relying on this advice. He meant that when Moon did things his father told him to do, he got into trouble. *Advice* means suggestions or recommendations from other people. You can use that word: "I gave my friend advice because _____. Good advice helps _____." What word?

Sentence Composing

Expand:

Sanders clutched the bars tightly.

Let's add details here. Why did this happen? Remember that if we start to add a phrase that begins with *because,* we can choose to add to the beginning or the end of the sentence.

Combine:

Officer Pete came through the door.
Officer Pete looked around.

Let's think about meaning first. If these are two similar ideas, we should combine with a comma plus *and.* If they are contrasting, we should use a comma plus *but.*

(continued)

Text-Based Writing

Think about Moon's position. He didn't know what a court is. He didn't really know what a lawyer is. He didn't know how long he would be in the jail. Write a letter from Moon to Pap describing what happened. Include events and feelings.

DAY 23: CHAPTERS 43 AND 44

Read-Aloud

We have a new character today, Judge Mackin. Think about what his speech and actions reveal about him as a character. What was motivating him?

After we read today, I'll ask you to make more predictions.

[Chapter 43, after: "I don't know, either," he said.]

How would you describe Officer Pete?

[After: "Did I ask you a question?"]

Why did Moon keep talking out in the courtroom?

[After: ". . . you're getting' any kind of special treatment."]

Now we know something about Judge Mackin, and I think it's important. When Mr. Wellington was first talking to Moon, he said that because Sanders was mean and had a daddy who was a judge, Moon had to be careful. Sanders did not act like a policeman should act. When he started acting badly in the courtroom, Judge Mackin says that he didn't care about the other judge. So I think that Sanders was not going to be allowed to be mean to Moon any more.

[After: "Who said I was lost!"]

Why do you think Sanders was telling so many lies?

[After: "Stop fancy-pantsin' around and get on with it."]

Do you think Judge Mackin liked Mr. Wellington? Why?

[Chapter 44, after: "I don't know."]

How do we know that Officer Pete and Judge Mackin were different from Sanders? Talk it over with your partner.

[After: "You're a dangerous man to be in front of," the judge said.]

Why did the judge say that Sanders was a dangerous man to be in front of?

[After: . . . and the aspirin bottle was gone.]

Why did Mr. Wellington have Moon demonstrate his shooting?

[After: . . . and I'll think of some more stuff before we get back to town.]

Why did Hal drive in and out so quickly?

Help me summarize today's events.

(continued)

Teach Tier 2 Words

One of the words from our book today was *commotion*. What word? *Commotion* means confusion and noisiness. At the end of a big game, there might be a commotion on the field. In our book, Judge Mackin closed the courtroom because the case had made such a commotion. There were reporters and cameras everywhere outside the courtroom because the case was so unusual. *Commotion* means confusion and noisiness. You can use that word: "If there is a commotion in this classroom, _____." "_____ would be a good commotion." What word?

Another of the words from our book today was *irrelevant*. What word? *Irrelevant* means not connected or important to a question or problem. If you want to know how tall someone is, his or her hair color is irrelevant. In our book, Mr. Wellington said that facts about Moon's father were irrelevant to the case. This means that nothing Pap had done could hurt Moon. *Irrelevant* means not connected or important to a question or problem. You can use that word: "When I think about irrelevant things during reading, I _____." "How people look is irrelevant when you are deciding to be their friend, because _____." What word?

Sentence Composing

Expand:

So that the truck leaned into a hard turn.

This is a fragment. It is telling why something happened, but it doesn't have a subject and a verb. We have to fix it with a complete sentence at the beginning or the end.

Combine:

Hal waved at us.
The bloodhounds heard me.
They tripped around in the garbage trying to stand up.

Let's combine with linking words that communicate the order of these three events.

Text-Based Writing

Perjury is lying in court. Write and make some predictions. What do you think was going to happen to Sanders? What about Moon? Give your reasoning.

DAY 24: CHAPTERS 45 AND 46

Read-Aloud

Pay really close attention to what Judge Mackin and Mr. Wellington said about what should have happened to Moon. It gives us a good picture of the real problem in this story.

(continued)

Today, think carefully about how Moon was feeling. Later, you'll have a chance to write a letter from Moon to Pap telling about those feelings.

[Chapter 45, after: "Boy, what're we going to do with you now?"]

What did Judge Mackin mean when he said that Moon needed something different?

[Chapter 46, after: The judge stood up, tapped the top of the car, and then turned away.]

Why did the Judge get Moon's hats?

[After: . . . I put everything into the envelope again and looked out the window.]

I can make an inference here. I have to think about things we learned in different parts of the book. Mr. Wellington found Moon's uncle because of Pap's watch. The watch was the only thing that Pap left for Moon. Even though Pap got Moon into this bad situation in the first place, in a way he saved him too.

How do you think Moon was feeling about the fact that he would be living with other kids? Tell your partner.

Teach Tier 2 Words

One of the words from our book today was *operates*. What word? *Operate* can mean when a doctor performs surgery to help people. But it also can mean to work or run. Only an adult can operate a car. Our cafeteria operates really well. In our book, Judge Mackin laughed when Moon said that Hal shouldn't get in trouble for driving without a license because he was a good driver. He said that Moon still didn't know anything about how the world operates. He meant that Moon didn't understand the rules. *Operate* can mean work or run. You can use that word: "I can operate a _____ better than my mother." "I want to learn to operate a _____." What word?

Another of the words from our book today was *hovering*. What word? *Hovering* means staying above without touching. You might see a hummingbird hovering over a garden. A helicopter can hover over a building. In our book, Moon got a short memory of a man that might be his uncle hovering over him. I think that the author wants us to be sure that this was his real uncle, and that Moon might have a chance at a real life. *Hovering* means staying above without touching. You can use that word: "I was hovering over my brother's crib because _____." "If I could fly, I would hover over _____." What word?

Sentence Composing

Expand:

I looked at the hand.

Let's add some dialogue here. Who do you think *I* refers to? What would that character say next?

Expand:

You're still property of the state.

(continued)

Let's turn this into dialogue. Who is talking? How can we add words and punctuation to signal that?

Text-Based Writing

Moon's life would be totally changed soon. Write a letter from Moon to Pap about what happened and how Moon was feeling.

DAY 25: CHAPTERS 47 AND 48

Read-Aloud

When authors resolve a story—that is, bring it to a conclusion—there is a difference between a good ending and a happy ending. We know that Sanders would be put in jail. We know that Moon was going to have a family. What about the other characters? Watch for how the author resolves *their* stories.

As I read, think about how Kit's life was now better because of Moon. You can write about that later.

[Chapter 47, after: "They're prob'ly lyin' in the shade down at the shop."]

Was this a good ending for the dogs? Why or why not?

[After: "You get in touch with me if you ever need anything."]

Mr. Mitchell really seems like a nice man. Before, I thought he was a bad father to Hal because he let him do dangerous things. But I was wrong. He was doing the best he could for Hal. And he was really kind to Moon. When you read, sometimes you think the wrong thing. If you read on and realize that you were wrong, you can self-monitor and correct your mistake.

[After: "Just as long as he doesn't cause trouble."]

Why did Mr. Wellington let Moon stay at the hospital?

[After: "Are you okay?" he asked me.]

What do you think was the meaning of Moon's dream? Talk it over with your partner.

[Chapter 48, after: "I know you do. Nothin' wrong with that."]

The smoke messages might not work for talking to dead people. They might work for helping live people. How had Moon's letters helped him?

Do you think Moon was right to want to leave and go to Mobile?

Teach Tier 2 Words

One of the words from our book today was *intensive*. What word? *Intensive* means very strong or forceful. When you are mad, you might give someone an intensive stare. In our book, Kit was so sick that he was moved to the intensive care unit. That is a place even more special than a regular hospital room. There are people trying to help 24 hours a day. They can't be interrupted by visitors. *Intensive* means very strong or forceful. You can use

(continued)

218

that word: "I have intensive interest in _____." "You need intensive training to learn to _____." What word?

Another of the words from our book today was *unconscious*. What word? *Unconscious* means still alive but not able to think. If you got hit hard in the head, you could be knocked unconscious. In our book, Kit was already unconscious when Moon got to the hospital. He was so sick that he couldn't see or hear. *Unconscious* means still alive but not able to think. It's like being asleep. You can use that word: "If I saw someone who was unconscious, I would _____." What word?

Sentence Composing

Expand:

Gradually I began to think of my new uncle.

Let's tell why. We can start our reason with *because* or *since*.

Expand:

He wouldn't know you were there.

Let's give contrasting information here. Start your addition with *even though*.

Text-Based Writing

How was Kit's life better because of Moon? Moon was going to live with his uncle, so could this be a good ending instead of a happy one?

DAY 26: CHAPTERS 49–51

Read-Aloud

When we finish our book today, I will give you a chance to write one last letter from Moon to Pap. I want you to pretend that he has now been living with his uncle's family for a year.

[As the story resolves, it may be best not to interrupt the narrative with modeling or questions. Instead, if the students want, read these chapters twice.]

Now that we've finished the book, let's pretend that the author, Watt Key, will be visiting our classroom. What are some good questions you'd like to ask?

Text-Based Writing

Write one last letter from Moon to Pap. Pretend that he has been living with his uncle's family for a year. What will have happened? How will he feel? How will he feel about Pap?

Sample Tier 1 Narrative Writing Unit

The lesson plans below bring concepts from this book together. This is a 7-day narrative writing unit from *Bookworms K–5 Reading and Writing*. To see more open-access lessons of this type, please contact the publisher, Open Up Resources (*https://openupresources. org*). Each day's lesson requires 45 minutes.

Within the curriculum, this unit comes just after students have read *Steal Away Home* by Lois Ruby, historical fiction with an embedded mystery, originally published in 1994 by Macmillan (and reprinted in 1999 by Aladdin). The text is 192 pages, with a Lexile of 890L. The writing unit presented here draws on lessons about mystery writing learned from the reading of this book. Students have already reviewed the genre-based characteristics of narratives, applied those characteristics to the specific case of mysteries, and used a simple graphic organizer to plan their mystery.

DAY 1

Teacher Instruction

Today you will begin to work on the introduction of your mystery. We know that in the beginning of a narrative we need to introduce the characters, identify the place and problem, and set the event sequence in motion. We can call this *establishing the situation*. One way to establish the situation is by using a direct statement. We have used this technique before when we told the setting, time, characters and problem by directly stating them to our reader. If I directly state the situation, I might write:

> *We had just bought an old house, and my parents decided to knock down a wall to make our kitchen and living room larger. When they were knocking down the wall, they found the craziest thing inside.*

This technique works fine, but there are other ways to establish the situation that might grab the reader's interest quickly and make my mystery sound more interesting to the reader.

A different way to establish the situation is to use dialogue. I could give similar information to our readers by having my main characters talk about the situation instead of directly stating the information. I could write:

> *"Hey, everyone come in here quickly. You will never believe what I just found unless you see it for yourselves," yelled my dad. "What in the world is that?" asked my sister Kate. "Oh, my goodness!" I shrieked. "That's crazy!"*

Another way to establish a situation is by using a question to draw your audience in. I might write:

(continued)

Have you ever discovered an unusual item and wondered how in the world it got there? Well, that is exactly what happened in our house this week.

An additional way is to describe a snapshot of time to establish the situation. I could write:

Hammers pounding. Wood cracking. Then complete silence until my dad broke the silence and hollered.

A fourth way to establish the situation is to try to connect to the audience. For this example, I might write:

If you have ever been inside an old house, you know it is full of odd-looking things. It could even contain something mysterious.

These are just four new ways to establish a situation in a narrative. I'll write these on an anchor chart: direct statement, dialogue, question, description of snapshot in time, connect to the audience.

Now I need to decide which one I like the best. Hmm . . . I think I will establish my situation with dialogue, so I'll circle that one.

Turn to a partner and discuss the four new ways to establish the situation. Then decide which way you might try today.

Student Work Session

Students will work independently to finish their graphic organizers and then work on their introductions. Gather those students together who are struggling to get started. Review the students' graphic organizers with them, and help them to verbalize their introductions.

Student Sharing

I read some interesting and attention-grabbing introductions today. Find someone whom you have not worked with recently, and share your introduction. Provide feedback to your partner that may help to enhance his or her introduction even more.

DAY 2

Teacher Instruction

A mystery can be made more suspenseful and exciting if the author is able to build tension throughout the plot. There are several ways to build tension, and today we are going to talk about a few before you begin writing.

One way to build tension is to have the main character come close to solving the mystery, but fail a few times before finally finding the solution.

(continued)

A second way to build tension is to have the main character get into trouble and have a difficult time getting out of the situation.

Another way is to give the main character a weakness that interferes with solving the mystery. For example, the character has a fear of spiders, but needs to crawl under the house to look for clues.

Another way to build tension is to find more mysterious items or discover strange clues.

I'll list the ways you can build tension to make your mystery more suspenseful: character comes close to solving, character gets into trouble, character has a weakness, more mysterious items/strange clues.

I want to give you a lot of time to write today. The first thing you need to do is finish your introduction. Then you will start working on the middle of your mystery. Choose at least one of the ways we discussed today to build tension, in order to make your mystery more suspenseful and exciting for your readers. You may sit near a partner for support. Gather your materials and find a good place to work.

Student Work Session

Students need to finish their introductions today and then begin working on the middle of their mysteries. Gather students together who are struggling to get started on the middle sections of their mysteries.

Student Sharing

I am very proud of your hard work today to make your mysteries suspenseful. Find a new partner and share what you have written so far. Provide feedback to your partner that would help make his or her mystery even more exciting.

DAY 3

Teacher Instruction

Yesterday you worked hard on the middle of your story. We can add details to this section of the story to help bring the story to life for the reader. One way to do that is by using dialogue. It helps the reader know how the characters think and how they feel about a situation. I have mentioned using dialogue throughout the year and shown you examples in my writing. Some of you also added dialogue in your first narrative.

Today we are going to review the use of dialogue, and then you will have time to add some dialogue to your mystery. We have read dialogue in all of our shared reading narratives. Professional authors are experts at using dialogue. Let's look at an excerpt from *Steal Away Home.* [Display and read aloud from pages 43–44.]

I have noticed that many of you often use the word *said* when you are writing dialogue. There are a lot of different words that you could use that would explain a character's

(continued)

thoughts and feelings better than *said.* Look through what we just read again. Find words that the author used other than *said* when she wrote dialogue.

You have all read dialogue in other books. Turn and talk with a partner, and discuss other words that you may have seen that we could use instead of *said.* [Create a list.]

Now I want to show you how to add dialogue to your own writing. I have a draft from [name of student volunteer] from yesterday, and he [or she] is allowing us to use it as an example. I'll read it to you first.

This is a perfect spot to add dialogue. When I add something to my writing, I don't need to erase or start over. Remember, I can use a caret to show what I am going to add, or I can write the new part on a sticky note and put it on my draft where I want it to go. I'll use a caret today, and I think I'll write [provide appropriate dialogue].

Notice how I put quotation marks in front of the first word that the character said. What else do you notice that I did to the first word after the first quotation marks? When I snap, whisper your answer out loud.

You have to capitalize the first word after the quotation marks. Notice how after the last word that the character said, I need another set of quotation marks, and then I have to chose a word to use to tell how the character spoke. I don't want to use *said.*

Today I want you to finish the middle part of your draft, and then go back and decide where dialogue could make your story more interesting and add it in. First, share your story with your partner, and work together to identify spots to add dialogue. You may move to a good spot and get started.

Student Work Session

Each student sits with a partner. The partners should share their drafts with each other and then collaborate to add dialogue to their mysteries. Monitor and offer support as needed. Pull students together who may be struggling to add dialogue. Help them to find at least two spots to add dialogue.

Student Sharing

I was very entertained today when I was walking around and you were adding dialogue. You were laughing and having fun writing what you thought your characters would say. Find a different partner and share your mystery.

DAY 4

Teacher Instruction

We have talked about how building tension and adding dialogue can make a mystery more exciting for your readers. Today we will talk about another way to create excitement in your story: by using cliffhangers.

(continued)

Cliffhangers are sudden events that cause shock and surprise for your readers. In books, a cliffhanger often comes at the end of a chapter and then is resolved in the next chapter. Authors use cliffhangers to keep the readers wanting to read more. They hook the reader to want to finish the story.

For our purpose, you could add a cliffhanger to the end of a paragraph and then resolve it in the next paragraph. You don't want to overuse cliffhangers. Depending on the length of your paper, one or two cliffhangers will be enough. I will share some examples of cliffhangers with you, and then you can decide which type would fit best in your mystery.

One type of cliffhanger is a sudden, shocking revelation or discovery. A character could all of a sudden find a clue or figure something out, but the author doesn't tell the reader what it is until the next paragraph. I could do that by using dialogue too. I could end a paragraph with this:

> *"Oh, no. I can't believe what I am seeing," gasped John.*

Then I could tell my reader about what I saw in the next paragraph. Would you want to keep reading if you had read that? I know I would.

Another type of cliffhanger is to place a character alone in an unusual or uncomfortable place. I could write:

> *I creep into the crawlspace. It is dark, narrow, and full of spiders.*

I would end the paragraph there, leaving my readers wanting to know more.
A third way to create a cliffhanger is to have a character get ready to explain how the mystery was solved, but have to do something else first. If I was going to use this type of cliffhanger, I might write:

> *"Well, it's been a long investigation searching for clues and asking a lot of questions, but we finally know what happened. Before I can tell you the whole story, I have got to get some sleep. I'm exhausted."*

Again, you can see how this would keep the reader wanting more. There are numerous ways to create cliffhangers, but I'll share one more. This example has the main character lose something very important and then find it in the next paragraph. For this type, I could write:

> *I have been looking everywhere, but I can't remember where I put it. I will retrace my steps, and hopefully it will show up. If not, I don't know what I will do.*

Today as you are continuing to work on the middle section of your mystery, you can continue to build tension, add dialogue where it makes sense, and choose one or two cliffhangers to add to the end of a paragraph. Remember that the resolution to the cliffhanger should be in the next paragraph. I will leave my examples up and write a list of the four types of cliffhangers we discussed: sudden clue, alone in an unusual place, explain everything later, lose something.

(continued)

You should be finished with the middle section of your mystery by the end of writing today. We will work on the conclusion soon. You may gather your things and work near a partner for support.

Student Work Session

Each student will sit near a partner. The partners should continue to add to their mysteries, including dialogue, tension, and at least one cliffhanger. Pull students together who may have a difficult time completing their middle sections today without your support. Help them choose some places to add dialogue and build tension, and find one place to add a cliffhanger.

Student Sharing

You worked very hard today to finish the middle section of your mystery. I could tell you really enjoyed adding cliffhangers today. They are sure to hook your reader to keep reading until the end.

Each of you, share the cliffhanger(s) you used with a new partner. Partners, give feedback to help the writers make their cliffhangers the best they can be to hook the reader.

DAY 5

Teacher Instruction

You have spent several days adding details to your mystery to make it exciting for your reader. We are going to talk about another technique today. The art of writing a good narrative is to create a picture in the reader's mind by using only your words. Sometimes we find ourselves repeating the same or similar words or phrases several times in a piece of writing, which makes our story boring and not vivid for our reader at all.

Earlier this week, we created a word list for other ways to say *said.* Today we will create a few more word lists for some common words. I chose the following words that I see used repeatedly in your writing. Think of some other words or phrases that are synonyms or have the same meaning as *run, like, funny, good, bad,* and *nice.* I will write them on the chart as you say them.

Now that we have our chart started, how can we use it to improve our writing? I will show you how to replace some words in your writing with words from this list or other words we can think of. Would one of you like to share your writing?

First, I will read through the piece. As I am reading it, give a thumbs-up if you hear a word or phrase that you think could be replaced. I will underline the words, and we will come back to them after we read the whole piece.

I've underlined a few words. Let's go back and look at them. Here is the word *like.* Look at the chart and choose a different word to replace *like.* I also underlined *really like.* This is a phrase that I see a lot in your writing. Look at the chart and choose a replacement. Give a

(continued)

thumbs-up if you chose *admire.* Or give a thumbs-up if you think *treasure* sounds better here.

Today I would like you to follow this same procedure to add more interesting words to your story. If you find other words that are not on our list, add them to a sticky note so that we can add them later. You may work near a partner to support each other as you replace some ordinary words with more interesting words. You may find your spots and get started.

Student Work Session

Students replace common words with more interesting words. Monitor and offer support; as needed, work with students who are having difficulty choosing words to replace.

Student Sharing

You made some careful decisions today with your word replacements. They will help your reader to stay interested in your story. Please share any new words you thought of to add to our word list.

DAY 6

Teacher Instruction

You have been working for the past several days on improving your mysteries. We have talked about the importance of word choice and keeping the interest of our readers, so we certainly don't want to end our stories with *That's the end of my story.* Today I am going to show you a few different ways to end your mystery in an interesting way.

One way is to have the narrator share a reaction about how he or she is feeling after this experience. If I were going to write a reaction, I could have my main character say:

> *"Well, it was a lot of hard work, but I am glad my family worked as a team to solve the mystery," John sighed. "I don't think I ever want to go through that again!"*

Another way to end a narrative is to circle back to the beginning scene. If I were going to choose this ending, I could write:

> *The next morning the demolition picked up right where it left off. Lots of hammering and banging could be heard as I lay in my bed trying to get some much-needed rest. Solving mysteries is exhausting work.*

A third way to end a narrative is with a sequel starter. I could do that by writing:

> *We thought our investigating days had come to an end until Dad hollered from the living room, "Guys, come quick! Look what I just found!"*

Now I need to decide which ending I like the best. I'm going to choose circling back to the

(continued)

beginning scene, so I will circle that one. I will create a chart to help you remember the different ways to end a narrative: reaction of a character or narrator, circling back, sequel starter.

Today I want you to choose which ending technique you will use. Write out the ending first, and make sure it will work with your mystery; then add it to your story. You may gather your things and move near a partner for support.

Student Work Session

Students will continue working on their drafts by writing endings and choosing one. They can also read through their drafts again and add more descriptions, vivid word choices, and dialogue if needed. Work with students who may have difficulty writing an ending. Help them choose which one to try and guide them through the writing.

Student Sharing

As I was walking around today, I was thinking again about how much your writing has improved so far this year. You have learned many techniques that good writers use. Find a partner with whom you have not worked recently, and share your endings.

DAY 7

Teacher Instruction

Yesterday we tried out new endings, and you completed your drafts. Today we will revise and edit our own pieces thoughtfully with the checklist, and try something new today for peer editing. Then you will complete your final copies.

I know that you know how to use our editing and narrative checklists to improve your writing. I have seen you do this several times. So instead of modeling my thinking when using the checklist again, I want to show you how to give constructive feedback when you are editing and revising with a peer. Using the checklist is a really good place to start, but being able to tell authors one or two things they did really well, and one change that would make a big difference, is really helpful. May I have a volunteer to share his or her writing? I'll read it aloud first. [Read the volunteer's work.]

Wow! That was a really strong narrative piece, but just telling our friend that this piece was strong doesn't help her [or him] at all. Hmm. . . . Let me look at the checklist. The checklist has "Do I use dialogue to develop the events?" She did that, so I can make that my positive comment. I am going to write that down as my positive, because I definitely want her to do that again.

+ Dialogue

OK, one more positive note. This ending . . . this ending is awesome. I can see that she tried one of our new techniques and ended with an idea for a sequel. I want to give her positive feedback about that.

(continued)

+ Ended with sequel starter

Now I need to find something really important that she can do better. I want to pick something big, so that I can help her make this piece really strong. Hmm. . . . We spent a lot of time discussing how to build tension in a mystery to keep the reader in suspense. I see that she did that one time in the beginning, but I don't see any other attempts at tension building. I am going to write:

– Tension building?

I want to talk to her about why it is not in here and see if I can help.

Turn and tell your partner what you noticed I did. I named specific things that [our volunteer] did well. I used the checklist to guide thinking. I gave meaningful feedback that would really help make the piece better. Today when you go off to revise and edit with a peer, I want you to do the same thing.

Student Work Session

Students will work on revising, editing, peer revising and editing, and finishing up their final copies. Work with students who need additional support.

Student Sharing

Students will post their final copies on their desk or on their screens, and students will be able to walk around the room and read their final copies. For each piece that a student reads, the student should leave a positive note.

Informal Decoding Inventory

This inventory is in two parts. Part I (from Walpole & McKenna, 2017), except for the last subtest, assesses skills used to decode single-syllable words. We include it here to help teachers identify the word recognition needs of students in upper elementary grades who need intensive interventions. The full inventory should only be used for students who are dysfluent and also cannot read the last subtest in Part I, Multisyllabic Words, when this is administered separately (as the Multisyllabic Decoding Screening; see Chapter 4). Part II assesses skills used to decode multisyllabic words. We recommend that teachers administer Part II after teaching the multisyllabic decoding lessons (see Appendix F) to guide reteaching.

ADMINISTERING PART I

Short Vowels

Point to **sat**. Say, "What is this word?" Go from left to right on the scoring form (top to bottom for the child), repeating this question for each word in row 1. It is fine if the student reads across the line without prompting. Repeat the procedure for row 2 (nonsense words). (Note: If the student cannot pass this subtest, consider placing the student in a Tier 3 intensive intervention program and using the assessments accompanying that program.)

Consonant Blends and Digraphs

Point to **blip**. Say, "What is this word?" Go from left to right on the scoring form, repeating this question for each word in row 1. It is fine if the student reads across the line without prompting. Repeat the procedure for row 2 (nonsense words).

R-Controlled Vowel Patterns

Point to **card**. Say, "What is this word?" Go from left to right on the scoring form, repeating this question for each word in row 1. It is fine if the student reads across the line without prompting. Repeat the procedure for row 2 (nonsense words).

Vowel–Consonant–e

Point to **stale**. Say, "What is this word?" Go from left to right on the scoring form, repeating this question for each word in row 1. It is fine if the student reads across the line without prompting. Repeat the procedure for row 2 (nonsense words).

(continued)

Vowel Teams

Point to **neat**. Say, "What is this word?" Go from left to right on the scoring form, repeating this question for each word in row 1. It is fine if the student reads across the line without prompting. Repeat the procedure for row 2 (nonsense words). For nonsense words *feap* and *tead,* accept either the long- or short-/e/ sound.

Multisyllabic Words

This subtest contains only real words, and they progressively differ in syllable type. Point to **flannel**. Say, "What is this word?" Go from left to right on the scoring form, repeating this question for each word.

SCORING PART I

Part I of this inventory includes six subtests that progress in difficulty. The first five address single-syllable decoding; the last addresses multisyllabic decoding. Each subtest contains 10 real words and 10 nonsense words, except for the Multisyllabic Words subtest, which (as noted above) contains only real words. Grouping decisions are based on the first subtest the student fails to pass. It is not necessary to total scores across subtests, but simply to identify the highest level of proficiency. Use a criterion of 8 correct for real words and 6 for nonsense words as indicating proficiency with a particular word type.

ADMINISTERING PART II

Compound Words

Point to **batman**. Say, "What is this word?" Go from left to right on the scoring form, repeating this question for each word in row 1. It is fine if the student reads across the line without prompting. Repeat the procedure for row 2 (coined and nonsense words).

Closed Syllables

Point to **dentist**. Say, "What is this word?" Go from left to right on the scoring form, repeating this question for each word in row 1. It is fine if the student reads across the line without prompting. Repeat the procedure for row 2 (nonsense words).

Open Syllables

Point to **lotus**. Say, "What is this word?" Go from left to right on the scoring form, repeating this question for each word in row 1. It is fine if the student reads across the line without prompting. Repeat the procedure for row 2 (nonsense words).

Vowel–Consonant–e Syllables

Point to **confine**. Say, "What is this word?" Go from left to right on the scoring form, repeating this question for each word in row 1. It is fine if the student reads across the line without prompting. Repeat the procedure for row 2 (nonsense words).

(continued)

R-Controlled Syllables

Point to **fiber.** Say, "What is this word?" Go from left to right on the scoring form, repeating this question for each word in row 1. It is fine if the student reads across the line without prompting. Repeat the procedure for row 2 (nonsense words).

Vowel Team Syllables

Point to **chowder.** Say, "What is this word?" Go from left to right on the scoring form, repeating this question for each word in row 1. It is fine if the student reads across the line without prompting. Repeat the procedure for row 2 (nonsense words).

Consonant–le Syllables

Point to **bubble.** Say, "What is this word?" Go from left to right on the scoring form, repeating this question for each word in row 1. It is fine if the student reads across the line without prompting. Repeat the procedure for row 2 (nonsense words).

SCORING PART II

Like the first five subtests in Part I, each Part II subtest contains 10 real words and 10 nonsense words. Likewise, because real words may be identified at sight, a higher criterion (8 correct, or 80%) is used for mastery. For nonsense words, the criterion is 6 correct (60%), but remember to count as correct pronunciations that are reasonable, even if they include different syllable divisions. Students cannot check their pronunciations against meaning, so they may divide and pronounce some syllables incorrectly.

Informal Decoding Inventory, Part I
Teacher Protocol

Name: _____ Date: _____

Short Vowels									
sat	pot	beg	nip	cub	pad	top	hit	met	nut
						Total			
mot	tib	han	teg	fet	lup	nid	pab	hud	gop
						Total			

Consonant Blends and Digraphs									
blip	check	clam	chin	thick	frank	mint	fist	grab	rest
						Total			
clop	prib	hest	chot	slen	bund	bist	hald	slub	shad
						Total			

R-Controlled Vowel Patterns									
card	stork	term	burst	turf	fern	dirt	nark	firm	mirth
						Total			
fird	barp	forn	serp	surt	perd	kurn	nirt	mork	tarst
						Total			

(continued)

Vowel–Consonant–e

stale	hike	dome	cube	blame	chive	cute	prone	vane	brine
							Total		
bame	neme	hile	pome	rute	nube	vope	clate	vike	pene
							Total		

Vowel Teams

neat	spoil	goat	pail	field	fruit	claim	meet	beast	boast
							Total		
craid	houn	rowb	noy	feap	nuit	maist	ploat	tead	steen
							Total		

Multisyllabic Words

flannel	submit	cupid	spiky	confide	cascade	varnish	surplus	chowder	approach
							Total		

Informal Decoding Inventory, Part I
Student Materials

sat	blip	card	stale	neat	flannel
pot	check	stork	hike	spoil	submit
beg	clam	term	dome	goat	cupid
nip	chin	burst	cube	pail	spiky
cub	thick	turf	blame	field	confide
pad	frank	fern	chive	fruit	cascade
top	mint	dirt	cute	claim	varnish
hit	fist	nark	prone	meet	surplus
met	grab	firm	vane	beast	chowder
nut	rest	mirth	brine	boast	approach
mot	clop	fird	bame	craid	
tib	prib	barp	neme	houn	
han	hest	forn	hile	rowb	
teg	chot	serp	pome	noy	
fet	slen	surt	rute	feap	
lup	bund	perd	nube	nuit	
nid	bist	kurn	vope	maist	
pab	hald	nirt	clate	ploat	
hud	slub	mork	vike	tead	
gop	shad	tarst	pene	steen	

Informal Decoding Inventory, Part II: Multisyllabic Decoding Inventory
Teacher Protocol

Name: _____ Date: _____

Compound Words									
batman	blackmail	carpool	flashlight	baseball	corndog	crosswalk	battlefield	frostbite	bootstrap
							Total		
catboy	sundog	paintrag	oatfarm	raincan	skywatch	dogrun	meatman	bluestar	hattree
							Total		

Closed Syllables									
dentist	tunnel	compact	hundred	flannel	banquet	submit	contest	blanket	gossip
							Total		
sindict	pladchet	suncrip	bunpect	wunnet	blensim	pefdimp	stindam	flanpeck	winsprick
							Total		

Open Syllables									
lotus	lunar	cupid	spiky	pony	final	spiny	ivy	rely	equal
							Total		
rulab	cluden	diler	slony	nicot	fodun	siny	pady	pilem	byliss
							Total		

(continued)

Vowel–Consonant–*e* Syllables

confine	athlete	conclude	concrete	compose	stampede	suppose	endure	cascade	recline
							Total		
depide	repale	wranblise	mondrine	slindome	lompise	sisdike	dimcline	plinsipe	indube
							Total		

R-Controlled Syllables

fiber	super	furnish	serpent	varnish	jogger	surplus	servant	clergy	diner
							Total		
borniss	sirper	winler	wupper	sonnor	darber	burclust	perstat	birvick	biver
							Total		

Vowel Team Syllables

chowder	ointment	approach	mushroom	pillow	meadow	bounty	treatment	maroon	discreet
							Total		
grinlow	shoopoy	spoinap	haynick	reemin	slighnat	crainem	moanish	flaiwat	scoatal
							Total		

Consonant–*le* Syllables

bubble	dandle	cattle	struggle	bugle	people	eagle	drizzle	whistle	sprinkle
							Total		
buble	scanfle	fangle	baddle	magle	dafle	cogle	pubble	butle	baitle
							Total		

Informal Decoding Inventory, Part II: Multisyllabic Decoding Inventory
Student Materials

batman	dentist	lotus	confine
blackmail	tunnel	lunar	athlete
carpool	compact	cupid	conclude
flashlight	hundred	spiky	concrete
baseball	flannel	pony	compose
corndog	banquet	final	stampede
crosswalk	submit	spiny	suppose
battlefield	contest	ivy	endure
frostbite	blanket	rely	cascade
bootstrap	gossip	equal	recline
catboy	sindict	rulab	depide
sundog	pladchet	cluden	repale
paintrag	suncrip	diler	wranblise
oatfarm	bunpect	slony	mondrine
raincan	wunnet	nicot	slindome
skywatch	blensim	fodun	lompise
dogrun	pefdimp	siny	sisdike
meatman	stindam	pady	dimcline
bluestar	flanpeck	pilem	plinsipe
hattree	winsprick	byliss	indube

(continued)

fiber	chowder	bubble
super	ointment	dandle
furnish	approach	cattle
serpent	mushroom	struggle
varnish	pillow	bugle
jogger	meadow	people
surplus	bounty	eagle
servant	treatment	drizzle
clergy	maroon	whistle
diner	discreet	sprinkle
borniss	grinlow	buble
sirper	shoopoy	scanfle
winler	spoinap	fangle
wupper	haynick	baddle
sonnor	reemin	magle
darber	slighnat	dafle
burclust	crainem	cogle
perstat	moanish	pubble
birvick	flaiwat	butle
biver	scoatal	baitle

Multisyllabic Decoding Lessons

WEEK 1: COMPOUND WORDS

Today we will work with compound words. Compound words contain two words that are joined together to make up a new word. We will divide each compound word into its parts, read each part, and then read the parts together to read the compound word. The challenge is to figure out where to divide the word. For compounds divide after the first word.

herself	bookcase	footstep	soapstone	racehorse
anyone	doorknob	crossroad	keyhole	workshop
himself	armpit	household	afterthought	cardboard
yourself	countryside	rainstorm	manlike	gravestone
throughout	classroom	housework	likewise	swordfish
everyone	workday	storeroom	bookstore	southeast
everybody	racetrack	fireball	schoolmate	grapevine
somehow	airline	burnout	seaside	graveyard
something	farewell	cornfield	shoelace	thumbnail
somewhere	doorbell	fieldtrip	roommate	windburn

Spelling Practice

Now that we practiced reading compound words, let's try to write some compound words. Say the word to yourself. Divide it into two separate words. Spell each word. Remember to check to make sure there is at least one vowel in each word.

chopstick	catfish	dustpan	racetrack	bookstore
pitfall	boxcar	classroom	armpit	cardstock
passport	yardstick	pathway	likewise	grapevine

(continued)

WEEK 2 THROUGH WEEK 6: PREFIXES AND SUFFIXES

Prefixes (Days 1 and 2): Today we will work with prefixes. A prefix is a word part used at the beginning of a word. You need to know a lot of prefixes. To divide and read words with prefixes, find the prefix, read the root word, and then read the prefix and root word together. Remember that the prefix changes the meaning of the root word.

Suffixes (Days 3 and 4): Today we will work with suffixes. A suffix is a word part used at the end of a word. You need to recognize suffixes when reading longer words. To divide and read words with suffixes, find the suffix, read the root word, and then read the root word and suffix together. Remember that the suffix changes the meaning of the root word.

Prefixes and Suffixes (Day 5): Today we will work with words with prefixes and suffixes. A prefix is a meaningful word part at the beginning of a word. A suffix is a meaningful word part used at the end of a word. To divide and read words with prefixes and suffixes, find the prefix, find the suffix, read the root word, and then read the prefix, root word, and suffix together. Remember that the prefix and suffix change the meaning of the root word.

(continued)

Week 2: *un-, re-, -ful, -ly*

Day 1	Day 2	Day 3	Day 4	Day 5
un- means not. For example, the word *unable* means not able (to do something).	*re-* means again or back. For example, the word *repaint* means to paint again.	*-ful* means full of. For example, the word *painful* means full of pain.	*-ly* means in the manner of. For example, the word *suddenly* means something that happens quickly, without warning.	*un* means not. *-ful* means full of. *-ly* means in the manner of.
unscrew	rebuild	fearful	softly	ungracefully
unknown	rework	wishful	nicely	frightfully
unpack	remake	gleeful	sadly	untactful
unclean	reborn	needful	lively	unthoughtful
unplug	rewrite	thoughtful	kindly	unfaithfully
unsafe	reuse	cheerful	motherly	ungratefully
unfair	regain	boastful	fatherly	dreadfully
unkind	restate	peaceful	sisterly	peacefully
unreal	revisit	dreadful	brotherly	boastfully

Spelling Practice

Now that we practiced reading words with prefixes and suffixes, let's practice spelling them. Say the word to yourself, break it into syllables, and spell each one. Remember to think of the parts we discussed today, and check to see that there is at least one vowel in each syllable.

unplug	remake	cheerful	fatherly	faithfully
unreal	reuse	mindful	sadly	unmindful
unscrew	regain	thoughtful	softly	frightfully

(continued)

Week 3: *over-, mis-, -ed, -ness*

Day 1	Day 2	Day 3	Day 4	Day 5
over- can mean in excess, or too much. For example, the word *overflow* means additional flow. *over-* is a two-syllable prefix.	*mis-* means bad or badly. For example, the word *misfortune* means to have bad fortune, bad luck.	*-ed* shows past tense and refers to something that happened in the past. *-ed* sounds like /t/, /id/, or /d/, depending on the base word.	*-ness* means with and is at the end of nouns. For example, the word *darkness* literally means with dark.	*over-* means in excess. *mis-* means bad or badly. *-ed* shows past tense and refers to something that happened in the past. *-ness* means with and is at the end of nouns.
overpower	misfit	trusted	kindness	youthfulness
overgrow	mistrust	blessed	sweetness	mistrusted
overcook	mismatch	heated	coolness	cheerfulness
overrun	misjudge	marked	chillness	colorfulness
overgrown	misread	barked	fairness	restfulness
overdo	misspell	cheered	loudness	wastefulness
overstep	mistreat	boasted	goodness	mismarked
overplant	misuse	worked	greatness	overmatched
overplay	miscount	helped	nervousness	misspelled
overstay	misplace	lifted	sickness	misguided
Spelling Practice				
Now that we practiced reading words with prefixes and suffixes, let's practice spelling them. Say the word to yourself, break it into syllables, and spell each one. Remember to think of the parts we discussed today, and check to see that there is at least one vowel in each syllable.				
overplay	misplace	cheered	sickness	restfulness
overplant	misjudge	lifted	sweetness	mismatched
overstep	mistrust	dressed	goodness	mistrusted

(continued)

Week 4: *pre-, dis-, -able; -er, -ar,* and *-or; -ed*

Day 1	Day 2	Day 3	Day 4	Day 5
pre- means before. For example, the word *preheat* means to heat something before using it.	*dis-* means the opposite of. It means not, just like the prefix *un-*. For example, the word *disapprove* means not to approve (something).	*-able* means able to. For example, the word *manageable* refers to something that can be managed.	*-er* and *-or* can mean one who (does something). For example, the word *teacher* literally means a person who teaches.	*pre-* means before. *dis-* means the opposite of. *-able* means able to. *-ed* shows past tense and refers to something that happened in the past.
pregame	discharge	laughable	pitcher	previewed
prebake	dislike	enjoyable	banker	distractable
precook	disown	suitable	buyer	disbanded
prepay	distrust	valuable	editor	discovered
preschool	disarm	workable	actor	prescribed
preview	disagree	teachable	dancer	prejudged
prepaid	disallow	trainable	painter	disordered
preset	disinfect	washable	leader	avoidable
prescribe	disorder	wearable	worker	disarmed
prejudge	disbelief	readable	pointer	dismounted

Spelling Practice				
Now that we practiced reading words with prefixes and suffixes, let's practice spelling them. Say the word to yourself, break it into syllables, and spell each one. Remember to think of the parts we discussed today, and check to see that there is at least one vowel in each syllable.				
prepay	disagree	workable	banker	avoidable
precook	disorder	washable	pointer	disjointed
prescreen	discharge	suitable	worker	disbanded

(continued)

Week 5: *fore-, trans-, -ing, -en, -ed*

Day 1	Day 2	Day 3	Day 4	Day 5
fore- means before, or in front of. For example, the word *forearm* refers to the part of your arm in front of the elbow.	*trans-* means across or beyond. For example, the word *transport* means to carry across a distance.	*-ing* is an ending for verbs that you are using all the time.	*-en* means to make more. For example, the word *lighten* means to make lighter.	*trans-* means across or beyond. *-ing* is an ending for verbs. *-en* means to make more. *-ed* shows past tense and refers to something that happened in the past.
foresee	transplant	flossing	blacken	toughened
forelegs	transpose	praying	sharpen	transported
foresight	transform	laughing	moisten	strengthened
forefather	transcribe	playing	strengthen	foretelling
forewarn	transport	planting	frighten	loosening
forethought	transact	throwing	lengthen	lightened
foretell	transatlantic	barking	quicken	forewarned
forehead	transverse	blasting	toughen	transfixed
foremost	transmit	tracking	brighten	transplanted
forefinger	transpire	drawing	broaden	sharpening
Spelling Practice				
Now that we practiced reading words with prefixes and suffixes, let's practice spelling them. Say the word to yourself, break it into syllables, and spell each one. Remember to think of the parts we discussed today, and check to see that there is at least one vowel in each syllable.				
forefather	transport	blasting	toughen	strengthened
foremost	transform	tracking	brighten	transplanted
foresight	transact	praying	moisten	sharpening

(continued)

Week 6: *under-, after-, -some, -ment, pre-, -ful, re-, -ness*

Day 1	Day 2	Day 3	Day 4	Day 5
under- means below or less than. For example, the word *underpaid* means being paid less than you deserve. *under-* is a two-syllable prefix.	*after-* means later than a specific event or point in time. For example, the word *afternoon* means the time after 12 P.M. *after-* is a two-syllable prefix.	*-some* changes a word into an adjective. You are using words with the suffix *-some*. For example, *handsome* means good-looking or attractive.	*-ment* means an action or process. For example, the word *government* means the action of governing, ruling a state.	*pre-* means before. *-ful* means full of. *re-* means again. *under-* means below, less than. *-ness* means with and is in nouns. *-ment* means action or process.
underage	aftershave	lonesome	statement	understatement
underground	afterworld	handsome	placement	repayment
understate	afterlife	fearsome	movement	underimprovement
underpants	afterthought	wholesome	payment	pretreatment
underplay	aftertaste	tiresome	treatment	gleefulness
underarm	aftereffect	awesome	improvement	resettlement
underfed	afterglow	bothersome	shipment	gracefulness
underlie	afterward	gruesome	retirement	underpayment
undereat	aftershock	loathsome	advancement	prepayment
undermost	aftermath	meddlesome	agreement	blissfulness

Spelling Practice

Now that we practiced reading words with prefixes and suffixes, let's practice spelling them. Say the word to yourself, break it into syllables, and spell each one. Remember to think of the parts we discussed today, and check to see that there is at least one vowel in each syllable.

underfeed	afterschool	bothersome	shipment	gracefulness
understate	aftercare	tiresome	agreement	blissfulness
underground	aftermath	troublesome	treatment	understatement

(continued)

Week 7: Closed Syllables

Today we will work with words that have closed syllables. A syllable is called closed if the vowel is followed by one or more consonants. The word *stamp* is a closed syllable. So is the word *an*. If you find a closed syllable in a word, the vowel sound will be short. The challenge is to figure out where to divide the word. A strategy you can use is to place a dot underneath each vowel. Then decide how to divide. Remember: In a closed syllable, the vowel is followed by one or more consonants, and its sound is short. So divide after the consonant. When you have double consonants, break the word between them. Blends are usually not divided, and digraphs are never divided. Divide the syllables, decode them, and blend them. If your word doesn't sound right, divide it in a different way.

Practice Words (Sample Talk)

Here is my first word. I will mark the vowels. Now I will look for double consonants to help me to divide. I will divide between two consonants. I will now read each part and blend them. If the word sounds right, I have divided it correctly.

Day 1	Day 2	Day 3	Day 4	Day 5
absent	muffin	conquest	contest	puffin

Words

met	ship	dash	fluff	plump
shed	loft	stump	brush	dusk
velvet	submit	lesson	contrast	attract
bottom	gadget	blanket	fabric	affix
pilgrim	dentist	suffix	fossil	attempt
trumpet	common	insect	gallop	wisdom
cactus	faster	hammer	glutton	nostril
custom	expel	puppet	cannon	husband
blossom	basket	until	canvas	collect
ribbon	compass	pallet	falcon	pumpkin

Spelling Practice

Now that we practiced reading words with closed syllables, let's spell some words with the same patterns. Think of the vowel sound within each syllable when you spell it.

bottom	compass	blanket	canvas	wisdom
velvet	common	puppet	fabric	husband
trumpet	gadget	insect	contrast	attract

(continued)

Week 8: Open and Closed Syllables

Today we will work with words that have open syllables. A syllable is called open if the vowel is not followed by one or more consonants. The word *he* is an open syllable. If you find an open syllable in a word, the vowel sound will be long. The challenge is to figure out where to divide the word. A strategy you can use is to place a dot underneath each single vowel. Then decide how to divide. Remember: In an open syllable, the vowel is not followed by one or more consonants, and its sound is long. So divide after the vowel. Divide the syllables, decode them, and blend them. If your word doesn't sound right, divide it in a different way.

Practice Words (Sample Talk)

Here is my first word. I will mark the vowels. Now I will think if I should divide after the vowel or after the consonant. I will now read each part and blend them. If the word sounds right, I have divided it correctly.

Day 1	Day 2	Day 3	Day 4	Day 5
ivy	navy	gravy	pupil	apron

Words

be	hi	fry	eject	she
unit	event	music	equal	frugal
cozy	fever	python	recent	puma
moment	hotel	pupil	bypass	bacon
nomad	focus	aphid	human	hyphen
rely	student	raven	pilot	blatant
retry	silent	lady	stupid	mucus
moment	depend	total	evil	vacant
baby	basic	robot	brutal	program
even	bonus	result	fatal	strident

Spelling Practice

Now that we practiced reading words with open syllables, let's spell some words with the same patterns. Think of the vowel sound within each syllable when you spell it.

nomad	bonus	music	evil	strident
unit	depend	robot	brutal	bacon
baby	focus	raven	recent	frugal

(continued)

Week 9: Closed, Open, and Vowel–Consonant–*e* Syllables

Today we will work with words that have closed syllables, open syllables, and vowel–consonant–*e* syllables. In a vowel–consonant–*e* syllable, there is a single vowel and a consonant, followed by a final /e/ that indicates that the vowel is long. The word *fate* is a vowel–consonant–*e* syllable, and so is the word *blame*. If you find a vowel–consonant–*e* syllable in a word, the vowel sound will be long. The challenge is to figure out where to divide the word. A strategy you can use is to place a dot underneath each vowel. Then decide how to divide. Remember: In a vowel–consonant–*e* syllable, the pattern you see is vowel–consonant–*e*. So when the vowel–consonant–*e* does not come at the end of a word, divide after the *e*. For each word, divide the syllables, decode each one, and blend them. If your word doesn't sound right, divide it in a different way.

Practice Words (Sample Talk)

Here is my first word. I will mark the vowels. Now I will look for the pattern vowel–consonant–*e*. I will now read each part and blend them. If the word sounds right, I have divided it correctly.

Day 1	Day 2	Day 3	Day 4	Day 5
collide	revise	migrate	pavement	define

Words

rake	space	frame	flute	brute
mistake	supreme	donate	pollute	stampede
estate	athlete	microbe	dictate	divide
ignite	humane	cascade	crusade	explode
conspire	reduce	chloride	refuge	precede
mandate	define	volume	deplete	inquire
compose	restate	concede	decade	expire
translate	rephrase	suffice	impede	debate
rotate	deduce	immune	extreme	acquire
divine	define	polite	before	impure

Spelling Practice

We will practice spelling some words with closed, open, and vowel–consonant–*e* syllables. Think of the vowel sound for each syllable type when you spell it.

compose	athlete	donate	refuge	stampede
ignite	supreme	volume	deplete	expire
estate	humane	immune	dictate	divide

(continued)

Week 10: *r*-Controlled Syllables

Today we will work with words that have closed syllables, open syllables, and *r*-controlled syllables. An *r*-controlled syllable has a vowel followed by an *r* that changes the vowel sound. The word *car* is *r*-controlled. So is the word *bear*. The challenge is to figure out where to divide the word. A strategy you can use is to place a dot underneath each vowel. Then decide how to divide. Remember: In a closed syllable the vowel will be short; in an open syllable, the vowel will be long, and in an *r*-controlled syllable, the vowel will not be long or short because of the *r*. Divide the syllables, decode each one, and blend them. If your word doesn't sound right, divide it in a different way.

Practice Words (Sample Talk)

Here is my first word. I will mark the vowels. I will then decide where to divide the word. I will now read each part and blend them. If the word sounds right, I have divided it correctly.

Day 1	Day 2	Day 3	Day 4	Day 5
barber	harvest	farmer	tamper	blubber

Words

far	sir	her	fur	or
garment	letter	sermon	butter	fever
circus	thermos	after	carbon	turnip
skirmish	sturdy	marshal	rattler	afford
parchment	dinner	further	garlic	current
carpet	perhaps	barley	person	worry
monster	perfect	burden	farther	minor
worker	marker	furnish	merchant	robber
server	confirm	burlap	suburb	alert
surplus	kernel	border	hermit	thirty

Spelling Practice

Now that we practiced reading words with closed, open, and *r*-controlled syllables, let's spell some words with the same patterns. Think of the vowel sound within each syllable when you spell it.

garment	perfect	further	hermit	afford
carpet	confirm	border	garlic	alert
monster	diner	sermon	carbon	turnip

(continued)

Week 11: Vowel Teams

Today we will work with words that have open, closed, *r*-controlled, and vowel team syllables. In a vowel team syllable, there are two vowels working together to make one sound. The word *main* has a vowel team and so does the word *clown*. Remember that *w* and *y* can work as vowels. A strategy you can use is to place a dot underneath each single vowel and an underline below a vowel team. Then decide how to divide. Remember in a closed syllable the vowel will be short. In an open syllable the vowel will be long, and in an *r*-controlled syllable the vowel will not be long or short because of the r. Divide the syllables, decode them, and blend them. If your word doesn't sound right, divide it in a different way.

Practice Words (Sample Talk)

Here is my first word. I will mark the vowels and underline the vowel teams. I will now read each part and blend them. If the word sounds right, I have divided it correctly.

Day 1	Day 2	Day 3	Day 4	Day 5
seasons	contain	steamer	retrieve	healthy

Words

glow	float	fear	bear	pearl
maintain	fairway	faucet	compound	portrait
flounder	applaud	weather	roundup	instead
allow	boarder	harpoon	coastline	relief
crayon	mistook	preacher	enjoy	mushroom
ointment	county	feather	blackout	townsfolk
raccoon	autumn	daughter	tiptoe	beneath
approach	baboon	rooster	widow	repeat
complain	tattoo	slaughter	window	pillow
balloon	ready	jawbone	willow	freedom
meadow	feedback	seesaw	mildew	campaign

Spelling Practice

Now that we practiced reading words with closed, open, *r*-controlled, and vowel team syllables, let's spell some words with these patterns. Think of the vowel sound within each syllable when you spell.

balloon	tattoo	daughter	willow	feedback

(continued)

Week 12: Consonant–*le* Syllables

Today we will divide and read words that have a consonant–*le* syllable. The consonant–*le* syllable, as its names indicates, is a consonant followed by *le*. The consonant–*le* syllable type is at the end of words. The syllable before it can be any of the types we discussed. When you see a consonant–*le* syllable at the end of a word, always divide before it. Divide the syllables, decode each one, and blend them. If your word doesn't sound right, divide it in a different way.

Practice Words (Sample Talk)

Here is my first word. I will mark the vowels and underline the vowel teams. I will look for the consonant–*le* pattern and divide before it. Then I will look at the first part of the word and decide what type of syllable it is. I will now read each part and blend them. If the word sounds right, I have divided it correctly.

Day 1	Day 2	Day 3	Day 4	Day 5
candle	able	saddle	fable	cattle

Words

cripple	cable	double	eagle	noodle
grapple	noble	sprinkle	people	beetle
turtle	cycle	riddle	staple	beagle
crumble	maple	mumble	noodle	whistle
simple	title	idle	pickle	bridle
muscle	steeple	ample	freckle	riddle
ruffle	fable	rifle	poodle	giggle
drizzle	bugle	stifle	steeple	whittle
puzzle	marble	gargle	dawdle	dribble
jungle	sniffle	hurdle	wrinkle	mingle

Spelling Practice

Now that we practiced reading words with the different syllable types, we will spell them. Think of the vowel sound and pattern within each syllable when you spell.

jungle	noble	mumble	poodle	beagle
simple	title	riddle	eagle	dribble
candle	marble	sprinkle	people	whistle

(continued)

251

Week 13: *-ed* and *-ing*

We have worked with the suffixes **-ed** and **-ing**. We said that these suffixes appear always in verbs. Today we will work on some of the spelling patterns for these suffixes.

Day 1	Day 2	Day 3	Day 4	Day 5
In a verb where the base word ends in a final *e*, we will add only *d* when creating the past tense. The *-ed* will make the sound /d/, /id/, or /t/, depending on the base word.	In a verb where the base word ends in final *e*, we will drop the *e* when adding *-ing*.	In a verb where the base word ends in a short vowel followed by a single consonant, we double the final consonant before adding *-ed* or *-ing*.	In a verb where the base word ends in a long vowel followed by a single consonant, we add *-ed* or *-ing* without changing the base word.	In the following words, either the base word ends in a final *e* and the *e* was dropped, the final consonant was doubled, or there was no change. Remember what we discussed during the week, and identify the base word after reading the word.
used	hoping	nodding	moaned	riding
waved	writing	hopped	boasted	smiling
skated	closing	sniffed	meeting	tuning
traded	framing	planned	mailing	shouting
shaped	waving	swimming	cleaning	waited
glazed	skating	stopped	eating	seemed
based	making	rubbing	dreaming	voted
spiked	moving	permitted	preaching	fanning
grated	having	begging	greeting	flopping
cared	taking	dropped	snowing	slipped

You may ask the students to spell some of the words after they practice reading them.

(continued)

Week 14: Changing *y* to *i* or No Change

We have worked with the suffixes **-ed** and **-ing**. We will examine the endings *-ies* and *-ied*, as well as changes in words that end in *y*. We will work on some of the spelling patterns for these suffixes.

Day 1	Day 2	Day 3	Day 4	Day 5
In a verb that ends in a consonant plus *y*, we first change the *y* to *i* before adding -ed or -es. In a verb that ends in a vowel plus *y*, we do not need to change the *y* before adding -s or -ed.	In a singular word that ends in *y*, we add an -s to make it plural when there is a vowel before the *y*. If there is a consonant before the *y*, we drop the *y* and add *-ies*.	In a verb that ends in *y*, there is no change when adding -ing.	In a word that ends in a consonant followed by *y*, we change the *y* to *i* before adding a suffix.	Read the words, and identify the root word and the changes that happened to *y*.
cried	days	crying	armies	delaying
applies	pennies	hurrying	fanciful	deliveries
occupied	juries	applying	variance	adversaries
supplies	monkeys	portraying	appliance	tendencies
conveys	abilities	studying	ordinarily	joyful
conveyed	buddies	terrifying	emptiness	accompanied
employed	families	qualifying	burial	thirstiness
qualifies	personalities	enjoying	dutiful	verified
replied	surveys	tidying	alliance	certified
horrified	delays	employing	ladies	petrifying

You may ask the students to spell some of the words after practicing reading them.

(continued)

253

Week 15: Combinations of Syllable Types

You know all the syllable types, and you know how to divide and read words with two syllables. Today we will divide and read words that have more than two syllables. The challenge is to determine where to divide the word. A strategy you can use is to place a dot underneath each vowel and an underline below a vowel team. Blends and vowel teams are usually not divided. Digraphs are never divided. Remember that the real test is to ask if the word you read sounds right. If it doesn't, divide it in a different way.

Practice Words (Sample Talk)

Here is my first word. I will mark the vowels and underline the vowel teams. I will now read each part and blend them. If the word sounds right, I have divided it correctly.

Day 1	Day 2	Day 3	Day 4	Day 5
prosecute	compromise	pantomime	personalize	instrument

Words

speculate	persistent	compressor	stimulate	example
porcupine	argument	assembly	validate	ignorant
turbulent	evacuate	dictator	advocate	assignment
recorder	scholastic	fabricate	increasing	neighborhood
understand	refinement	determined	announcement	domestic
department	mechanism	technical	compromise	attainment
hibernate	synchronize	congratulate	absolute	retirement
camcorder	departure	customer	eradicate	government
delightful	dissatisfy	progressing	insulate	storekeeper
laborer	professor	murderer	singular	quadruple

Spelling Practice

Now that we practiced reading multisyllabic words, let's try to spell them. Say the word, break it into syllables and try to spell each syllable. In the end, check to see if each syllable part is represented correctly.

porcupine	departure	customer	insulate	ignorant
camcorder	refinement	dictator	singular	domestic
hibernate	evacuate	congratulate	stimulate	example

(continued)

Week 16: Accent and Schwa Sound

Today we will work with the schwa sound. The schwa sound is the /uh/ sound and can be heard in the unaccented syllable of multisyllabic words. For example, in the word *about*, the *a* makes the /uh/ sound. The first syllable is unaccented and it is pronounced with a schwa. We will read some multisyllabic words that have schwa syllables. Divide the words using what you know about the syllable types, decode each part, blend them, and decide if the word sounds right. Then pay attention to the unaccented syllable. Remember, the schwa sound can be in any unaccented syllable, regardless of the vowel letter you see.

Day 1	Day 2	Day 3	Day 4	Day 5
-*al* is a suffix and in multisyllabic words makes the schwa sound. Words that end in -*al* can be nouns or adjectives. The word *signal* is a noun, and the -*al* is unaccented.	-*ic* is a suffix, and it can be in words that are nouns and adjectives. The accent in these words is always before the ending -*ic*.	-*ant* and -*ance* are at the end of words. These endings have the schwa sound and are unaccented.	-*ive* is unaccented and makes the schwa sound as in *active*.	In three-syllable words, the open middle syllable is unaccented, and it has the schwa sound.

Words				
vital	horrific	tolerance	fugitive	pharmacy
general	terrific	attendance	captive	legacy
personal	athletic	defiant	narrative	tentacle
arrival	patriotic	abundant	relative	argument
global	pathetic	hesitant	massive	metaphor
internal	sarcastic	relevant	perceptive	singular
eternal	statistic	occupant	respective	innocent
nocturnal	angelic	reluctance	negative	alphabet
funeral	ceramic	compliance	sensitive	antelope
identical	electric	significance	massive	octopus

You may ask the students to spell some of the words after practicing reading them.

(continued)

255

Week 17: Accent in Two- and Three-Syllable Words

Today we will work with the two- and three-syllable words and examine their accent. In words with two syllables, the accent usually is on the first syllable. Sometimes, though, the accent may be on the second syllable. Divide each syllable based on its type. Then pay attention to the accent. The syllable that is mostly stressed has the primary accent. The syllable that has a less strong accent has a secondary accent.

Day 1	Day 2	Day 3	Day 4	Day 5
-it and *-et* are suffixes of multisyllabic words. They usually are pronounced as /it/.	*-ate* is a suffix and can have the /it/ or /et/ sound.	*-ate* is a suffix. It is pronounced /it/ when it is unaccented and the word is a noun or an adjective. It is pronounced with a long ā and has a secondary accent when the word is a verb.	*-ine* is an unaccented suffix and is pronounced /in/. In two-syllable words, the accent is on the first syllable.	*-ain* is an unaccented suffix and is pronounced /in/. In two-syllable words, the accent is on the first syllable.
Words				
poet	accurate	estimate	feminine	chieftain
planet	adequate	illuminate	masculine	captain
quiet	literate	literate	doctrine	fountain
orbit	pirate	chocolate	engine	bargain
credit	fortunate	climate	famine	chaplain
audit	private	senate	examine	certain
limit	certificate	donate	imagine	porcelain
toilet	compassionate	ornate	medicine	villain
implicit	delicate	vaccinate	Madeline	mountain
closet	desperate	validate	determine	curtain

You may ask the students to spell some of the words after practicing reading them.

(continued)

Week 18: Accent in Two- and Three-Syllable Words

Today we will work with the two- and three-syllable words and examine their accent. In words with two syllables, the accent is usually on the first syllable. Sometimes, though, the accent may be on the second syllable. Divide each syllable based on its type. Then pay attention to the accent. The syllable that is mostly stressed has the primary accent. The syllable that has a less strong accent has a secondary accent.

Day 1	Day 2	Day 3	Day 4	Day 5
-ine can be also pronounced /en/. When it is pronounced /en/, the accent is on the second syllable for two-syllable words. For three-syllable words, the first syllable has the primary accent and the last the secondary.	*-ice* is an unaccented suffix that is usually pronounced with a schwa sound and forms nouns.	*-tion* is an unaccented suffix that forms nouns. It is pronounced (shun). The syllable before *-tion* is always accented.	*-age* is an unaccented suffix. In words with more than one syllable, it is pronounced /ij/.	*-ture* is an unaccented suffix. It is pronounced /chur/. *-sure* is also an unaccented suffix, and it is pronounced /zhur/.

Words				
chlorine	justice	ignition	cabbage	composure
vaccine	office	repetition	garbage	pleasure
sardine	crevice	election	savage	future
figurine	apprentice	starvation	advantage	puncture
Pauline	novice	quotation	language	gesture
routine	notice	frustration	cottage	literature
magazine	practice	commotion	voyage	departure
submarine	accomplice	rotation	wreckage	adventure
marine	cowardice	perfection	shortage	mixture
machine	service	position	bandage	fracture

You may ask the students to spell some of the words after practicing reading them.

Fluency and Comprehension Sample Plans

SAMPLE LESSON FOR A FOURTH-GRADE FLUENCY AND COMPREHENSION GROUP

Option 1

If you want to teach a self-contained, 15-minute lesson, first read aloud for 5–6 minutes to estimate the number of pages that students will be able to read in a day. Then divide the text into daily segments. Whole chapters are ideal, but this may not be realistic. List page numbers in the left-hand column below. Finally, start to read. At the end of each segment, compose three or four inferential questions. Try to start them with *how* or *why*. All lessons will take the same format: (1) choral reading of a new text segment, (2) partner or whisper reading of the same text segment, and (3) using the questions to engage in a comprehension discussion.

Option 2

If you want to have students read chorally with you for the full 15 minutes, reread with partners outside of your small-group time, and then discuss the text segment the following day, you will be able to assign more than one of the daily segments below each day.

Title and Author: *Esperanza Rising* by Pam Muñoz Ryan
Lexile Level: 750L

Reading	Questions for Discussion
1–8 1924/ Las Uvas (Grapes)	Why did Papa say that the land was alive? Why was it an honor for Esperanza to receive the knife from Papa? How was Esperanza's clothing different from the servants' clothing? Why? Why was the harvest Esperanza's favorite time of year?
8–15	What do we know about Esperanza's life, based on her birthday traditions? How did Esperanza and Mama react to Esperanza's "bad luck"? Why would bandits try to hurt the people who owned land? What lesson did Abuelita teach Esperanza when they crocheted together?

(continued)

Reading	Questions for Discussion
16–22	Why did Mama laugh when Esperanza said she wanted to marry Miguel?
	Do you think Esperanza should have told Miguel about the river? Why?
	Why didn't Esperanza and Mama like Tío Luis and Tío Marco?
	What was Esperanza's bad news, and how did she find out about it?
23–28 Las Papayas (Papayas)	Why does the author describe the blanket and shawl as feeling heavy?
	Why was Señor Rodríguez overcome with grief when he delivered the papayas?
	Which of the gifts do you think was most important to Esperanza? Why?
	Why do you think Abuelita said that the doll looked like an angel?
28–33	How did Mama and Esperanza feel about her uncles' constant presence?
	Why was Papa's estate divided between Mama and Tío Luis?
	Do you think Mama should have sold the house to Tío Luis? Why?
	Do you think Mama should have agreed to marry Tío Luis? Why?
34–38	Why did Miguel and his family plan on leaving for the United States?
	How did Esperanza feel about Hortensio, Alfonso, and Miguel leaving?
	What do you think Esperanza and her family would do without Papa?
39–44 Los Higos (Figs)	What do you think was the significance of Esperanza's dream?
	How do you think Abuelita hurt her ankle during the fire?
	Why did Mama, Abuelita, and Esperanza think the uncles started the fire?
44–50	Why did Mama consider Tío Luis's proposal? How did Esperanza react?
	Would Papa want Mama and Esperanza to go to the United States?
	How were Mama, Abuelita, and Esperanza like the phoenix?
	Why did Esperanza's comment make everyone laugh?
50–57	Where did Abuelita go, and why did she go with Mama and Esperanza?
	Why did Mama and Esperanza dress in clothes from the "poor box"?
	How did this event show how much their lives had changed?
	How do you think Tío Luis would react when he found out that they left?
58–65 Las Guayabas (Guavas)	Why did Mama, Esperanza, and Hortensia have to hide in the wagon?
	How did Hortensia help Esperanza relax when they were hiding?
	How did Miguel show that he was smart and brave?
	How did Esperanza's train ride with Papa compare to the wagon ride?

(continued)

Reading	Questions for Discussion
65–72	How did this train ride compare with Esperanza's train ride with Papa?
	Do you think Esperanza really understood how her life had changed?
	Why was Mama upset with Esperanza's reaction toward the little girl?
	Why was Esperanza glad when the little girl got off the train?
72–80	What do you think Alfonso and Miguel were carrying in the oilcloth? Why?
	Why wouldn't Miguel be able to work at the railroad if he stayed in Mexico?
	Why do you think Mama explained the family's situation to Carmen?
	Why did Miguel explain the difference between rich and poor people?
81–85 Los Melones (Cantaloupes)	Why do you think the people in the first cars were passed through quickly?
	How do you think the people who were sent back to Mexico felt?
	What do you think was in Alfonso and Miguel's secret package? Why?
85–93	How do you think Esperanza felt when Isabel questioned her wealth?
	How had Isabel's life been different from Esperanza's?
	Why do you think Esperanza couldn't hear the heartbeat of the land?
	How did Miguel help Esperanza come back to reality?
93–99	How was the San Joaquin Valley different from Aguascalientes?
	Do you think Marta liked Esperanza? Why or why not?
	Why did Marta support the workers going on strike?
	Why didn't Esperanza like Marta?
100–106 Las Cebollas (Onions)	How did the camp compare to Rancho de las Rosas?
	Why was Mama happy to be at the camp?
	Why wasn't Esperanza happy at the camp?
	Do you think Esperanza was telling Isabel the truth about being rich? Why?
106–113	How did Esperanza feel about having to watch the babies?
	Why didn't Esperanza like Mama's hair?
	Was it a good thing that everyone in camp knew each other's business? Why or why not?

(continued)

Reading	Questions for Discussion
113–120	Why didn't Esperanza tell Isabel that she didn't know how to sweep?
	Why did Esperanza feel humiliated while sweeping the camp's platform?
	Why was Miguel not able to find work at the railroad?
121–129 Las Almendras (Almonds)	Why was Alfonso and Miguel's secret important to Esperanza?
	Did you know that Alfonso and Miguel had brought Papa's roses? How?
	How did Esperanza's actions during bath time reveal her ignorance?
	Why didn't Isabel's father like it when Marta came to their *jamaicas*?
129–138	Why did Esperanza feel alone at the fiesta?
	Why did Marta and her friends want to strike? Why didn't the workers?
	Had Esperanza's feelings toward Marta changed? If so, how?
	Why did Mama say that she would pray for Esperanza?
139–143 Las Ciruelas (Plums)	Why did Esperanza think that Abuelita would be proud of her?
	Do you think it was a wise choice to feed the babies plums?
	How did Esperanza figure out a way to make the sick babies feel better?
	Why do you think no one questioned Esperanza when they got home?
144–153	Why did Esperanza like spending time with Melina?
	Do you think the strike was a good idea? Why or why not?
	What were the effects of the dust storm on the men and women?
	How did the dust storm affect the strike?
153–157	How did the dust storm affect Mama's health?
	How come Mama got Valley Fever and others had no symptoms?
	For how long did the doctor think Mama might be able to live?
	What do you think Esperanza would do if she lost Mama too?
158–164 Las Papas (Potatoes)	Why did Esperanza and Mama both need Abuelita?
	How did Esperanza deal with the valley of Mama being sick? Why was Mama depressed in addition to being sick?
	What was Esperanza's plan to help take care of Mama?
164–172	How did Esperanza plan to make money to bring Abuelita?
	What was repatriation, and how might it affect workers who went on strike?
	Does repatriation sound fair to you? Why or why not?
	Why did Marta's aunt and uncle say that she could not stay with them?

(continued)

Reading	Questions for Discussion
173–178	How was Christmas celebrated at El Rancho de las Rosas?
	Why did Esperanza tell Isabel that she couldn't remember the gifts?
	How was what Esperanza wanted different from what Isabel wanted?
	What did Esperanza mean when she promised to be *la patrona?*
179–184 Los Aguacates (Avocados)	How had Esperanza's work ethic changed since she arrived in California?
	Why didn't Esperanza recognize her hands as her own?
	Why did Hortensia rub the avocado mixture on Esperanza's hands?
	Why couldn't Mama have any visitors for at least a month?
185–193	Why did Miguel drive to the Japanese market instead of closer stores?
	Do you think people would look at Esperanza and think she was uneducated?
	Why did Esperanza buy a piñata even though she was saving money?
	How was the camp where Marta and Ada lived different from Esperanza's?
194–198	Why did Esperanza give the children in the camp the piñata?
	Why did Marta tell Esperanza and Miguel to be careful?
	How did Miguel and Esperanza feel about the strike?
	Why did Miguel begin to remind Esperanza of Papa?
199–204 Los Espárragos (Asparagus)	Why did one of the strikers throw a rock at the woman?
	Who hired the guards, and who were they protecting?
	Who do you think put a rattlesnake in one of the crates? Why?
	Why did Miguel say that things would get worse?
204–213	Why did immigration deport the strikers but not the workers?
	Why did Esperanza help Marta disguise herself as a worker?
	Why did Marta say that she misjudged Esperanza?
	Why was the field no longer crawling with people as it once was?
214–220 Los Duraznos (Peaches)	How was the Queen of the May chosen? Was it fair? Why or why not?
	How was the new camp for people from Oklahoma better? Why was it better?
	Why would the Mexicans only be allowed to swim on Friday afternoons?
	Why did Miguel have to dig ditches instead of working on the railroad?

(continued)

Reading	Questions for Discussion
221–225 Los Duraznos (Peaches)	Why did Miguel argue that life was better in California than in Mexico?
	Why did Esperanza tell Miguel that he was still a second-class citizen?
	Do you think that Esperanza still thought she was a queen? Why?
	Why did Miguel leave? Was it Esperanza's fault?
225–233	Were you surprised that Isabel did not win Queen of the May? Why?
	Why did Esperanza give Isabel the porcelain doll?
	Why was Mama proud of Esperanza?
	Who do you think took the money orders from Esperanza's valise?
234–239 Las Uvas (Grapes)	How do you think Esperanza felt about Miguel taking her money?
	Why was Esperanza concerned when she saw Alfonso?
	Why did Miguel take Esperanza's money orders?
	Why did Esperanza think she saw *un fantasma*, a ghost, of Abuelita?
240–247	How do you think Mama felt when she saw Abuelita?
	How did Miguel sneak Abuelita away from Tío Luis and Tío Marco?
	What was the significance of mountains and valleys?
	How did Esperanza measure time? How was it similar to the chapter titles?
247–253	What does *"Aguántate tantito y la fruta caerá en tu mano"* mean?
	How did this saying apply to Esperanza's life over the past year?
	How did Esperanza's birthday compare to the birthdays of her past?
	Why did Esperanza say, "Do not ever be afraid to start over," to Isabel?
255–262 Author's Note	How did the real Esperanza compare to the main character in the story?
	How was the real Esperanza's life different from the fictional story?
	Why was the Deportation Act passed, and what were the effects?
	What does the word *esperanza* mean in Spanish? Why is that significant?

(continued)

SAMPLE LESSON FOR A FIFTH-GRADE
FLUENCY AND COMPREHENSION GROUP

Option 1

If you want to teach a self-contained, 15-minute lesson, first read aloud for 5–6 minutes to estimate the number of pages that students will be able to read in a day. Then divide the text into daily segments. Whole chapters are ideal, but this may not be realistic. List page numbers in the left-hand column below. Finally, start to read. At the end of each segment, compose three or four inferential questions. Try to start them with *how* or *why*. All lessons will take the same format: (1) choral reading of a new text segment, (2) partner or whisper reading of the same text segment, and (3) using the questions to engage in a comprehension discussion.

Option 2

If you want to have students read chorally with you for the full 15 minutes, reread with a partner outside of your small-group time, and then discuss the text segment the following day, you will be able to assign more than one of the daily segments below each day.

Title and Author: *I Am Malala* by Malala Yousafzai with Patricia McCormick
Lexile Level: 830L

Reading	Questions for Discussion
1–4 Prologue	How do we know that Malala misses things about her old life?
	How has life changed for her father?
	How do we know her father is proud of her?
4–7	How were Malala and Moniba's experiences similar to those of other students you know?
	Why do you think Malala included her thoughts about death?
	Why do you think the men asked the students to identify Malala?
11–15 As Free as a Bird	Why do you think Malala gave us so many insignificant facts about herself?
	Based on what we know so far, how would you describe Malala's family?
	Do you agree with Malala's commitment to avoid revenge? Why or why not?
16–20	How were the lives of men and women different?
	How did Malala feel about the tradition of purdah (covering)?
	Why was Malala's relationship with her father unusual?

(continued)

Reading	Questions for Discussion
21–24 Dreams	What is fasting, and why would a feast be an important family tradition? How was life different for Malala's country relatives than for her own family? How was life different for women in Afghanistan under the Taliban?
25–28 A Magic Pencil	Why did Malala want a magic pencil? How did her experience at the rubbish heap change her? What was special about her family?
29–31 A Warning from God	How did the earthquake change things? What would people have needed to survive? Why could those who came to help easily influence people?
32–36 The First Direct Threat	Who was the mufti, and why was his visit important? What evidence do we have that Malala's family members were good Muslims? Why was the school so important to its students?
39–43 Radio Mullah	Why do you think people used the earthquake as a threat? How was the Radio Mullah influencing people's ideas? Did Malala's family have any connection to the bombers of 9/11 in New York City?
44–47 The Taliban in Swat	What specific actions was the Radio Mullah encouraging, and why were they controversial? Why was it hard for Malala to accept the new rules that people were making? How did her family try to maintain a regular life?
47–51	If women obeyed the Pakistani Taliban, what would life be like for them? Why was it dangerous for Malala's father to travel to Islamabad? How do you think Malala felt about the letter on the school gate?
52–55 No One Is Safe	Why was the newspaper article a brave act? Why was Benazir Bhutto an inspiration? How do you think Malala felt when Bhutto was assassinated?
56–59 Candy from the Sky	Why were the toffees so surprising? How did the curfew change life for people? What kind of life did Malala's family have to get used to?
60–62 2008: What Terrorism Feels Like	Why were the compliments of teachers so important? What do the students' actions tell us about their character traits? Why was it important that the television channels were cut off?

(continued)

Reading	Questions for Discussion
62–65	Why would the Taliban destroy a girls' school at night?
	How does Malala say that war and terrorism are different?
	How did the family face fear at night and find courage in the morning?
69–72 A Chance to Speak	Why was the democracy event at the school surprising?
	What character traits would you assign to Malala now?
	What does it mean to "find one's voice"? Can there be both a literal and a figurative meaning?
73–78 A Schoolgirl's Diary	Why did the girls stop coming to school?
	Why was it risky for Malala to write the diary?
	Why was the diary like a magic pencil?
78–80	How did Malala misunderstand the man on the phone?
	How did Moniba figure out that Malala was the diary author?
	How was her identity revealed more broadly?
81–85 Class Dismissed	Why did the video journalists decide to include Malala in their work?
	Why didn't all of the girls come to school that last day?
	How did the girls work to make their last official day of school special?
86–89 Secret School	How did American television influence Malala?
	Why did children begin to play war games?
	Why were the elementary schools opened, while the schools for older girls remained closed?
90–92 Peace?	Why was the peace deal controversial?
	What does it mean that Malala was wise beyond her years?
	How was she both standing up for what was right and putting herself in danger?
92–95	How do you think women in Pakistan reacted to the video of the young woman being beaten?
	Why didn't the reactions of people outside Pakistan make it easier on the people in Malala's town?
	How can we tell that things were getting much worse for the family?
96–99 Displaced	Why did they have to pack and leave so quickly?
	How would you describe the journey?
	What is an IDP?

(continued)

Reading	Questions for Discussion
99–103	How did Malala continue her education in the mountains?
	How did Holbrooke respond to Malala's request for an education?
	Why did people forget Malala's birthday?
104–106 Home	How had Swat and Mingora changed in the time that the family had been hiding in the mountains?
	Why had the school survived?
	How were the events shaping Malala's own hopes for the future?
107–110 A Humble Request and a Strange Peace	How did life return to normal?
	How did the flooding change things again?
	What was confusing about the position of the Taliban in Pakistan?
111–114 Good News at Last	How did the world continue to notice Malala?
	Why was she determined to be a politician?
	Why could this be a problem for her?
117–119 A Death Threat against Me	Why was the direct threat to Malala from the Taliban so dangerous?
	Why did it upset her father so much?
	How did she decide to deal with it?
120–122 The Promise of Spring	How was the field trip to the White Palace similar to a field trip you might take?
	Why did it become controversial?
	How did the letter show that the ideas of the Taliban were still strong?
123–126 Omens	Why does Malala's age of 15 seem so surprising?
	How do we know that her father was afraid?
	How do we know that she was afraid?
127–130 A Day Like Any Other	Why is the chapter entitled "A Day Like Any Other"?
	Why were the seating arrangements on the bus important?
	Why were the details about Atal important?
133–136 A Place Called Birmingham	What had actually happened to Malala?
	Why couldn't she speak?
	Why did the alphabet card help her?
136–137	Where was Malala?
	Why was she worried about the hospital bills?
	Where was her father?

(continued)

Reading	Questions for Discussion
138–140 Problems, Solutions	How do we know that Malala had suffered some brain damage? How do we know that she was also still herself? Why do you think her family was not with her?
140–142	Why was the newspaper picture so important? Why did the doctors tell Malala not to cry? Why did they tell her father not to cry?
143–145 A Hundred Questions	Why hadn't the doctors told Malala what had happened to her? Why hadn't they given her a mirror before? How did she react when she saw the damage to her face?
146–148 Passing the Hours	Why would the hospital want to take a picture of Malala? Why would she want to cover her hair with a scarf? How was Malala still like a regular teenager?
148–150	How had Malala survived the attack? Why did she get such fantastic medical care? Why was there a piece of her skull in her abdomen?
151–154 We Are All Here Now	Why was it important that Malala moved to a different room in the hospital? Why did Malala finally cry? Why didn't her father answer her question?
154–156	Why was Malala's father so sad? Why was the family shocked at how she looked? How did she show she was strong?
157–160 Filling in the Blanks	How did specific people intervene to save Malala's life? Why was her family not included in decisions? Why did her father decide not to travel to Birmingham with her?
161–164	Why did Malala's father think it was his fault? How did the Taliban react to the story? Why wasn't anyone actually arrested?
165–166 Messages from Around the World	How had people found out about Malala's story? Why was it so hard for her to understand? How did her reactions reveal that she was still a regular teenager?

(continued)

Reading	Questions for Discussion
167–171 A Bittersweet Day	How did Malala participate in her recovery? How did her family start to return to normal? Why did the meeting with the Pakistani government officials occur in private?
172–175 Miracles	How was life different for the family now that they were in England? Why did Malala miss her old friends and her old life? How was her physical recovery progressing?
176–178 This New Place	Why was it so hard for the family in Birmingham? How were they adjusting? Why did the boy warn the family?
178–181	How was school different for Malala? Why did she think she had to be so careful about her actions? What does it mean to say that people have much more in common than the things that make them different?
182–185 The One Thing We All Know	Why couldn't the family return to Pakistan? How were they adapting to their life? Why did Malala's father start to cook breakfast?
186–188 Anniversary	How did Malala take advantage of her opportunities? Why did she understand the people who want to focus on the attack? How did the publicity she was getting help other people?
189–193 One Girl Among Many	How did Malala react to New York City? Why did she write her United Nations speech for people around the world? Why does she see her life as a responsibility and a gift?
195–197 Epilogue: October 2015	How is the life of Malala's mother inspirational? How is the education of girls in England different from Malala's experience in Pakistan? Why does she have to study even harder than she used to?
198–200	How has Malala's personal life continued? Why is the work to support education for all children still important? Why is she working for children in other countries?
201–204	Why was Malala awarded the Nobel Peace Prize? How has Malala's life changed? How has she remained the same?

Text Structure Graphic Organizers

Sequence

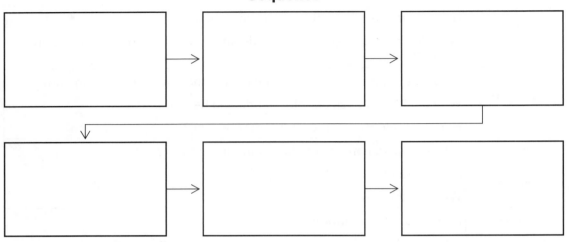

Compare/Contrast

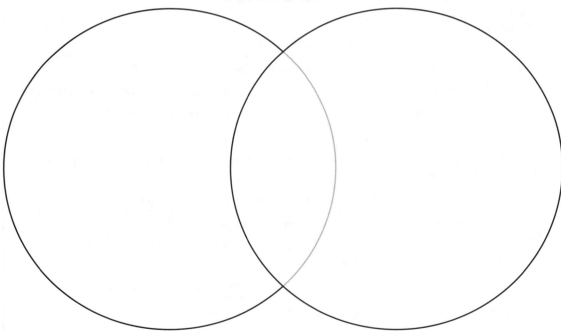

(continued)

Cause/Effect

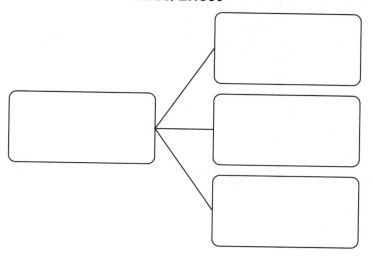

Problem/Solution

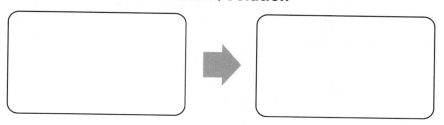

Description/Listing

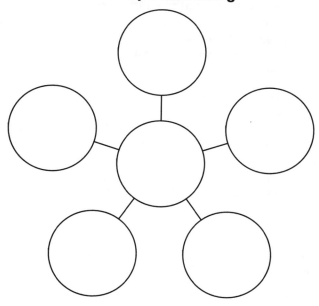

Vocabulary and Comprehension Sample Plans

FICTION SAMPLE LESSON
FOR A VOCABULARY AND COMPREHENSION GROUP

Option 1

If you want to teach a self-contained, 15-minute lesson, first read silently for 7 minutes to estimate the number of pages that students will be able to read in a day. Then divide the text into daily segments. Whole chapters are ideal, but this will depend on chapter length. List page numbers below. Then start to read. At the end of each segment, choose two vocabulary words to teach after reading, identify a strategy to highlight in a reading guide, and compose three or four inferential questions. Try to start them with *how* or *why*. All lessons will take the same format: (1) Update the story map and set a purpose for reading, (2) have students read silently, (3) use the questions to engage in a comprehension discussion, and (4) teach two new words.

Option 2

If you want to take the full 15 minutes to teach vocabulary and engage in discussion before assigning a new text segment for students to read silently outside of your small-group time, you will be able to assign a longer text segment each day. After the first day, all lessons will take the same format: (1) Discuss the previous day's text segment, (2) teach two new words, (3) update the story map and set a purpose for reading, and (4) have students read silently.

Title and Author: *The Thief* by Megan Whalen Turner
Lexile Level: 920L

The Thief: Chapter 1	
Introduce book	We are going to begin a complicated fantasy, set in the past. You will see that the author writes as if it is historical fiction, but we have to begin knowing that it is not. Listen as I read the author's own notes from the back of the book, titled "The real world behind Gen's world." You can see that even a fantasy is influenced by fact.
	From these introductory resources, we know that we will be on a quest, or a mission. Since it is fiction, we know that we have to be on the lookout for characters, setting, and a problem. In each chapter we will have multiple events to keep track of, so once we begin the quest, we will keep track of events chapter by chapter in a running story map. We'll also have to be sure to keep track of all the place names, since they are made up.

(continued)

Set purpose for reading	Decide who is narrating the story, and look for details about that character.
Highlight a strategy that will help students read silently	[p. 3. I had wanted everyone to know that I was the finest thief since mortal men were made, and I must have come close to accomplishing the goal.] After you read about Gen calling himself "the finest thief since mortal men were made," you might want to self-monitor. Think about why a thief would want everyone to know he was the best. Think about why Gen seemed so proud of his crime in public. You might be able to make a hypothesis to check later.
Lead inferential discussion	1. Why was the narrator chained in his cell? 2. Why were the guards careful to check on the prisoner? 3. What does the author mean by saying that there were temples to the old gods and a basilica to the new gods? 4. What had the prison been before it became a prison? 5. What is a magus? 6. Why did Gen need to let his eyes adjust when the magus took him out of his cell? 7. Why didn't the magus want Gen to sit? 8. Why did the magus want Gen's services? 9. Who else was in the chamber with the magus and Gen? 10. What had made him successful? 11. Why did the king show Gen the gold?
Teach vocabulary	*In-va-ders* (closed, open, *r*-controlled) is a noun that means armies who enter a country to take over its land and resources. We will see that the setting of this book is a region where there have been many invasions. *Invasion* is the noun form. *Invade* is the verb. *Meg-a-ron* (closed, unaccented, closed) is a noun that means a house with a large hall in the center. It was a type of house built in Mycenae, a city in ancient Greece. *Mega-* means big, so we should think of a megaron as a very large house.
The Thief: **Chapter 2**	
Describe text structure	Update the story map.
Set purpose for reading	Think about why the journey was so difficult for Gen.
Highlight a strategy that will help students read silently	[p. 28. The smells of the prison floated down the road with me, and I think even the horse underneath me objected.] Your understanding of this chapter will be deepened if you take the time to make sensory images. Use clues from the author to think about what Gen looked and smelled like. Then visualize how that look and those smells may have influenced his relationships with the rest of the people on the journey.

(continued)

Lead inferential discussion	1. Why was the noonday sun so painful for Gen? 2. Why was the magus angry about the packing job? 3. Why did Gen think the journey would be long? 4. Why didn't Gen want to get onto the horse? 5. What details does the author provide about the city they passed through? 6. Why didn't the magus want Gen to speak to his friend? 7. How did Gen figure out what time of year it was? 8. Why was Gen so much more tired than the others? 9. Why did Gen finally get to wash? 10. Why did Gen want to keep his own shoes? 11. Why was it so difficult to clean Gen's sores?
Teach vocabulary	*Cir-cu-it-ous* (r-controlled, open, closed, suffix) is an adjective that means longer than necessary. A circuitous route is not straight from one place to another. *Circuitous* is related to the word *circle*. *In-dis-tinct* (closed, closed, closed) is an adjective that means not clear. The prefix *in-* means not, and *distinct* means clear. If something is indistinct, it looks or sounds blurry.
The Thief: **Chapter 3**	
Describe text structure	Update the story map.
Set purpose for reading	Think about Gen and how his actions reveal his character.
Highlight a strategy that will help students read silently	[p. 43. "Prison," I said.] It will help to self-monitor again. You are going to get more information about how Gen thought and talked about himself. Remember in Chapter 1, we were surprised about his bragging. Now that Gen was with the magus, he was still telling things that others might consider secret. When you see strange information like this, it's good to stop and think about it, and then to hold it in mind for later.
Lead inferential discussion	1. Why did Pol have to carry Gen up to the rooms? 2. Why did Gen like having long hair? 3. How did Pol make sure that Gen didn't escape during the night? 4. Why did Pol wash Gen instead of letting him do it himself? 5. Why was the innkeeper kind to Gen in the morning? 6. Why was the magus asking Sophos and Ambiades questions about trees? 7. Why was Gen still so hungry at lunch? 8. Which of the apprentices was a future duke? 9. Why did the magus want Sophos and Gen to take riding lessons? 10. Why would sleeping lightly be a virtue? 11. What did Gen think of being a soldier as a career?

(continued)

	12. Why was that controversial? 13. Why couldn't they have used a cart? 14. What do we learn about Gen's crime? 15. Why did Gen think he was the most important person on the trip?
Teach vocabulary	*Ap-pren-tice* (closed, closed, irregular) is a noun that means a person who is learning from someone else who is called a *master.* An apprentice learns things that can't be learned in regular school. You might be an apprentice carpenter or jeweler. *Dis-grun-tled* (closed, closed, consonant–*le*) is an adjective that means angry or not satisfied. *Disgruntled* is related to the word *grunt,* because if you are disgruntled, you might grunt.

The Thief: Chapter 4	
Describe text structure	Update the story map.
Set purpose for reading	Think about how the author provides us with information about the setting—really, the three kingdoms of Sounis, Eddis, and Attolia.
Highlight a strategy that will help students read silently	[p. 66. I wondered if he'd told Pol.] Stop and summarize during this chapter. There is a central mystery here about what they were going to steal. Look back and figure out what we know about it. Create a brief summary in your mind about what their goal was and which characters had the most information about it. If you make that summary in your mind, you can update it later if there are more clues.
Lead inferential discussion	1. Why was the magus quizzing the apprentices on history? 2. Why was Gen able to rest longer than on previous days? 3. Why did they set out on foot instead of on horses? 4. Why didn't Gen carry a pack? 5. How had the landscape changed? 6. Why was there tension among Sounis, Eddis, and Attolia? 7. What is a succession? 8. How was Hamiathes's Gift related to the old gods—very much like the Greek gods in the Greek myths? 9. How did the Gift keep things peaceful? 10. Why was Gen so upset that Hamiathes's Gift was from a myth? 11. Why did the magus think he could find it? 12. What is the magus's motivation to steal the Gift? 13. What does it mean when the King's Thief is capitalized? 14. Why couldn't Gen be King's Thief? 15. What was Sounis's real motivation to marry Eddis?

(continued)

	16. Who was Polyphemus, and why did people think he built a road?
	17. What do we learn about Sophos's father?
Teach vocabulary	*Ten-a-cious* (closed, open, suffix) is an adjective that means willing to keep trying. Someone who is tenacious does not give up. *Tenacity* is the noun form.
	Pan-the-on (closed, open, closed) is a noun that means all of the gods in a religion. Ancient Greeks worshiped a pantheon of gods; Hindus currently worship a pantheon. *Pantheon* is sometimes also used to mean a place where religious ceremonies take place.

The Thief: Chapter 5	
Describe text structure	Update the story map.
Set purpose for reading	Think about the relationship between Ambiades and Sophos.
Highlight a strategy that will help students read silently	[p. 92. My father wanted me to be a soldier, but he's been disappointed.]
	This story is complicated, so I have to stop and summarize quite frequently. The author is giving us more information about Gen, but it's hidden in the details. Make sure that you make a quick list in your mind about what we know about Gen's background. What facts do we learn about his mother, and which of them are hard to make sense of?
Lead inferential discussion	1. What did the myth of creation explain?
	2. How did Gen feel about religion?
	3. How did he feel about mythology?
	4. What was the magus's explanation for differences between his versions of the myths and Gen's mother's?
	5. What happens when the magus insulted Gen's mother?
	6. Why would Gen and the King's Thief of Eddis have the same name?
	7. What can we tell about the characters by their reaction to the temple?
	8. What do we learn about Pol?
	9. Why was Sophos embarrassed when he asked about Gen's father?
	10. What do you think the myth of the birth of Eugenides explains?
	11. Why was Ambiades watching Gen sleep?

(continued)

Teach vocabulary	*Hea-then* (vowel team, closed) is a noun or an adjective that is used as a put-down; it means a person who does not believe in religion.
	Tem-per-a-men-tal (closed, *r*-controlled, irregular, closed, closed) is an adjective that means likely to change moods often. A temperamental person can be hard to get along with. The noun form is *temperament.*

The Thief: **Chapter 6**	
Describe text structure	Update the story map.
Set purpose for reading	Think about how the author keeps providing us with more and more information about each character and his motivations.
Highlight a strategy that will help students read silently	[p. 112. I didn't want them to think I liked being clean, but the cool water was refreshing.] In this chapter, it helps to spend some time on Gen's character traits. You have to infer them from what he said and did *and* what he thought. Remember that since the author provides us access to Gen's thoughts, we can compare and contrast what he wanted others to know about him with what he was really like.
Lead inferential discussion	1. Compare and contrast the Sea of Olives and the dystopia. 2. How was Pol helping the two apprentices? 3. Why were the travelers now in danger? 4. How were the cloaks of Ambiades and Sophos different? 5. Why did Ambiades start to torture Gen again? 6. What was unusual about the comb that Gen took from Ambiades's pack? 7. What do we find out about Ambiades's family? 8. What natural laws does the myth explain? 9. What does it tell us about the god of thieves?
Teach vocabulary	*En-vy* (closed, open) is a noun or a verb that means a feeling of jealousness of other people's things. It can be used positively ("I envy you") or negatively ("He was filled with envy"). The adjective form is *envious.* *Dys-to-pi-a* (closed, open, irregular, unaccented) is a noun that means an imaginary place where everything is awful, especially the environment. If all of the plants and animals on earth were killed, there would be a dystopia. Many fantasies are set in an imaginary dystopia.

(continued)

	***The Thief:* Chapter 7**
Describe text structure	Update the story map.
Set purpose for reading	Now focus on the descriptions of the geography and how it influences the characters.
Highlight a strategy that will help students read silently	[p. 135. I have an overabundance of relations, and I wonder if I am better off than you.] Take the time to synthesize during this chapter. Stop reading and think about everything we now know about Gen's original crime. What was it, and why did he do it? Does Gen seem to be telling the truth or not?
Lead inferential discussion	1. Gen had done bad things before. Why did the magus beat him this time? 2. Why did Gen stay with the journey, even though he was humiliated? 3. Why did the apprentices decide to fish? 4. Why did they tie Gen up? 5. Why did Gen agree not to tell the magus what they had done? 6. What do we learn about Sophos's relationship with his father? 7. What do we learn about Pol? 8. Why were there more abandoned farms in Attolia than in Sounis? 9. What do we learn about the magus's family? 10. What do we learn about Gen's family? 11. What do we learn about why Sounis wanted to annex Attolia? 12. What was the dystopia? 13. How did Gen thank Pol for giving him the pain berries? 14. What happened when Sophos and Ambiades practiced their sword fight? 15. Why did Ambiades get so mad at Gen? 16. Why did they decide to go into the dystopia without Ambiades? 17. What was strange about the end of the chapter?
Teach vocabulary	*Plague* (irregular) is a noun meaning a horrible disease that kills most of the population. There was a great plague in Europe that killed thousands of people. There were no medicines that could cure it. *Sur-plus* (r-controlled, closed) is a noun or adjective that means extra. You could have surplus goods that are used for export. You could have surplus cash to use for entertainment.

(continued)

The Thief: Chapter 8	
Describe text structure	Update the story map.
Set purpose for reading	Think about all of the different obstacles that were used to hide Hamiathes's Gift.
Highlight a strategy that will help students read silently	[p. 155. You already knew then? I asked.] There are important developments in this chapter, and it will help you to stop and synthesize. Think about the tools. Synthesize facts about the tools, so you can identify some unexpected issues with the magus and the quest in general.
Lead inferential discussion	1. What were the important details in the dream that Gen was having? 2. What do you think the author's purpose was in including the myth of Eugenides and the Great Fire? 3. Why did the river stop flowing? 4. What did it reveal behind the waterfall? 5. How was Gen's task related to the river? 6. How did Gen get his tools back? 7. What had happened to previous thieves and their parties? 8. Why was it important that Gen knew how he had 6 hours of oil? 9. What was true from Gen's dream? 10. How were the first and second doors of the chamber different? 11. Why was the maze different from a traditional temple? 12. What strange substance was found throughout the maze? 13. Why did Gen become panicked? 14. What dangers did he face as he escaped the maze?
Teach vocabulary	*Su-per-sti-tion* (open, *r*-controlled, irregular, suffix) is a noun that means a belief in the supernatural—things like curses and ghosts. A person who is filled with superstition is superstitious. *Superstitious* is the adjective form. *Maze* (VC-*e*) is a noun that means a series of paths set up to make people lost. It can be made of hedges or hallways, but they include turns that all look alike.
The Thief: Chapter 9	
Describe text structure	Update the story map.
Set purpose for reading	Look for evidence that Gen had inherited the cleverness of Eugenides.
Highlight a strategy that will help students read silently	[p. 188. The thought of stealing something from the Great Goddess was too awful to contemplate, and I could not do it.] There is a lot of interesting action in this chapter, but you should take the time to make some inferences about Gen's

(continued)

	character traits. Create a picture of him that links his thoughts on religion, his thoughts on stealing, and his thoughts on family traditions. Remember that inferences are new ideas that are constructed by combining specifics.
Lead inferential discussion	1. Why was the woman in the dream putting a second mark by Gen's name in her scroll? 2. Why was it strange that all of the bones were in the back of the maze? 3. Why did Gen look for the Gift among the bones? 4. Why didn't he take all of the jewelry he found? 5. What did he need the rope for? 6. How did Gen use what he learned? 7. What was new about his dream? 8. What was significant about the rocks moving? 9. How was the third night in the maze different? 10. Why did Gen decide to try to break the Obsidian? 11. What did Gen find at the top of the stairs? 12. Why was Gen reluctant to take the stone? 13. How did he know that he had not offended the gods? 14. What did he learn about his own feelings about the old religion? 15. Why was Gen caught in the river?
Teach vocabulary	*Fate* (VC-*e*) is a noun meaning the idea that a person's life is already planned in advance by the gods. The plural, *fates,* is also used to mean imaginary gods who do this planning. *Fated* is the adjective form. *Ret-ri-bu-tion* (closed, irregular, open, suffix) is a noun that means punishment for a crime. It is not mean; it is fair punishment. If a crime is very serious, the retribution will be very serious.

The Thief: Chapter 10

Describe text structure	Update the story map.
Set purpose for reading	Think about what was unnerving to Gen about the soundless horses.
Highlight a strategy that will help students read silently	[p. 201. I shrugged and wiped my hands on my pants, but my pants were muddy and my hands only ended up dirty as well as wet.] Check the inferences you made about Gen in the last chapter. Given the new information here, do they still hold up, or do you have to revise them? Remember that inferences are ideas you make yourself, based on new information. You should be able to tell why you think what you think.

(continued)

Lead inferential discussion	1. What did Gen do when he woke alive? 2. Why did the others think he was dead? 3. How had the previous searchers disappeared? 4. Why did this party survive? 5. How did they know that the stone was real? 6. How had Amiades behaved while they were gone? 7. How were Amiades's and Sophos's actions in the surprise attack different? 8. What did they do to try to find the lost stone? 9. Why was the stray horse important? 10. What was the magus's plan to deal with the lost stone? 11. Why did they need Gen to steal food? 12. What did the magus mean when he kept saying that they would all go to the block together? 13. How did the god of thieves help Gen steal the horses? 14. Why did Gen decide to separate from the rest? 15. Why did Sophos give him his sword? 16. Why did Gen jump down from the rock instead of hiding? 17. What happened to him in the end?
Teach vocabulary	*Trea-son* (vowel team, closed) is a noun meaning a crime that is usually punished by death. It means that you have turned against your country. The adjective form is *treasonous.* *Un-nerv-ing* (closed, r-controlled, closed) is an adjective that means losing courage or confidence. The prefix *un-* means not; the root *nerve* can mean courage. Something is unnerving if it surprises you and scares you.

The Thief: Chapter 11 (first half, to p. 235)

Describe text structure	Update the story map.
Set purpose for reading	Think about what more we learn about Gen and his family.
Highlight a strategy that will help students read silently	[p. 221. Ambiades had told them about the trail.] You are going to have to stop during this chapter to synthesize, but it won't be about Gen. You will need to go back and revise what you think you know about Ambiades. Make sure that by the end of this chapter, you can describe Ambiades differently.
Lead inferential discussion	1. How did the magus treat Gen when they were both in prison? 2. Why were the magus and Sophos so impressed with Gen's fighting? 3. Where had Gen learned how to fight? 4. What clue had Gen used to know that Ambiades was a traitor? 5. How did Ambiades die? 6. How was it different from how Pol died?

(continued)

	7. Who actually stole the food from the saddlebags? 8. Why did the river destroy the temple? 9. Why did the Queen dress like Hephestia? 10. How did the magus try to help Gen? 11. Why was the Queen surprised that Gen didn't take her offer?
Teach vocabulary	*Im-pov-er-ished* (closed, closed, *r*-controlled, closed) is an adjective that means poor, or living in a state of poverty. Someone who is impoverished would not have everything he needed. *Weal-thy* (vowel team, open) is an adjective that means rich, or living in a state of plenty. People who are wealthy have what they need and the money to buy extra things. *Wealth* is a noun that means riches.

The Thief: Chapter 11 (second half)

Describe text structure	Update the story map.
Set purpose for reading	Look for evidence that Gen's relationship with the magus had changed.
Highlight a strategy that will help students read silently	[p. 253. Getting across the makeshift bridge had been well done, and the god of thieves agreed, although some might not recognize his sign of approval.] Don't skip over interesting details in this chapter. You are going to have to bring to mind facts about Eugenides and things that happen in this chapter, and make an inference.
Lead inferential discussion	1. How did the gods help Gen to keep hope? 2. What did Gen do to help the magus and Sophos? 3. Why didn't the magus want Gen to come with them? 4. Why was there a secret door to the outside ledge of the castle? 5. Why was it dangerous that they had followed the river in the wrong direction? 6. How was Gen's ideal place different from what the others might have thought? 7. What do we learn was the magus's real motivation to get the Gift to his king? 8. How did they escape from the guardsmen who were following them? 9. Why weren't they afraid of the guns? 10. How did they end up at the end of the chapter?

(continued)

| Teach vocabulary | *Bribe* (VC-*e*) is a noun or a verb that means a crime where one person influences another person to do something by providing money or a gift. It is usually, but not always, a bad thing. You might bribe your younger brother to leave you alone by letting him borrow your basketball. |
| | *Gin-ger-ly* (closed, *r*-controlled, suffix) is an adjective or an adverb that means very carefully. You would walk gingerly across a garden so that you would not damage the plants. |

<table>
<tr><td colspan="2" align="center">The Thief: Chapter 12</td></tr>
<tr><td>Describe text structure</td><td>Update the story map.</td></tr>
<tr><td>Set purpose for reading</td><td>Look for surprises!</td></tr>
<tr><td>Highlight a strategy that will help students read silently</td><td>[p. 257. That will be the Attolian guard, said the magus.]

In this chapter, you should spend some time visualizing the setting. Think about the geography. Make sure that you are picturing the physical distance between Attolia and Eddis.</td></tr>
<tr><td>Lead inferential discussion</td><td>
1. Why didn't the guards from Eddis give the prisoners back to the guards from Attolia?
2. Why was it so surprising that the Queen knew Gen and called him Eugenides?
3. Why was it so surprising that Gen had had the Gift all along?
4. Why was it so surprising that he was the Queen's thief instead of a common thief in Sounis?
5. Why was the magus surprised that the minister of war was Gen's father?
6. Why was it surprising that only Pol knew Gen's identity, but didn't tell?
7. What was surprising about Sophos's identity?
8. What was surprising about the Queen's plan for the Gift?
</td></tr>
<tr><td>Teach vocabulary</td><td>*Suc-cinct* (closed, closed) is an adjective that means brief and clear. When you write an opinion, it is important to be succinct. The adverb form is *succinctly.*
Cha-grin (irregular, closed) is a noun that means a feeling of embarrassment. You would feel chagrin if someone saw you doing something unkind.</td></tr>
</table>

(continued)

NONFICTION SAMPLE LESSON FOR A VOCABULARY AND COMPREHENSION GROUP

Option 1

If you want to teach a self-contained, 15-minute lesson, first read silently for 7 minutes to estimate the number of pages that students will be able to read in a day. Then divide the text into daily segments. Whole chapters are ideal, but this will depend on chapter length. List page numbers below. Then start to read. At the end of each segment, choose two vocabulary words to teach before reading, identify a strategy to highlight in a reading guide, and compose three or four inferential questions. Try to start them with *how* or *why*. All lessons will take the same format: (1) Teach two new words, (2) describe structure and set a purpose for reading, (3) have students read silently, and (4) use the questions to engage in a comprehension discussion.

Option 2

If you want to take the full 15 minutes to teach vocabulary and engage in discussion before assigning a new text segment for students to read silently outside of your small-group time, you will be able to assign a longer text segment each day. After the first day, all lessons will take the same format: (1) Discuss the previous day's text segment, (2) teach two new words, (3) describe structure and set a purpose for reading, and (4) have students read silently.

Title and Author: *Grand Canyon* by Jason Chin
Lexile Level: 1000L

Grand Canyon: Pages 1–12	
Introduce book	We are going to read about the Grand Canyon in the state of Arizona. Even though this book is nonfiction, the author teaches readers about the Grand Canyon through a story about a girl and her father hiking into the canyon. Listen as I read the inside front cover and the statistics on the first page.
	From these introductory resources, we know that the Grand Canyon is 277 miles long, an average of 10 miles wide, and 1 mile deep. Grand Canyon National Park is located in the northwest part of Arizona, and it is home to many plants and animals, including fossils of things that lived long ago.
Teach vocabulary	*Can-yon* (closed, closed) is a noun that means a deep valley with steep rock walls. A canyon often has a stream or river flowing through it. The page before the title page tells how canyons are formed. A river cuts down into the earth to form a canyon, which grows wider through weathering and erosion. The Grand Canyon is an example of a canyon; it was formed by the Colorado River.

(continued)

	Sed-i-ment (closed, unaccented, closed) is a noun that means material (such as sand and mud) that sinks to the bottom of a liquid. Sediment can be carried through water and eventually build up to form rock layers.
Describe text structure	The author uses a description/listing structure to describe the characteristics of four ecological communities found in the Grand Canyon. Preview the diagram on the right-hand side of page 4. The author begins by describing the Riparian region before describing the Desert Scrub, Pinyon–Juniper Woodland, and Ponderosa Pine Forest. As you read each page, first examine the text features, including figures and other illustrations with captions, before reading the text.
Set purpose for reading	Begin on pages 1–2, the illustration of the mountain lion after the title page. As you read, look for the plants, animals, and rock layers in the Riparian region.
Highlight a strategy that will help students read silently	[pp. 9–10. Starting more than a billion years ago, layers of sediment (such as sand and mud) piled up on top of the basement rocks. . . . The youngest layers are at the top and the oldest layers are at the bottom.] When you look at the illustrations showing how layers of sediment formed layers of rock, it will help you to self-monitor. Think about the sequence of events by which layers of sediment formed the Grand Canyon. Think about why the oldest layers are at the bottom and the youngest layers are at the top. You might be able to make a hypothesis about how the canyon was carved.
Lead inferential discussion	1. Why do you think the canyon is hotter and drier at the bottom than the top? 2. Why are there different ecological communities at different elevations? 3. Using the text and illustrations on page 4, can you tell what oases in the desert are? 4. What plants and animals live in the Inner Gorge? Why do they live there? 5. How old are the rock walls in the Inner Gorge? How do you know? 6. Is the Grand Canyon getting deeper? If so, how is it getting deeper? 7. Why would you pass younger rock layers if you hike up out of the canyon? 8. Why are there ripple marks preserved in the Grand Canyon Supergroup?

(continued)

Grand Canyon: Pages 13–22	
Teach vocabulary	*Cliff* (closed) is a noun that means a high, steep surface of rock or earth. Rock climbers often scale steep cliffs when hiking up to the top of a mountain. *Slope* (VC-*e*) is a noun meaning ground that slants downward or upward. A slope can be steep, or it can be slight or gentle. The verb form is *to slope.*
Describe text structure	Update the description/listing text structure graphic organizer with important details about the Riparian region of the Grand Canyon and the Inner Gorge.
Set purpose for reading	Begin on pages 13–14, the illustrations of the girl and her father in the desert. As you read, look for the plants, animals, and rock layers in the Desert Scrub and the Pinyon–Juniper Woodland regions of the Grand Canyon.
Highlight a strategy that will help students read silently	[pp. 17–18. The sea covered the Grand Canyon region many times in the past. . . . Different types of sediment became different types of rock.] It will help you to make an inference by thinking about previously learned information when you look at the illustrations showing how different types of sediment became different types of rock. Remember that layers of sediment turn into layers of rock over a long period of time. Then think about which type of rock was oldest: sandstone, mudstone and shale, or limestone.
Lead inferential discussion	1. Do you think it is easy or difficult to climb out of the Inner Gorge? Why? 2. What plants and animals live in the Desert Scrub? How have they adapted? 3. How was the rock layer known as the Bright Angel Shale formed? 4. Why are some of the caves in the Redwall Limestone inaccessible? 5. Why are the California condors close to extinction? 6. Compare the illustration on the bottom of page 18 showing the different types of rock with the diagram of rock layers on the bottom of page 17. 7. How old are the sandstone, shale, and limestone in the Desert Scrub? 8. What plants and animals live in the Pinyon–Juniper Woodlands? Why? 9. How do we know what animals lived near the Hermit Formation long ago?

(continued)

	*Grand Canyon:* **Pages 23–34**
Teach vocabulary	*Weath-er-ing* (vowel team, *r*-controlled, suffix) is the noun form of the verb *to weather.* To weather means to wear away or change the surface of something because of the effects of the sun, wind, or rain over a long period of time. For example, rocks can be worn down by weathering over millions of years.
	E-ro-sion (open, open, suffix) is the noun form of the verb *to erode.* To erode means to gradually destroy something by natural forces such as wind or water. For example, centuries of erosion by wind can cause grooves to form in rocks.
Describe text structure	Update the description/listing text structure graphic organizer with important details about the Desert Scrub and Pinyon–Juniper Woodlands regions.
Set purpose for reading	Begin on page 23, the illustration of the girl and her father looking at the bighorn sheep. As you read, look for the plants, animals, and rock layers in the Desert Scrub and the Pinyon–Juniper Woodland regions of the Grand Canyon.
Highlight a strategy that will help students read silently	[pp. 27–28. When rock breaks apart, it's called weathering. . . . Often shale erodes beneath limestone or sandstone, and the cliff wall gives way.]
	It will help you to ask questions about cause-and-effect relationships to aid understanding of the differences between weathering and erosion and between cliffs and slopes. Ask yourself what causes weathering, what causes erosion, and what the effects of erosion are on different types of rocks.
Lead inferential discussion	1. How have bighorn sheep adapted to living on steep cliffs? 2. How is a fossil formed? Why are there different types of fossils? 3. What are cross-beds in the Cocino Sandstone, and how were they formed? 4. Why is there more vegetation as you approach the rim of the canyon? 5. What is the difference between weathering and erosion? 6. Why do the Grand Canyon's walls have both cliffs and slopes? 7. How was the limestone of the Kaibab Formation formed? 8. What plants and animals live in the Ponderosa Pine Forest? Why?

(continued)

Grand Canyon: **Pages 35–40**	
Teach vocabulary	*E-col-o-gy* (open, closed, open, open) is a noun that means the study of the relationships between living things and their environments. The root *eco-* means environment, and the suffix *-logy* means the study of a subject. The adjective form is *ecological.* A scientist might study ecological communities. *Ge-ol-o-gy* (open, closed, open, open) is a noun that means the study of rocks and layers of soil in order to learn about the history of the earth. The root *geo-* means earth, and the suffix *-logy* means the study of a subject. The noun *geologist* refers to a scientist who studies geology.
Describe text structure	Update the description/listing text structure graphic organizer with important details about the Ponderosa Pine Forest region of the Grand Canyon.
Set purpose for reading	Begin on page 35 under the heading "The Grandest Canyon." As you read, look for the plants, animals, and rock layers in the Desert Scrub and the Pinyon–Juniper Woodland regions of the Grand Canyon.
Highlight a strategy that will help students read silently	[p. 38. Canyons are carved by rivers . . . on the carving of Grand Canyon.] Take time to synthesize information when reading about how canyons are carved and how the Colorado River contributed to carving the Grand Canyon. Group important details by the sequence of events that take place when a canyon is carved, and link them to what is known about the Grand Canyon.
Lead inferential discussion	1. How do you think the Grand Canyon received its name? 2. Why have so many people visited and lived in the Grand Canyon? 3. Why are there different ecological communities in the Grand Canyon? 4. Look back at the illustration of the mountain lion on pages 1–2. Which ecological community do you think the lion is in? Why? 5. Why do geologists study sedimentary rocks, rock structures, and fossils? 6. How are canyons carved by rivers? Why don't all rivers carve canyons? 7. How was the Grand Canyon carved by the Colorado River? 8. How do the rock layers in the walls tell the story of the Grand Canyon?

References

Allington, R. L. (1977). If they don't read much, how they ever gonna get good? *Journal of Reading, 21*, 57–61.

Allington, R. L. (1983). Fluency: The neglected reading goal. *The Reading Teacher, 36*, 556–561.

Anderson, R., & Pearson, P. D. (1984). A schema-theoretic view of basic processes in reading. In P. D. Pearson, R. Barr, M. Kamil, & P. Mosenthal (Eds.), *Handbook of reading research* (Vol. 1, pp. 255–291). New York: Longman.

Armbruster, B. B., & Anderson, T. H. (1988). On selecting "considerate" content area textbooks. *Remedial and Special Education, 9*, 47–52.

Ash, G., Kuhn, M., & Walpole, S. (2009). Analyzing "inconsistencies" in practice: Teachers' continued use of round robin reading. *Reading and Writing Quarterly, 25*, 87–103.

Ayto, J. (2011). *Dictionary of word origins: The histories of more than 3,000 English-language words.* New York: Arcade.

Baumann, J. F., Edwards, E. C., Boland, E. M., Olejnik, S., & Kame'enui, E. J. (2003). Vocabulary tricks: Effects of instruction in morphology and context on fifth-grade students' ability to derive and infer word meanings. *American Educational Research Journal, 40*(2), 447–494.

Baumann, J. F., Edwards, E. C., Font, G., Tereshinski, C. A., Kame'enui, E. J., & Olejnik, S. (2002). Teaching morphemic and contextual analysis to fifth-grade students. *Reading Research Quarterly, 37*(2), 150–176.

Baumann, J. F., Font, G., Edwards, E. C., & Boland, E. (2005). Strategies for teaching middle-grade students to use word-part and context clues to expand reading vocabulary. In E. H. Hiebert & M. L. Kamil (Eds.), *Teaching and learning vocabulary: Bringing research to practice* (pp. 179–205). Mahwah, NJ: Erlbaum.

Baumann, J. F., & Graves, M. F. (2010). What is academic vocabulary? *Journal of Adolescent and Adult Literacy, 54*, 4–12.

Baumann, J. F., & Kame'enui, E. J. (Eds.). (2012). *Vocabulary instruction: Research to practice* (2nd ed.). New York: Guilford Press.

Baumann, J. F., Ware, D., & Edwards, E. C. (2007). "Bumping into spicy, tasty words that catch your tongue": A formative experiment on vocabulary instruction. *The Reading Teacher, 61*(2), 108–122.

Beck, I. L., & McKeown, M. G. (1994). Outcomes of history instruction: Paste-up accounts. In M.

Carretero & J. F. Voss (Eds.), *Cognitive and instructional processes in history and the social sciences* (pp. 237–256). Hillsdale, NJ: Erlbaum.

Beck, I. L., McKeown, M. G., & Kucan, L. (2008). *Creating robust vocabulary: Frequently asked questions and extended examples.* New York: Guilford Press.

Beck, I. L., McKeown, M. G., & Kucan, L. (2013). *Bringing words to life: Robust vocabulary instruction* (2nd ed.). New York: Guilford Press.

Beerwinkle, A. L., Wijekumar, K., Walpole, S., & Aguis, R. (2018). An analysis of the ecological components within a text structure intervention. *Reading and Writing, 31*(9), 2041–2064.

Benjamin, R. G., Schwanenflugel, P. J., Meisinger, E. B., Groff, C., Kuhn, M. R., & Steiner, L. (2013). A spectrographically grounded scale for evaluating reading expressiveness. *Reading Research Quarterly, 48*(2), 105–133.

Berninger V. W., & Winn, W. D. (2006). Implications of advancements in brain research and technology for writing development, writing instruction, and education evolution. In C. MacArthur, S. Graham, & J. Fitzgerald (Eds.), *Handbook of writing research* (pp. 96–114). New York: Guilford Press.

Best, R. M., Floyd, R. G., & McNamara, D. S. (2008). Differential competencies contributing to children's comprehension of narrative and expository texts. *Reading Psychology, 29*(2), 137–164.

Biemiller, A. (2012). Teaching vocabulary in the primary grades. In J. F. Baumann & E. J. Kame'enui (Eds.), *Vocabulary instruction: Research to practice* (2nd ed., pp. 34–50). New York: Guilford Press.

Biemiller, A., & Slonim, N. (2001). Estimating root word vocabulary growth in normative and advantaged populations: Evidence for a common sequence of vocabulary acquisition. *Journal of Educational Psychology, 93*(3), 498–520.

Blachowicz, C., & Fisher, P. J. (2015). *Teaching vocabulary in all classrooms* (5th ed.). Boston: Pearson.

Blanton, W. E., Wood, K. D., & Moorman, G. B. (1990). The role of purpose in reading instruction. *The Reading Teacher, 43*, 486–493.

Boothby, P. R., & Alvermann, D. E. (1984). A classroom training study: the effects of graphic organizer instruction on fourth graders' comprehension. *Reading World, 23*, 325–339.

Bowers, P. N., & Kirby, J. R. (2010). Effects of morphological instruction on vocabulary acquisition. *Reading and Writing, 23*(5), 515–537.

Brindle, M., Graham, S., Harris, K. R., & Hebert, M. (2016). Third and fourth grade teacher's classroom practices in writing: A national survey. *Reading and Writing, 29*(5), 929–954.

Brophy, J. E. (1983). Classroom organization and management. *The Elementary School Journal, 83*, 264–285.

Brown, L. T., Mohr, K. A. J., Wilcox, B. R., & Barrett, T. S. (2018). The effects of dyad reading and text difficulty on third-graders' reading achievement. *Journal of Educational Research, 111*(5), 541–553.

Brown-Chidsey, R., Bronaugh, L., & McGraw, K. (2009). *RTI in the classroom: Guidelines and recipes for success.* New York: Guilford Press.

Buly, M. R., & Valencia, S. W. (2002). Below the bar: Profiles of students who fail state reading assessments. *Educational Evaluation and Policy Analysis, 24*(3), 219–239.

Carbone, E. (2006). *Blood on the river: James Town 1607.* New York: Viking.

Carlo, M. S., August, D., McLaughlin, B., Snow, C., Dressler, C., Lippman, D., . . . White, C. E. (2004). Closing the gap: Addressing the vocabulary needs of English-language learners in bilingual and mainstream classrooms. *Reading Research Quarterly, 39*(2), 188–215.

Carlo, M. S., August, D., McLaughlin, B., Snow, C., Dressler, C., Lippman, D., . . . White, C. E. (2008). Closing the gap: Addressing the vocabulary needs of English-language learners in bilingual and mainstream classrooms. *Journal of Education, 189*(1–2), 57–76.

Carter, M., & Ivey, A. (2017). *Steal away home.* Nashville, TN: B&H.

Catts, H. W., Compton, D., Tomblin, J. B., & Bridges, M. S. (2012). Prevalence and nature of late-emerging poor readers. *Journal of Educational Psychology, 104*(1), 166–181.

Cervetti, G. N., Barber, J., Dorph, R., Pearson, P. D., & Goldschmidt, P. G. (2012). The impact of an integrated approach to science and literacy in elementary school classrooms. *Journal of Research in Science Teaching, 49*(5), 631–658.

Chall, J. E. (1996). *Stages of reading development* (2nd ed.). Fort Worth, TX: Harcourt Brace College.

Chall, J. E., Jacobs, V., & Baldwin, L. (1990). *The reading crisis: Why poor children fall behind.* Cambridge, MA: Harvard University Press.

Ciullo, S., & Mason, L. (2017). Prioritizing elementary school writing instruction: Cultivating middle school readiness for students with learning disabilities. *Intervention in School and Clinic, 52*(5), 287–294.

Clark, K. (2009). The nature and influence of comprehension strategy use during peer-led literature discussions: An analysis of intermediate grade students' practice. *Literacy Research and Instruction, 48*(2), 95–119.

Coker, D. L., & Ritchey, K. D. (2015). *Teaching beginning writers.* New York: Guilford Press.

Creech, S. (1994). *Walk two moons.* New York: HarperCollins.

Cunningham, A. E., & Stanovich, K. E. (1997). Early reading acquisition and its relation to experience and ability 10 years later. *Developmental Psychology, 33,* 934–945.

Curtis, C. P. (1995). *The Watsons go to Birmingham—1963.* New York: Delacorte Press.

Cutler, L., & Graham, S. (2008). Primary grade writing instruction: A national survey. *Journal of Educational Psychology, 100*(4), 907–919.

Dahl, R. (1964). *Charlie and the chocolate factory.* New York: Knopf.

Davis, Z. T., & McPherson, M. D. (1989). Story map instruction: A road map for reading comprehension. *The Reading Teacher, 43,* 232–240.

Deeney, T. A. (2010). One-minute fluency measures: Mixed messages in assessment and instruction. *The Reading Teacher, 63,* 440–450.

Deeney, T. A., & Shim, M. K. (2016). Teachers' and students' views of reading fluency. *Assessment for Effective Intervention, 41*(2), 109–126.

Deshler, D. D., Ellis, E. S., & Lenz, B. K. (1979). *Teaching adolescents with learning disabilities: Strategies and methods.* Denver, CO: Love.

Dewitz, P., Jones, J., & Leahy, S. (2009). Comprehension strategy instruction in core reading programs. *Reading Research Quarterly, 44*(2), 102–126.

Diliberto, J. A., Beattie, J. R., Flowers, C. P., & Algozzine, R. F. (2009). Effects of teaching syllable skills instruction on reading achievement in struggling middle school readers. *Literacy Research and Instruction, 48,* 14–27.

Duffy, G. G. (2014). *Explaining reading: A resource for explicit teaching of the Common Core standards* (3rd ed.). New York: Guilford Press.

Duke, N. K. (2000). 3.6 minutes per day: The scarcity of informational texts in first grade. *Reading Research Quarterly, 35,* 202–224.

Duke, N. K., & Pearson, P. D. (2002). Comprehension instruction in the primary grades. In C. C. Block & M. Pressley (Eds.), *Comprehension instruction: Research-based best practices* (pp. 247–258). New York: Guilford Press.

Dwyer, J., Kelcey, B., Berebitsky, D., & Carlisle, J. F. (2016). A study of teachers' discourse moves that support text-based discussions. *The Elementary School Journal, 117*(2), 285–309.

Eldredge, J. L. (2005). *Teaching decoding: Why and how* (2nd ed.). Upper Saddle River, NJ: Pearson.

Eldredge, J. L., Reutzel, D. R., & Hollingsworth, P. M. (1996). Comparing the effectiveness of two oral reading practices: Round-robin reading and the shared book experience. *Journal of Reading Behavior, 28,* 201–225.

Elleman, A. M., Olinghouse, N. G., Gilbert, J. K., Compton, D. L., & Spencer, J. L. (2017).

Developing content knowledge in struggling readers. *The Elementary School Journal, 118*(2), 232–256.

Englert, C. S., Mariage, T. V., & Dunsmore, K. (2006). Tenets of sociocultural theory in writing instruction research. In C. A. MacArthur, S. Graham, & J. Fitzgerald (Eds.), *Handbook of writing research* (pp. 208–221). New York: Guilford Press.

Englert, C. S., Raphael, T. E., & Anderson, L. M. (1992). Socially mediated instruction: Improving students' knowledge and talk about writing. *The Elementary School Journal, 92*, 411–449.

Englert, C. S., Raphael, T. E., Anderson, L. M., Anthony, H. M., & Stevens, D. D. (1991). Making strategies and self-talk visible: Writing instruction in regular and special education classrooms. *American Educational Research Journal, 28*, 337–372.

Fisher, D., & Frey, N. (2014a). Addressing CCSS anchor standard 10: Text complexity. *Language Arts, 91*(4), 236–250.

Fisher, D., & Frey, N. (2014b). Content area vocabulary learning. *The Reading Teacher, 67*(8), 594–599.

Fitzgerald, J., & Shanahan, T. (2000). Reading and writing relations and their development. *Educational Psychologist, 35*(1), 39–50.

Foorman, B. R., Smith, K. G., & Kosanovich, M. L. (2017). *Rubric for evaluating reading/language arts instructional materials for kindergarten to grade 5* (REL 2017-219). Washington, DC: U.S. Department of Education, Institute of Education Sciences, National Center for Education Evaluation and Regional Assistance, Regional Educational Laboratory Southeast. Retrieved from *http://ies.ed.gov/ncee/edlabs*.

Friend, M. (2016). Welcome to co-teaching 2.0. *Educational Leadership, 73*(4), 16–22.

Fritz, J. (1977). *Can't you make them behave, King George?* New York: Coward, McCann & Geoghegan.

Fuchs, D., Fuchs, L. S., Mathes, P. G., & Simmons, D. C. (1997). Peer-Assisted Learning Strategies: Making classrooms more responsive to diversity. *American Educational Research Journal, 34*, 174–206.

Ganske, K. (2008). *Mindful of words: Spelling and vocabulary explorations 4–8.* New York: Guilford Press.

Gibbons, G. (1992). *Recycle!* Boston: Little, Brown.

Gilbert, J., & Graham, S. (2010). Teaching writing to elementary students in grades 4–6: A national survey. *The Elementary School Journal, 110*(4), 494–518.

Gillespie, A., & Graham, S. (2014). A meta-analysis of writing interventions for students with learning disabilities. *Exceptional Children, 80*, 454–473.

Goodwin, B. (2011). Don't wait until 4th grade to address the slump. *Educational Leadership, 68*(7), 88–89.

Graham, S. (2006). Strategy instruction and the teaching of writing: A meta-analysis. In C. A. MacArthur, S. Graham, & J. Fitzgerald (Eds.), *Handbook of writing research* (pp. 187–207). New York: Guilford Press.

Graham, S. (2018). A writer(s) within community model of writing. In C. Bazerman, A. Applebee, V. Berninger, D. Brandt, S. Graham, J. Jeffery, P. Matsuda, . . . S. K. Wilcox (Eds.), *The lifespan development of writing* (pp. 272–325). Urbana, IL: National Council of Teachers of English.

Graham, S., Bollinger, A., Booth Olson, C., D'Aoust, C., MacArthur, C., McCutchen, D., & Olinghouse, N. (2012). *Teaching elementary school students to be effective writers: A practice guide* (NCEE 2012-4058). Washington, DC: National Center for Education Evaluation and Regional Assistance, Institute of Education Sciences, U.S. Department of Education.

Graham, S., & Harris, K. (2005). *Writing better: Effective strategies for teaching students with learning difficulties.* Baltimore: Brookes.

Graham, S., Harris, K. R., & Chambers, A. B. (2016). Evidence based practice and writing instruction. In C. A. MacArthur, S. Graham, & J. Fitzgerald (Eds.), *Handbook of writing research* (2nd ed., pp. 211–226). New York: Guilford Press.

Graham, S., Harris, K. R., & Mason, L. (2005). Improving the writing performance, knowledge, and self-efficacy of struggling young writers: The effects of self-regulated strategy development. *Contemporary Educational Psychology, 30*(2), 207–241.

Graham, S., Harris, K. R., & McKeown, D. (2013). The writing of students with learning disabilities: Meta-analysis of self-regulated strategy development writing intervention studies and future directions: Redux. In H. L. Swanson, K. Harris, & S. Graham (Eds.), *Handbook of learning disabilities* (2nd ed., pp. 565–590). New York: Guilford Press.

Graham, S., & Hebert, M. A. (2010). *Writing to read: Evidence for how writing can improve reading: A Carnegie Corporation Time to Act report.* Washington, DC: Alliance for Excellent Education.

Graham, S., Kiuhara, S. A., Harris, K. R., & Fishman, E. J. (2017). The relationship among strategic writing behavior, writing motivation, and writing performance with young, developing writers. *The Elementary School Journal, 118*(1), 82–104.

Graham, S., MacArthur, C., & Fitzgerald, J. (2015). *Best practices in writing instruction* (2nd ed.). New York: Guilford Press.

Graham, S., MacArthur, C., & Hebert, M. (2018). *Best practices in writing instruction* (3rd ed.). New York: Guilford Press.

Graham, S., McKeown, D., Kiuhara, S. A., & Harris, K. R. (2012). A meta-analysis of writing instruction for students in the elementary grades. *Journal of Educational Psychology, 104,* 879–896.

Graham, S., & Perin, D. (2007). *Writing next: Effective strategies to improve writing of adolescents in middle and high schools: A report to Carnegie Corporation of New York.* Washington, DC: Alliance for Excellent Education.

Graves, M. F. (2006). Building a comprehensive vocabulary program. *New England Reading Association Journal, 42*(2), 1–7.

Graves, M. F. (2011). Ask the expert. *The Reading Teacher, 64*(7), 541.

Graves, M. F., Baumann, J. F., Blachowicz, C. L. Z., Manyak, P., Bates, A., Cieply, C., . . . Von Gunten, H. (2013). Words, words everywhere, but which ones do we teach? *The Reading Teacher, 67*(5), 333–346.

Guthrie, J. T., McRae, A., Coddington, C., Klauda, S., Wigfield, A., & Barbosa, P. (2009). Impacts of comprehensive reading instruction on diverse outcomes of low- and high-achieving readers. *Journal of Learning Disabilities, 42,* 195–214.

Hairrell, A., Rupley, W., & Simmons, D. (2011). The state of vocabulary research. *Literacy Research and Instruction, 50*(4), 253–271.

Hall, C., Roberts, G., Cho, E., McCulley, L., Carroll, M., & Vaughn, S. (2017). Reading instruction for English learners in the middle grades: A meta-analysis. *Educational Psychology Review, 29*(4), 763–794.

Hall, L. A. (2012). Moving out of silence: Helping struggling readers find their voices in text-based discussions. *Reading and Writing Quarterly, 28*(4), 307–332.

Harris, K. R., Graham, S., Aitken, A., Barkel, A., Cunningham, J., & Ray, A. (2017). Teaching spelling, writing, and reading for writing: Powerful evidence-based practices. *Teaching Exceptional Children, 49,* 262–272.

Harris, K. R., & Graham, S. (2009). Self-regulated strategy development in writing: Premises, evolution, and the future. *British Journal of Educational Psychology Monograph Series II, 6,* 113–135.

Harris, K. R., Graham, S., & Mason, L. H. (2006). Improving the writing, knowledge, and motivation of struggling young writers: Effects of self-regulated strategy development with and without peer support. *American Educational Research Journal, 43*(2), 295–340.

Harris, K. R., Graham, S., Mason, L., & Friedlander, B. (2008). *Powerful writing strategies for all students.* Baltimore: Brookes.

Hart, B., & Risley, T. R. (1995). *Meaningful differences in the everyday experience of young American children.* Baltimore: Brookes.

Hasbrouck, J., & Tindal, G. (2017). *An update to compiled ORF norms* (Technical Report No. 1702). Eugene: Behavioral Research and Teaching, University of Oregon.

Hebert, M., Bohaty, J. J., Nelson, J. R., & Brown, J. (2016). The effects of text structure instruction on expository reading comprehension: A meta-analysis. *Journal of Educational Psychology, 108*(5), 609–629.

Henk, W. A., & Melnick, S. A. (1995). The Reader Self-Perception Scale (RSPS): A new tool for measuring how children feel about themselves as readers. *The Reading Teacher, 48,* 470–482.

Hiebert, E. H., & Mesmer, H. A. E. (2013). Upping the ante of text complexity in the Common Core State Standards: Examining its potential impact on young readers. *Educational Researcher, 42*(1), 44–51.

Hirsch, E. D., Jr. (2006). Reading-comprehension skills? What are they really? *Education Week, 25*(33), 42–52.

Hosp, M. K., Hosp, J. L., & Howell, K. W. (2016). *The ABCs of CBM: A practical guide to curriculum-based measurement* (2nd ed.). New York: Guilford Press.

Hoyer, K. M., & Sparks, D. (2017). *Instructional time for third- and eighth-graders in public and private schools: School year 2011–12.* Washington, DC: National Center for Education Statistics, U.S. Department of Education.

Israel, S. E. (Ed.). (2017). *Handbook of research on reading comprehension* (2nd ed.). New York: Guilford Press.

Jeong, J., Gaffney, J., & Choi, J. (2010). Availability and use of informational texts in second-, third-, and fourth-grade classrooms. *Research in the Teaching of English, 44,* 435–456.

Johnson, P. (2008). *Ice to steam: Changing states of matter.* Vero Beach, FL: Rourke.

Johnston, S. S., Tulbert, B. L., Sebastian, J. P., Devries, K., & Gompert, A. (2000). Vocabulary development: A collaborative effort for teaching content vocabulary. *Intervention in School and Clinic, 35*(5), 311–315.

Kamil, M. L., Borman, G. D., Dole, J., Kral, C. C., Salinger, T., & Torgesen, J. (2008). *Improving adolescent literacy: Effective classroom and intervention practices: A practice guide* (NCEE Report No. 2008-4027). Washington, DC: National Center for Education Evaluation and Regional Assistance, Institute of Education Sciences, U.S. Department of Education.

Kear, D. J., Coffman, G. A., McKenna, M. C., & Ambrosio, A. L. (2000). Measuring attitude toward writing: A new tool for teachers. *The Reading Teacher, 54*(1), 10–23.

Kieffer, M., & Lesaux, N. (2007). Breaking down words to build meaning: Morphology, vocabulary, and reading comprehension in the urban classroom. *The Reading Teacher, 61,* 134–144.

Kim, Y.-S., Wagner, R. K., & Foster, E. (2011). Relations among oral reading fluency, silent reading fluency, and reading comprehension: A latent variable study of first-grade readers. *Scientific Studies of Reading, 15*(4), 338–362.

Kintsch, W. (1994). The role of knowledge in discourse comprehension: A construction-integration model. In R. Ruddell, M. R. Ruddell, & H. Singer (Eds.), *Theoretical models and processes in reading* (4th ed., pp. 951–995). Newark, DE: International Reading Association.

Klauda, S. L., & Guthrie, J. T. (2008). Relationships of three components of reading fluency to reading comprehension. *Journal of Educational Psychology, 100*(2), 310–321.

Klingner, J. K., Vaughn, S., & Boardman, A. (2015). *Teaching reading comprehension to students with learning difficulties* (2nd ed.). New York: Guilford Press.

Kovaleski, J. F., & Black, L. (2010). Multi-tier service delivery: Current status and future directions. In T. A. Glover & S. Vaughn (Eds.), *The promise of response to intervention: Evaluating current science and practice* (pp. 23–56). New York: Guilford Press.

Krashen, S. (2012). Direct instruction of academic vocabulary: What about real reading?. *Reading Research Quarterly, 47*(3), 233–234.

Kuhn, M. R. (2005). A comparative study of small group fluency instruction. *Reading Psychology, 26*(2), 127–146.

Kuhn, M. R. (2014). What's really wrong with round robin reading? *Literacy Daily*. Retrieved from *www.literacyworldwide.org/blog/literacy-daily/2014/05/07/what's-really-wrong-with-round-robin-reading*.

Kuhn, M. R., & Stahl, S. A. (2003). Fluency: A review of developmental and remedial practices. *Journal of Educational Psychology, 95*(1), 3–21.

LaBerge, D., & Samuels, S. J. (1974). Toward a theory of automatic information processing in reading. *Cognitive Psychology, 6*, 293–323.

Lane, K. L., Harris, K., Graham, S, Driscoll, S., Sandmel, K., Morphy, P., & Schatschneider, C. (2011). Self-Regulated Strategy Development at Tier 2 for second-grade students with writing and behavioral difficulties: A randomized controlled trial. *Journal of Research on Educational Effectiveness, 4*(4), 322–353.

Lesaux, N. K., Crosson, A. C., Kieffer, M. J., & Pierce, M. (2010). Uneven profiles: Language minority learners' word reading, vocabulary, and reading comprehension skills. *Journal of Applied Developmental Psychology, 31*(6), 475–483.

Li, D., Beecher, C., & Cho, B.-Y. (2018). Examining the reading of informational text in 4th grade class and its relation with students' reading performance. *Reading Psychology, 39*(1), 1–28.

Liebfreund, M., & Conradi, K. (2016). Component skills affecting elementary students' informational text comprehension. *Reading and Writing, 29*(6), 1141–1160.

Lipka, O., Lesaux, N., & Siegel, L. (2006). Retrospective analyses of the reading development of grade 4 students with reading disabilities: Risk status and profiles over 5 years. *Journal of Learning Disabilities, 39*, 364–378.

Lou, Y., Abrami, P. C., Spence, J. C., Poulsen, C., Chambers, B., & d'Apollonia, S. (1996). Within-class grouping: A meta-analysis. *Review of Educational Research, 66*, 423–458.

Lubliner, S., & Smetana, L. (2005). The effects of comprehensive vocabulary instruction on Title I students' metacognitive word-learning skills and reading comprehension. *Journal of Literacy Research, 37*, 163–200.

MacArthur, C. A. (2012). Strategies instruction. In K. R. Harris, S. Graham, & T. Urdan (Eds.), *APA educational psychology handbook: Vol. 3. Application to learning and teaching* (pp. 379–401). Washington, DC: American Psychological Association.

MacArthur, C. A., Graham, S., & Fitzgerald, J. (Eds.). (2016). *Handbook of writing research* (2nd ed.). New York: Guilford Press.

Manyak, P. C., Gunten, H. V., Autenrieth, D., Gillis, C., Mastre-O'Farrell, J., Irvine-McDermott, E., . . . Blachowicz, C. L. Z. (2014). Four practical principles for enhancing vocabulary instruction. *The Reading Teacher, 68*(1), 13–23.

Marzano, R. J. (2004). The developing vision of vocabulary instruction. In J. F. Baumann & E. J. Kame'enui (Eds.), *Vocabulary instruction: Research to practice* (pp. 100–117). New York: Guilford Press.

Mason, A. (2007). *A history of Western art*. New York: Abrams Books for Young Readers.

McCardle, P., Chhabra, V., & Kapinus, B. (2008). *Reading research in action: A teacher's guide for student success*. Baltimore: Brookes.

McKenna, M. C., Franks, S., Conradi, K., & Lovette, G. (2011). Using reading guides with struggling readers in grades 3 and above. In R. L. McCormick & J. R. Paratore (Eds.), *After early intervention, then what?: Teaching struggling readers in grades 3 and beyond* (2nd ed.). Newark, DE: International Reading Association.

McKenna, M. C., & Kear, D. J. (1990). Measuring attitude towards reading: A new tool for teachers. *The Reading Teacher, 43*, 626–639.

McKenna, M. C., Kear, D. J., & Ellsworth, R. A. (1995). Children's attitudes toward reading: A national survey. *Reading Research Quarterly, 30*, 934–956.

McKenna, M. C., & Robinson, R. D. (2011). *Teaching through text: Reading and writing in the content areas* (2nd ed.). New York: Guilford Press.

McKenna, M. C., & Stahl, K. A. D. (2009). *Assessment for reading instruction* (2nd ed.). New York: Guilford Press.

McKeown, M., Beck, I., & Blake, R. (2009). Rethinking reading comprehension instruction: A comparison of instruction for strategies and content approaches. *Reading Research Quarterly, 44*, 218–253.

McMaster, K., Fuchs, D., & Fuchs, L. (2006). Research on Peer-Assisted Learning Strategies: The promise and limitations of peer-mediated instruction. *Reading and Writing Quarterly, 22*, 5–25.

McNamara, D. S. (Ed.). (2007). *Reading comprehension strategies: Theories, interventions, and technologies.* New York: Erlbaum.

McNamara, D. S., Ozuru, Y., & Floyd, R. G. (2011). Comprehension challenges in the fourth grade: The roles of text cohesion, text genre, and readers' prior knowledge. *International Electronic Journal of Elementary Education, 4*(1), 229–257.

Meisinger, E. B., Bradley, B. A., Schwanenflugel, P. J., & Kuhn, M. R. (2010). Teachers' perceptions of word callers and related literacy concepts. *School Psychology Review, 39*(1), 54–68.

Menke, D. J., & Pressley, M. (1994). Elaborative interrogation: Using "why" questions to enhance the learning from text. *Journal of Reading, 37*, 642–645.

Meyer, B. J. F. (1987). Following the author's top-level organization: An important skill for reading comprehension. In R. J. Tierney, P. L. Anders, & J. Nichols Mitchell (Eds.), *Understanding readers' understanding: Theory and practice* (pp. 59–76). Hillsdale, NJ: Erlbaum.

Meyer, B. J. F., Young, C. J., & Bartlett, B. J. (1989). *Memory improved: Reading and memory enhancement across the life span through strategic text structures.* Hillsdale, NJ: Erlbaum.

Moody, S. W., Vaughn, S., & Schumm, J. S. (1997). Instructional grouping for reading: Teachers' views. *Remedial and Special Education, 18*, 347–355.

Musti-Rao, S., Hawkins, R. O., & Barkley, B. A. (2009). Effects of repeated readings on the oral reading fluency of urban fourth-grade students: Implications for practice. *Preventing School Failure, 54*(1), 12–23.

Nagy, W. E., & Anderson, R. C. (1984). How many words are there in printed school English? *Reading Research Quarterly, 19*, 304–330.

Nagy, W. E., Anderson, R. C., & Herman, P. A. (1987). Learning word meanings from context during normal reading. *American Educational Research Journal, 24*, 237–270.

Nagy, W. E., Herman, P. A., & Anderson, R. C. (1985). Learning words from context. *Reading Research Quarterly, 20*, 233–253.

Nagy, W., & Townsend, D. (2012). Words as tools: Learning academic vocabulary as language acquisition. *Reading Research Quarterly, 47*(1), 91–108.

National Center for Education Statistics. (2012). *The nation's report card: Writing 2011* (NCES 2012-470). Washington, DC: Author.

National Commission on Writing in America's Schools and Colleges. (2003). *The neglected "R": The need for a writing revolution.* New York: College Board.

National Governors Association Center for Best Practices (NGACBP) & Council of Chief State School Officers (CCSSO). (2010). *Common Core State Standards for English language arts and literacy in history/social studies, science, and technical subjects.* Washington, DC: Authors.

National Reading Panel. (2000). *Report of the National Reading Panel: Teaching children to read: An evidence-based assessment of the scientific research literature on reading and its implications for reading instruction.* Washington, DC: National Institute of Child Health and Human Development.

Ness, M. (2011). Explicit reading comprehension instruction in elementary classrooms: Teacher use of reading comprehension strategies. *Journal of Research in Childhood Education, 25*(1), 98–117.

O'Connor, R. E. (2014). *Teaching word recognition: Effective strategies for students with learning difficulties* (2nd ed.). New York: Guilford Press.

O'Connor, R. E., Swanson, H. L., & Geraghty, C. (2010). Improvement in reading rate under independent and difficult text levels: Influences on word and comprehension skills. *Journal of Educational Psychology, 102*(1), 1–19.

Olinghouse, N. G., & Leaird, J. T. (2009). The relationship between measures of vocabulary and narrative writing quality in second- and fourth-grade students. *Reading and Writing, 22*(5), 545–565.

Olinghouse, N. G., & Wilson, J. (2013). The relationship between vocabulary and writing quality in three genres. *Reading and Writing, 26*(1), 45–65.

Open Up Resources. (2018). Bookworms K–5 Reading and Writing. Retrieved from *https://openupresources.org/bookworms-k-5-reading-writing-curriculum*.

Palincsar, A. S., & Brown, A. L. (1984). Reciprocal teaching of comprehension-fostering and monitoring activities. *Cognition and Instruction, 1*, 117–175.

Parsons, A. W., Parsons, S. A., Malloy, J. A., Gambrell, L. B., Marinak, B. A., Reutzel, D. R., . . . Fawson, P. C. (2018). Upper elementary students' motivation to read fiction and nonfiction. *The Elementary School Journal, 118*(3), 505–523.

Paulsen, G. (1987). *Hatchet.* Austin, TX: Holt, Rinehart & Winston.

Pearson, P. D., & Gallagher, M. C. (1983). The instruction of reading comprehension. *Contemporary Educational Psychology, 8*, 317–344.

Petscher, Y., & Kim, Y.-S. (2011). The utility and accuracy of oral reading fluency score types in predicting reading comprehension. *Journal of School Psychology, 49*(1), 107–129.

Philippakos, Z. (2018). Using a task analysis process for reading and writing assignments. *The Reading Teacher, 72*(1), 107–114.

Philippakos, Z. A., & FitzPatrick, E. (2018). A proposed tiered model of assessment in writing instruction: Supporting all student-writers. *Insights into Learning Disabilities, 15*(2), 149–173.

Philippakos, Z. A., & MacArthur, C. A. (2016). The effects of giving feedback on the persuasive writing of fourth- and fifth-grade students. *Reading Research Quarterly, 51*, 4.

Philippakos. Z. A., & MacArthur, C. A. (2019). *Developing strategic young writers through genre instruction: Resources for grades K–2.* New York: Guilford Press.

Philippakos. Z. A., MacArthur, C. A., & Coker, D. L. (2015). *Developing strategic writers through genre instruction: Resources for grades 3–5.* New York: Guilford Press.

Philippakos, Z., MacArthur, C., & Munsell, S. (2018). Collaborative reasoning with strategy instruction for opinion writing in primary grades: Two cycles of design research. *Reading and Writing Quarterly, 34*(6), 485–504.

Philippakos, Z. A., Overly, M., Riches, C., Grace, L., & Johns, W. (2018). Supporting professional development on writing strategy instruction: Listening to the voices of collaborators as carriers of change. *School–University Partnerships, 11*(4). Retrieved from *https://napds.org/wp-content/uploads/2018/08/5-Final_Philippakos-6_18.pdf*.

Philippakos, Z. A., & Williams, L. (2018, November). *Writing in science: Integrating writing strategy instruction across the curriculum.* Paper presented at the meeting of the Association of Literacy Educators and Researchers, Louisville, KY.

Pikulski, J. J., & Chard, D. J. (2005). Fluency: Bridge between decoding and reading comprehension. *The Reading Teacher, 58*(6), 510–519.

Pinnell, G. S., Pikulski, J. J., Wixson, K. K., Campbell, J. R., Gough, P. B., & Beatty, A. S. (1995). *Listening to children read aloud.* Washington, DC: National Center for Education Statistics, U.S. Department of Education.

Pittelman, S. D., Heimlich, J. E., Berglund, R. L., & French, M. P. (1991). *Semantic feature analysis: Classroom applications.* Newark, DE: International Reading Association.

Pressley, M., & Allington, R. L. (2015). *Reading instruction that works: The case for balanced teaching* (4th ed.). New York: Guilford Press.

Pressley, M., & Wharton-McDonald, R. (1997). Skilled comprehension and its development through instruction. *School Psychology Review, 26*(3), 448–466.

RAND Reading Study Group. (2002). *Reading for understanding: Toward an R&D program in reading comprehension*. Santa Monica, CA: RAND. Retrieved from *www.rand.org/pubs/monograph_reports/MR1465*.

Rasinski, T. V. (2003). *The fluent reader: Oral reading strategies for building word recognition, fluency, and comprehension*. New York: Scholastic Professional Books.

Rasinski, T. (2006). Reading fluency instruction: Moving beyond accuracy, automaticity, and prosody. *The Reading Teacher, 59*(7), 704–706.

Rasinski, T., Rikli, A., & Johnston, S. (2009). Reading fluency: More than automaticity?: More than a concern for the primary grades? *Literacy Research and Instruction, 48*, 350–361.

Reutzel, D. R. (1985). Story maps improve comprehension. *The Reading Teacher, 38*, 400–404.

Ritchey, K. D., Palombo, K., Silverman, R. D., & Speece, D. L. (2017). Effects of an informational text reading comprehension intervention for fifth-grade students. *Learning Disability Quarterly, 40*(2), 68–80.

Roberts, G., Torgesen, J. K., Boardman, A., & Scammacca, N. (2008). Evidence-based strategies for reading instruction of older students with reading disabilities. *Learning Disabilities Research and Practice, 23*, 63–69.

Roehling, J. V., Hebert, M., Nelson, J. R., & Bohaty, J. J. (2017). Text structure strategies for improving expository reading comprehension. *The Reading Teacher, 71*(1), 71–82.

Rogers, L., & Graham, S. (2008). A meta-analysis of single subject design writing intervention research. *Journal of Educational Psychology, 100*, 879–906.

Rotherham, A. J., & Willingham, D. T. (2010). "21st-century" skills: Not new, but a worthy challenge. *American Educator, 34*(1), 17–20.

Saddler, B. (2012). *Teacher's guide to effective sentence writing*. New York: Guilford Press.

Sanacore, J., & Palumbo, A. (2009). Understanding the fourth-grade slump: Our point of view. *The Educational Forum, 73*(1), 67–74.

Scammacca, N., Roberts, G., Vaughn, S., Edmonds, M., Wexler, J., Reutebuch, C. K., & Torgesen, J. K. (2007). *Interventions for adolescent struggling readers: A meta-analysis with implications for practice*. Portsmouth, NH: RMC Research Corporation, Center on Instruction.

Schumm, J. S., Moody, S. W., & Vaughn, S. (2000). Grouping for reading instruction: Does one size fit all? *Journal of Learning Disabilities, 33*, 477–488.

Schwartz, R. M., & Raphael, T. E. (1985). Concept of definition: A key to improving students' vocabulary. *The Reading Teacher, 39*, 198–205.

Shanahan, T. (2017). The instructional level concept revisited: Teaching with complex text [Blog post]. Retrieved from *https://shanahanonliteracy.com/blog/the-instructional-level-concept-revisited-teaching-with-complex-text*.

Shanahan, T. (2018). Comprehension skills or strategies: Is there a difference and does it matter? [Blog post]. Retrieved from *https://shanahanonliteracy.com/blog/comprehension-skills-or-strategies-is-there-a-difference-and-does-it-matter*.

Shany, M., & Biemiller, A. (2010). Individual differences in reading comprehension gains from assisted reading practice: Pre-existing conditions, vocabulary acquisition, and amounts of practice. *Reading and Writing, 23*(9), 1071–1083.

Silverman, R. D., Coker, D., Proctor, C. P., Harring, J., Piantedosi, K. W., & Hartranft, A. M. (2015). The relationship between language skills and writing outcomes for linguistically diverse students in upper elementary school. *The Elementary School Journal, 116*(1), 103–125.

Silverman, R. D., Martin-Beltran, M., Peercy, M. M., Hartranft, A. M., McNeish, D. M., Artzi, L., & Nunn, S. (2017). Effects of a cross-age peer learning program on the vocabulary and comprehension of English learners and non-English learners in elementary school. *The Elementary School Journal, 117*(3), 485–512.

Simmons, D. C., Fuchs, D., Fuchs, L. S., Hodge, J. P., & Mathes, P. G. (1994). Importance of instructional complexity and role reciprocity to classwide peer tutoring. *Learning Disabilities Research and Practice, 9*, 203–212.

Slavin, R. E. (1987). Ability grouping and student achievement in elementary schools: A best-evidence synthesis. *Review of Educational Research, 57*, 293–336.

Somervill, B. A. (2011). *Animal cells and life processes.* Boston: Heinemann.

Sparks, R. R., Patton, J., & Murdoch, A. (2014). Early reading success and its relationship to reading achievement and reading volume: Replication of "10 years later." *Reading and Writing, 27*(1), 189–211.

Spear-Swerling, L. S. (2016). Common types of reading problems and how to help children who have them. *The Reading Teacher, 69*(5), 513–522.

Stahl, K. A. D., & Bravo, M. A. (2010). Contemporary classroom vocabulary assessment for content areas. *The Reading Teacher, 63*(7), 566–578.

Stahl, S. A., & Nagy, W. E. (2005). *Teaching word meanings.* Mahwah, NJ: Erlbaum.

Stanovich, K. E. (1986). Matthew effects in reading: Some consequences of individual differences in the acquisition of literacy. *Reading Research Quarterly, 21*, 360–407.

Strecker, S. K., Roser, N. L., & Martinez, M. G. (1998). Toward understanding oral reading fluency. *National Reading Conference Yearbook, 47*, 295–310.

Strickland, W. D., Boon, R. T., & Spencer, V. G. (2013). The effects of repeated reading on the fluency and comprehension skills of elementary-age students with learning disabilities (LD), 2001–2011: A review of research and practice. *Learning Disabilities: A Contemporary Journal, 11*(1), 1–33.

Swan, E. A. (2002). *Concept-oriented reading instruction: Engaging classrooms, lifelong learners.* New York: Guilford Press.

Swanborn, M. S. L., & de Glopper, K. (1999). Incidental word learning while reading: A meta-analysis. *Review of Educational Research, 69*, 261–285.

Swanborn, M. S. L., & de Glopper, K. (2002). Impact of reading purpose on incidental word learning from context. *Language Learning, 52*(1), 95–117.

Swanson, E., Edmonds, M. S., Hairrell, A., Vaughn, S., & Simmons, D. C. (2011). Applying a cohesive set of comprehension strategies to content-area instruction. *Intervention in School and Clinic, 46*(5), 266–272.

Sweet, A. P., & Snow, C. E. (Eds.). (2003). *Rethinking reading comprehension.* New York: Guilford Press.

Taylor, S. E. (1989). *EDL core vocabularies in reading, mathematics, science, and social studies.* Orlando, FL: Steck-Vaughn.

Torgesen, J. K., & Miller, D. H. (2009). *Assessments to guide adolescent literacy instruction.* Portsmouth, NH: RMC Research Corporation, Center on Instruction.

Toste, J. R., Capin, P., Vaughn, S., Roberts, G. J., & Kearns, D. M. (2017). Multisyllabic word-reading instruction with and without motivational beliefs training for struggling readers in the upper elementary grades: A pilot investigation. *The Elementary School Journal, 117*(4), 593–615.

Trainin, G., Hiebert, E. H., & Wilson, K. M. (2015). A comparison of reading rates, comprehension, and stamina in oral and silent reading of fourth-grade students. *Reading Psychology, 36*(7), 595–626.

Troia, G. A. (2009). *Instruction and assessment for struggling writers: Evidence-based practices.* New York: Guilford Press.

Troia, G. A., & Graham, S. (2016). Common core writing and language standards and aligned state assessments: A national survey of teacher beliefs and attitudes. *Reading and Writing: An Interdisciplinary Journal, 29*(9), 1719–1743.

Vadasy, P., & Sanders, E. (2008). Benefits of repeated reading intervention for low-achieving fourth- and fifth-grade students. *Remedial and Special Education, 29*, 235–249.

Walpole, S., & McKenna, M. C. (2006). The role of informal reading inventories in assessing word recognition. *The Reading Teacher, 59*, 592–594.

Walpole, S., & McKenna, M. C. (2007). *Differentiated reading instruction: Strategies for the primary grades.* New York: Guilford Press.

Walpole, S., & McKenna, M. C. (2009). *How to plan differentiated reading instruction: Resources for grades K–3.* New York: Guilford Press.

Walpole, S., & McKenna, M. C. (2017). *How to plan differentiated reading instruction: Resources for grades K–3* (2nd ed.). New York: Guilford Press.

Walpole, S., McKenna, M. C., Amendum, S., Pasquarella, A., & Strong, J. Z. (2017). The promise of a literacy reform effort in the upper elementary grades. *The Elementary School Journal, 118*(2), 257–280.

Wanzek, J., Petscher, Y., Otaiba, S. A., Rivas, B. K., Kent, S. C., & Schatschneider, C. (2017). Effects of a year long supplemental reading intervention for students with reading difficulties in fourth grade. *Journal of Educational Psychology, 109*(8), 1103–1119.

Wanzek, J., Vaughn, S., Wexler, J., Swanson, E. A., Edmonds, & Kim, A. H. (2006). A synthesis of spelling and reading interventions and their effects on the spelling outcomes of students with LD. *Journal of Learning Disabilities, 39,* 528–543.

Wanzek, J., Wexler, J., Vaughn, S., & Ciullo, S. (2010). Reading interventions for struggling readers in the upper elementary grades: A synthesis of 20 years of research. *Reading and Writing: An Interdisciplinary Journal, 23*(8), 889–912.

Wehmeyer, M. L., Shogren, K. A., Toste, J. R., & Mahal, S. (2017). Self-determined learning to motivate struggling learners in reading and writing. *Intervention in School and Clinic, 52*(5), 295–303.

Wigfield, A., Guthrie, J., Perencevich, K., Taboada, A., Klauda, S., McRae, A., & Barbosa, P. (2008). Role of reading engagement in mediating effects of reading comprehension instruction on reading outcomes. *Psychology in the Schools, 45,* 432–445.

Williams, J. P., Hall, K. M., & Lauer, K. D. (2004). Teaching expository text structure to young at-risk learners: Building the basics of comprehension instruction. *Exceptionality, 12*(3), 129–144.

Willingham, D. T. (2006–2007). The usefulness of brief instruction in reading comprehension strategies. *American Educator, 30*(4), 39–50.

Willingham, D. T. (2017, November 25). How to get your mind to read. *The New York Times.* Retrieved from *www.nytimes.com/2017/11/25/opinion/sunday/how-to-get-your-mind-to-read.html.*

Wilson, J. (2018). Universal screening with automated essay scoring: Evaluating classification accuracy in grades 3 and 4. *Journal of School Psychology, 68,* 19–37.

Wolf, M., & Katzir-Cohen, T. (2001). Reading fluency and its intervention. *Scientific Studies of Reading, 5*(3), 211–239.

Wood, E., Pressley, M., & Winne, P. H. (1990). Elaborative interrogation effects on children's learning of factual content. *Journal of Educational Psychology, 82,* 741–748.

Zutell, J., & Rasinski, T. V. (1991). Training teachers to attend to their students' oral reading fluency. *Theory into Practice, 30,* 211–217.

Index

Note. *f* following a page number indicates a figure.